DAMON RUNYON

BOOKS BY JIMMY BRESLIN

FICTION

The Gang That Couldn't Shoot Straight
World Without End, Amen
.44 (with Dick Schaap)
Forsaking All Others
Table Money
He Got Hungry and Forgot His Manners

NONFICTION

Can't Anybody Here Play This Game?
The World of Jimmy Breslin
How the Good Guys Finally Won
The World According to Breslin
Damon Runyon

DAMON RUNYON

JIMMY BRESLIN

TICKNOR & FIELDS
NEW YORK 1991

For information about permission to reproduce selections
from this book, write to Permissions, Ticknor & Fields,
Houghton Mifflin Company, 2 Park Street, Boston,
Massachusetts 02108.

Library of Congress Cataloging-in-Publication Data
Breslin, Jimmy.
Damon Runyon / by Jimmy Breslin.
p.   cm.
ISBN 0-89919-984-4
1. Runyon, Damon, 1880–1946 — Biography.
2. Authors, American — 20th century — Biography.
3. Broadway (New York, N.Y.) — Biography.   I. Title.
PS3535.U52Z57   1991
818'.5209 — dc20   91-16073
[B]   CIP

Printed in the United States of America

1 2 3 4 5 6 7 8 9 10 AGM

DAMON RUNYON

ONE

THIS ALL STARTED when Lyndon Baines Johnson told the president of the University of Texas, "Buy everything in the whole frigging world." So the librarians went out and bought the first photo ever taken, and a Gutenberg Bible, and all the papers of Beckett, Joyce, Yeats and Faulkner, which they placed in the main research collection building, seven stories of precious manuscripts.

Then, following orders to the decimal, they also bought the Hearst morgue from New York. It is kept in the research building annex, the oldest building on the campus of the University of Texas. It belongs in a cage. Out front are oak trees that have ravens squalling in the branches. The man in charge of the morgue is Ken Craven, whose job usually kept him busy studying the manuscripts and papers of Samuel Beckett and storing them in acid-free boxes. Now he leads you into the silence of a large ground-floor room that is crowded with rows of dented olive-green filing cabinets. The cabinets fill the room and march through a doorway and into another room and fill this one too.

Ken Craven sighed as he looked at the cabinets. "It's just driving me crazy," he said.

He pulled open one of the *M* drawers. In the front was a large card, which said everything about the Hearst system of thought and filing:

MENTAL HEALTH.
SEE INSANITY

The newspapers, the *Journal* and *American,* later combined, were dedicated to "noise in the news" and had an editorial view of the world from inside a bedroom, or at the rail of a police desk at night. These tales were printed in newspapers that practiced bribery, extortion, calumny, also known as slander, and two kinds of lies, bald-faced and by omission. Anybody on the staff who performed an act without malice was regarded as a dreadful amateur. There was great confusion in the office, for sometimes the sins being committed at typewriters were greater than the ones being written about. There was no situation so bad that a fresh edition of the morning *American* or evening *Journal* newspaper couldn't make it worse. Yet the working conditions were the best in the history of the business, for nobody died at an early age of that worst of maladies, seriousness.

Ken Craven, standing with his files, was saying that "people working on books come here from all over the country to look up rich miscreants. Hearst always had the best gossip. But we have trouble finding things. These newspapers of yours, they filed the woman under the husband's name. Man comes down here from Minnesota doing the eighth definitive book on Gloria Vanderbilt, we can't find anything under her name. How do I know you had to know the names of all the husbands? We finally figured out Stokowski and we found her in there."

"Pasquale di Cicco," I said.

"Who?"

"Pat di Cicco from Astoria," I said. "That's in Queens County, where I come from. The guy's father grew broccoli in his cellar. Pat went over to Manhattan and told everybody he was the Broccoli King. He got next to that Gloria Vanderbilt once and that took care of that. 'I am in love with the Broccoli King,' she said."

Craven grabbed the old brass handle of a *D* drawer and pulled it open. Several envelopes, thick with clippings and covered with dust, were under the name of Thomas E. Dewey, gangbuster district attorney of Manhattan, governor of New York, twice a Republican presidential candidate. He lost to Harry Truman in 1948, in the greatest election upset ever. Behind the Dewey envelopes, you now came to a series of envelopes for "di Cicco, Pat (Husband of Gloria Vanderbilt)."

There was one packed envelope after the other, many more than for Dewey, for any bindlestiff can prosecute people and get enough rich men around him to run for President, but only the greats step out of a cellar in Astoria and make it with a millionairess.

Ken Craven opened the drawer for *B*. "No Nellie Bly. But now look at this." He walked down the aisle to the start of the *S*'s. Here was "SEAMAN. ROBERT L. (HUSBAND OF NELLIE BLY)."

"Now, can you tell me who Seaman is?" he asked.

"Sure I can. He's the man Nellie Bly married."

Craven wears a green plaid shirt and suspenders. In the shirt pocket is a list of work to be accomplished in the research center next door on some frivolous collection such as Samuel Beckett. He left me alone with the old metal filing cabinets and now the room was thick with cigarette and cigar smoke and through the open window the sound of ravens turned into truck horns. The grounds outside the windows now became South Street in New York City, and it was crowded with news delivery trucks and a city bus and big old trucks from the Fulton Fish Market down the street.

A ship's whistle blared in the air. There, outside the windows, the Texas oak trees became the East River and here was an old freighter sitting in the water off Pier 44 East River, waiting for the longshoremen to walk over from Mutchie's Bar, South Street and Market Slip; all the streets down here at this end of town were called slips because they ran right into the docks. Suddenly, the room I am in is filled with the sound of typewriters.

My business here concerned Damon Runyon, who was the columnist for the Hearst papers and who rose above his newspapers by writing with what was then an original style. He lifted the style, the first person present, entirely from Coleridge, but liked it so much that he said it was his own. He did add one nuance: he used no contractions. But it was still a copy of Coleridge. Literary people are so gullible that they believed Runyon had invented writing in the first person present. He then moved up to short story writing, with an astounding number of the stories being turned into movies, at least a couple of them as good as the country has had. He had a successful play on Broadway, *A Slight Case of Murder*. After his death, a collection became the wonderful musical *Guys and Dolls*.

He ate at some of the great dinner tables of the country, but he hated legitimate people and loved thieves. His characters became known as Runyonesque, a word that is one of the dozen most used descriptive words today. He understood that a newspaper was the literary underworld and that all these people sitting at typewriters who were on the way to nowhere suffered from phenomenal jealousy. When Runyon decided that at least many people in city rooms who smiled at him actually couldn't stand his name, he decided to engage in pain. He showed sportswriters earning $50 a week his checks for thousands from movie companies.

I am here, leaning against these filing cabinets, because more than anybody else I've ever heard of, he beat the New York newspaper business. Beat it to a pulp. And his life gave off a reflection of more than three decades of the city of New York, and it has almost become the official record of the times. He practically invented at least two entire decades of his times, and had everybody believing that his street, Broadway, actually existed. So much of it never happened. What do you care? What does anybody care? Go to any library and the illusion is there as fact. The Roaring Twenties, the Golden Age of Sport, Broadway, the warmhearted guys and dolls. He did something practically nobody else could do. He put a smile into a newspaper, which usually has as much humor as a bus accident. Other newspaper columnists who feigned importance left stirring accounts of the Bretton Woods Monetary Conference.

I worked for $156.50 a week on those Hearst editions that filled the last envelopes of these files in Austin. That was in the years just before time finally took care of the Hearst style. The Western Union telegraphers, who sat in an alcove behind the sports department, all talked about the days when they had handled Damon Runyon's copy. They always love a Big Guy in memory. A couple of the old guys on the news desk had spent several vacations with Runyon at his movie studio bungalows. I was in my early twenties at the *Journal-American* and whenever anybody mentioned Runyon to me, I will tell you exactly what I said. I said, to hell with him, I'm better, I'm J. B. Number one. All the older guys used to go insane when I pulled that, particularly Jimmy Cannon, who wrote a sports column and always claimed that Runyon had nominated him as official successor. I said to Cannon, well, in that case to hell with you too.

Now all these years later, here with these green cabinets, I am remembering that one of the most personal stories I heard about Runyon was how Jimmy Cannon snuck around with Runyon's wife, Patrice. One guy, Sam Becker, Runyon's lawyer, had the physical evidence of a watch engraved with "To Jimmy. Love Patrice." Some successor.

And now, here in this old building in Austin, Texas, just because I was leaning on the drawer marked *C*, I decided to pull it open. My fingers begin to pick their way though Campbell, Canfield, and I come to Carbo, and inside the envelope is packed with clippings, at least a few of them carrying the byline of Damon Runyon. I finger a Runyon clipping with a red date stamp on it, September 4, 1931.

Now the envelope moves as if it is breathing, and from the clip there comes a rough voice that speaks from behind a closed door on the fourth floor of the Cambridge Hotel at 60 West 68th Street in Manhattan, New York City.

"Yeah, what do you want?"

"Western Union. Telegram for Mr. John Paul Frankie Carbo."

"Put it under the door."

"I'm sorry, mister, but I need you to sign."

Inside the door, a young woman's voice said, "Who's that, Frankie?"

"Telegram."

"Don't open no door, Frankie. Are you crazy?"

"Forget about it. I know what this is. They got a fighter, Freddie Steele, coming in for me on the train. That's the one going to win a title. You're telling me don't answer the door."

"Frankie, don't," the young woman shrieks.

There is the sound of the door lock snapping and the door opening and the telegram man saying, "Police department. You're under arrest."

"Frankie! I told you. Bulls!"

There is the sound and grumbling of at least a quartet of detectives.

"What's your problem?" Frankie says.

"You mean you don't know?" the detective says.

"Frankie, make them show you a warrant."

"Here," the detective said.

"Let me see that!" the girl said.

There is a crackle of fresh paper and then at least a gasp. "Frankie, this says you murdered somebody! Who is this guy they say you murdered?"

"It never took place," Frankie said.

"You're under arrest for shooting Mickey Duffy," the detective said.

Suddenly, standing up in the file drawer is Frankie Carbo, who is only twenty-seven but turning gray already. That was his nickname, Mister Gray.

Now there appears a man leaning against the wall, holding a small pad and a gold pen, a thin man with a straight face and blue eyes that are merry behind round wire-rim glasses. He has on a light brown plaid suit that doesn't have a wrinkle. A flowered tie has a big stickpin. He shows a gold wristwatch and an enormous pinkie ring on his note-taking hand.

Frankie Carbo stands with his feet slightly spread and a smirk on his lips. He looks at the man in the brown plaid suit. "It's over nothin', Damon," he says. The plaid suit smiles.

Frankie Carbo holds a hat in his free hand, which is an exact description because the detective is putting a handcuff on the other one. The hat is a pearl-gray snap-brim from Moe Penn Hatters, Pitkin Avenue, Brownsville, Brooklyn, the home of Murder, Inc.

His girlfriend, Miss Vivian Lee, now rises from the clips and stands next to her boyfriend, Frankie. She turns to Damon Runyon. "I am a legitimate person," she announces. "I got a job dancing. Put that in, Mister Runyon. Vivian Lee is the kind of girl you bring home with you to your mother. She knows what I am the minute she sees me."

Miss Vivian Lee has bright red hair and blue eyes that are narrow in anger. The chest is dewy. She wears a long print dress. She holds a large yellow straw sunhat. Miss Vivian Lee slaps her big straw hat on and pulls it down so that it covers her face to the chin.

Frankie Carbo brings up his snap-brim pearl-gray hat as if to inspect it.

Frankie Carbo now puts the hat over his face.

He and Miss Vivian Lee, handcuffed to each other, step out of the file drawer and walk past the photographers, who can get no photos of their faces.

And now everybody is gone and I listen to these files, groaning with past wrong but saying nothing you can catch. As I am left alone in this room, I might as well start talking. I am going to tell you a story about a guy, Runyon, and newspapers and a city and deliver much of it with one hand in these file drawers and the rest of it, a lot of it, straight from memory, and I am about the only one who can do it because of the life I've lived. I must have heard a thousand conversations about the man and his times from all parts of town because I spent so much of my life, too much of it, in bars and police stations, in racetrack receiving barns, fight gyms and political clubhouses. I don't think that anybody working New York today has been in more places or heard more, or has so many street memories, and so when I tell you this story and I put down what people say, the conversation was told to me long before we met each other as reader and writer.

I spent the full five years at John Adams High, Ozone Park, Queens, whose back door was about a furlong from the place where wallets die, the last turn at Aqueduct Race Track.

After high school, I then went into the only business that would support somebody like me at the time, the newspaper business. The first job I ever had was right there in Queens County, at a place called the *Long Island Daily Press*, which is now good and dead. When I was there, each Saturday the paper ran a page of photos of young women who were engaged. That some might have been pregnant rather than ecstatic was their business. Ours was to present them in the best light available, you might say. The photo retouch artist, Al Camera, used an airbrush liberally on all pictures of young women who did not appear particularly endowed. "No flat-chested girl appears in my paper," he said. Thus, the Saturday engagement page took your breath away. Guys with no connection to the young women used to buy the paper to look at this page full of big hussies. Not one of the engaged young women ever complained.

I went on working for newspapers, and during all my years in the trade, I have been around so many people, from so many places, standing in bars over the long hours that are the open seacocks that scuttle many lives, hearing so many tales and recounted conversations that, as I told you, I now can stand here in this room in Texas with the files and give you as much of this story from memory as from clips.

I spent five years at Hearst and the same at the Scripps-Howard feature service, where the sports editor was Harry Grayson, who once worked the fight beat with Runyon and then wrote stories about Runyon taking a share of the fight promotions. After work for so many evenings over so many years, I went up to an office on 42nd Street and Broadway and sat with Ned Brown, who was ancient by then, but was still putting out a wrestling magazine with his daughter. He had been a medical student who became the boxing writer for the *New York World* and hung out with Runyon, and did some scheming with him, including judging fights.

In those years running around the streets, there was Eddie Reynolds and Bunny Jacobs, who ran the theater ticket agency across from the Forrest Hotel on West 49th Street, and when I got there, the sidewalk in front of the place was still called Jacobs Beach. Frankie Carbo sat in the Forrest bar with a Scotch and stared at the cigar in his hand and said, "We need charity." Then he left to shoot somebody. He liked to think of himself as a fight manager, but as the Runyon clip tended to indicate, he was really a standby killer for the Mafia. Upstairs in the hotel was Eddie Borden, one of the rare completely honest humans, and who also was the Broadway broad jump champion. And then there was Butch Tower and Toney Betts and Champ Segal, dreaming of great scores with hot horses. Artie Bieler, who shot Vincent Coll, sat with me on the hospital steps while my son was born. A woman was inside giving birth while he talked to me for hours about old murders.

Later, at the *New York Herald Tribune* newspaper, I had a column and started a great run, and continued it wonderfully well and for a long time, and sometimes when I think of this, I am so delighted with myself that I could sing a song.

And you better do the same thing. For if you do not blow your own horn, there is no music.

Anyway, when I first started my run at the *Herald Tribune,* my friend was Damon Runyon Jr. He put my column on the syndicate wire each night. He didn't drink by then and had a lovely daughter and was living in his father's old suite at the Forrest.

After forty years in newspapers, I have a girlfriend, although she is hardly a girl anymore, working in many news morgues from here to El Paso. Also, in my travels I've been in the public library in every place in the country I've been in, and as a library is the last repository of American manners, along with the nation's history, I have made friends forever with as many librarians as I have met. Books don't seem to encourage crossness. So as I'm talking to you, I not only have these old dented files in this room in Austin, Texas, but right there on the desk in the corner is the phone. If I use it, I have the use of a hundred years of files in towns all over the country. One group of files must be used in person. They are in the sub-basement of the courthouse at 60 Centre Street in Manhattan. When I used it, the floor was covered with so much water from an underground creek that clerks had to wear high rubber boots. The electricity is off because of the water, so you use a flashlight to find precious records of old trials, which, the moment you touch them, start flaking.

Now in the big barren room in Austin, I hear someone lighting a match. It is down the line of files, at the *RU–RY*. I walk over to the *RU–RY* and start to pull out the drawer. A hand comes out to stop me. I brush it aside and open the drawer. My fingertips blacken as I fly through the envelopes. "The Runt — Slays Classmate." "Runstrom — Prison Escapee." And then we come to "Runyon," and the first envelope says, "Runyon, Mrs. Damon," and there are other "Mrs. Damon" envelopes after that, all preceding those under the name of Damon Runyon, which take up the rest of the drawer. All his years of columns are here. As I began to pull out the first envelope for Mrs. Damon Runyon, both the guy's hands come down on mine, big pinkie ring and nicotine-colored fingers clamping on mine, trying to stop me from pulling the clips on his wife. But there was absolutely no way to stop me from getting them out. In fact, the envelopes jumped out of the drawer. She was the second wife and she wanted to be known.

When the housekeeper walked across the room in her smart flowered dress, she sounded like a broom on a tile floor. Her name was Patrice and she had to be at least in her mid sixties on this night, and that is being a nice guy, but the dress was cut as low as they go for someone who doesn't dress this way to take money directly from men. "I am a virgin," she would announce. She had been married twice, but that really doesn't make any difference, because very little else about this whole story fits, either.

Her eyes were large and dark, and atop them was a pile of blond hair, which might seem strange, being that the eyes were so dark, but if she could say that she was a virgin, then certainly she could be blond.

Now, at seven o'clock at night, her employer, Bill Dougherty, walked into the living room, and immediately her face showed displeasure. People were coming for dinner and Dougherty wore no tie. Long ago the housekeeper had announced to Dougherty, "This is my place as much as yours." His response was to dismiss what she had said, primarily because of a fear of truth. Periodically, he would try to fight back, but she had endless will to keep such a battle going and he did not.

"Don't you think you'd look better in a tie?" the housekeeper said to Dougherty softly, her voice liquid and beckoning.

"Why?"

"Please. You know I'm right about these things. My husband Damon used to take an hour to pick out the proper tie for the day."

"I'm not living on Broadway. These are people I do business with."

"I just thought that perhaps it would look nice on you. Oh, dear, I don't know. Perhaps I am bothering you. Wouldn't you like a nice martini?"

"No. I drink enough outside the house without doing it inside, too."

"Wouldn't you just have one to relax you?"

"I'm perfectly relaxed."

"No, you are not. I can see that you are tight as a man who has to fight Joe Louis. I insist you have a drink."

"I told you don't push. You'll have me crazy. You go too far."

"I do not."

"You sure as hell do. Why do you want me to have a drink, anyway? So you can have one, too?"

"I do not drink," she said.

He shrugged. He had never seen her swallow a drop in the house, although half the time at night she was clinging to the doorway. He once had been the general manager of a beer company, and knew a little about alcohol. He was sixty-two, a big man with sharp features and a deadpan face that broke into totally unexpected smiles. In daily business he was austere and proper, and suddenly he would run from the office to follow fire engines. He stopped at all accidents. Here in his home, supposedly to cook, dust and make beds, was Housekeeper Patrice Amati Runyon. The night before, she put on white gloves and went for a drive in her white Jaguar. After midnight, she was barside, Florio's on the Boston Post Road, and gave away the car to a landscape worker. He was maybe twenty-five. Later, she decided she didn't want to give him her Jaguar. At 3 A.M., Patrice the Housekeeper called her employer, Dougherty, who came down to the bar and drove her to the landscape worker's house, which was one flight over a liquor store. Patrice reclaimed the keys and started a fight between the landscape worker and his wife and drove off in her Jaguar with one white glove held in the air, as if she had just won at Indianapolis.

She stood at the front window and looked down the long driveway at the last light of day blazing off the Sound, which was as flat as slate. She sighed. "Oh, Bill, isn't it lovely? I feel like I'm standing in my living room in Miami, Two Seventy-two Hibiscus Island, that is where I lived. Oh, my beautiful white house. I would stand in the living room and I would have to squint when I looked at the water. The sun placed diamonds on it. Dear Damon would be upstairs typing on his white typewriter. Everything in the house was white. That is my favorite color. You know that. My Jaguar is white. My ermine isn't white, but it's so beautiful. Have you given any thought to the one hundred and fifty thousand dollars so I can have my body frozen in California when I die?"

"Never mind freezing you. What about getting the lobsters out of the freezer?" Dougherty said.

"The girl has it well in hand," the housekeeper said. "I am a virgin and I want to be frozen so I can come back in five hundred years. It only costs one hundred fifty thousand. Why aren't you looking at me?"

"Let me ask you something. Do you ever bother to look in the kitchen?"

"Why are you being so fresh to me?" she said.

"Jeez, I do pay you to work."

"What's that supposed to mean? That you own me? That you can get so fresh with me?"

"I don't think I said anything so insulting."

"You said 'work.' "

She was about to become furious at him, but at this moment the first guests arrived.

She didn't know either of them. She went to the door and threw her arms around the woman. "You first," she said. She kissed the woman on both cheeks. She kissed the ruddy-faced man on the cheek. She led them inside. "What will you have to drink? I know what. A nice martini."

She didn't wait for an answer, and went to the cocktail table and held a bottle upside down, as if it had fallen from a shelf, and when the gin ran over the sides of the glasses, she pulled the bottle up. She put in some vermouth, which ran over the sides, too. She shook it like she was working behind a bar, and handed the drinks to the couple, both of whom buckled on the first sip.

"Oh, dear," the wife said.

"Boy," the husband said.

"I should have made you mint juleps," the housekeeper said, smiling sweetly. "This is Derby time, is it not?"

"Oh, I forgot all about that. When is the race?" the man said.

"Tomorrow is the first Saturday in May, isn't it?" she said.

"Sure is."

"Well, that's Derby day. Do you know something? I don't believe I know the field for this race. Oh, I do know one horse, Dust Commander. That's because Bobby Lehman owns him. From the Lehmans, you know. But isn't that a perfectly horrid name? Dust Commander, indeed. I hope the horse loses with such a name. My horse was named Angelic. She was a fine filly. She won a stakes race at Saratoga. Angelic was my own horse. Damon, he was my late husband, was partners with me in Tight Shoes. We were going to run him in the Kentucky Derby."

"Really?" the woman said drily.

"Oh, yes. Nineteen forty. Two weeks before the Derby we were at Jamaica Race Track and we ran Tight Shoes in a sprint against a colt — oh I can't recall his name, but I certainly can tell you the owner. John Hay Whitney. Yes, dear Jock. He was so young and handsome then.

Did Jock Whitney die? I can't think of everything I should know. Anyway, Tight Shoes ran such a marvelous race. I know the name of Jock Whitney's horse now. Calory. He was a one-to-four shot. Well, we win by six. Basil James rides for us. He gets him there in one twelve and two. I remember going into the winner's circle and Hirsch Jacobs, our trainer, said to me, 'How does it feel to finish ahead of a Whitney?' Hirsch and I laughed. Then he said, 'I believe you ought to take a chance with this horse in Louisville. If I were you I would announce that I was shipping the horse down on the Cincinnati Limited tomorrow morning. Attach him to the train in a private horse car. Send a wire to Louisville right now and tell them the horse is coming.' So I just turn around to my husband Damon and I say, 'Oh, Damon, the horse runs in the Kentucky Derby?' Damon just smiles and says 'Carissima mía, whatever you want.' He took off his glasses and began to wipe them. He always did that when he didn't want you to see that he was excited or emotional. I turned to the press steward and said, 'Please announce that Mrs. Patrice Amati Runyon and her husband Damon Runyon are shipping their colt Tight Shoes to Louisville aboard the Cincinnati Limited tomorrow. He will run in the Kentucky Derby on May 4.' "

"How did you do in the race?" she was asked.

"Oh, poor Tight Shoes. He got sick and damn near died the day he got to Louisville. He never made the Kentucky Derby. Gallahadion won. Mrs. Mars owned the horse. She's from the Mars candy company. Milky Way bars. Do they still have them? I remember kissing Mrs. Mars right as the horse went under the wire. She was in the next box to us."

She glanced at the dining room table: salt shakers! "Oh, excuse me. I must attend to something." She smiled. The dress went *shoosh-shoosh* as she walked toward the kitchen, where Princess Starr Bright, the Indian girl she had hired to do the work for her, stirred a vat of clam chowder.

"You filthy squaw!"

Princess Starr Bright looked up.

"You ignorant redskin sonofabitch! I told you that you were never to use salt shakers for company. You use the little dishes. Salt in a silver dish. Oh dear, where are they? You should catch a good beating. You should be out jumping on corn for some big ignorant buck. No wonder you people commit suicide so much. You people are such victims!"

Outside, Bill Dougherty sat with the guests.

"Is she really the housekeeper?" the man asked.

"That's what she is," Dougherty said.

"And you have another girl inside the kitchen?" the woman asked.

"Oh, the other girl doesn't work for me," Dougherty said.

"Who does she work for?"

"She works for the housekeeper."

"The housekeeper works on a budget?"

Dougherty closed his eyes. "I don't know. I tried to be a simple guy when my wife died. This woman has me so effed up — excuse me, but that's the way it is. I don't know whether I'm here or gone." He didn't want to start telling the people who the housekeeper was. If they heard from his mouth that she was Patrice Runyon, the widow of Damon Runyon, the New York newspaper columnist whose typewriter invented the Broadway world with the stories about guys and dolls, which became one of American's most famous Broadway musicals, they would say that, sure, Bill has the old broad living with him and instead of saying it's his cousin, he tries to pass her off as the housekeeper. He also knew that Patrice would tell them so many things by the end of the night that they would consider her crazy and leave it at that.

Now other guests arrived, and as there were twelve for dinner, Patrice the Housekeeper was too busy mixing drinks to talk about herself. At dinner, Patrice drummed these long fingernails on the table and told each guest where to sit.

"And you are . . . please, you have to tell me your name again."

"Martin Siegel. This is my wife, Mimi."

"Of course. I'm getting so horrible with names. Did you ever have a Champ Segal in your family?"

"We had a Siegel who was club champion at Whippoorwill."

"Oh, that's not quite the Champ Segal I'm thinking of. The Champ Segal I knew shot people."

Then she stepped into the kitchen.

"Get that soup, you effin' Indian!"

Patrice the Housekeeper sat down at a place she had set for herself. She was next to a man named Mattone, who had a large wholesale hardware business that purchased a screw manufactured by one of Cannon's businesses.

"You're the housekeeper?" Mattone said to Patrice.

"Yes."

"That's all right. It doesn't bother me."

"Did you know Al Capone? That's *Mister* Al Capone."

"Let me ask you," Mattone said.

"Yes?"

"Is this the first thing you ask every Italian you meet?"

"Yes. Because Mister Capone is their natural hero, don't you think? He certainly was one of mine, and I'm not even close to Italian. I'm Castilian Spanish. When I used to eat with Mr. Capone, we always had gold plates."

"You work for him?" Mattone asked.

"Oh, dear no. I was a dinner guest. My husband Damon and I went to Capone's all the time in Miami. We lived at Two Seventy-two Hibiscus Island and he was at Ninety-three Palm Island, which was just a few yards over a bridge. A footbridge, really. Damon and I would stroll over there sometimes for dinner. We had this marvelous Italian food heaped on gold plates."

"Gold-*colored* plates," Mattone said.

"Oh, not at all. Mr. Capone would only eat from real gold. When we dined out at an exclusive restaurant, some of his people carried gold plates for him in this big bass fiddle case. They had gold plates and machine guns in the case. They would go to the dinner table and order the waiter to remove the restaurant plates and they would snap open the case. First, Mr. Capone's people would take out the gold plates. The others dining were ecstatic over the gold, but that stopped soon enough. Under the gold plates were these Tommy guns. You ought to have witnessed the sight of all these stunned people in the restaurant. Frozen stiff! I mean, positively terrified when they saw the Tommy guns. One of the men with Mr. Capone would snap the case shut. You were left with all this . . . gold! It was so exciting to walk up to a table in a restaurant and see the whole place looking at the plates on the table. Of course you understand that by now the case had been snapped shut and they were unable to see the machine guns, but I must say they certainly knew that they were there. I didn't care. The least bit of light over the table would make the gold glow. I used to be thrilled just to eat lettuce."

"I'll bet you were." Mattone squirmed. He decided that Dougherty was a civic hero for giving a job to this poor demented old broad rather than leave her in a home someplace. He also was beginning to wish she would go into the kitchen where she belonged and tell her stories to herself.

"I didn't like Mr. Capone's dishes as well as I liked the plates Mrs. Roosevelt served me lunch on," she said.

Hearing this, Mrs. Mimi Siegel asked across the table, "Where was this?"

"In the White House. We were upstairs in the family dining room. Damon was in the solarium with Mr. Harry Lenny, the fight trainer he got to help Mr. Roosevelt with his exercise." Patrice rose. "If you'll all excuse me. I must go inside and check on how the girl is doing with the lobsters."

She went into the kitchen. Princess Starr Bright said, "Do you need anything?"

"Shut up, you filthy Indian."

In one move she took out a Coca-Cola and splashed some in a glass, pulled a gin bottle down from a cabinet, filled the glass to the top. She gulped the drink down and immediately made another.

"I told you I hate Indians, so don't talk to me."

She had about seven good slugs of gin in her within, what, ten minutes?

Patrice the Housekeeper walked out of the kitchen like a fighter going up to the ring. "You!" she snarled at Dougherty. He looked down rather than get into a fight. Patrice dipped the spoon in and out of her soup noisily but took none of it. She said to Mattone, "Do you like Frank Sinatra?"

"The greatest."

"A slob in my husband Damon's movie."

"What movie?"

"*Guys and Dolls.* I don't know who was worse, Frank Sinatra or Marlon Brando. My God, when I think of the real people. Champ Segal and Butch Tower. Arnold Rothstein. Good God, Owney Madden! Then they make me sit through Marlon Brando singing. A big fat stumblebum. And this Frank Sinatra. That takes care of him as a person of action."

"He's some swinger," Mattone said.

"In my husband's movie he is a two dollar bum," Patrice said, the softness dissolving on the words and turning into acid. "My friend Bob Hope would've been so much better."

Watching Mattone, Dougherty said to himself, What would he do if he knew this witch was telling the truth?

A year and a half before, Dougherty had placed an ad for a housekeeper. One day, a woman in a white Jaguar pulled up with the ad in her hand. She wore one white glove and held the ad in the uncovered hand, obviously to keep it from smudging a glove. Before coming to the door, she stood in the driveway and looked over the land and the view of the Sound. She walked quite confidently up to Dougherty and gave her name as Mrs. Gridier.

"I of course have references," Mrs. Gridier said.

"Would you mind if I checked them?" Dougherty said.

"Of course not. I have them written down for you."

When she left, Dougherty looked at the names. One was Ralph Pulis, vice president, trust division, Chase Manhattan Bank, New York, New York. I never saw a maid with references like this, Dougherty told himself. He called the Chase bank, and later that day Pulis called him back.

"She is the widow of Damon Runyon, the writer," Pulis said. "She receives from us about thirty-five thousand dollars a year in royalties from the play *Guys and Dolls*. I can't estimate how much she will get next year, because they do the play in England a lot and we don't know what the grosses are right away. When theater groups decide to do it around the country here, we don't hear about it until the contracts arrive. We never can tell. But it is about thirty-five thousand a year."

"She really was married to Runyon?"

"Absolutely," Pulis said. "There is one thing I can tell you about but I don't have the record here. She is the owner of the Amati diamond. It belonged in her family. It is 31.12 carats. That makes it one of the ten largest stones in the world at this time."

Now, in the midst of dinner, Patrice the Housekeeper decided that she wanted another drink. In the kitchen, when she opened the green glass Coke bottle to go with her gin, her past came pouring into the glass. As usual, the remembrances made her angry. No matter how she tried to twist her memories, it all came out that once she had a big guy.

Damon Runyon invented the Broadway of *Guys and Dolls* and the Roaring Twenties, neither of which existed, but whose names and phrases became part of theater history and the American language. "The building of castles in the air made dreamers of us all," his friend Gene Fowler said. Runyon's people, Nicely-Nicely and Nathan Detroit and the Lemon Drop Kid and Little Miss Marker, were famous all over the world. He started the characters off in newspapers, then took them into short stories, following which they became huge American movies. He left nothing for anybody who followed. Just about. While there are still plenty of thugs around who seem lovable at first, it all winds up with them selling drugs to kids. At least in Runyon's time, the drugs were going to high rollers and other nitwits. In New York now, the Lady Boncile takes the bail money for boyfriend C.J. and she buys a liquor store and he sits in a cell. But the money all comes from selling crack to thirteen-year-olds, and I don't know how to make that bright and funny. Anybody trying to write a column today winds up writing about zoning changes.

He made the gangsters so enjoyable that they could walk off a page and across a movie screen. Twenty-six of his short stories became part of the American art form, the movie. He stressed fine, upstanding, dishonest people who fell in love, often to the sound of gunfire that sounded harmless. His stories were based on people on Broadway and 50th Street in Manhattan, in front of an all-night delicatessen called Lindy's. He had the most admiration for Arthur Bieler of Tenth Avenue, an undertaker's delight, who in real life rarely missed when shooting at people he didn't like.

"The secret of my success is that I always keep my machinery in good operating condition," Bieler told him proudly.

Many of his people and their actions in real life were frightening to temporal authorities, but what does this have to do with the most important work on earth, placing merriment into the hearts of people? Damon Runyon's Broadway was the only major street in the world where love was a topic of conversation. His first movie, *Lady for a Day*, was nominated for the 1933 Academy Award as Best Picture of the Year, and also the star, May Robson, and the director, Frank Capra, were nominated.

Runyon's second movie, *Little Miss Marker*, created the biggest star in the world, Shirley Temple. And there was *The Big Street*, which is an American movie, probably a great one, that reflects the country, a large door pulled completely back, with feelings open for all to see, and not the silent, pained face of some piece of porcelain on leave from the Royal Shakespeare and reflecting so much inner writhing over nothing. Lucille Ball, its star, said *The Big Street* was her favorite movie, and it certainly should have been, for she was stunningly beautiful and the acting was the best she ever did.

Runyon gave the American gangster movie someplace to go. The first three big gangster movies were *Little Caesar*, *The Public Enemy*, and *Scarface*. They appeared in 1930, 1931, and 1932. You had Edward G. Robinson as Rico, a bloodthirsty homosexual; James Cagney, who wanted to kill everybody in the house; and George Raft flipping a nickel as part of the Capone mob. After these movies, the only thing left was to have the movie tough guys get into drinking blood. Yet in 1933 here came Runyon's short story "Madame La Gimp" onto the screen as *Lady for a Day*. Gangster humor gave the gangster movie room to survive.

The best way to write stories about good guy gangsters was to live with thieves, which was great with him. The boundary between Runyon and gangster was so fine that it was his genius that he somehow was always able to leave one deserted patch, one long scar running like an unseen traffic line down Broadway, as a border marker. Always, he dressed and acted like a gentleman. He never swore in front of a woman, nor permitted others to do so. He could become as formal as a drawing room, with demeanor suitable for the saddling enclosure at Belmont. Yet he often forgot himself, and in the finest dining rooms in the city spat on the floor to punctuate something he was saying. He was supposedly a newsman who dealt in facts, yet superstitions from dark winter nights in the empty West often directed his life. If he forgot something and had to return to the house for it, he walked in, sat down, spat, crossed his feet, patted one shoulder and said aloud a series of numbers. He refused to enter a room with a hat on the bed. At large parties, when great numbers of coats and hats were on a bed, he would slam the door so he couldn't see. A comb on the street caused him to walk away, as the comb meant a woman with witch powers was nearby and could determine his life for the day. If he knew her, it was fine. She could blow on his dice. But he was afraid of an unknown. In covering gangsters, he refrained from making personal appearances at time of gunfire, and therefore expected his people, no matter how upset they were, to use weaponry either before he showed up or after he left.

Which was the case with his friend Harry (Champ) Segal. He was from the family that started Segal Lock, which later became the first safety razor company. But it was always said of him, "The family makes the locks and the Champ picks them." One night Runyon went to night court because the Champ had just shot a couple of people. "They fucking deserved to get shot," the Champ explained. A detective had come into Champ Segal's bar and, drawn by the smell of fresh cordite, found a big gun with the initials *HS* on it.

"I can prove it's not my gun," the Champ told the judge.

"How?" the judge asked.

"Because I don't own a gun," Champ Segal said.

When he was released due to postponement, Champ Segal asked Runyon, "If I go back inside and ask them, would they give me my gun back?" Runyon said nothing. His small foot pawed the boundary between them.

Not that he was so terrified about being corrupted; Runyon stole milk from babies. Oh, he did not take the milk right out of the babies' mouths, for that still would be a most abominable act, and this is essentially a very romantic guy, a gentleman. He only stole money from the charity that raised milk money for the babies. As it was no small charity, and it was run by the wife of a newspaper publisher and involved no public funds, he was therefore not some common bum filching change.

He said aggressively, "I need the money. Besides, babies cry even when you give them the milk."

He lived during Prohibition and the Depression and came from the West and understood his city better than anybody of his time. Right away, he figured out that New York had more religious fanatics than any city aside from Mecca in season. He backed the winner, the Roman Catholics. That his first wife, the former Ellen Egan, was a Catholic had only a little to do with this, because he had been raised among people who felt that Catholics should be shot second only to Indians. What convinced him was the overwhelming number of Catholics in New York. "They have to be ahead upstairs. Therefore, the losers might truly weep." But he was not out there on his knees. He would accompany a heartbroken prostitute to St. Malachy's, the show business church, in order to write a story, but aside from that, he made only those appearances needed to display affiliation. He wrote notes to the nuns at his daughter's grammar school, took the cardinal to championship prizefights and would restrain himself from attending the racetrack on Good Friday.

But while the Catholics were first in church steeples, the Protestants were first in banks. There was no way to crack that league. "When you give a Presbyterian a bank, you might as well give him a machine gun," he said. As the Rockefellers owned Chase Manhattan Bank, he deposited money there. "I ride winners only," he said. After these two institutions, he knew the remainder of the city was wet cardboard. Any known person could sit at any of the great dinner tables in town. The work that made him, however, required him to live with gangsters, touts and gamblers. Which he didn't mind a bit because he loved them:

1:30 A.M., corner of Broadway and 49th Street. Ptl. Rouse, post 17, found 16-year-old, Manny Manishor, 128 Houston Street, engaged in coin tossing for money with several men. Manishor said men were in contest to see who would take Manishor to his doctor. Boy said he had stomach ache. Abraham Goldberg volunteered to take boy. They left. Ptl. Rouse to post 17.

Some minutes later, when Manny Manishor returned to the sidewalk in front of Lindy's all-night delicatessen, he yelled for his money. He had a way of spinning a coin off his fingers that made it drop dead, right at the crack in the sidewalk, and got him all the money. Now he wanted his end and nobody was there. "I play in the schoolyard, all the kids pay. I come here the first time and all the big shots run. Put in the paper that they're all deadbeats," Manny complained to Runyon, who fell in love with him forever.

Runyon came out of a time when the day's news arrived by ink. His newspaper business was the literary underworld, filled with people in lowly positions, most of whom were so incapable of controlling their own lives that it was a feat to pay any bill. Their home lives were at least crumbling, but they judged others with great disdain and rigidity. On Runyon's paper, the editorial writing about economics was done by Gene Fowler of Denver, who, having blown his train ticket money on whisky, had to accompany a casket from Denver to Albany in order to get within scheming distance of his job in New York.

He arrived in Manhattan by boat and then wrote scathingly of the mayor's budget.

As with all weak people, the criticism and backbiting by reporters occurred only during office gossip. After this, they all proceeded to genuflect in print for a rich man or a politician. They had no access to public funds, the most stolen article in all of crime, so only rarely could a news reporter be found in jail. Yet they constantly perpetrated the worse crime, the sin of omission, by not persistently attacking the alliance of builders, bankers and politicians who, stealing tax money, form the criminal class in this country. Even worse than this thievery, the amount of effort used in pilfering tax money took the attention of government away from anything important.

Even with all this horrible weakness, newspaper work habits caused reporters to put excitement into the American language. City rooms were places where fragments of thoughts kept spitting around as people tried, and with so little time, to put together two or three different circumstances into one story. Yet the art of thinking through was spo-

radic in any newspaper. In the 230 years of American newspapers, there
have been about seventy-five columnists worth reading, and of these
only a pitiful few, Benjamin Franklin probably being the best, could
cling to a thought long enough to see it to the end. For everyone else,
there always was great security in being late and forced to work rapidly, for then no calls could be allowed from some filthy loan company.
At the same time, because words and phrases are formed by nervous
energy, the language was strengthened by people writing while looking at a city room clock that moved too fast. You had Runyon, of the
New York American, watching Franklin D. Roosevelt being sworn in
while Runyon's employer, William Randolph Hearst, urged him to write
critically of Roosevelt. "The man has a handicap, you know," Hearst
said, reading the text of the speech.

Runyon shook his head. He typed out as a phrase in the lead of his
column: "Never knock a winner."

He watched his friend Regret pull his pants pockets inside out on
Broadway to show what had happened to him at Jamaica Race Track.
"All horseplayers die broke," he wrote that night. Another friend, Ir-
vin Cobb, rewrite desk, *New York World*, watched a man who was
shot while simply walking along the street. Back in the city room, Cobb,
nerves rattling, made the typewriter carriage jump up and down as he
tried to figure out how to describe it. Suddenly the phrase "innocent
bystander" jumped onto a page for the first time. As news reporting
was a business for children who gloated over something that for the
moment only they knew, following which there was a need for immediate gratification, big cold beer and whisky next to it, Cobb rewarded
himself after work by going to a whorehouse. He heard one of the girls
trying to describe a customer she hated. "The man was a . . . stuffed
shirt!" He shook with anticipation of writing this into the first piece he
could.

On newspapers, Runyon wrote sports and covered murder trials.
When he finished such work, he went into a Park Row drugstore that
was a Prohibition speakeasy for newsmen, where one night Don Mar-
quis of the *Sun* had pasted to the wall a first page made up for the *New
York American* of December 25. The huge red headline said, "CHRIST
IS BORN."

When Runyon turned from news to delivering myths, they became
one of the few things ever to spring out of the Broadway cement and
last. In New York history, there is O. Henry, and on the other side of
the street is Runyon. He felt he had been born a poet, and the first

writing Runyon ever did was poetry; two collections were published when he was in his twenties. Afterward, even at moments of highest flying success, he felt he was somehow cheating. Poetry required his most precise effort, and he wanted to see which hilltop he could reach. He was, of course, able to make a living only by writing about prize-fighters and gangsters, and therefore dropped the role of poet.

He loved one thing about being a poet — the strain of dictator that every poet has in him. How marvelous it is to find such a quality within you! He used real people walking on the sidewalk as the basis for his fictional characters. When he was through distorting them, directing them through his stories, he made the real persons believe every word they read, and soon they began acting accordingly.

With Patrice the Housekeeper, the illusion started on the night that Runyon and his usual party of one or two purportedly legitimate individuals, and the rest certainly not, took her to the West Side nightclub owned by Texas Guinan, a large, coarse, talkative woman. Patrice had just arrived in town, and he was getting her a job as a dancer at the club. This didn't just come about, as if the two had met while changing trains at 42nd Street. Rather, there was quite a history to their knowing each other, about which we will tell you all as we go along with this story.

Most of such history has to do with Damon Runyon, a thin man who walked on tiny feet, which took a size 5½B shoe. He had a solemn face that was controlled by pale blue eyes that distilled all they saw into three words: "Get the money." He wore round wire-rim glasses over the eyes. As the eyes usually were fixed and stern, the face took on the same look, but the face always was at the point of folding into a smile, for Runyon did not go a quarter of an hour without somebody causing laughter. At the same time, the face had to be ready to jump into the frozen stage, for when offended or angered at something that did not go precisely the way he wanted it, Runyon had a cold glare that caused family and friends to be afraid of mentioning even the weather for fear they would be shot by the eyes. His hair was slapped straight back, and by now — he is forty-five on this particular night in his life, in the year 1925 — some of it on the forehead was at least withering. Many times in his newspaper column he had advocated that men be allowed to wear hats indoors, and cited strict Jewish religious groups and not his own fear of baldness. While he wore more jewelry than a bride, all of it was cheap costume stuff. If he had to come up with the real for a broad, such as he sure was going to have to soon for this Patrice, then he did what he had to do. But for himself, he wanted the wrist to gleam and the tie-clasp to look like a million, but he didn't want to pay for it. He didn't want to be caught wearing swag jewelry, which is the only kind he would think of buying. Much of the jewelry Patrice wore over the years was as hot as a live fire, but he figured nobody ever would bother her. The famous Amati diamond, of course, was all hers. He also kept his money for something important, like betting on a horse. He was smoking cigarettes and drinking coffee; he drank about forty cups a day and had a cigarette with each. On this occasion, he wore a subdued brown plaid suit and a yellow tie, arrived at after an hour and a search of perhaps a half-hundred other ties.

Runyon sat at a table with a man who looked like a priest and kept his hands folded as in prayer. He was Edward Frayne, sports editor of the *New York American*. The other man at the table was a young, dark, handsome hoodlum named Frank Costello, who was thirty-four and had certain changes taking place in his life. He found he liked talking to people better than he did shooting them, and thus he wondered about the usefulness of the gun in his life. He had served a year in 1915 for wearing one, and by now he was increasingly confident of his ability to survive without one about. I can steal with my mind, he assured himself. Of the two — Frayne, the legitimate job holder, and Costello, a young and willing gangster — it was no contest as to the better thief. You had to keep extra lashings on an ocean liner if Frayne was on the dock. He was with his wife, who never questioned where a dollar came from. Costello was with a dark-haired girl named Jeannie, and he made it plain he would kill with bare hands anybody who looked at her. Runyon appeared to be with Patrice. He held her hand, and they scarcely exchanged words while gazing at each other. However, he expected the others at the table to act as if he were not with a woman, and this they did, talking to him familiarly and to her as if she were an innocent bystander. He had a wife, Ellen, who was home on Broadway and 95th, where he felt she belonged, taking care of two children.

Taking care of them well, too, for there was no worry about money in his house. He regarded himself as an excellent husband and parent, and his only unease about his home was that now and then in the dawn air as he passed his wife's bedroom, he thought he smelled whisky. Just because he was out all night with girlfriends didn't mean that she could sit home and drink. Common drunk. She slept in the largest bed sold in New York, with the tufted headboard painted with restful garden scenes. When he slipped into the room on a couple of occasions, intending to search for bottles, the last breezes of the night would cause the large cut-glass chandelier to tingle, and he would retreat, fearing that the sound would awaken her.

Runyon's bedroom was an armory. There were several shotguns, some leaning against the wall and others in leather carrying cases. On the dresser was a curved machete and a large .45, whose aiming required the arms of a piano mover. Hanging on the closet door was his army uniform with ribbons from the Spanish-American War. A football and major league baseballs were on one chair. A good Irish maid kept the place in such order that he felt it was absurd when his wife expressed any dissatisfaction with her life. Why, look what he had done for her: he had given her a fine home and, to complete his duties, two children so that she could spend her days covering babies with kisses. That he never got home until dawn, and on many occasions failed to arrive at all, was merely because he was following a clear path through a merciless world.

Which, he told himself, was precisely what he was doing right now in this saloon. He was out with Frank Costello, and even if he and Costello didn't like each other ("I had despise for the guy a lot of times," Costello had said) they needed each other enough — Runyon, the story; Costello, the respectability — to suffer through hours together at a table. For her part, Patrice tilted forward the usual couple of degrees to give her front some real good exposure.

Runyon also was waiting for the owner, Texas Guinan, to make her way, caterwauling, through out-of-town suckers. When she arrived, Costello stood and held the chair for her. This is why Costello became known as the Prime Minister of the Underworld.

"Hello, sucker," Texas Guinan said to him. "That's real coffee," she told Patrice, indicating Runyon's cup. "Look at what I got for you, honey. He ain't even a drunk."

Guinan broke Runyon's unwritten rule about identifying relationships, but she was a loudmouth with a license around town to say anything, and on this occasion it was even more permissible. She was to hire the nineteen-year-old Patrice as a dancer. Whether Patrice could dance well enough for a big-city show line was irrelevant. Texas Guinan had such a small dance floor that all her chorus line did was hop around like nervous little birds.

"Where are you from?" she asked Patrice.

Patrice knew enough not to mention Mexico and was figuring out what to say when Costello brought the waiter over for drinks. "The little girl will have Coca-Cola," Texas Guinan said. She knew exactly what would happen the moment she said "little girl": Runyon would quiver from shoe to hairline. For years, Guinan had been presenting some big-chested hillbilly chorus girl to audiences and calling out, "Give the little girl a big band." Always, some big butter-and-egg man from out of town would crawl onto the dance floor and try to bite Texas Guinan's little girl.

And now right here at the table Runyon went into shock. "Damon don't know what hit him," Costello later remembered.

Patrice sipped the Coke.

"I went to school in Texas," Patrice said.

"So did I, honey," Texas Guinan said.

"I went to school in New Mexico, too."

"That's one place I missed," Texas Guinan said.

"You've got a little Spanish to your voice," Runyon said.

Patrice kept her mouth shut.

"I make you for a Spanish countess," he said.

"He got a story in his mind already," Costello said.

"You are a countess from Spain."

"You bet she is," Texas Guinan said.

"A countess. Trained in dance. Here between throne topplings."

She swallowed the rest of her Coke.

"I have a job," Patrice said.

"Give the little girl a big hand," Texas Guinan said.

Everybody at the table clapped. Runyon did not let go of Patrice's hand.

Months after this, he was in bed in his penthouse on the roof of the Forrest Hotel on 49th Street. He was still a trifle married, but he also had to have someplace to live with his girlfriend Patrice, who was here beside him in bed. He wore a dressing gown and pajamas, smoked a cigarette and worked on a short story called "Madame La Gimp." It was about a busted valise of a woman out on Broadway who once had been a dancer and somehow had banged up her leg and walked with a limp. "I seldom see her but what she seems to have about half a heat on from drinking gin," he wrote at the start. Of course this part of it couldn't be Patrice, because as she had shown in Texas Guinan's night-club, she did not drink at this time. But throughout the story, he wrote in longhand that Madame La Gimp was "ginned up." In the story she had had a daughter out of wedlock, and had sent the daughter to a distant relative in Spain. Madame La Gimp cleaned houses in a place on Park Avenue and used the stationery from one rich man's house when she wrote to the daughter in Spain. The daughter then wrote to say that she not only was marrying the son of a Spanish nobleman, but the nobleman's whole family was coming to New York to meet the rich Madame La Gimp. A street guy named Dave the Dude, who was Frank Costello in fiction, arranged for a party in the Park Avenue apartment. They found a card and pool cheat to pose as Madame La Gimp's enormously wealthy husband. The guests were pulled from tables at Lindy's Restaurant on Broadway and dressed by a Broadway show costume place. In the story, a butler announced the guests: " 'Vice President of the United States, the Honorable Charles Curtis,' and in pops Guinea Mike, and I say as much to Dave the Duke, who is running around every which way looking after things, but he only says, 'Well, if you do not know it is Guinea Mike, then will you know it is not Vice President Curtis?' "

When Runyon finished the story, he handed it to Patrice and told her, "This is you. Learn this the way you learned your Hail Marys. But just don't read that you're a countess from Spain. Glom the whole thing. Live the story. Anybody with me is at least a countess, anyway."

May Robson played Patrice in Frank Capra's first big movie, *Lady for a Day*. Patrice saw it a dozen times on Broadway. She became May Robson. Years later, when there was a remake and Lucille Ball played the part with Bob Hope, Patrice saw it in a movie house in New Bedford, Massachusetts, for two straight weeks and became Lucille Ball. But always she was a Spanish countess. Better, she was the owner of the Amati diamond.

Now, in the kitchen at Bill Dougherty's house, she was so engrossed in remembering this particular story about her life that she never noticed the Indian carrying out coffee. She had another drink. In the story, the phony husband they got for Madame La Gimp was a man named Judge Henry G. Blake, who was far from a judge, but had such a distinguished bearing that he could pass for anything. In the end, both Blake and Madame La Gimp believe the story they are acting in and they get married.

Dougherty looks just like Judge Blake, Patrice decided. She poured herself another drink. By the time she came out of the kitchen, unsteadily, she was a Spanish countess, the dinner guests were gone and the master of the house was up in bed.

TWO

O N THIS DAY of October 8, 1880, in another Manhattan, out in Kansas, sitting in the darkness of the wheat and corn fields with only little lights from candles and weak gas lamps showing in the pitch dark, Libbie J. Damon Runyan went into labor in a bedroom off the small living room of a house on the corner of Fourth and Osage. The house cost $800. As there were not enough trees in the new prairie town for wood fires, a coal fire, the smoke heavy and bitter, burned in the living room fireplace. The doctor, Charles Little, who lived on the corner of Fifth and Osage, came across the street to the Runyan house and delivered the baby. Afterward, he sat in the living room with the father and toasted the mystery of childbirth with whisky. Alfred Lee Runyan walked the doctor across the street to his house and continued for another block to the newspaper office where he worked as a printer-writer. He stood at the type case and picked out a birth announcement.

The next day his paper, the *Manhattan Enterprise*, whose masthead announced it was "An Advocate of Purity," reported:

FOUND: A small male dog, partly greyhound, came to my place September 29th. 509 P. H. Mjungdahl, McDowell Creek.

REMEMBER: C. E. Miller keeps nothing but good driving horses.

FOR SALE CHEAP: One cook stove, as good as new. Enquire of Judge Brown at his offices.

MARRIED: WILKINSON-CALVIN

Sept. 30 by Rev. R. D. Parker, Marshall E. Wilkinson and Miss Florence J. Calvin. Both report they are very happy.

DIED: CONNOR — On Sept. 24th, Robert, son of James Connor, aged 8 months.

MILLER: In Riley Centre, September 27th, of typhoid, malaria, Miss Jane Miller, aged 11 yrs. 4 months and 5 days.
BORN: RUNYAN — To A. L. Runyan and wife, a son

In Manhattan, New York City, on the same day, the old record for recidivism, one day, New York State penal system, falls and a new record is established by ex-convict Otto Walters, a man of many outstanding characteristics, one of which was not good intentions. Released amidst great hope by warders at Sing Sing Prison in the morning, Walters rode down to Grand Central Station, where for about a half hour he experienced the thrill of freedom. Then he got down to business. In two hours, Otto Walters managed to make himself a prominent part of the day's events as recorded by the *New York Times* newspaper:

CONVICT CAUGHT
Man Again Apprehended
by Alert Police

The story beneath, supplemented by ancient police records, indicates that Otto Walters, upon being released from Sing Sing that very morning of October 8, immediately displayed rehabilitation by entering the store of A. J. Christen at 208 Broadway and requesting to see some watches. He had been living by a calendar and now he wanted a watch. Mr. Christen, the proprietor, produced a tray of them. Thereupon, Mr. Otto Walters caused the tray to spill on the floor. As Mr. Christen bent over to pick up the watches, he noticed that Mr. Walters was stuffing a silver chronometer into his pocket. Mr. Christen, proprietor, let out a prolonged scream. This attracted Detective Moran of the 14th Precinct, who had Walters back in a cell in the Tombs jail in time for late afternoon peanut butter.

And to complement Walters's great performance, another New York endeavor immediately takes place. The taking of money from suckers, who can't wait to give it to somebody anyway, occurred on a large scale. For Damon Runyon's birth date, the October 8, 1880, issue of the *New York World* newspaper reported:

GREAT DAY OF SPORT AT JEROME PARK
But Joy Is Diluted By Bettors' Riot

. . . Sport at Jerome Park race track yesterday was seriously affected by the "scratching" of a big favorite within an hour of the time

fixed for the race. Under the old system of pools it made little difference, for all money was returned, but under the "play or pay" book
system, all the money bet on a "scratched" horse is lost. The horse
"scratched" yesterday was Checkmate, who had been a big favorite.
Consequently, when it was announced at 1:10 P.M. that "Checkmate
does not start," the betting ring became a whirlpool of noise and excitement caused by bettors punching bookmakers.

At the very sound of the announcer's voice in New York, the first
squall of a newborn baby started in the house on Osage Street in Manhattan, Kansas. The cry went out of the house on Osage Street, and up
into the sky, where it became completely understandable, because it
became the motto of America: "Never give a sucker an even break."

Because of this sudden and widespread influence caused by one birth,
it is all the more necessary at this point to look into how the Runyans
got to this country, for in showing the years and ability and movements
involved in establishing a single talent, we have a marvelous picture of
how pride can overcome humility and truth.

As far as he was concerned, his ability was the result of immaculate
conception. Of his family's past, he said the greatest thing ever to happen to him was that he stopped drinking before he got to New York, or
otherwise he would have wound up a sodden bum, capable of doing
nothing, like his father and the family that had gone before him. "They
were nothing but some Huguenot horse thieves," Damon Runyon said.
"Anything I have, I worked hard for. I sure didn't get any help from
anyplace. The only thing I ever got was a wire asking for money."

The first records show that a family named Rognion was in Poitiers,
in the Poitou province of France, in 1645, and they turned their backs
on every Catholic in France by embracing Calvinism. The Rognion
heretics became known as Huguenots. Nobody knows where such a
word comes from, although it is used in all history books. The American Society of Huguenots, in New Paltz, New York, thinks the word
might originate from the meetings held by French Calvinists at the
Hughes Gate in Paris. Yet the society feels unsure. In 1665, decent
French Catholics drove them into the sea, and the Rognions ended up
in New Jersey, where the name was changed to Renoyan.

A couple of centuries later, one of the Renoyans, William, who was
Damon Runyon's grandfather, was a printer in New Jersey. In 1852,
he headed west with eighty families to find gold in the mountains; they
believed that somewhere out on the plains there would be a waterway
that would take them all the way to the West Coast. Renoyan traveled

with his printing equipment: chests of type, stocks of paper and ink, and a printing press of such weight that it required extra lashings, for if it shifted, a boat would list dangerously. At the Ohio River, the families loaded their belongings and parts for ten prefabricated houses onto a steamer called the *Hartford* and sailed to the mouth of the Blue River in Kansas, where, as they debated whether to land or try somewhere else, the *Hartford* chose their futures by running aground. They waded off the ship and went through the weeds and onto flat land that glistened in the sun and spread out for so many miles, the view so constant because of the treeless ground, that all became confused and unsteady simply by standing still. They lugged their prefabricated houses off the *Hartford* and set them up on the flat prairie land where, perhaps to reassure themselves in the loneliness, they named their village Manhattan.

William Renoyan established a newspaper called the *Manhattan Independent.* He changed his name to Runyan, either to join an America of names shortened as they hit the prairie or more likely to save a character count.

The settlers arrived in time to experience the effects of the Kansas-Nebraska Act of 1845. The law had caused newspaper work to be in the middle of the fight between abolitionists and slavery. Guns appeared at all printing stones as violence spread to almost any subject the newspapers touched. Colonel Dan R. Anthony, a publisher, was horsewhipped, beaten and seriously wounded by gunfire. J. Clarke Swayze, editor of the *Topeka Daily Blade,* said John W. Wilson of the *Topeka Commonwealth* was padding his printing bills. Wilson blew him away with a .45. Carry Nation printed the *Smasher's Mail* and Moses Harman put out a paper called *Lucifer the Light Bearer,* which called for free love on the Prairie and drew gunfire from citizens. The only publishing law worth observing was to remain alive. Libel was a word most could neither spell nor comprehend. Sol Miller, editor of the *Kansas Chief* at White Cloud, wrote that when Editor Thomas J. Key of the *Constitutionalist* was born, "there was a double birth; one was a baby and the other a calf — the baby died shortly afterwards."

As putting out a paper usually was work a man did by himself, the stories of these years reflected the energy and anger of a single person, and you can track this from the past in the West to Runyon in New York.

William Runyan and "Runyan's wife" had a son, Alfred Lee Runyan, who was the father of Damon Runyon. As she was a woman in a prairie printing family, she was so unimportant to daily living that nobody took the time to write down her first name. When Alfred Lee Runyan was nineteen, he set type for a notice in the *Manhattan Independent* of October 10, 1868, that said the state of Kansas was sending volunteers into the badlands to fight the Indians who threatened white civilization.

On October 12, the Annual Report of the Adjutant General shows, Alfred Lee Runyan, a short guy with red hair and a belligerent chin, was one of the first volunteers at the Manhattan recruiting station, and was assigned to Company M, Nineteenth Kansas Volunteer Cavalry Regiment, which also did a lot of walking. General George Custer, of the Seventh, said, "The Nineteenth put to the blush the best regular infantry." When Al Runyan left for military service, the editor of the *Manhattan Standard*, apparently printed in the same shop, said, "He has promised to keep our readers posted as to the incidents and doings of the regiment." Of the 189 days that Al Runyan served, 111 were spent with Company M, mostly out in the field escorting wagon trains from camp.

Later, the writer Damon Runyon, in all the tales he told in New York, never mentioned the existence of his father's newspaper dispatches. Only a most indefatigable researcher uncovered them on the western plains. They provide indisputable evidence that writing is acquired by inheritance, and should be distributed in surrogate's court, because the one who receives the inheritance is almost sure to be a bald-faced liar and claim he learned by himself. Herewith the work of the father that was denied to the end by the son.

CAMP NORTH CANADIAN, IND. TER.
December 5, 1868
[Published January 2, 1869]
EDITOR STANDARD: — Instead of remaining at Wichita two or three weeks, we were on the march early Friday morning, the 13th of November. We marched over rolling country, very sandy, and towards night, camped on Standing Turkey creek, a small stream about 15 miles south-west of Wichita. Here we saw our first buffalo in the distance and one of our scouts, Apache Bill, killed two. The next day we saw buffalo in large herds, and carried the hind-quarters in on our backs.

At Medicine Lodge creek, we had a stampede and lost about 150 or 200 horses. We had to lay over here one day to hunt for them. All but seventy-five were recovered. . . .

Our horses were now so weak for want of corn that we had to walk nearly all the time. The only food they got was by digging under nearly fourteen inches of snow; and as the men were also weak for want of proper food, we had to march very slow. We camped that night on Round Pond creek, a small stream, but with a great deal of timber on it. Here the men suffered more than at any other time; and as it snowed all that night and the next day, it being also very cold, and the men being starved, a great many almost barefoot, they suffered almost beyond human endurance. Hundreds would have given anything they possessed for one good meal. I have seen five dollars offered for one small piece of buffalo meat, the size of a silver dollar. One man gave a good pair of buckskin gloves for one hard-tack. Many lay around the fires so nearly starved and frozen that they could scarcely move. Hunters went for buffalo, but returned unsuccessful, as there were none to be seen. It was a terrible state of affairs. They were all exposed to the bitter fury of the storm, without tents, and some of them froze their almost naked feet very badly that night. The men began to talk of the good qualities of horse and mule meat. The officers of the regiment did all they could to alleviate the sufferings of the men. To my own knowledge, the officers of Company "M" gave nearly all of their scanty stock of provisions to the men, and went without themselves. . . .

[The next day] orders came to leave the wagons, all unserviceable horses and all sick or dismounted men. We started late in the afternoon, about 450 strong, with a very different appearance from that we made marching out of Topeka, 1,000 strong. Then we marched out gaily, four in rank, close up, with fine, spirited horses, in good order, arms and clothing bright and clean. Now we marched out in single file, our line strung out about 5 miles, with broken down horses, hardly able to walk. Some of the men almost barefoot, with clothes burned nearly off them, getting too near the fire on cold nights; and thus we left "Starvation Hollow," as some of the men called it. Several of the horses gave out before night, and most of their riders took the back track. We marched about ten miles, through deep gullies and canyons, with walls from ten to one hundred feet high on either side. We camped in a deep ravine, with plenty of timber, though no water. It was very cold and disagreeable for the men to camp in the snow, and many froze their feet. We were on the march early next morning through a very rough country and deep snow, and at night encamped in a thick woods. In the evening several Indians were seen, for the first time, on the brow of a hill.

. . . We followed the course of the river and when we had marched about ten miles, the troops in the advance suddenly commenced cheering. Hardly knowing why, the whole regiment took up the cry and made the woods fairly ring. We then heard that scouts had come in with the inspiring news that Gen. Sheridan, with a train was only five miles ahead. It did not take us long to travel that five miles. We got into camp about sundown, and a great many of us got our tents pitched that night, and best of all, we had a good supper.

On Monday, the 7th Cavalry under Gen. Custer came in from having a fight with the Indians, south of here. They were on the march for three days and night[s], with hardly a thing to eat. One of the principal scouts, who was in the fight, told me that they killed the Indians' picket line about nine miles from their camp. They then surrounded the Cheyenne village, and about daylight made a charge, killing 60 Indians, capturing about 20 squaws and 30 papooses and killing about five hundred ponies after capture. The 7th, lost one captain and 19 men killed and about 15 wounded. Major Elliott and fifteen men missing. When last seen Major Elliott was pursuing wounded Indians about four miles from the command. It is assumed he has "gone up."

. . . The mails are very uncertain in this country, as the carriers from here to Fort Dodge are often killed by Indians.

Yours &c., A. L. R.

[Published January 16th, 1869]

EDITOR STANDARD: We laid over [one?] day at Fort Beecher and then started back with the empty train. Here we learned that Gen. Sheridan had the Indians surrounded somewhere in the Wachita mountains. . . . One man, belonging to Company "E," was frozen to death, about three weeks ago. He went after a bucket of water to the river, one cold, stormy night, and never returned. He was found, a week afterward, about a mile from camp, half eaten by the wolves. He must have suffered fearfully, wandering around over the prarie.

March 5th, . . . All along our route (which is the one Custar took to attack the Indians) we saw indications of recent occupation by the Indians and they must have been in very great numbers. . . .

On the 8th we reached our destination and camped about five miles from the battle field of Gen. Custar. The Nineteenth had not yet arrived, so we camped and prepared to make ourselves as comfortable as possible. The next day a party struck out to visit the battle field. Almost everything was burned. From appearances it looked as if there had been between forty and fifty lodges. Later accounts of the battle from eye witnesses, say that 7th were very glad to get out of there, and that there were more of the cavalry than Indians killed. . . . Thus the "glorious" victory of the 7th. . . .

By classifying his father only as a drunk, and because the father did drink a ton of alcohol and remain in obscurity while doing so, Damon Runyon grew up without being compared to the father's ability. Private Al Runyan rode and walked for day after day on mean, empty land, with little sleep and poor food, with the empty and endless plains causing the mind to slip into a daze, and he still was able to pick up a tablet and pencil and, shaking the the cobwebs out of his head, compose these understated, often thrilling news dispatches. Any detailed examination of Al Runyan's mistake in often spelling Custer's name with an *a* leads only to the conclusion that it was an attempt to drive Custer more clearly insane.

Private Al Runyan, Company M, Nineteenth Kansas Regiment, U.S. Army, was, at age twenty, living on the same lonely landscape with a general officer who, sword jingling, leather squeaking, was supreme over all in his presence, and when Al looked up at the general, he saw a bum and a bindlestiff in a soldier suit, and went to his tablet and wrote it, then dispatched the article to his newspaper in Manhattan, Kansas, only ten miles from Custer's house on the grounds of Fort Riley. Custer lived in a two-story semiattached stone house, 24A Sheridan, in the row of houses on the most preferred part of the fort. His front door opened to a sweeping, sweet-smelling, clipped, mowed, hand-policed parade ground. Number 24A had low green wood steps leading up to a small porch and front door. That Manhattan paper had to wind up on the porch somehow, but Custer and Runyan never did run into each other, the evidence for this being the fact Al Runyan came home alive. He was somewhat different from his famous son, who, often at moments of moral concern, either did nothing or announced, "I never bite the hand that feeds me."

FORT HAYS,
April 8, 1869
[Published April 17, 1869]
    EDITOR STANDARD: — My last letter was dated at Washita River, Indian territory. . . .
    On March 28, 1869, we started at noon with a loaded train south to meet Custar. We camped on Wolf creek and next afternoon about 3

o'clock we met Custar. The 7th looked "hard." In fact, they had seen hard service. The 18th [19th] was dismounted at Fort Cobb, and Custar took a tour through the Washita mountains, marching between 25 and 35 miles a day, which nearly used them up. Custar overtook the Indians and after nearly surrounding them demanded the white women which were captured on the Solomon and Republican rivers last autumn. After parlying some time, he succeeded in getting them, but not until nearly all the Indians had left. He got three chiefs which he captured by enticing them into camp upon pretence of making peace. He then commenced making presentations to hang them, which brought in the white women, and Gen. Custar then kept both Indians and women.

Captain Payne reports that both Miss Morgan and Miss White, the former of whom was captured by the Sioux and traded to the Cheyennes, and the latter who was taken by the Cheyennes about seven months since, were rescued by the command and restored to their friends. Their captivity has been an unremitting scene of cruelty, torture and degradation. Both of these unfortunate women are pregnant, having been compelled by torture to submit to the brutality of their captors. Mrs. Morgan who was a bride of a month, expresses a hope, however, that her offspring may be white and not of that fiendish race that glories in the murder of women and children. They were compelled to do the drudgery of the lodge, to bring the wood, herd the ponies, etc. Twenty five backloads of wood, which had to be brought from a long distance, was the daily task load of each. They were scarcely clothed at all, and were suffering from intense cold. They attempted to warm their hands at the fire, when the Indians would seize them, and hold their hands over the flames until blistered.

The recital of the many brutalities to which these poor women were subjected should inspire every one with a desire for the condign punishment of the savages, and nothing less than death is appropriate or adequate to their deserts.

The rescue was effected by threats to hang three Cheyenne chiefs who were prisoners in our camp. The savages resorted to subterfuges to delay in the matter, but when Custar ordered the chiefs hung forthwith, and had the ropes adjusted for that purpose, the women were brought in immediately. Their only clothing consisted of an old flour sack each, tied around their waists, and, as will be imagined, they were in a most pitiful and suffering condition. . . . It is related of the 7th that after the Indians' camp had been destroyed, they pursued a blind squaw, which had been left, with their best horses, but she, knowing the country, made her escape.

At Camp Supply Co. M was dismounted, and we had to "hoof it" to Fort Dodge, at the rate of 25 to 35 miles per day, which was the utmost cruelty on the men, almost all with blistered feet. Custar may gain a name for making long marches in short periods, but he wears out men and animals in doing so. He has few friends among the privates of the 7th and 19th. . . . A.L.R.

Runyan and the rest boarded a train and fired rifles out the window into the sky all the way to Manhattan. In 1876, Damon Runyon's father married the mother-to-be, Libbie J. Damon of Abilene, who was a descendant of John White, who landed in Massachusetts Bay in 1638. Al had a job at the weekly *Junction City Union*, just outside the gates of Fort Riley. On June 29, 1876, a soldier walked in and put down a short notice, which read:

> HEADQUARTERS, DEPARTMENT OF DAKOTA,
> CAMP ON LITTLE BIG HORN RIVER, JUNE 27, 1876.
> Sad news has been received of a terrible fight between Indians and United States troops Northwest from the Black Hills, on the Little Big Horn river, a branch of the Yellowstone, in Montana; and General Custer and two hundred sixty one killed and fifty two wounded.

Al Runyan had time only for placing a short box in the paper: "Terrible News." A week later, the paper ran a long story under a tiny headline, "Terrible Indian Fight." He copied a story in the *Chicago Tribune*, the only method small papers had for obtaining national news.

> Proceeding up that river about twenty miles, Custer struck a very heavy Indian trail, which had previously been discovered, and pursuing it, found it led, as he supposed it would lead, to the Little Big Horn river. Here he found a village of almost unexampled extent and at once attacked it with the portion of his force which was immediately at hand. . . .

Al Runyan's obituary for Custer consisted of spending many hours at the type case, setting a story stolen from a larger paper. He spelled Custer correctly. His wife was home packing. He had decided to move back to Manhattan and start a family.

THREE

IT WAS four years later in Manhattan that, as we told you earlier, Al Runyan picked out the metal letters announcing the birth of his son, then known as Alfred Damon Runyan. One difficulty at the time of this birth was that Manhattan, Kansas, had a severe honesty problem, and because of it the father was barely able to feed the son.

Manhattan had too much apparent honesty, and no American newspaper ever survived a plague like this. Oh, the men of Manhattan were not so completely inhuman that they did not steal. But so much of it was done in private or by bank paper, and that always seems legitimate when you first look at it. There also were not enough decent homicides to raise the circulation of the Runyan newspaper, the *Manhattan Enterprise*, by as much as a dozen copies. If it weren't for whisky the thing would have gone under for sure. Starting in Europe, printing always was an accomplice of alcoholism, and the heritage was not lost when it reached the plains and mountains of the West.

First the work. Newspaper language was controlled by the labor of printing by hand, which often made the sentence dependent upon the nimbleness of the printer-writer's fingers. The metal type was stored in a wooden case divided into little compartments which had the most used letters, such as *a, t, r, s,* and *e,* in a small circle at the center of the case. The less used letters were set around them. A printer snatched metal letters out of the compartments and arranged them in words and lines in a composing stick. Over the course of an hour and usually more, he'd have an entire column in a long tray, after which he started on the next column. Printers had to learn to identify letters that were cast upside down and backwards. But even the best had trouble with the *p* and *q,* grabbing the wrong one out of the type case so frequently that the expression "Mind your p's and q's" went into the American language. The other common error was to pull out an n and use it for a u. This caused people who wrote stories in longhand always to place a line under the u and above the n in their copy in order to help the printer. Only some newspaper stories were written in longhand; most were composed aloud while picking the type. The writers were not so great at things like sentence construction. Which did not cause readers to squawk, as many barely understood a headline. In the case of A. L. Runyan, he wrote the stories as he picked type, talking it aloud, his hands going at a type case that he knew by heart. He put his sentences and paragraphs into type as he picked the type and put it into a tray. When he had a column he placed it in a form, a metal frame the size of the newspaper page.

He worked in light fit for a cat. When the page form was filled with eight columns of type — laid out backward and upside down — he cranked the metal frame tight. The type, squeezed in, was banged with a wood mallet to keep it at equal height, and with a shout the page was inked and put on a cart and pushed to a handpress. The upside-down-and-backwards type now came out, on paper, as the day's news.

Now the alcohol. After the newspaper was out on the streets, the writer-printers ran for quick whisky, because they still had to put every letter of type back into the case, with each letter going to its right place, or there would be no paper the next day. They were disorderly people in a trade that called for attempted meticulousness. Newspaper families were neglected and generally shattered and lived under the same roof only because there was no other.

Then, for survival, the two, work and whisky, had to be put together.

Libby and Al Runyan, Damon Runyon's parents, also had three daughters. All four children learned to read using the father's old dispatches from Custer's army, and afterward the day's newspaper. At age eight, Alfie Damon Runyan sat in the semidarkness of his father's newspaper shop, and when the father had just finished handsetting the entire first page of the paper, the boy ran up and pushed the cart to the press. He tripped, and rather than fall he gripped the edge of the cart tightly for balance. The cart tipped and here went the first page onto the floor with a smacking sound. The type went all over the place. Five hours of work were gone. Always, the eight-year-old boy remembered the sudden shock of a clout on his head. The father stood outside and held his arms to the sky and said, "What did I do to deserve such a thing?" Then he walked in fury toward the stone house that the last of the stagecoaches used as a station.

Inside, there were two itinerant printers heading for San Francisco. A. L. Runyan, swallowing whisky with them, said he was sure that he was a much faster typesetter than they were. The itinerants sneered. One had worked in Boston, where printing was an art. "I will bet you a bottle of whisky I can set type faster than you two," Runyan said. Half stiff, he and the two printers went back to the shop. The guy from Boston sure could handset type: he did a column in forty-three minutes. "I can't match you," Runyan said. He waited for the guy to set a second column. Then he awarded the guy from Boston the bottle. As the guy left, grinning with pride, A. L. Runyan had about one column left to set until the page was back in order and he could print his newspaper.

Soon, A. L. Runyan sent announcements of typesetting contests to all newspapers on the plains, with the winning printer receiving a free bottle of whisky. Drunken tramp printers pounded the plains into cloudbanks of dust as they headed to the contests. Regularly, entire editions of the *Manhattan Enterprise* were finished at the cost of a single bottle of whisky.

At this time, small papers were able to start everywhere, for there was no competition from large city dailies. This was before rural free delivery, so the Kansas City paper never could reach as far as Manhattan. When the last tracks of the Manhattan, Alma and Burlington Railroad were spiked down, Manhattan grew, but Al Runyan, who could snare words from the wind, substituted whisky and barroom tantrums for sense. He began signing papers with Kansas bankers, who regarded 24 percent interest as common and were famous for tight smiles that killed more people on the plains than smallpox. Soon, Al Runyan stood at a type case and put together a closing notice and sold the house on Osage Street to people called Williams for, records show, $1,000.

Al Runyan moved his wife and family to Clay City, then to Wellington, Kansas. Copies of his newspapers no longer can be found, but Dee, clerk of the probate court at Sumner County Courthouse in Wellington, has in file cabinets many pages of handwritten testimony that show all the hours and days Al Runyan wasted filing papers in court and sitting through hearings when he merely had to sit down and write. It was the one useless trait he left his son. From all this, Al Runyan learned only one thing. Kansas bankers thought it was being close to God when they charged 24 percent interest. He told this to his son, who never took a bank loan in his life. If he needed money for betting, he went to a legitimate Broadway loan shark.

When his wife Libbie became ill with consumption, A. L. Runyan took her and the children to Pueblo, Colorado, which was on a high plateau a few miles from the first Rockies. Pueblo sat on western sandhills, which was a great place for a writer to be from. Pueblo had many of the appearances of the West, with its low stone buildings and its horses, but on the corner of Santa Fe and 8th Street it also had the Grand Hotel, which had one hundred bedchambers, top floor as good as the first, a billiard room and a bar that was the most magnificent in all of Colorado, and clearly had pretensions to being eastern. The mining and a steel mill on the edge of town caused a large number of prostitutes to take over entire buildings.

While Pueblo was surrounded by a sparkling sky, the town itself was dedicated to the destruction of the human body, with the air virtually grainy from lead and coal mine smokestacks. There were forty saloons in a three-block area on South Union Street. No sin went untouched, or unreported. Over 127 newspapers were published in the history of Pueblo, 35 of them in foreign languages. A. L. Runyan took a job as a printer on the *Chieftain* newspaper, which was in a red stone building with a curved front and an alley behind it, which served as an outdoor saloon and whorehouse. He also discovered the Arkansas Saloon, which had a long bar, a large team of bartenders and free Limburger cheese.

Libbie Runyan was able to put her son, still age eight, into the Hinsdale School, Pueblo School District 6, where one teacher, Miss Smith, remembered, "He could spell very well." A school fire later destroyed many records and more were destroyed in a flood.

On March 3, 1888, Libbie Damon Runyan, age thirty, died of consumption in her home on 8th Street in Pueblo. The newspaper obituaries state she left a husband and four children. She was buried in an unmarked grave in the Oddfellows Cemetery, which since has been allowed to be overgrown with weeds. "The grave was unmarked because nobody marked it," the town historian, Eleanor Fry, says. Eleanor attended a convention of the Association of Gravestone Studies at Worcester, Massachusetts, in order to improve her work in restoring the Oddfellows Cemetery. While doing so, she discovered that Esther Baldwin, one of Pueblo's prominent women, and Maria Lockhart, the town's most famous whore in the 1880s, are buried together with a joint headstone. Esther is buried under the name of Sara Lee Fox, but old Pueblo court records show that Esther died first and that her will left everything to prostitute Maria Lockhart, who obviously was linked financially and perhaps personally with Esther. "There'll be the biggest scramble you ever did see come resurrection day," historian Eleanor Fry says.

The only thing Damon Runyon ever remembered about the funeral of his mother was the picture taken by his young eyes of his grandmother, then fifty-seven, who was standing on the railroad platform holding the youngest of his three sisters. The grandmother obviously was filled with sympathy for Al Runyan. He had taken her beautiful daughter and returned her dead at thirty, and now, at her age, the grandmother suddenly had a new family of three girls. There could be no other way, for it was obvious that the father couldn't take care of himself. She did not dare look at the boy lest she wind up with him, too. Al Runyan stood with his son on the train platform and helped them board. The three little girls stared at him with large eyes, which had been called upon to look at the face of their mother in a box. When the father kissed them, they had no idea of its finality. The train was gone and the boy went with his father back to a rooming house. He never saw his sisters again, nor could he recall his father ever mentioning them. The father barely talked to him about anything more personal than the weather, and he wasn't around to do that so often.

The Pueblo city directory shows that there was no listed residence for the Runyans in 1889. In order to show the fact checking done on a man whose personal life was lived to avert all facts, we can report that they lived for a time as squatters in a shack. In 1890, A. L. Runyan was at 512½ Main Street. The directory states "no dependants," which is correct, for by now the three daughters were at their mother's family home back at Junction City, in Kansas, and Alfie Runyan the son, was already out on the streets earning his own money. The city directory shows that in 1892 the father moved into the Mount Pleasant Boarding House, on the corner of Summit and 6th Street, where father and son took turns sleeping in the single bed.

A. L. Runyan usually went from work at the *Chieftain* to his personal bar, the Arkansas, and when it closed he hung around on the streets and killed the last part of the night by talking with other newspaper workers. In the winter, however, he had to leave the freezing streets early, and came in and slept on the floor next to the bed. Alfie got out of bed as early as 5 A.M. to make room for the father. He would then doze in a doorway until the first delivery driver's horse and wagon sounded on the empty streets. He followed the wagons and took bread and a quart of milk left in doorways of stores not open yet. Once — that he later talked about — his shoes fell apart, and the moment his father came home and removed his, Alfie was out of bed. He had on two or three pairs of socks and put his feet in his father's shoes. He came into school with his feet flopping on the floor.

Early one morning, there was a noise at the door of their room and the father walked in with a woman. He was breathing heavily with whisky and, undressing her, he pushed the son over into a corner of the bed, against the wall, and pulled the girl in with him. Alfie closed his eyes and pretended that the thrashing about right at his side was not occurring. When all was still and silent, he slipped out of bed and went to school.

Alfie, living practically alone, and without company for most of the hours outside school, had no criteria for behavior or speech other than his father's, and on the rare occasions he was with his father, the father spoke only to other men. As Alfie was embarrassed to imitate these adults when speaking to children his own age in school, he mostly fell silent. Holidays consisted of watching his father raise a glass in the Arkansas and clap people on the back in season's greetings, and then the next day, cold and gray, father and son would stand in front of the saloon and wait for it to open and serve Christmas dinner.

There were many men living with no families, and they crowded the restaurants on a holiday. But as Damon Runyon remembered it, he was the only boy in the place on most Christmases. He remembered eating in complete silence. Since he had no hearth or kin on Christmas, and he could see what others had merely by walking a block or two and looking at Christmas trees in the windows of houses, he became afraid of his own emotions. At any big occasions in Pueblo, he retreated inside himself, found a cold empty chamber with pale light, sat down in it and waited for the cheerfulness around him to pass. As his lonely life left him subject to no demands that he enter a conversation, he almost never talked. He appeared to have insides made of plate glass. He saw everything and felt nothing. If somebody pressed a face to the pane of glass and looked in for too long, he merely pulled the shade down.

The most exciting thing was being near anybody who lived outside of normal life. One day he waited at the 8th Street rail station for an hour until the sheriff arrived with a man in manacles named Robertson, who had tried to rob the First Pueblo Bank. Seeing Alfie, the attempted robber said, "Son, you better hope the sheriff here has the carfare, because I left all my money back in the bank." The sheriff and a couple of old men hanging around the station had a fit of laughter. Alfie stayed around the station for hours, talking about Robertson's farewell. When he walked back onto the streets and fell in with highly marvelous law-abiding people, he again enveloped himself in silence.

He could be found in the alley behind the *Chieftain*, smoking cigarettes after school. A widow named Browning lived on the second floor of a nearby building, with her back door opening on a staircase leading to the alley. At dinnertime, when she called for her own children, she always saw the Runyan boy looking up the stairs longingly. He was dirty and wore ripped clothes, but she couldn't bear to leave him alone outside. She brought him up to dinner, where he always seemed to be sitting next to her favorite, Edna. Alfie also sat across from Edna in school. He never talked to her; all he did was look. One day, he got Edna in an empty classroom and pushed her up against the wall. When the teacher came in, she threw him out of school. He also was thrown out of dinners. One day Mrs. Browning opened her door and here on the scrubbed staircase wall was a huge black scrawling: "Alfred Damon Runyan." The mother despised what she saw. The daughter Edna hated it so much that she ran out of the house to look for him. Mrs. Browning caught up with her and, free hand swatting the girl, dragged her home. He never was able to speak to her, so one day in school he passed her a note, which the teacher intercepted. The note, saved over the years and purportedly in Damon Runyon's printing — and it could very well be, for he remembered writing a lot of notes — said, "Meet me behind the paper today and I'll let you have a drag on my cigarette." The teacher threw him out of class.

Much of his days were spent in libraries, reading Rudyard Kipling aloud in the corner of a room. He loved that stirring, tough man's rhythm of poetry, which should have been printed on leather. Then he'd go out to the street and light a cigarette to look tough. Sometime during the first week of February in 1892, Alfie Runyan, now eleven, came to work at the *Pueblo Chieftain* with a poem that had been written in longhand. He was not in rags but in a cap, a British-cut suit, highly polished shoes and severe face. The father had groveled, borrowed, connived, in order to mark properly what he felt was the start of a serious writing career. Had he known that for doing this he would go down in his son's memory as a drunken bum, the father undoubtedly would have left the small ingrate out in the cold, where he belonged.

Alfie remained as fixed as a tailor's dummy while the photographer, using a five-pound Speed Graphic on a tripod and a tablespoon of flash power, took a photo that ran in the *Chieftain* on February 6, 1892, along with his poem.

CREEDE

Written for the Chieftain:
When gold was discovered in Creede
It was just the same as planting a seed.
Crowds rushed there to dig the gold,
And it was just lately the Last Chance was sold.
Of course they had to have railroads,
For how could the mines ship the loads?
The rush is like a human tide,
And miners are seen on every side.
So just go there and make some money,
And then come back and see your honey.
— Alfie Runyan, aged 11.

It was only a year later when the boy got a job as a reporter on the *Pueblo Evening Press* newspaper, immediately extolled Miller's Clothing in order to get a strong discount on another suit and started drinking whisky in the Home Café because he was a newspaperman.

When he was fifteen, there was one night when he wriggled to the front of a crowd of several thousand pressed around the Colorado and Southern Railroad's station for the lynching of a man named Kimblern, who was either black or mulatto. He had killed Dave Allen, one of the proprietors of the Home Café. Kimblern was caught in Denver, and two sheriffs wired Pueblo that they were bringing him back. A freight train came thundering down the tracks at 11:37 P.M. when some people, thinking the train was running past them with the prisoner aboard, fired shots at the engine. So many jammed the station that the train had to stop up the tracks, far up from the station. The train stood motionless as people crowded up to it, and many climbed up and ran through the cars looking for the black man. After that, the train was permitted to pull into the station, and its passengers stepped off into the torchlights of the mob.

Alfie Damon Runyan stood in the cinders and gravel of the railbed as Kimblern was pulled off the train by sheriffs, who immediately shrugged and walked away. For a moment, Kimblern looked just like a fighter rising from a knockdown and, his hands at his sides, walking with dumb resignation into the punch that would send him into oblivion.

The young reporter looked right at the guy and the guy looked at him. "At least I thought he looked at me," Damon Runyon recalled. "I yelled, 'Are you sorry you did it?' I see the guy doesn't know where he is."

Kimblern took a death step and got one foot on the ground when he was swept away by the howling mob. They had a rope, and the prisoner, manacled hand and foot, was thrown to the ground and dragged around the front of the train and out to Santa Fe Avenue and 8th Street. A young man clambered up the foot pegs to the crossarm of a pole and threw the rope over. When they didn't get the body high enough for those in the rear of the large crowd to see, many screamed, "Burn him!" At least they could see a burning body. Somebody pulled hard on the rope and Kimblern now dangled just under the crossarm, thirty feet from the ground.

Alfie Runyan went to the *Evening Press* and read his notes to the city editor, who wrote the story. After this, he ran to the Home Café, where he drank rye until he decided to seek women. There was a shop opposite the train station that had eight barber chairs and two bathtubs. The baths cost twenty-five cents and the water was warmed by coal stoves. Two young women soaped backs and washed them and of course did anything else as long as you had the money. The town was filled with women who were loose by profession.

After the barbershop, Runyan and Chester Letz, another young reporter, bought a dollar bottle of whisky and went to 1st Street to see Nellie White, who gave working-press rates, particularly during those hours when paying customers were home asleep with their wives. Runyan, the child reporter, attended the whorehouse without uttering a word. After drinking whisky and falling in love with one of Nellie White's girls, Runyan took her to see the man swinging from the pole. When a woman on her way to buy milk saw Runyan and his lady sitting on the curb, she stopped on the street, with the body hanging directly overhead, and scowled at the two.

Seeing this, Runyan's lady said, "You got a daughter?"

"I do and she's not like you."

"That's good." She patted Runyan's shoulder. "How would you like it if I ask him to call on your daughter when he gets off work at two in the morning?" Which always has been the retort of anybody who works nights and knows who you meet when you leave work after midnight.

At 8 A.M., the coroner pulled up in a wagon, set up a ladder and cut the rope. People going to work stopped to watch. The body fell to the street with a last thump as Runyan and the prostitute sat on the curb and held hands. He did not like the hanging all that much, although it was part of his times and certainly of his business. Right now, the comforting hand of one of Nellie White's girls, with whom he was desperately in love in the morning, made him forget to notice the hanging.

Aside from nights when the two found themselves on the same story, Runyan's father was distant. Sometimes in saloons, he would talk to Alfie at great length about newspaper work, but little beyond it. He could not talk to his son about anything personal, except how to acquit himself in a saloon fight, about which the father thought he knew everything and of course knew nothing. In attempting to fight, he spent more time on a saloon floor than the spittoons. But the father understood the beginnings of a writer.

"You quote the teller for the bank and not the president of the bank," he announced one day at the bar. "Identify your thoughts with those of a working man, a carpenter rather than a mill owner." Sitting alongside was Hume Lewis, the city editor of the *Chieftain*. Lewis had been educated at Harvard and rode a nickel-plated bicycle. When he heartily agreed, young Runyan was impressed to the bone with what he had heard.

"And another thing you do is stick with what you know. If you see and hear something, then you don't need anything more. The worst thing can happen is for you to use somebody else's brains. Look around. You'll see most fellas'd rather purloin what they hear some fella sounds smart sayin' than spend any of their own sense. Fellas cave in when they hear a dime's worth of glibness. Listen to anybody, but know ye that you cannot succeed by relying on any brain other than your own. That's not so bad, either. You're a bright boy."

In the highly personal matter of saloon fighting, the father taught, "Whenever anything happens, just start going to your right as fast as you can. Most of these bindlestiffs out here only throw a right hand. Big roundhouse punches. If you're going to the right, you'll be out of their reach. When they miss, you bang them with everything you got." The son was small, had exceptionally thin arms and legs, and was best off being trained for spectator.

Then came the first thrill of youth in Pueblo, the appearance of the most dangerous man alive, sure of sight and shot, Bat Masterson.

"I'm dead tired of killing," he announced in the billiard room of the St. James Hotel, a four-story white sandstone building on Santa Fe in which prizefights were staged in the main dining room. A crowd stood along the walls and watched him line up shots.

"How many you kill?"

"How high can you count?"

"Do you remember them?"

"Son, I don't look at the faces. I shoot for the belt buckle. Don't matter what the man shows on his face. I want to see the blood spread across his belly!"

This was just after a prizefight in the dining room. Fireman Jim Flynn of Pueblo — proper name Hector Chiariglione — had just boxed one Mexican Pete. Flynn could fight. Later, he would be seen in a main event at Madison Square Garden in New York in which he delivered a major beating to a big-city tough guy, Carl Morris. Mexican Pete, however, was unschooled in anything but suffering. Flynn won easily. Bat Masterson promoted the show, along with Otto Floto, the 250-pound sports editor of the *Denver Post* and an influential figure in Colorado boxing, and also anything else on which he could place his hands. As was the custom, they had music at the fight, delivered by Schriever's Band and a singer, Ed C. W. Keefer, whose best number was "The Persian Serenade." The crowd was served doughnuts and lemonade, and the ticket takers passed out corncob pipes. The difficulty in having music came afterward, when the musicians demanded their pay.

Now Masterson was walking around the billiard room with the gate receipts in his pockets. Shorty Adams, a Pueblo fight man, walked in with Flynn, the winner of the main event. Masterson put down his cue stick and led them into a smoky little office used by the bar and billiard room manager. Runyan, who had the run of the hotel, stood in the doorway of the room with a notepad.

Masterson sat at the desk and looked up at the fighter and shook his head sadly. "We just didn't make it tonight," he said wearily.

"What am I supposed to do?" Shorty said.

"Get mad, I suppose," Bat said.

"My boy here already bled once. What's he supposed to do, bleed again?"

Bat put his head down sadly. A loud sigh went into the air. "I can give you this, but it's like a piece of my life."

He went into his pocket and brought out a sheriff's badge with his name on it.

"Do you know what this means to me?" he asked Flynn. "This here is the story of my life."

Shorty and the fighter looked at the badge in church silence.

"You know where I had this on?" Bat said.

"Is this — ?"

"The OK Corral."

"I'll be."

"Sad to say, a man has to do things like that sometimes," Bat said.

"How many of the people at the OK Corral did you kill?" Fireman Flynn asked.

"Who knows? I know two of the Clanton brothers. After that I prefer to keep things hazy. That was a slaughter, and I don't know if I'm so proud I was there. I did what I had to do. That was killin' people. Course, they ain't the first I ever done in. I must of shot twenty men out here. That's shot dead. I don't even count fellas who lived with lead in them."

"You killed that many?" the fighter said.

"I'm afraid so."

"Did they say anything to you before?"

"Before they went away?"

"Uh-huh."

"Son, in all my gunfights, the only words I ever wanted to hear was the coroner saying, 'I declare this man to be ex-pired.' "

"You stayed around for that?" the fighter asked.

"Son, I'm the closest thing to Doubting Thomas you ever met. I wanted to stay there and not just put my finger but my whole hand into that man's chest cavity and feel the heart to make sure it's like it should be, as still as a doorknob."

The fighter was reluctant to touch the badge.

"Go ahead," Bat said.

Fireman Jim Flynn read the badge. "It says, 'Sheriff of Tombstone.' "

"You bet it does. Go ahead, take it."

The fighter picked it up.

"Where does this leave me?" Shorty said.

"You and I are going to meet again down the road and I'll make it up to you," Bat said. "But I don't know if I'll see the boy here again." Now he looked at Fireman Jim Flynn and stood up and poked his finger in the fighter's chest. "Mind you one thing. Now you've got my badge. But you don't have a license to kill with it. Only one person allowed to kill with that badge and that's me. I know a badge like this can be dangerous. People have it in their pocket get to believin' that they're me.

I got twenty notches. Kill no more behind that badge, you understand?"

"Yes, sir."

Masterson removed his finger and now, head down, as if hiding tears, he clutched Fireman Jim Flynn's arm and mumbled goodbye.

Runyan, in the doorway, said, "Was that hard on you?"

"I guess so," Bat said. The next fighter walked in, the loser, with a large contusion under the left eye. Masterson became somber. Wearily, the chair squeaking, he shifted around, went into his pocket and took out a sheriff's badge from Tombstone.

"Do you know what this means to me?"

Later that evening, Masterson's partner, Otto Floto, came into the bar with his eyes fiery red. "Where's mine?" he yelled. "You didn't pay anybody else. I'm sitting in there like a good fella, waiting for you to come in and at least pay me. I had enough of your act."

Otto Floto stepped into the middle of the white tile floor and in one motion shucked his jacket and brought his fists up. It was a return match. They had first fought in Denver on the street in front of Bert Davis's cigar store, again over money belonging to a prizefighter, which was all right, except some of it was destined for Floto and never got there. The tale was that it was one of the great street fights ever seen. It was related by Masterson himself.

Now, in the bar in Pueblo, people exulted as Masterson came around a pool table, reluctantly surrendering his cue to somebody, very reluctantly, and advancing on Floto with hands raised. They were both boxing experts, with Floto, the sports editor, using many pounds of printing metal to excoriate a fighter who could not hook off a jab, and Masterson, as promoter, always insisting that fighters must smile upon being hit hard, even when in most excruciating pain. "I want you to teach bravery to the crowd," he'd say.

When they fought in this billiard room, Floto never landed a punch. Almost immediately, his face became crimson. He sucked mightily for any air in the room. His arms were limp and he had to kick Masterson in the stomach. Masterson fought like a senior citizen. The highlight of the fight was a prolonged clinch.

Everybody else became excited and punched each other. Little Alfie Runyan confidently picked a fight with some big ol' horseback rider. He hit the horseback rider and moved to his right, and did real well, except that the rider was a southpaw. As Runyan traveled to his own right, he managed to rush himself and chin directly into the cowboy's best punch, and even in his own written recollections he noted it was "quite a punch, particularly with the two-way action of a little man moving right into a big punch. It was reported to me later that even one of Nellie White's most brazen girls couldn't bring me up out of the smoke." He only had one or two other fights in his life, but in his recollections he mentioned a full thousand.

In saloons all over the West, Masterson said he shot a million people, including a god-awful lot during a Pueblo railroad war. Nobody ever could say with certainty that he ever had killed anybody, even at the OK Corral, where, according to the oral history, thousands were shot. Whenever shooting opened up, Masterson could be found on the ground behind a wall, firing into the sky.

President Theodore Roosevelt, who always disregarded the truth in discussing physical exploits, offered him the post of marshal of Oklahoma. Cornered, Masterson wrote to Roosevelt, "I would be bait for grown-up kids who fed on dime novels. I would have to kill or be killed. No sense to that." Even the letter is suspect, however. A later look at his sentences indicates he used a ghost for the letter to Roosevelt.

Years later, Bat Masterson would become Sky Masterson in the Broadway musical and movie *Guys and Dolls*, with Marlon Brando trying to play him in the film, and he would be the teller of what might be Damon Runyon's most famous anecdote: " 'Son,' my father told me, 'there will come a time when you are out in this world and you will meet a man who says that he can make a jack of hearts spit cider into your ear. Son, even if this man has a brand-new deck of cards wrapped in cellophane, do not bet that man, because if you do, you will have a mighty wet ear.' "

The other characters Runyan carried with him when he eventually reached New York were Cleveland George, Kid Switch and Sheriff John Tobias of the town of Queever, who had to keep the jail full so town merchants could sell supplies to the place. Sheriff John let anybody needing a place to sleep use it, providing they pled guilty to some amateur charge. Most of them pled to vagrancy. "Novices could plead guilty to the charge of carrying a concealed weapon — a razor being a weapon in these parts." The merchants of Queever felt warmth and security as they walked past the jail and heard the babble of a full house. The citizens of the rest of the county, who paid taxes, "didn't understand anything about it, which is the way it is with most taxpayers."

In the year 1898, when the United States moved against an insurrection in the Philippines, Runyan was seventeen and a half and needed

to be eighteen to join the army, but he went anyway to the post office
for an enlistment form. He saw it as a ticket to adventure, and his father saw a bed to himself. When the father signed the enlistment form,
he used "Runyan" and his son signed "Runyon," with an *o*. The *o* was
originally acquired when he had a job at the *Pueblo Evening Press*.
This introduction of a new newspaper here is not as sudden and strange
as you might at first believe. Nobody said hello or goodbye when they
worked on Pueblo newspapers. People changed jobs by walking around
the corner. At his new paper, the *Press*, the editor had decided to give
the young reporter a byline and misspelled it when writing it in pencil
at the top of the story. Runyan thought the editor had changed the
name on purpose. He decided that if the boss wanted it, then that's
what he would get. He needed pay to spend on cigarettes, whisky, and
hussies much more than he needed an *a* in his last name. But for a time
he continued to use both spellings.

When Runyon went with the contingent from Pueblo up to Camp
Alma Adams, outside of Denver, an officer pulled him out like a weed
and told him to go home, that he was not only too young but too small
to be away from home overnight. He snuck into a barracks and pretended he was a soldier. When the troops were loaded on a train to San
Francisco, he jammed in with them and wound up in Camp Merritt,
where he walked around until he found a sergeant from the Thirteenth
Minnesota Volunteers who needed a bugler. Runyon signed papers and
was assigned to Company L. His bum notes drew attention to his size:
a little guy standing in the sand with a caved-in chest and skinny wrists
trying to get enough breath to blow the next string of cracked notes
through his horn.

The *Minneapolis Tribune* reported, in its "Notes from Our Fighting
Men," that "Company L has what is billed as the world's largest soldier, Vern Hanson of International Falls. Hanson is six foot four. He is
said to weigh 230 pounds. Company L also has what it believes to be
the world's smallest soldier. This is Alfred Damon Runyon. He is five
foot six and weighs perhaps 125. He is an interloper from Pueblo, Colo.,
where they must have no food."

On June 26, 1898, when the Thirteenth Minnesota was ordered to
pack for shipment overseas, there was much apprehension over the
chances of little Runyon being under fire of savages in the Philippines.
Runyon suddenly was confined to his tent. The band ahead of them
blaring and thumping, the Thirteenth left camp and went on a thrilling
march through all of San Francisco and out to the troopship *City of*

Para, sailing for Manila and war. Runyon remained in his tent. The Thirteenth Minnesota landed at Manila harbor on July 31, and two days later the city had fallen. When word reached Camp Merritt that the danger was over, Private Runyon was ordered to the docks and onto a troopship to Manila. He loved the triple-tier bunks and greasy soup served out of a tin bucket. On September 1, 1898, he reported to his company's tent. Company L was stationed in the Sampoloc district, which suffered an overcrowding of prostitutes. Thus in Runyon's war there were two great cries:

> You may fire when ready, Gridley.
> > — Admiral Dewey at Manila Bay
> Hey, soldier!
> > — Anastacia Bailerino at Sampoloc.

Always, he said she was the first love of his life. He failed to return on his first pass and said it was because of her. He wrote of her as being "as lovely a maiden as ever came down the pike. Her complexion was the shade of heavily creamed coffee, her eyes were black, her hair a raven's wing." After drinking as much as he could swallow on Christmas Eve of that year, he woke up unable to move. It was beyond a hangover, for an eighteen-year-old should be able to have a clear head by noon at the latest, particularly on a holiday such as Christmas. Runyon remained in bed, with the whisky inside him metabolized into poison. Not only was he not built to fight with his fists, but his insides also were not constructed for sturdiness in this man's world he loved so much. His liver was as weak as a glass chin. It would take him years of pain and unimaginable insanity before he realized this.

The glory of service in the Philippines came down to the middle of the night in a stone corridor of Bilibad Prison in Manila, with water on the floor and dirty prisoners three and four in a cell. Private Runyon, Thirteenth Minnesota, on guard duty, was startled by the metallic sound of something being rapped against the bars.

"That's yours," a sergeant called to Runyon.

"Mine?"

"That's the order. If you leave it in there till morning, it causes fights."

Runyon went to the cell, unlocked it, and a grinning prisoner handed him a full slop bucket. The smell caused Runyon to gag. He walked down the long cellblock, boots splashing dirty water, and emptied the stinking bucket down a hole in the floor. He later reported being wounded twice in the Philippines, and this surely was one of the occasions.

In the army, like his father before him, he finally sat down with a pad and pen and began writing about the life around him. Outside of the one published poem, it was the first writing he had ever done in his life, all previous newspaper work consisting of reciting facts to a person who did the writing. In the *Pueblo Chieftain* of March 8, 1899 — between advertisements for a dozen eggs selling at fifteen cents and for Hood's Pills, which cured sick headaches, coated tongue, gas in the stomach and bad taste in the mouth — there was a news report:

Some Observations by a Colorado
Boy with the Minnesotas.
PRIVATE ALFRED D. RUNYAN
Letter full of Interesting Personal
Mention and Opinions

Alfred D. Runyan, now with Company A, Thirteenth Minnesota Volunteers in Manila, writes an interesting letter to the Chieftain. . . . Young Private Runyan, has shown great aptitude for newspaper work and before leaving Pueblo was a reporter on the Pueblo Evening Press. . . .

Insurgent scares have been the order in Manila for the past few days, but now that these have subsided somewhat the task of going home is again revived. It was a veritable reign of terror here for about a week, the rebel chief, Aguinaldo, issued several proclamations in which he broke off friendly relations with the United States army and an attack was expected every day. All the natives in town went into the provinces and all Spaniards in the suburbs moved into the walled city. An immense number of supposed friendly natives made for the insurgent lines to shoulder guns for Aguinaldo. One day a Minnesota policeman shot a dog down and the report went out that the attack had begun. Soldiers downtown flew for their barracks, pressing street cars, cabs and every other conveyance into service, whether the owners would or not. Everyone closed up business and Spaniards made for the walled town.

The foreigners flung out their flags and closed their homes. In an incredibly short time, the army of the Pacific was under arms and men were being hurried to the trenches. For several days everybody was in suspense but now things are more peaceful and natives are returning to their homes. . . .

Smallpox continues to decimate the ranks of the army but it seems to have now settled on the twentieth Kansas which loses several men a day from the dread disease. Poor old William Bell of C Company, Colorado Regiment, from Pueblo, died the other day from smallpox. He was an old man who served at Leadville during the strike. In Pueblo he worked at the Fire Brick Works.

Nearly half the "non coms" of C Company have been reduced and forty of the company are under arrest, the boys claim, for sending the dispatch asking to be sent home. Sergeant Hiram Wallace was among those reduced and the boys immediately bought him a fine diamond ring to show their regard for him. He is very popular in Company C and the boys swear by him. Yage Hamilton of D Company, thirteen Minnesota, has been in the hospital but is again on duty. Yage's company polices the worst district in town, Zinondo, and smallpox and every other disease is rampant there. This is where the Kansas regiment are quartered.

Certainly our company feeds just as well as if we were home, but then we have a company fund of six thousand dollars and the other companies in the regiment have funds nearly as large. This is due to the generosity of James J. Hill, president of the Great Northern Railroad and to other citizens of the Northwest. Besides these funds the regiment has a fund of $15,000, of which each company draws $50 a month. With it, a splendid regimental hospital has been established and various other benefits given the boys. To show you how we live, I will give our company bill of fare for today:

BREAKFAST OATMEAL AND MILK, STEAK AND POTATOES, TOAST, COFFEE, BUTTER. DINNER RICE SOUP, BOILED RICE AND MILK, BOILED MEAT AND POTATOES, COFFEE, BREAD AND BUTTER. SUPPER STEAK AND FRIED POTATOES, FRIED ONIONS, BAKED SALMON, FRIED RICECAKES, BREAD AND BUTTER, TEA AND PRUNES.

We are given no special instructions, just told to use our own judgment. When we first commenced this duty in Manila we carried rifles. Now we have to carry a big revolver, a regulation policeman's club and whistle. At night we carry a dark lantern — as if we didn't have enough already to carry. I will wager that no police force in the United States is any harder worked than we are. Robberies, murders and all such crimes are common but they are confined to the natives. There is a police station in every district and a central station in the walled town. All are connected by telephone.

There are two courts, the inferior and superior provost courts. The lower court does wonderfully quick work. I had a couple of old native women down there one day on the charge of selling "vino" (the native

drink) without a license. The names of the parties were read and I
was called. "What do you know of this case," asked the judge. I told
my story. "Ten days" said the magistrate before I finished and the
women were led away. It all took about five minutes. Several American soldiers have been stabbed by apparently innocent and harmless
looking natives and it does not pay to take any risks. But I fear I will
weary your readers if I keep this up. So hoping that I have told you
something of interest I will close.

All records of the Thirteenth Minnesota show that Runyon was never
close enough to any shooting to be hit by anything but a bad case of
floating ringworms, which lasted a year. On one of those nights spent
standing guard at Bilibad Prison he found a stone corner with a sharp
projection that he immediately backed into and, he claimed, wore the
stone down scratching the "Manila itch" between his shoulders. The
Thirteenth's memorial book shows that his outfit was stationed in a district of Manila whorehouses. He was disciplined for being AWOL on
one occasion. "Drunk and got lost. Returned of own volition two days
later." In July of 1899, the Thirteenth Minnesota was put on steam-
ships and returned to the United States.
     "Where did you go when you were wounded?" he was asked one day
when he was back in Pueblo and was barside, the Home Café. He had
returned with the Thirteenth Minnesota from Manila and was discharged in San Francisco. He had separation pay, which might have
been as much as fifty dollars, and roaming through San Francisco as a
returning hero, he found it extraordinarily pleasant until he ran out of
money, which took much less than a week. People were at first cool
and then nasty. At least here in Pueblo nobody got mad when he told
his war stories.
     "China," Alfie Damon Runyon answered.
     "Where?"
     "To Peiping to train Chinese troops."
     As he was only in the Philippines for eleven months, and a trip to
Peking in those days would have taken months, it seems he did not put
a boot outside the Manila whorehouse district.
     Here in the bar, he twitched in what he said was the pain of old
wounds, but happened to be his pet ringworm. He frequently went
into the men's room, from which there often came thudding sounds as
he imitated a horse while rubbing his back against the wall. He came
out and announced to the bar that the Chinese were the greatest fighters in the history of the world. He took a mop handle and in the sun

coming through the saloon windows began to do the manual of arms, making the mop handle slap in his hands. There were tens of millions of Chinese troops ready to enter the war on the side of the Americans against the dread Philippine insurgents, Runyon announced to the saloon. Around this time he wrote: "The Chinese infantrymen walk a thousand miles to report for duty. This gives officers a disciplinary problem, for there is no way to punish a Chinese infantryman by having him march guard duty. The Chinese regarded long periods of walking as relaxation. They do have difficulty in performing the manual of arms because they are used to carrying objects horizontal on the shoulder and not keeping it vertical as military life demands. I could do no more than assist in training. When my wounds healed, I was back in action in Manila."

In the bar, he stopped talking and his foot went to the rail.

FOUR

THE CITY DIRECTORY shows A. L. Runyan, "no dependants," living in Pueblo in 1893, 1894 and 1895. In 1896, when the father got into fights at the *Chieftain* and moved to a Colorado City paper, the initials change to A. D. Runyan, living in Pueblo with "no dependants." From 1897 until 1899 Damon lived alone in the Fifth Avenue Hotel. He was unlisted in 1899 and part of 1900. From 1900 until 1902, he was listed as living at 802 Summit in Pueblo, and in 1902–1903 he was at 808 Santa Fe. It was in the directory for those years that the last name became Runyon. Damon kept it as Runyon with an *o* and the father stayed with the *a*. In 1903 and 1904 A. D. Runyon was listed as being at 111 East 4th Street.

The *Chieftain* editor was about to fire him for whisky, so Runyon got a job on the *Colorado Springs Gazette,* in a temperance town, and moved into a rooming house on South Nevada Avenue. He worked until 2 A.M., at which hour Runyon went out in stiff high collar, necktie, short jacket with belted back and English cap pulled down over one eye and sought the Devil. Only a block away in the temperance town was a drugstore with bar in the back room. The druggist's wife demanded that he be home by 3 each night. But another block away, the Elks Club of Colorado Springs, with a great big bar and a running poker game, never closed. If he did leave the Elks, he had to pass a restaurant called MacRae's, which served whisky in coffee cups. The fact that there were three places is vital information, because Runyon, operating on newspaper money, could establish moderate tabs at three places and not owe so much money in one place that the saloon owner would beat him up.

When Runyon was missing from work, he was in bed in his room, unable to move. He had a body that begged for whisky but could metabolize almost none of it. The alcohol turned into formaldehyde, which is the reason, based on medical knowledge, that people say they got "pickled" or "embalmed" last night. Runyon's hangovers lasted for days, and often a week. The illness from whisky, and the simultaneous burning need for it, often lined up on either side of his skull and raced at each other, illness against uncontrollable thirst. The resultant explosion being awful. Once, Runyon walked into the *Gazette* city room and tried to stab his friend Cecil Connors with scissors used for cutting copy paper. He was lugged to St. Francis Hospital for a few days, until, like laundry in a sunny backyard, he was adjudged dry.

When he felt well enough to forget hangover and delirium, he could hardly wait to accompany his friend Cecil on a train to cover a prizefight in Pueblo. The feature of the excursion was a liquor barrel. When he finally showed up in Colorado Springs many days later, he was asked to find work elsewhere. He was in St. Joseph, Missouri, then back to Pueblo. The 1904–1905 Pueblo city directory states: "Moved to Denver."

Runyon arrived in the town just after Bat Masterson departed. Masterson's departure did not suit his own arrangements and it also came quite close to preventing him from becoming such a marvelous Runyon character later on. In May of 1902, Masterson was at a bar in Denver. He was causing great laughter by telling about an offer he had from a newspaper in New York, the *Morning Telegraph*. "Imagine me working indoors?" Bat said. "Why, I'd go to shoot one man and the bullet'd go through him and hit six others."

It was on this very day that a sheriff with a large gun came up to him at the bar and asked him to make a small choice: either get out of Denver right away or be killed.

Masterson stared at the drink in his hand and said, "Do editors spell for you?"

Masterson was offered the newspaper job because the editor, W. E. Lewis, wanted to match his brother, who was a novelist, by writing his own book and using Masterson as the central character. On the train to New York, Masterson sat with a minister, George H. Snow of Salt Lake City, son of the president of the Church of Jesus Christ of Latter-day Saints. He loved the thrill of gambling but could not keep his cards straight, which is a problem. All across the American heartland, Bat Masterson sat and dealt cards without shuffling the deck, and each time, the minister beamed and said, "Thank you." When the train roared into Pennsylvania Station, the Mormon owed him his shoes.

That first night, Masterson went to the Hotel Metropole, on 42nd and Broadway, and contracted with the manager, Poole, to publicize the bar. At noon the next day, Bat went to get paid from Minister Snow at 69th Street and Columbus Avenue, where there was always a concentration of Mormons. New York City Police Officer Richard Clare, on duty under the el at Columbus Avenue, did not like the looks of Masterson, gun bulge showing, as he appeared to be pressing this gentleman. Officer Clare made inquiries. When the Mormon minister explained that he had to pay a gambling debt to this gunman, the cop's hand clapped on Masterson's shoulder. "You're a common lot," he said. He took Masterson in. At the police station, Detective Sergeant Gargan took away Masterson's gun and charged him with carrying a concealed weapon. He was released on $500 bond, which Poole, of the Metropole, arrived to post. When Bat asked for his gun back, the police refused him. Detective Sergeant Gargan immediately showed Masterson's gun to reporters. "Notice that it doesn't have one notch on it," he noted.

Masterson missed jail because the Mormon failed to show in court. Bat went to work on the *Morning Telegraph*, which was printed in an old car barn on Eighth Avenue. He also got a no-show job as an assistant U.S. marshal at the federal courthouse. The job paid $2,000 a year, a sum that should have caused decent people to riot. Bat lived at 300 West 49th Street, a few doors off Times Square, and after work he went directly to the Hotel Metropole. He was to be there for years.

Runyon, following Masterson to Denver, found a job as a news reporter on the *Denver Post*. He wasn't in the place two days when he glanced over to the other side of the editorial room and saw Charles Van Loan — a large man whose face advised that he was utterly devoid of any sourness — take a drink of water out of a pitcher. Now, there are many ways that people take in water, but the drinker's gulp, with the hand shaking the cup of folded copy paper as if it contained ice, tells you more about the person than a complete biography. As Van Loan put the paper cup down, he happened to notice Runyon. Van Loan's eyebrows arched.

"What is that?" Runyon said some moments later when the two were barside, Denver Press Club.

"It's what I drink," Van Loan said. He showed him the bottle. It was something called North Platte.

"Let me see what it tastes like," Runyon said. The steward, Jimmy Wong, poured him a fine drink of North Platte.

"This tastes good," Runyon said.

That was all the words either of them needed for the first day. It took several shape-ups at the bar over the weeks before Runyon finally mumbled that he was going to be a poet. Van Loan announced he was going to be a fiction writer. On the bar, Runyon wrote the start of a poem:

> A big, black hearse; 'twas Dougal's hearse,
>   Creaked down through Union Street,
> And old, old echoes were aroused
>   By the horse's heavy feet.

"You ought to go someplace and finish it," Van Loan said.

"All poetry gets written before you take up a pencil," Runyon said. "It's in the dreaming."

"All of anything gets written before you write," Van Loan said. "But you still have to write it."

"I'll stay with dreaming before I begin the manual labor," Runyon said. He held out his glass for another North Platte.

He put in a lot of time dreaming after this. One payday, he went alone to the Windsor Hotel, which had a sixty-foot bar that was studded with three thousand silver dollars. Calamity Jane had put four shots into the ceiling when the bartender refused to serve her because she was a woman. In the *Denver Post* library, Runyon had found that the poet Eugene Field had once written a poem on paper and traded it for free whisky. Carl Sandburg had worked at the hotel, and Robert Service, Robert Louis Stevenson and Rudyard Kipling had been in the bar drinking whisky right at this very spot where Runyon, drink in hand, stood amidst the gleam of three thousand silver dollars.

Kipling.

He arranged himself at the bar. Cigarettes on the left, drink in the middle and notebook on the right hand. He smoked, sipped and wrote furiously into the notebook for long hours. Then he ripped out some pages and held them out to the bartender.

"What can I do for you?" the bartender said.

He handed the bartender his poem, which was straight from his long hours of reading Rudyard Kipling in the library in Pueblo.

> There's a sting to the breeze of the morning;
>   There's a lash in the breath of the sea;

> And hark! The bells, the convent bells,
> Chant a gloomy litany.
> There's a gloomy mist on the rice fields
> That softens the morning glare —
> And mark the shells, the shrapnel shells,
> As a band strikes up an air: . . .

"It's nice," the bartender said, handing it back.

"I'm giving it to you for the whisky," Runyon said.

"You're fuckin' well not," the bartender said.

"They used to do it here," Runyon said.

"Well, I wasn't workin' then," the bartender said. He walked off.

Runyon went back to the Press Club and had North Platte on credit. Each time he took a drink, he became even more filled with the noble thoughts of poetry. He stared across his glass of North Platte and felt breezes coming across a bay and a sky stained blue, and here in the smoke he exhaled he saw a man with a dynamite bomb in his hand — O pity the earth an' the sea! Troops paraded through the smoke over the bar and he saw the band of the First Colorado marching up the sea beach, with shot and shell raining upon them, and he could hear them playing "There'll Be a Hot Time." A sting in the breeze, a lash from the sea. Steady all! What's here? Soldiers!

Runyon sat motionless on the stool and dreamed. He also was exceptionally gloomy. He never had known that an inspiring thought weighs as much as a sack of cement, and if you have enough inspiring thoughts you can't square your shoulders at the bar.

"He thinks up things," Jimmy Wong said, watching Runyon in gloom at the Press Club.

"He must be burying his mother, shovelful by shovelful," Charley Van Loan said.

At work as a reporter one afternoon, he was in the cellblock behind the courtroom where Mrs. Elektra Beard, a society matron, had just been convicted on six counts of looting the children's hospital fund of $2,120. As she had spent the money on clothes, the jury hated her. She sat in the cell with her hands folded in her lap. Reporter Runyon was at the cell door.

"Mr. Beard will come for me in a few minutes," she said. "He will help me put on my gloves and then we will go home. I'm awfully tired and want to rest."

When Beard, the husband, appeared, he was catatonic. "The appeal," he murmured.

"Tough one," Runyon said.

"The lawyer said the only grounds for appeal have to be on a wrong fact," the husband said.

"What does he think was wrong?"

"Nothing. They had the facts right in this one. The only one wrong is our lawyer if he thinks I'm going to pay what he's asking for to put in an appeal that has no chance."

Beard attempted to console his dazed wife before the guards asked him to leave. Mrs. Beard looked up and said to Runyon, "What is the matter? Mr. Beard did not kiss me when he left. This is the first time he ever left me without kissing me. I don't understand."

Outside, Runyon caught up with the husband. He suggested the Press Club and the husband agreed. At the bar, they each had several North Plattes and now the husband muttered, "Jail for a woman."

"That's too bad," Runyon said.

"Yeah, well. If she thinks I'm going to go broke on her appeal."

Runyon was silent.

"I never saw a quarter of that money, anyway. I remember one morning, you know, I'm not blind, I could see that something was going on, she had on a new dress every half hour and her purse was so full that she was going to hurt her back carrying it. Well, anyway, I told her, 'If you have any loose cash, remember that we're partners in this marriage.' Do you know what she told me? She told me, 'Go out and get your own. After me, you come first.' "

"She shouldn't have stolen from the poor," Runyon said.

"If you can't steal from the poor, who are you going to steal from, the rich?"

Now the husband had another North Platte. He bellowed, as if announcing a train arrival, "She is going to do six months as sure as there are bars on the windows." The glass hit the hardwood. "Next time she'll know enough to give her husband some of it."

Suddenly, for the first time in so long, Runyon felt mirth and the thrill of larceny in him. This painful nobility of a poet that was tyrannizing his life was dispelled. He looked into his glass and now he knew forever how he felt about life: "I love people who steal!"

After work that night, he went to a crap game in the horse barns on Oxford Street, and a guy he called Silent Sam, the quietest man in seventeen states, was throwing dice. The Sphinx was a noisy slob compared to him, Runyon thought. Then Silent Sam threw the dice and they came out the wrong way. "Damn!" he said.

They sure were startled to hear that from him. Even the horses in the stalls — and they were pretty tired horses from pulling the trolley cars all day — were surprised. All over the building you could hear the clop of hooves. As the dice continued to go wrong, he began to talk more. "He can't make a point but he can churn the air," Runyon said. He couldn't wait to write something real. Put your bravery and your bugles away.

> . . . you can write it in ink or chalk —
> You can be born dumb, you can be born numb —
> Them Dice'll Make You Talk!

It was a long way from being published.

As he did in school back in Pueblo, he also used writing as a social exchange. After many cups of coffee in Dan's Luncheonette, he became so enthralled with the waitress that he wanted to reach over the counter and paw her whole body. But he could not get himself to speak to her. She also had a boyfriend who was a frequent visitor. The boyfriend looked like the front end of a locomotive. When the guy was not present one day, Runyon wrote her a note, right while he had his coffee, and put it next to him on the empty counter. She was busy and didn't pick it up. At which point the boyfriend appeared. "Who left this?" he roared. He walked to the far end of the counter to question his girlfriend. Runyon snatched the note and stuffed it into his mouth, chewed a couple of times and swallowed.

At the *Denver Post*, the city editor thought Runyon drank too much and transferred him to the sports department. The sports editor, Otto Floto, was so delighted to find that Runyon could write, even if he did overwrite, that he had him fill up the sports column, which ran under Floto's name. Otto himself was too busy for such grubby work as writing his own column, for he was often out promoting prizefights.

One night, Van Loan, needing money rather desperately, stayed after work in the empty city room and started writing his fiction. He was at it until 2 A.M., then he hurried the three blocks to the Denver Press Club and found the steward, Jimmy Wong, obviously having trouble with Runyon, who was alone inside the poker room, insane on North Platte.

"He is a demon," Wong said. Which became Runyon's nickname in Denver.

Van Loan approached Runyon's table. "Didn't you ever leave?" he demanded.

Runyon had a small pile of copy paper with him. He wrote on it, "I did my stint."

"Are you so drunk you can't talk?" Van Loan said.

Runyon wrote, "Yes."

"Let me see the paper," Van Loan said. He grabbed the sports section from under Runyon's arm.

Otto Floto's column, written by Runyon, was right there, under the heading

VIRTUE INCREASES UNDER A WEIGHT OR BURDEN
by Otto Floto, who has carried some heavy load

Runyon sat back haughtily with a cigarette in his mouth and a North Platte in his hand. He wrote, "I wrote the headline myself."

"Did anybody see it before you sent it down?" Van Loan said.

"I show my work to nobody."

Van Loan went to the bar. He thought that Runyon's contribution to insanity would somehow be the straw that broke the camel's back around here. And that was some big back to break, too. The owners of the *Denver Press* newspaper, F. G. Bonfils and Harry Tammen, walked around with the minds of circus men. So much so that they went into business with Floto and bought a traveling circus. They became celebrities, and as the level of fame of a publisher most often depends on the amount of his irresponsibility toward readers, their paper frequently was a fraud and a fake. The worse sin for a reporter was not producing a sensation. Their most famous news-page headline, eight columns of it, read, "DOES IT HURT TO BE BORN?" Still, here at barside, Charley Van Loan thought that, seeing that publishers can make up for their own irresponsibility by murdering somebody else for the same thing, Runyon was going to be in trouble for the headline. When Runyon finally collapsed in the card room, Van Loan brought him to his room and threw him in like a dead deer.

Sure enough, the next working day at the newspaper, Otto Floto came over to Van Loan. "Keep an eye on that Runyon for me, will you?"

"Why?" Van Loan said.

"I hear that he drinks," Floto said. "He don't even talk. He writes notes. I never heard of anybody this crazy."

On another night, Runyon threw a drink over a man in Gahan's on Larimer Street. Runyon posed like John L. Sullivan, arms out, fists held upside down. He was about to start his famed rushing to the right when the big guy casually reached out and took hold of Runyon by the celluloid collar. The big guy now lifted. Some moments later, the owner, deciding that Runyon was being choked to death, pulled the big guy off. He called Van Loan and asked him to take this little guy out of the place before he was killed.

As the writing of poetry demanded more time than a job as a plumber, and paid about a hundred times less, he understood that he needed a side business requiring neither work nor passion, preserving all strength and spirit each day for his poetry. His business, however, had to come up with the money. It didn't have to be a fortune of money, but at the same time he wasn't some dimwit who thought that the sky would provide. He stood at the bar of the Denver Press Club and thought about uncertain cash, which he knew was a disease tougher than typhus. At work one day he was told that he was being assigned to Otto Floto's traveling circus for a month as referee for the boxing sideshow. There was a country boy named Jess Willard, as thick and tall as a tree, who was paid to meet all comers, usually consisting of half-drunk farm boys boiling up from the crowd and challenging Willard for a five dollar purse. A few pushes and a punch had the farm boys yearning for the oat field. In the course of one of these matches, on a Sunday afternoon in Boise, an Idaho grain worker caught Willard with a right hand that caused his big hairy legs almost to bend in half. Years later, Runyon would go broke on the memory of that punch.

Runyon found that the job of circus boxing referee was exactly what he needed. It didn't dominate his mind and allowed many spare hours in quiet towns for his verse writing. This opportunity for a delightful life began to unravel the moment he glanced at the admission booths set up outside the circus. He spent long periods of time talking to ticket takers, or standing on line with buyers, in an attempt to understand what went into the phrase "paid attendance." As interest in gate receipts rose, poetic beauty dipped. When he finished his month with the circus and was back in the newsroom, Runyon became obsessed with writing stories about business leaders who were heavy advertisers in the newspaper. He felt that he could gain approval of the newspaper bosses and the big advertisers at the same time. He was named business writer of the year by Henry L. Doherty, general manager of the Denver Gas and Electric Company, who took Runyon to a convention of electric light people in St. Louis.

Runyon now decided that he knew everything about business and that he could apply his new science to his old game, sports, and become the first great sports businessman. He announced that he was starting a Colorado State Baseball League. He awarded franchises from a bar stool and soon decided that one league was not enough and that he would form three separate leagues. He hardly had carfare to get to any ballpark. After this, he patrolled the Denver gyms and traveled for hours through the night to fight clubs in small towns, looking for a heavyweight champion of the world. He dreamed of sitting on a wood folding chair in the half-light of a fight gymnasium and writing page after page of poetry. All the while, right up overhead, his prizefighter would be knocking the very front teeth out of sparring partners while getting ready for a huge money match. The thought of money sparked him to talk. "Champions are born, not made," he announced, barside, the Denver Press Club. "I think I will comb the nurseries and elementary schools for my champion. You can tell a heavyweight champion the first time you put your eyes on him."

One night, Runyon entered the Press Club under a moon and emerged into shocking morning sunlight. He arrived at the newspaper plant on Champa Street to find a crowd scuffling on the sidewalk. On the balcony, one of the paper's owners, F. G. Bonfils, threw bright copper pennies down to a crowd of street urchins. He was amazed when people felt he was cheap for throwing pennies and asked him for more. Bonfils called out, "Jesus never asked for money!" The other owner of the paper, Harry Tammen, was an honest rogue, one who would commit suicide rather than degrade human beings, but as he could not stomach being so thoroughly reasonable, he was considered as reliable as sand while Bonfils, with a patrician nose and waxed mustache, was compared in steadiness to the western slope of the Rockies. As Bonfils threw his bright pennies down on this particular morning, Runyon noticed one kid tussling for the coins. He had jet black hair and was about seven. He pushed and punched his way to the penny every time one hit the pavement. Older kids tried to shove him away, and being much bigger they usually succeeded at first shove in toppling the kid onto his back. Whereupon he came off the sidewalk with both hands flailing at anybody in sight. When one of his punches landed, these larger boys were surprised and hurt, particularly when the little black-haired kid threw a low blow, which was every other punch.

Runyon took out a handful of change and gave it to the black-haired urchin, who gave his name as Jack Dempsey. He said he was in from a western-slope town with his mother and two brothers and sisters. The mother had been sick with altitude illness on the western slope and she came to Denver, the Mile High City, to recuperate. When the family got on the train, the mother had the children cram into one seat, as if playing, while Jack hid on the floor. She tried to pay for only three children, but the conductor counted heads and demanded another half-fare which the mother did not have. The conductor was about to throw Jack off when "a rich man" on the train paid the conductor. They now were staying at Dempsey's aunt's house in Denver. He was saving pennies and selling newspapers so he could have carfare home to his father. Runyon extolled him for being a good, strong, purposeful boy. Then he went into the office to work. He was not to see Dempsey again for fifteen years. When reminded of this morning in front of the newspaper, Runyon said he remembered it well, although it was clear that he didn't know anything about it.

In Denver a couple of years later, among those out on the street corners selling newspapers was Eugene Fowler, a gangling, extroverted kid who someday would become a famous name, first at the *Denver Post*, then in New York and Hollywood. While selling the *Post*, he hooked up with the same street kid, Blackie Dempsey, and they tried to get a spot at midday on the busiest street corner for newspaper sales, 16th and Broadway. Only a bear could survive there. Pretenders were given a swat, had their papers taken away and were kicked toward home. Fowler did not mind a good fistfight, and he had a habit of laughing when punched. Blackie did not laugh. Right off, he was thrown into the Broadway gutter by a bigger guy. Blackie got up and came back, not out of pride or to prove toughness, but vengeance. As he could not reach the taller kid selling papers, he got his black hair right up against the tall kid's midsection. There was a loud scream as the big kid dropped his papers and ran off clutching his body where the Dempsey kid had just tried to bite his stomach off. All those years later, Runyon said that he had been raised in the same shed with Dempsey, and whatever he wrote about Dempsey had the authority of a testament and as such was to earn Runyon plenty. Whatever Runyon claimed, Dempsey said was true.

Runyon's actual mistiness about Dempsey came because he was interested in more important things than fistfighting, such as whisky and bad girls.

While walking through the city room one night, the city editor of the *Denver Post* was summoned.

"Say," muttered the girl at the typewriter, heavily painted, totally unfamiliar with the machine.

"What's the problem?" he said.

"Giving a write-up to Denver. I don't know how to make big letters."

"What for?"

"I'm giving a big write-up to Denver."

"You are?"

"How do you spell 'orgy'?"

"How did you get in here?" the city editor asked.

"With Runyon. He went to the toilet. He don't feel good."

And that was the end of that job. As he had no way to last more than a few days without being on a payroll, Runyon went to the *Rocky Mountain News* and begged for a tryout. He needed the job, so he went right for what he knew was absolutely irresistible to an editor: a story knocking anybody who isn't white. The city of Denver was planning to raise a pioneer monument at the intersection of Colfax Avenue and Broadway. Runyon found that the sculptor planned a great statue of an Indian dressed for war and sitting on a pinto pony. He noticed that around the base of the statue were white men and women crouching in terror. He ran from the office with the copy.

"Savages!" Captain Jack Howland snapped. They were in the lobby of the Brown Palace Hotel. Howland, a former Union army officer and famous Indian fighter, sold his oil paintings in the lobby. His works became more popular every year, and he was considered an art authority in Denver. Howland's finger tapped the drawing of the proposed Indian statue. "If this savage was alive, I'd get a shootin' iron and he wouldn't be alive. I didn't risk my scalp so I could retire and glorify these filthy savages."

Runyon ran this quote in the paper and started a campaign to get rid of the Indian statue. The editor of the *Rocky Mountain News* was named Keating, and Runyon, drunk or not, became Keating's new favorite. The newspaper's campaign to change the statue was successful, and the sculptor had to put up one of Kit Carson.

He was half poisoned by whisky one night — not any bad whisky, just whisky taken in such vast amounts that he wound up catatonic for days. When he came to, he was mortally afraid of trying again right away. He sat for hours in a rooming house and began a short story that came from his imagined military experiences. He wrote while smoking Turkish oval cigarettes and putting Zymol Trochets into his hot, seared throat. He wrote in a room with the shades drawn against the heat and with his typewriter on a table facing a wall. "It is the only way for a writer to write," he always said. "The only scenery needed is the imagination. Even a potted geranium gets in the way." His first story was about unemployed soldiers in a Colorado militia unit that was supposed to help break a strike of mine workers. Runyon's soldiers, and the miners and their wives, beat off an attack in the snow by some rich militiamen from Denver. He titled it "The Defense of Strikerville."

The story used a narrator's voice that showed the beginnings of a style that was to develop into one that became instantly recognizable as Runyon's. In "Defense," in place of a narrator speaking in the first person, which would become his style, Runyon simply quoted the man for the length of the story: " 'Lemme tell you about that,' said Private Hanks, sitting up. 'Lemme relate the sad circumstances of J. Wallace Hanks' enlistment in the Colorado State milish, and if you all don't weep, you haven't got no hearts.' "

Hanks, of course, was Runyon. Later Runyon would change the narrator to a nameless man, who would still be Runyon but would speak in something Runyon was certain he alone had discovered, the first person present. He ended "Defense" with a scene that was weak, but it was an early version of what was to become a typical Runyon ending: tough guys assist an impoverished damsel in distress as all readers smile at the warmth. Runyon mailed the story to *McClure's Magazine*, which paid him $25 and asked him to write more.

"The Defense of Strikerville" appeared in the *McClure's* issue of February 1907. The author was twenty-seven and now had his first fiction published. His next story was "The King of Kavanaugh County," which ran in the April issue. It started by saying, "A white party dress will attract a great deal more attention in the slum district of Denver than it will at the party for which it is designed. Especially is this true if a pretty girl is wearing the dress." Pitting rich against poor. The rich woman was Miss Laurene Mason and the representative of the poor was Con Kavanaugh, who had a saloon in which the men blew their money over his bar, and he gave it back to their wives, who lived in a building called the Rat Pit. Of course Con was better than Laurene, the society woman, until she saved herself by learning at the end how wonderful Kavanaugh was and how brutal were her rich gentlemen.

"Kavanaugh" was first fiction, juvenile in parts, written in straight third person and without the speed of word or turn of phrase that was needed. The heartbeat, however, was in there somewhere, immature but still strong, and reading it now, it becomes obvious that all Runyon needed was for an editor simply to encourage him to cut down on playing big drinker, remain seated and writing, and soon enough Runyon of Denver would have a body of short stories that could be put into a book. As long as he just kept working, the country would have a major writer in Runyon before he reached thirty.

He struggled somewhat through the whole of 1908, but he was still using whisky, which specializes in stopping people in their tracks. And so here he is in Boulder, this spring morning in 1909, sprawled on the fresh green lawn of the University of Colorado quadrangle in a long-sleeved shirt and bow tie, body propped by an elbow, flask in his back pocket, tearing dandelions out of the ground by their very roots. He was so entranced by a beautiful coed in a white sunhat that sometimes he grabbed grass instead, and this caused him to become angry because his job was to grab dandelions.

The coed sat a yard or so away on the grass and gently plucked dandelions. "You don't slide them out of the ground. You yank the daylights out of them!" Runyon said. Between them was this fresh, wet, green and yellow pile Runyon and the coed had gathered thus far in the university's annual Dandelion Picking Contest. All across lawns that were yellow with dandelions until they ran to the treeline marking the start of the slope to the Rockies were large equal squares of greensward marked off by stakes and string fences, giving each square about the same amount of dandelions. The contest was to see who could most beautify the campus by amassing the highest pile of dandelions, that being determined by a judge with a yardstick. As Dandelion Picking was a team sport, one coed and one young man, some of the teams didn't even pluck more than a stem or two and spent the rest of the time holding hands. Runyon, being a fierce competitor, kept looking about to see if anybody had a higher pile. Soon, he had the coed in the sunhat yanking dandelions until they had the highest pile in the early going.

The contest was an outgrowth of the university president's call for more outdoor sports. "The book worm, if he exists, may be at fault in being too mechanical and unreflecting in enjoying no outdoor exercises." He also called smoking "slow suicide, moral and physical." Therefore no smoking was allowed in the annual Dandelion Picking Contest, a rule that caused Runyon to rip dandelions at a furious pace.

He could barely wait to take this coed off somewhere so he could smoke and get out that pint flask he had on his hip.

The contest was the major event of the spring week, for the flag rush had been postponed when the sophomores attacked the freshmen in the gym the night before. Runyon's coed in the big hat also was excitedly telling him about the school dance committee, which had just decided to end the practice of filling out dance cards in advance of the evening of the dance. The committee, all boys, had stated, "Whereas the making out of dance programs before the occasion of the dance itself is entirely undemocratic in spirit and essentially out of harmony with the best interests of all concerned . . ." What made this such an important story, the coed explained, was that a group of women, led by Miss Hallie Chapman, had met in the school chapel and endorsed the ban of naming dance partners in advance. Never before had coeds been so bold as to take a position on their own. Runyon took the girl for a drink and talked this over at length with her. The dandelion pile stopped growing, and his team failed to win the dandelion pull.

On a fall Saturday morning in 1909 Runyon, in checked overcoat and porkpie hat, looked excitedly out the window of the interurban car, which rolled over the tracks from Denver to Boulder. At one point, coming over a hill, here ahead was the town of Boulder and the red roofs of the university buildings, sitting at the bottom of the Rockies in a sight most thrilling, and even more so if you were going to a football game where the coeds got cold.

He is supposed to be writing short stories, but he sits at lunch in the Sigma Alpha Epsilon house, drinking in the back room, after which out to the game he goes, sitting in some grandstand while all these children cry into the sky, "Yeah Buffaloes!" The animal being the nickname of the University of Colorado football team.

You had to shoot him to keep him away from the dance that night. Runyon couldn't dance a little and never got off a chair, but he chatted up the young college women and took them outside for a drink. Much later, when the songfest began, he did his best to set up "a prospective mother for deflowering." They sang "Cuddle Up a Little Closer, Lovey Mine" and, standing in front of the school president's house, "Fly Away Kentucky Babe" and "Home Sweet Home."

He lost more time by covering land scandals and children in communes. By now he had a hundred times more of these incidents than any fiction writer ever needed. However, he did write poems in *Lippincott's* and *Munsey's* magazines. One paper, the *Denver Republican*, even wrote of him as "forging to the front as a poet."

One night in Denver he covered the reception for Mrs. Ruth Bryan Leavett, the daughter of William Jennings Bryan. Also on the story was Ellen Egan, a society writer. At night's end, he took her home to 1515 Downing Street, a duplex apartment in a row of attached stucco houses on a middle-class street. Two things happened on that street that night. One was the shock of being with anybody as pretty as Ellen Egan, who not only made an honest living but one many, many stations above restaurant cashier or tavern waitress. Bedazzled by the young woman, in wonder of her respectability, he fell instantly in love with her. On summer nights when he came to take her out, he wore high button boots, tight-top pants and a straw boater, a string anchoring the hat to his collar as sentry against breezes. Every time he pressed the doorbell, he was drawn closer to marrying her.

At the same time, the man couldn't be expected to behave himself just because he had a legitimate girlfriend. Runyon, deep in drink one night with two prostitutes who said they wanted to hear music, took the girls to a concert at Cheeseman Park, where Ellen Egan, in the audience, was mortified. Runyon walked out with the two girls and took a room in the Standish Hotel, and at some point the girls left. Midway through the night, the room clerk heard screams from Runyon's room. He went upstairs and found Runyon deranged. A doctor gave him an injection to calm him. Another doctor, from the Denver Boxing Commission, said that the heart was out of whack. Runyon looked up at a hospital room ceiling and pledged that he would never go against whisky again. He had been around enough abrupt endings in fight arenas to know that the knockout victim goes to the dressing room right away, and that is that. He now became obsessed with the alcoholism over which he had suddenly triumphed. At the same time, he had to keep this out of his writing. Even his newspaper stories suggested a barroom tough guy atmosphere, and his poetry and short stories absolutely required it. When people saw his name, they had to smell the barroom. To admit to being a nondrinker would put into a reader's mind such thoughts as clinic, sanitarium, vitamin shots into a pale flabby arm. Every one of his stories would play against a white sanitarium wall. Who needed that? So in print he remained at the bar. Out of a reader's sight, over the years, he wrote letter after letter about Alcoholics Anonymous.

> I think it may be one of the great movements of all time. Drinking is not hereditary as some rumpots like to alibi, but I think there are certain strains that are allergic to alcohol.
>
> I quit drinking in Denver and have not had a drink since. I quit because I realized that I got no fun out of drinking. Liquor only gave me delusions of grandeur that got me into trouble. It never made me happy and bright and sparkling as it does some people. It made me dull and stupid and quarrelsome. It made me dreadfully ill afterwards. I did not have the constitution to drink. It rendered me helpless.
>
> I quit because I saw that I was not going to get anywhere in the world if I didn't, and I wanted to go places. I was sorely tempted many times, usually in elation over some small triumph or when I was feeling sorry for myself, a strong characteristic of the drinker, but I managed to stand it off.
>
> It was never taking that first drink that saved me.
>
> I had to endure loneliness and even derision as a result of my abstinence for some years but it eventually became a matter of such general knowledge that no one pressed me to take a drink any more and finally I became positively famous for hanging out with drunks and never touching a drop.

This was at once a fine treatise and, as you will see, it also made him the Benedict Arnold of the barrooms. Had he known how much good that drinking by others was going to do for his career, he would have known enough to banish sin from his own life without any noise.

FIVE

HIS GOOD FRIEND in Denver, Van Loan, went to New York in 1909 to work on Hearst's *Evening Journal*. Early one evening, Van Loan was in Mike Iorio's saloon on Park Row with William (Bunk) Macbeth, who was a sportswriter for the *Journal*. Macbeth talked about the pitching that day of Christy Mathewson of the Giants. He then banged his glass down and announced he was going to the office to write a great story. Outside, he heard a groan and looked down at a man in the gutter. "You're nothing but a stumblebum," Macbeth said. "If I can go to work, you can stand on your own feet, you slob." Macbeth walked on to the office.

Sometime later, Van Loan emerged. He, too, heard a groan and saw the man in the gutter. Quickly, he went over and saw that the man had a badly broken leg. Van Loan called for an ambulance and accompanied the man to Bellevue, where the hospital attendant found the man's wallet, identifying him as Solomon S. Carvalho, executive vice president of Hearst Newspapers, Inc. Carvalho, who never swallowed alcohol in his life, had wound up in the gutter from a slip on the rain-slick curbstones.

When Van Loan saw the name and occupation of the man on the emergency room table, he stepped through the curtain and whispered, "I'm Charley Van Loan of the *Journal*. Charley Van Loan of the *Journal*. You just rest there. I'm going to call your wife. I'll handle everything. Charley Van Loan of the *Journal*."

Solomon S. Carvalho many weeks later swung into the *Journal* on crutches, and with a leg that would be short for the rest of his days. As he worked his way to his large office stuffed with antiques, he went past the sports department where Macbeth sat. Carvalho picked up scissors and began cutting copy paper to ribbons as Macbeth watched.

Van Loan regarded Carvalho as an insurance policy with a limp. He was right. The main Hearst nationwide wire service, Hearst Universal, suddenly requested only Van Loan as the man to entrain for San Francisco to cover the heavyweight championship between James J. Jeffries and Jack Johnson on July 4, 1910. All other sportswriters were told to remain at their desks. On the train ride, Van Loan decided that soon he could quit the newspaper business and live a splendid, satisfying life staying at home and writing short stories for magazines. If he fell on his face, he merely had to call on Carvalho and return to payroll. At this time we must assure you that it is absurd to think of Carvalho as being even remotely honest, and this you will see in good time in this story.

While Van Loan had a flowery style perfect for the times, he was unsure of plots. In San Francisco, the idea of this huge black devil, champion Jack Johnson, fighting James J. Jeffries, tough, quite white and small, caused politicians to call off the fight. On the night the fight was banned, in the uproarious drinking and arguing, Van Loan saw Runyon, who was also there to cover the fight, and thought of his short stories and also several news stories that he always had assumed were well-told fables. He suggested that Runyon come to New York and help him write stories. He, Van Loan, being known at the *Saturday Evening Post*, would of course be the author, but Runyon could contribute plot assistance, for which he would be paid. Until money showed, Van Loan would extend room and board, but not carfare,

Runyon later said that he rode the rods under freight trains and lived in hobo camps to reach New York. A recent letter testifies otherwise:

My grandfather, John William McGovern, was a boyhood friend of Damon and in 1905 my Grandfather and Damon Runyon set out to begin their own newspaper in Trinidad, Colorado. Their efforts at an independent newspaper were short lived and he went to Denver. When he decided to go to New York, he borrowed the train fare from my grandfather, who was a bookkeeper for a department store. My Grandfather would say that Damon would get drunk and send his work to publishers who send him rejections. Later, he laughed to see former stories from his early rejections in print when his name became famous. My Grandfather submitted the name Runyon for our baseball field and won the contest. Signed, Patricia Dirkson, 17 MacGregor, Pueblo, Colorado.

When Runyon arrived in New York in the fall of 1910, he took the Flatbush Avenue trolley to Van Loan's house in Flatbush, on East 17th Street off Beverly Road. He thought he was back in Kansas. The borough of Manhattan had two and a half million people and Brooklyn had trees, churches, homes with yards and a million less people. Runyon had one suitcase, and upon moving into a spare bedroom, he worked right away on plots that were great for Runyon but not for Van Loan. Runyon was not drinking, and filled the many idle hours by drinking coffee, smoking cigarettes and sitting in the same room with the Van Loans. With stomach unsoured by hangovers, he was able at all times to enjoy meals, particularly second helpings and many snacks. When Gertrude Van Loan went shopping, Runyon asked her to get more meat and also cigarettes. Van Loan and his wife began to have small arguments, which was unusual because Van Loan had the large man's desire to laugh rather than suffer even the mildest of differences.

One day, Runyon sat on the stoop of the Van Loans' house and was shining his shoes, holding them up to the light, when the ice and coal man arrived. In conversation, Runyon discovered that the man was from Bari, in Italy, and that nearly all the coal and ice men in Brooklyn were from that province. Runyon envisioned an organization of coal and ice men that could get into icebox manufacturing, and even design a coal stove, and thus all members could be far more than deliverymen and he, Runyon, much more than an unemployed poet. He could fulfill his dream of writing poems while something — a heavyweight champion, an association of ice men — churned out a living for him. He spent hours scribbling organizational notes and speaking to the coal and ice men who came to the house. After a week of this, Van Loan looked into Runyon's room, observed him typing furiously and inquired about this story on ice men. Oh, this isn't a story at all, Runyon said. These are organizational charts and lists for the new amalgam of coal and ice men.

"When do you write?" Van Loan asked.

"Haven't had much of a chance this week," Runyon said.

Van Loan went into the bedroom and wanted to smack his wife, but she, having heard the conversation, snarled first. "Runyon has to get a job," Van Loan decided. When he called the Hearst offices, he was stunned to hear that Executive Vice President Solomon S. Carvalho was on an extended trip and would not return for at least a couple of months.

Runyon announced one day that he was going to try a story of his own. Great, Van Loan said. A week later, Runyon said he was finished and needed carfare to Manhattan to deliver the story.

He took the story, "The Breed and the Ball," to Robert Davis, the editor of *Munsey's Magazine*. Van Loan came home several days later to find Runyon thrilled, but Gertrude was even more ecstatic. The magazine was buying Runyon's story for $65. Runyon dressed and went to Manhattan to get paid. Van Loan sent his heart with him. By now, Runyon had a bill for board and incidentals that hurt when Van Loan thought of it. When Runyon had the money in his pocket later that day, he went for a walk on Fifth Avenue. At a luggage store, he saw a trunk of yellow leather and brass. He went inside merely to examine it. He discovered that it was a shoe trunk, with compartments made of soft cloth for eight pairs of shoes and a larger space for riding boots. Runyon brought the empty trunk home on the subway.

"What's that?" Van Loan said mildly as Runyon carted it in.

"For my shoes," Runyon said.

He began to show Van Loan and his wife the inside of the trunk.

"That must have cost a lot," she said.

"Oh, sixty dollars or so," Runyon said.

That night, the Van Loans had a fight that ended with Charley leaving the house and going down to Cortelyou Road, where he got legless.

Runyon followed this smashing success by taking a stack of poetry over to Desmond Fitzgerald, a publisher, and some days later, Fitzgerald, elated with Runyon's tough guy poetry from the front lines — the poetry all the tougher, shrapnel everywhere, because Runyon never actually had been there — wrote that the book of poems would be published the next year. He included a check for $25 as an advance on royalties. Runyon went out with the check and bought a carton of cigarettes and many ties. One day after this, he asked Gertrude Van Loan if he could read her something. She nodded. He stood in the living room and began to read a letter of proposal to Ellen Egan back in Denver.

"When do you want to get married?" Gertrude said.

"Right away if she answers yes," Runyon said.

Gertrude went inside to bed. A week later, two things happened at once. Ellen sent a letter back saying she would marry Runyon but only if he had a good steady job. And, soon after, Solomon S. Carvalho returned from his extended trip and made the return call to Van Loan, who threw on his clothes and went into the city to see him. When he came back that night he told Runyon, "You're on a big-city paper."

Hearst had two dailies, the *American* in the morning and the *Journal* in the afternoon, printed at William Street in downtown Manhattan. The city room staffs were separate, but with a common aim: to get paid and to put noise into the news. Runyon was hired for the morning paper.

One evening in March 1911, the new sports reporter for the *New York American* sat at an old machine on a ledge against a bare old wall. After he was finished typing, he brought his copy over to the copy desk, where Harry Cashman, the sports editor, took it, read the byline "By Alfred Damon Runyon," grunted and said, "Only Protestants use three names." He crossed out the first name and left the byline as Damon Runyon. "That happens to be a good-looking byline," Cashman said. He tossed the story to a copy reader and picked up the next one. In an ad agency they would have given Cashman a week off for making such a decision. In a newspaper he had to do this once or twice an edition, and there were five to six editions a night.

That spring, Runyon wrote more letters to Ellen Egan in Denver. He was earning $40 a week and the future was bright. They decided by mail to marry in New York in May. The Van Loans were pleased to be hosts and witnesses. Ellen Egan and Alfred Damon Runyon were married on May 6, 1911, at Holy Innocents Roman Catholic Church, Beverly Road and East 17th Street, Flatbush, by the Reverend William Costello, pastor. That day, the Giants played in Boston and the Dodgers were at Philadelphia so there was nothing to distract anybody from the wedding. On the front page of the local newspaper, the *Brooklyn Daily Eagle*, there was a story from El Paso that President Díaz of Mexico notified the rebels in Juarez that he would like to have a conference with them about their demands that he resign. There also was the most used news headline in American newspapers: "CLAIM U.S. STEALS LAND." In this instance, the story had a local angle. Charles A. Moore, formerly a Brooklynite and now building a railroad across Turkey, wanted rights to any and all gold mines that might be found over the route of the line within a radius of twenty kilometers on either side.

After the wedding, the bride and groom went to the Van Loans' for champagne. Runyon had coffee, Van Loan popped open the wine, and all raised glasses and Runyon a coffee cup. In Van Loan's living room, he kissed his beautiful wife. Van Loan said he never had seen Runyon do this before. When Van Loan drained the last bottle, he clapped his hands and the four went up to Flatbush Avenue and rode the trolley through the spring evening in Brooklyn to Court Street, where they got off and walked a block to the St. George Hotel, which had a roof garden and an indoor room with a dance floor and a ceiling of stars. Van Loan had the bandleader announce the presence of newlyweds, and to much applause, Runyon and his new wife were called on to dance. He could barely move his feet. Ellen Egan smiled it away, but the bandleader, in true Brooklyn style, felt moved to call out, "I think it's time for the groom to take his lovely lady off on the honeymoon because as you can see, the man can hardly move."

Runyon, the Victorian, acted as if he had not heard this. He and Ellen finished the night at the St. George and afterward took a cab over to the Marseilles Hotel, on 113th Street and Broadway, where they stayed for a few days. Ellen looked for apartments in midtown Manhattan, but on her husband's $40-a-week salary there wasn't much that she liked. He took her out to Flushing, which was a long ride on the IRT train, but at the end of the line, at Main Street and Roosevelt Avenue, there were blocks of big old frame houses, many with signs for roomers. They took two rooms at the sum of $40 a month. Ellen liked the spacious neighborhood and her husband seemed in love with her, he really did, although the man was so afraid of his feelings that he had everything encased in ice. The time when he showed the most enthusiasm about anything was in midmorning, when he went to the number 7 train at the Main Street, Flushing, stop and started for work. The train began as a subway and then climbed onto narrow, high tracks that passed over marshlands. It ran as an el through what was then New York's bedroom, the blocks of four- and five-story apartment houses running up to the foot of the Queensborough Bridge. The el dived into a tunnel and under the river, and now the stops were Grand Central Station and Times Square, and Runyon thrilled at the signs because they told him instantly that he was where he belonged, at the very top of the big town.

SIX

HERE WAS this pinwheel of white shirts and flailing arms in the stands in left center field, and the motion was so distracting to the eye that Runyon couldn't keep up with the first major league baseball game he had ever attended, on May 20, 1911. He got up from his press seat behind home plate and walked through the stands to left center, to the bleachers, where people were leaning over the railing and handing down containers of big cold beer to a Giants pitcher, who took the beer, held up a baseball and made a couple of feints at the crowd, causing all hands to go high and bodies to strain. He flipped the ball into the stands and drank his beer and the bleachers fought wildly for his baseball. As Runyon didn't know the players' faces yet, he asked the fan alongside him who the pitcher was. "The greatest! Bugs Raymond!"

In the bullpen, Raymond downed the last of the beer. There was another yell — "Beer!" — and another container of big cold beer was handed down. Raymond feinted throwing another baseball and the crowd put up pleading hands. Runyon took a seat and watched Bugs Raymond and forgot about the game.

Before the game, he had been introduced to John McGraw, known as Little Napoleon. He had started in baseball at Allegany College, outside of Olean, New York, later renamed St. Bonaventure University. The student manager of the team, Joseph A. Broderick, claimed that McGraw was versed in the 1889 *Spalding's Guide*, which said, "Saloon and brothel . . . are the two great obstacles in the way of success of the majority of professional ballplayers." Meeting McGraw at the Polo Grounds, for an instant Runyon had a small boy's thrill: I am meeting the great McGraw! He was the king of his sport, a most important sport, too, and therefore probably the most important figure in

the city. Runyon quickly fought this feeling down and replaced it with
cold silence.

Reporters also had introduced him to Christy Mathewson — "Big
Six" — the Giants' great pitcher. Because of superstition, Mathewson
never pitched opening day. He had the nickname because at that time
a six footer was considered a huge American. Also, Sam Crane, a former Giants player who had a job as a Hearst sportswriter, saw an an-
tique fire engine called Big 6 that once was the grandest equipment
used by New York's volunteer fire department. "Pumps more water
than Niagara Falls," the sign in the museum boasted. Crane decided
that it reminded him of Mathewson, as the Giants' pitcher was a "flame
thrower." Crane applied similar logic to his daily sports stories, which
meant that the readers deserved journalism awards. Mathewson, however, never turned down the nickname. He was a nice, well-spoken
thirty-year-old, who stood by the batting cage and told Runyon, "I want
to write novels." Mathewson talked about his college days and his views
on life. "I think any man who cheats on his wife would betray his country, too." In 1905, when Mathewson pitched those three shutouts in
the World Series, Runyon, in Denver, wrote a sports column about
the accomplishment and named Mathewson a religious figure. He now
cringed as he remembered this. Who makes money with a saint unless
you own a church? Mathewson, a graduate of Bucknell College in
Pennsylvania, could play checkers against six other baseball players at
once and win easily. That it would take the six players together to make
change after pumping gas, which was where they belonged, took some
of the wonder out of Mathewson's triumphs. But Mathewson did remember batters' habits as if he had a card file with him on the pitching
mound, and over the months to come he would cause Runyon to write:
"Mathewson pitched against Cincinnati yesterday. Another way of
putting it is that Cincinnati lost a game of baseball. The first statement
means the same as the second."

But now, in the bleachers on opening day, Runyon suddenly was
excited at finding himself where he was most comfortable, off the beaten
track, and he could see clearly what he had to do for himself: "I can
spend a lifetime writing about Mathewson and I shall know enough
about Bucknell and other aspects of clean living to found a monastery.
Or, I can breathe freely and hang around Bugs Raymond and get the
money."

The next day, at noon, he took the train in from Flushing, changed
at Times Square for the Broadway line going uptown and decided he

sure had enough of this; he wouldn't halt a career as a poet in order to ride on subway trains like some cheap commoner. He got off at 72nd Street and Broadway. At that time everybody lived somewhere near there, from Abe Attell to John McGraw, most of the ballplayers, show-business people and this gangster Arnold Rothstein, and that was the one he really wanted to meet. He walked along with his portable type-writer in a red-and-white-striped case, looking into places, and then he heard noise coming from Walsh's, a dark narrow bar on Broadway. It was just around the corner from the Hotel Alamac, at Broadway and 71st, where many of the ballplayers lived. He stood in the doorway and made out the form of Bugs Raymond, sitting on a bar stool with as much activity as if he were riding a horse. Seeing Runyon in the door, he called out, "Do you want a drink, pal?" When Runyon said no, Ray-mond said, "Well, we do. Come in and put something on the bar."

Raymond had a big guy next to him. The guy was in a white shirt with sleeves rolled up and a flushed face. He wore sunglasses.

"This is my keeper," Raymond said, introducing him. "McGraw hired him to watch me. I'm full and he's Fuller."

It seemed like a pleasant quip except that the private detective was completely stiff, with Raymond close to it. When Runyon asked Ray-mond if he had considered the idea that he might wind up pitching that day, Raymond said, "McGraw says he's going to take my paycheck and give it to my wife. If she gets the money, let her pitch."

Runyon suggested that they walk part of the way uptown to the Polo Grounds, on Eighth Avenue and 155th Street, so perhaps Bugs's head might dry up en route. He led Raymond down to Riverside Drive. With full green trees and a grassy slope running down to the Hudson, silver in the sun and empty right across to the untouched Palisades, the walk up the drive gave the same view as seen by Indians padding along a hundred years before this. On the way, Raymond threw stones at telephone poles, dogs and pigeons. He threw with great energy, but also with all the preciseness of carelessly poured beer. He was a right-handed pitcher with what he claimed was a "three-speed" pitch. His fourth and fastest speed was swallowing alcohol. He was first heard of when he was on a team in Shreveport, and he made a bet he could drink two bottles of bourbon, eat a whole turkey and win a double-header, which he did.

As they walked, the river was on the left, and on the right were apartment houses that looked as if they had been built by sculptors. There were arches and parapets and cupolas, and everywhere possible the cement had a design — a Greek god's face at one corner, a crest at another. French windows looked out at the Hudson in many apartments. At 86th Street, Runyon pointed to the Clarendon House, which was where William Randolph Hearst lived. Raymond said he would give a boss exactly what he deserved, "a broken window." Runyon didn't know the floors. Raymond said he would just have to break any window as a message. He lifted a leg and, with a tremendous whip of the arm, threw a stone at a second-floor window. But he was wide to the right and it clincked off the building. Runyon pulled Raymond along. Throw no more stones at the hand that feeds. He also held on to Raymond as if he were a bankbook. Newspapers were the only agency of information, and readers did not know who their U.S. senators were but regarded a double play as an important matter. In newspapers across the country there was a need for conscious humor. There was an extraordinary amount of unconscious humor, particularly in the use of the rules of grammar, but no one on sports pages knew enough to step over the petty details of a daily game and tell newspaper readers about a big league drunk.

"What's McGraw going to do when he sees you?" he asked Raymond.

"Keep his mouth shut," Bugs said.

"Fella won't try to kill you?"

"I'll take his head off with one punch. I'll tell you something else. I would of knocked the first Napoleon on his ass, too."

During these days on the *American*, Runyon thought that everything in life was centered on a baseball park, but then one night he went to the Metropole to look up Bat Masterson, who was drinking Tom Collinses, as he did all summer, and then for the rest of the year, even on the bitterest of winter nights. Masterson was telling marvelous stories that featured gambling and guns. The bartender reported to Runyon that at crucial moments during a night, Bat would take out his marshal's badge from Tombstone and cry a little, all the while on the alert for takers. He never attempted this in Runyon's presence.

Also on this night, and on most others when Runyon was in the Metropole, the sound of a tuba rumbled through the barroom. Then a drum began to thump. Outside, a Salvation Army woman in bonnet led a band through the street of sinners. Runyon heard this so often over the years that finally he figured out what it meant: put together Bat Masterson, a k a Sky Masterson, and the Salvation Army woman,

whoever she was, call her Sarah Brown, and have her fall in love with
Sky. He titled the story, "The Idyll of Miss Sarah Brown," or "Guys
and Dolls," but it would be years before he wrote it.

He was more interested in simply standing on a couple of squares of
cement that formed a line of adventure. It was on Seventh Avenue
between 49th and 50th streets, and he discovered it one day when he
was looking for a "handbook" and was directed to a doorway inhabited
by Chuck Green, who booked horses and also sold costume jewelry
that appeared real. Runyon had to shout the name of the horse because
of the construction a few yards away. Workmen were putting up the
Rivoli Theatre, which looked like a Greek museum or great public
building, with eight Doric columns rising from the marquee. Inside,
there were 2,100 seats, and some already called it the most beautiful
building on all of Broadway. Of course to keep it in rhythm with just
about everything else of its time, the Rivoli wasn't even on Broadway.
It was on Seventh Avenue.

Two streets running parallel from uptown, one Broadway, the other
Seventh Avenue, merged as they entered Times Square, and appeared
to be one street bathed in the yellow and blue light of a Wrigley's Gum
sign. The streets entered Times Square by running on either side of
the Studebaker Building, 1600 Broadway, a high brown boulder sepa-
rating two rivers of metal. The building had an entrance on Broadway
and another on Seventh Avenue. The distance on 49th Street from
Seventh Avenue to Broadway was exactly fifty yards, merely half a
football field. Once in Times Square, the streets ran as a common boulevard through the overhead lights and theater lights, the crowds and
noise, always noise. The sound of Times Square always was louder than
anywhere else because the instant people stepped into the hot bright
lights, they became excited and raised their voices. At the downtown
end of the square, at the Times Tower, with the news bulletins moving
in a ribbon around the building, Times Square split into two streets
that, with regained identities, street signs proclaiming "Broadway" and
"Seventh Avenue," ran downtown.

On this day, Runyon bet races with Chuck Green and also bought a
tie clasp that was loud and phony. Later on, he would demand that
Green produce things a little bit less conspicuous, and therefore more
nearly authentic to the eye. Green now introduced Runyon to a short
bald man who was standing two doors down, outside the entrance to
Lindy's delicatessen. He was Leo Lindemann, the owner. He had seen
Runyon at a baseball game at the Polo Grounds. He invited Runyon

inside for coffee and a pastrami sandwich. "Make the door shut," Lindemann yelled at a waiter. The Yiddish-German construction delighted Runyon. By now he kept this language of New York rolling around in his ear all night. The pastrami, unknown in the West, became his favorite. After the sandwich, he went out and stood in the start of the evening with Lindemann as the first signs went on and turned Times Square and Broadway and Seventh Avenue into a crater of light.

"I never get used to it," Lindemann said.

Soon, Runyon would realize that this was the most magnificent street in the world for him. The Salvation Army band passes, with the woman in the bonnet out saving souls. Then along comes Mendel (Sugar Plum) Yudelowitz. His friend Champ Segal told him that if he wants to hang around, he has to dress like a killer. Now here is Mendel in a black suit, black shirt and a white tie. "Oh, Chemp," he calls out, "vere is my machine gun?" There is Pussy McGuire, who steals cats and sells them to rich old ladies.

Unser Fritz is also out there. He is a degenerate horse player who wears shoes with no soles and who touts millionaires. He is disheveled and in need of two dollars to bet a horse. He actually needs to blow the money on soap. He has been on the dead run for so long, starting with an afternoon in Saratoga when he beat an old man in a wheelchair. He isn't such a nice old man, don't worry about it. Runyon turns this section of Unser Fritz's times into "The Lemon Drop Kid," and that is fine for Bob Hope and Runyon's pocket. One night on Broadway Unser Fritz says, "All horse players die broke." Runyon steals that line and makes it his forever. Why not? That's what the street is for. Now, standing on Broadway, he takes a deep breath. Even the cement smells of larceny. He hears the sound of a subway train rumbling to a stop at the station right under his feet. It sounds like somebody blowing a safe.

At this point, it is necessary to tell you about the building of Runyon's part of town, the narrow blocks of foul-smelling sidewalks that run off Times Square. They are so important because the people who leave a city its art — a play, a song, a performance that affects others for years — almost always thrive in crowds and dinginess and in rooms made airless by dusty windows that are stuck forever. "I would go out this window, but I can't open it," Mop Top the handicapper told his psychiatrist, Dr. Ernie, after summoning him on an emergency visit one day. Mop Top had just destroyed Broadway again with a horse that could not lose. At this very hour, half the songwriters in America were in an an-

gry group on the sidewalk in front of Lindy's. Mop Top decided his life
was a failure and he wanted to go out the window. The psychiatrist
slapped his hands on the window frame, grunted and began to push at
the window to get it open. "I lose five hundred on the horse myself,"
he said.

At their gatherings on these streets, people detest each other and
find the conflict wonderful. Any proximity to violence increases the
tension that produces their best work. A song written in a meadow has
the emotion of dandelions. A short story comes out of a hotel room and
not a country estate. All great performances begin in a filthy rehearsal
room that has pipes running across the ceiling and is one flight over a
cheap restaurant. And to establish such an important environment, the
place must be founded on larceny, which much of the West Side of the
great city most certainly was.

New York was first built on water, with the world's best natural harbor and also the finest water supply system ever, fresh rain water spill-
ing off mountainsides and running down rivulets and streams and creeks
to the city, without hand or machine touching it, running by gravity,
coming down one foot every mile until it raced into the water tunnels
under the city at sea level. Still, there could be no city, and in particular no Broadway, without transportation, and that was as dishonest as
human hands could make it.

When Runyon still was in a crib, the best people in New York were
preparing his streets for him by arguing over how to steal while building elevated train tracks, and also a cable car on Broadway. On that
street people rode in stagecoaches that were pulled by two-horse teams,
which often became nervous and balky in the heavy traffic. Hand-painted
landscapes were on the rear door of the coaches, and there was a coin
box behind the driver's seat, with a lamp inside that was lighted after
dark so that the driver could look at the kind of money dropped into
the box. The driver used a little hole in his seat to pass back to passengers small sealed envelopes in bright colors that contained any combination of change of a dollar needed to pay the fare. The employees took
home everything but the reins.

Broadway had reached uptown to the southeast corner of 41st Street,
where a place called the Metropolitan Casino was thrown up to house
great concerts and comic operas. The joint busted out and the owners
knew what to do, and showed up at the building at night with gas cans.
One of them is dousing the joint with gas and the other is reading the
insurance policy. They are about to have a candlelight ceremony when

the owner reading the insurance policy clutches his chest. They don't have a dollar's worth of fire insurance. They turned it into a roller rink. Some yards up from the roller rink was a triangular block between Broadway and Seventh Avenue that had a private school and some two-story buildings with small stores on the first floor. The stores were doing wretchedly and the owners wanted to burn them down out of pure bad temper, but didn't want to be blamed if any schoolchildren went up with the flames. The triangular block, however, was of great interest to others, who saw it as a village square, and also to a man named Ochs, whose newspaper, the *Times,* was being published downtown, but needed a new building. The owner, Ochs, in 1901 kept talking about building a newspaper plant on the triangle and naming the whole place Times Square.

There was in Manhattan, New York, only a single file of gas street-lamps that came up Broadway a few blocks at a time. The streetlamps were not yet at 42nd Street and Broadway, which after nightfall sat in the darkness of a farm town.

A real estate lawyer in the Washington Heights section of Manhattan, Henry Morgenthau, spread a rumor that there would be a subway under the streets momentarily. The area was a prairie on the banks of the Hudson. Anybody developing it would have to put up houses with lawns, unless a subway appeared. At this time, a rumor in a neighborhood, sometimes capricious, in this instance based on greed, could be highly successful, for newspaper reporters worked only within blocks of the office, and word of mouth, particularly when it seemed as if the information were honestly acquired, was usually accepted. There was no radio, and the city of 3,678,800 had about 117,500 phones, half of them at Wall Street and below. Making a phone call consisted of picking up a phone and telling the operator, "Get me 4331." There were few chances of people speaking to each other casually and thus decreasing the vulnerability to rumor. There is much recognition of rumor in the language — "rumor monger" — but little ability to look back on its effect, for the newspapers caught only a prominent few. Nobody ever will know how much rumor controlled life. In this case, nothing stood between Morgenthau's whispers and the bank. He sold forty-four lots of land for an advance of 170 percent on equity of $300,000. He then bought land on the Lower East Side and built tenements. He began to circulate with politicians, Boss Croker the most prominent.

Whenever successful politicians and businessmen are together, it is a moment of hope being reawakened. The politician, who is impoverished by comparison to the man he stands alongside, always is at once frightened and enticed by the thought of entering the business world and earning a fortune. The merchant with his money in his pocket is in awe of a person who can stand before grubby crowds and earn their cheers. Each in the other's presence secretly wishes he had the other's role, and off by themselves they are insanely jealous of each other. Yet merchants and politicians seem extraordinarily friendly with one another, and form a closed society to which strangers never are admitted readily, unless the stranger has wondrous amounts of money, at which point he rapidly ceases to be a stranger. The money is often never brought into use, but the stranger must own much of it. How can you yearn to be the other guy if he doesn't have any money? The merchant, by using courtesy to the point of groveling, so flatters the politician that the impossible occurs and the politician becomes momentarily secure, and immediately feels a need to make the merchant richer. While it is understood that the politician takes money out of this, nobody realizes the miserable amounts of money they often accept. No amount is too small for a politician to grab, nor for a rich man to offer. As nearly all great fortunes in America are made on land stolen while the public's back is turned — and by people who want money but don't want to work for it, by men who use the title of builder and yet never have driven a nail into a board — nowhere was the relationship between politician and merchant closer than at the time the subways of New York were built.

When the subway was first being discussed in 1900, August Belmont, financier, could do so with confidence. He was born as Schoenberg, which in German means beautiful mountain. From the start, he liked counting other people's money. He worked for the Rothschilds in Paris and soon changed his name to Belmont, which means beautiful mountain in French. He also changed his religion to Presbyterian so that he could be accepted first by the Catholics in France and then by the Protestants in America, who resented it bitterly if a Jew earned forty dollars, but applauded wildly if one of their own took a mountain, river or lane from the public. Which is exactly how Belmont learned to steal streets. Upon arrival in New York, Belmont joined with an Irish thief, Tweed, to build the subways. And so one day in his private office, Chief Engineer William Barclay Parsons was startled as the door flew open and through it rushed a crowd of men who were quivering with greed. When he rose to stop them, he was pushed against the wall and pinned there. Boss Tweed entered, smiling. "It's all right," he told Parsons. "Old Augie knows about this." Augie being August Belmont, major financier of the Interborough Rapid Transit systems, the IRT. The crowd snatched at Parsons's most private route maps. A small group of men huddled around one end of a map and one of them kept tapping his finger on it.

"What is this now?" the man said. "Am I correct in saying that this is 181st Street?"

"I'm not supposed to say. It is confidential," Parsons said.

"It's all right," Tweed said. "These men are going to tell nobody." Tweed looked at the map himself. "This spot at 181st Street will be a station, am I correct?"

"Yes, an express station."

"Express!"

Chief Engineer Parsons's personal diary states, "One of the men actually leaned forward and kissed the map."

Real estate records show that Henry Morgenthau bought 140 lots at 181st Street and Broadway, which soon was to become a top city neighborhood with express subway service. One of the sellers was Levi P. Morton, vice president of the United States under President Benjamin Harrison. Morton signed his name, and beneath it, in big letters, said, "Vice President of the United States." If he had brains that could come out of a salt cellar, others at the table had more sense. Somebody snatched the papers away and made Morton sign a new set, this time with merely his name and no official title. Morgenthau announced they were going to auction off the lots. It so happened that the owner of the *New York Herald* newspaper, James Gordon Bennett, also had an intense interest in this out-of-the-way part of the city. He put the auction story on the front page of the paper. At the auction, the highest prices were paid by the ex–registrar of deeds, John Reilly. "He afterwards confided to me that he succeeded where we had failed in finding out that the subway was to have an express stop at 181st Street," Morgenthau claimed in his reminiscences. About the only way Reilly could get into a deal like this on his own would be to appear on Washington Heights with a brigade of infantry. Another big speculator was a man named Charles Barney, of whom a *New York Times* editorial said, "With his real estate operator's instinct he went again largely into realty investment on the upper west side along the route that was then known only to a few of the inner circle of subway financiers." One of Barney's moves was to buy all four vacant corners at Broadway and 86th Street on the Upper West Side of Manhattan. Which was like buying pyramids.

In order to raise more capital and buy more land and get more money, Barney formed a syndicate that included George Ramsey Sheldon, a New York banker who was treasurer of the New York County Republican Committee; a national Republican committeeman, Francis M. Jencks, who was president of the Safe Deposit Company of New York; and William Havemeyer, whose father had been a three-term mayor of New York and a bitter enemy in the struggle of reform Democrats against Boss Tweed some twenty-five years before this. Which now did not count, as land theft knows no political party.

It was unfortunate that Charles Barney was not smart enough to stop stealing even when he had to take his clothes out of the closet to make room for his money, and he continued into some impossibly corrupt real estate businesses. One day he woke up and found the only way he could see his way out was to blow his brains out, which he did. This did not stop his heirs, who founded Smith Barney stockbrokers and used as their motto, "We make money the old-fashioned way. We earn it." They should have said, "We steal it," but that's all right. This is America. The Morgenthau heirs went into saving the country and deploring corruption. Nobody returned any money.

The subway tunnel and tracks were built by burrowing through the gray, ominous rock with the same breath-gulping speed with which New York construction workers send buildings climbing out of the sidewalk, climbing, climbing, as the head tilts more each day to follow them, going twice as high and twice as fast as can be done in any other city in the world. And, while digging a tunnel through rock that was formed and settled a billion years ago, they blasted it at such a pace that they seemed to be seeking some sort of rapid satisfaction. Or, rather, they simply wanted to finish the job and leave quickly for the sunlight on top; burrowing into the earth always brings bloodshed.

When these tunnel workers, called sandhogs, started driving the tunnel under Broadway, a box of dynamite exploded at 41st Street and five sandhogs were killed. Two months later, Ira Shaler, the subcontractor for the section, was standing with Chief Engineer Parsons, who had worked on the Denver and Rio Grande Railway. In his diary of the IRT, Parsons said: "Started with Shaler at 34th Street and went through the east tunnel. Examined the work and then examined the rock at north end of the roof at 40th Street. Told Shaler I did not like the looks of it and he replied that it was perfectly safe, when all at once some rock fell, injuring him. Two weeks later, Ira Shaler died."

The building of the Columbus Circle stop, which became the station at the Hearst syndicate offices, took generations of work habits and construction art that were inherited by the sandhogs and artisans from the fathers who came to the country before them. The tunnel had to be dug under a part of the city's plumage, the 724-ton, 75-foot-high monument to Christopher Columbus. The Columbus monument is a large granite statue carried on a 50-foot-high shaft. The shaft is mounted on a three-tier pedestal, which rests on a foundation that is a 45-foot-square, 14-inch-deep pad of concrete and brick masonry.

They had to sink twin shafts on the north and south side of the monument's foundation, the shafts carried to a depth three feet below the foundation line of the subway tunnel construction. Sandhogs now had to drive a small tunnel 6 feet wide and 7 feet high from one shaft to the other beneath the foundation of the monument. They did this by drilling holes into the face of the rock, the holes arranged in circles within circles, and then stuffing the holes with dynamite and setting it all off, blowing the rock to chips. They cleaned up the debris, the muck, and started drilling again. With explosions twice a day, they turned rock into a tunnel. Up on the street, the statue of Christopher Columbus neither shook nor cracked. Concrete was then poured on the floor of the new tunnel, and 12-by-12 wooden columns were placed between the concrete floor and the foundation of the monument. With this temporary underpinning in place, workmen built a solid masonry foundation. A large steel girder, resting on two wooden trestles, was placed beneath the eastern edge and wedged tight against the monument's foundation. The girder went all the way up the main tunnel from 59th Street to 135th Street, where a storage yard was located. From then on, whenever trains barged into the Columbus Circle station, their sound and vibration often reached the sidewalk, but all 724 tons of Christopher Columbus was to stand unmoved and in glory, and New Yorkers could ride subway trains without being crushed by the statue.

There was the normal cost to those who built the station. In a union pamphlet celebrating the subway job, one worker, John McCann, of 345 Willis Avenue, the Bronx, wrote of losing his hearing permanently while blasting out the tunnel under the statue of Christopher Columbus.

Because of this, none of these people who profited were of any use as characters, for they took money for themselves, and with no style.

This subway, conceived by thieves and built by honest workers, giving Runyon his street called Broadway, also was absolutely marvelous, the barons such as August Belmont said, because it saw to it that "the poorer classes, the working men of this city, [would] be given the opportunity of leaving their work quickly in the busy centres of activity and getting quickly out into the bright sunshine and the air which will benefit their lives and their health. The purer we can make the homes of the people of this city, the better will be the city."

They did erect pure tenements, and all of them along the IRT route. Whether in downtown Manhattan or far up in the Bronx, each tenement apartment was identical. Here were block after block of tenements, five stories, or six with basements. All were one-bedroom apartments that were ninety feet deep, four to a floor, with a common cold water bathroom in the hall. People heated water on the stove and took baths in big pans in the kitchen, once a week or so. Hot water was the big event of the Roaring Twenties. The tenements were the equal of British coal-mine town row houses in using architecture to crush ambition from the instant a person touched the floor in the morning. They went to work on the subway each day with lives of unfulfilled potential. The same tenements ensured that neighborhoods would someday become slums.

Runyon stood in front of Lindy's for the first time. He found a career at his feet, in the most luxurious of all times in this city, the years before the gun. Oh, there were some great shootings, but they were rare and only for the guys, and had nothing to do with the common citizenry. They lived on streets where nobody ever heard a gun go off, and there was a chance to laugh, as great numbers of human beings from everywhere crowded together more and more each day. If they didn't love each other all that much, they did live with each other, and that is all that the country ever asked. The police still dealt with those small acts that touch the emotions and can last forever in stories and pictures. The 16th Precinct blotter reports:

Jan. 4, 1916
11:30 P.M.
Property of Deceased
Pocketbook Found in Taxi

Louis Calio 2504 23 Ave., Astoria, Hack Badge 5-55-86 Chauffeur 1711 Auto 018299 NY present and left property of deceased, Alice Sullivan

#855 3rd Ave. aided #3271 Ladies pocketbook containing $3.90 in US Currency, 3 pair of tortoise shell glasses. 2 cases. 3 pair of beads. 1 pawn ticket #40448. Al Shastenio 418 West 125 St., 1 Policy Hancock Insurance, 1 Ladies Umbrella, religious articles, 1 Large suit case and 1 small suit case containing Ladies wearing apparel. Also one black cat. Body ordered removed to morgue by Medical Examiner. Cat taken to station house.

The cat wound up drinking from a plate of milk in the doorway at Lindy's that night. A sergeant named Keating told the story. As best these things can be traced, the cat wound up being named Lillian in a short story that has held up for a long time.

May 5, 1916, 5:10 P.M. LOST PROPERTY Ptl. Bowers present with small box with pictures of child in front of street on 42 and Broadway. Also receipt for picture frame for Silas Bros. 8th ave and 42nd St. Ptl. Returned to post.

The plot and the emotion in this two-sentence report were to appear in at least several short stories. For they were written when people thought of children and pets as being important.

Now, a chubby man named Tommy Francis and his companion, Enrico Caruso, out for his evening walk. Tommy reminded Caruso that it was Runyon's racing story he had read aloud as Caruso steamed in his morning bath. Tommy was the racing adviser to both Caruso and the Unione Siciliano, or "Black Hand," and therefore read all papers. "I love you," Caruso exploded. Caruso was in constant euphoria from the praise he received wherever people heard him. In all the history of the great European cities, and now of this new, exciting, maddening, crowded place known as New York, there never had been heard such a voice as that of Enrico Caruso. "He sings like a god," one newspaper reviewer wrote, so the compliment from Caruso caused Runyon to become light-headed.

Caruso clutched Runyon's arm. "I never touch-a that woman's ass. Caruso sleeps with queens. But this ugly woman! If I touch her, I pat her on the head like a dog."

As this trouble always was the first thing on Caruso's mind — by now he had told it to every head waiter and doorman in the city — he immediately took over the sidewalk and, hands expressing his frustration and anger, told Runyon all about his case. Of course it was a case involving a girl. Over what else could Caruso get in trouble?

Well before this, on a Sunday evening, early for a horse and carriage that was to take him to dinner, Caruso decided to stroll up Fifth Avenue. He was dressed in slouch hat, tuxedo, white scarf and dashing cape. A doorman remembered seeing him with one hand inside the cape; the other held an elegant walking stick. At 69th Street, he entered Central Park and ambled into the first zoo building, the monkey house. Caruso was there only moments when a woman shrieked, "This man is molesting me!"

A policeman named James J. Cain rushed up. "What did he do?"

"He touched me here," she wailed, touching her backside.

"Why you dirty ginny," the cop said. (This is a quote taken directly from the court transcripts.) The officer clapped a hand on Caruso's shoulder. The woman gave her name as Hannah Graham, her address as 1756 Bathgate Avenue, the Bronx. She signed a complaint and left. Caruso was booked in the police station in the park's headquarters building, thrown into a cell and later taken to the municipal court on Lexington Avenue and 57th Street. His lawyer, Fred W. Sperling, who acted as if this were an altercation with an oboe player, demanded a trial. The court couldn't wait to give him one. The lawyer then decided to ask for a judge but no jury. The judge, Diefenhitter, forgot himself and clapped his hands, as if applauding an opera. All this publicity was to be his!

The prosecutor, Mathot, the third deputy police commissioner, was not a lawyer, but he detested Italians enough to prosecute them vigorously. And this is exactly what Caruso was regarded as by those who made their money in the court system — a ginny.

The greatest thing Caruso's lawyer did was to put Caruso on the stand so that he could deny the charges that he molested women. Men always leave little room for doubt when they deny immoral conduct.

While Caruso was on the stand, a woman in a veil rushed up the aisle and screamed, "That's the man!"

With the woman in the veil screaming, Mathot bellowed, "Isn't it a fact that at the beginning of the second act of *Parsifal* at the Metropolitan Opera House on the fourth of February of 1904 that this lady here in this veil whom you say you don't remember was standing downstairs in the rear of the seats and that you went up to her and stood behind her and done to her that which you are accused of having done in this here same case?"

Defendant Caruso: "I was sing on the stage that night. I wasn't near any woman except the soprano."

Q. What do you mean, near her?

A. On the couch.

Lawyer Sperling (to judge): "What does this have to do with Central Park?"

"He molested me!" the woman in the veil screamed again.

"In Rome, you say to me, 'Thank you!' " Caruso announced.

"This pig!" Mathot roared.

When the Caruso fans in the audience began to boo and hiss and call for justice, the prosecutor spun around and shouted at them: "Curs!"

Now the judge became impatient and he called out that Caruso was guilty and the fine was $10. Caruso never got over it. He never had needed a drop of self-control because he had so many women falling on him. He was now guilty of nothing except being born Italian. He was infuriated, and so were the rest of the Italians in New York. Joe (the Boss) Masseria, who was the boss in charge of everything, said that if the law wouldn't protect an Italian, then the outlaws would. It was he who sent his turf adviser, Tommy Francis, to be Caruso's companion. If Tommy needed some firepower, he only had to yelp. Now, talking in front of Lindy's, Tommy Francis said to Runyon, "You hear him? There's-a two ways to stoppa you in this town. One, shoot you. The second-a is . . ."

"Dolls," Caruso said.

"You just heard it from-a the master," Tommy said.

"Young dolls," Caruso said.

"Hear him?"

"Little girls," Caruso said.

They left. That night, Runyon assured himself that he was wise enough to stay away from the one thing that so surely destroyed all, from the greatest of talents, a Caruso, down to a bindlestiff right off the freights: a very young doll. The rule was simple: Don't let a doll ruin you and you can own the lights.

The first time Damon Runyon saw the Broadway he would make famous, the set was just going up. The rudimentary sign in unblinking 25-watt bulbs advertising "Lindy's" was only steps away from the new black metal and frosted glass kiosks of the 51st Street station of the IRT. As people in growing numbers pounded up the stairs and out of the subway kiosks and onto Broadway and 51st Street, the sky above the street was afire and became known as "the Great White Way." All of which began when into the dimness at Times Square came Jacob Starselsky, who was born in Ekatranislav, outside of Chernobyl in Russia, when it didn't have a nuclear plant. His family owned a lumber yard that was burned down during a pogrom, and the family was forced by swordpoint into a hut in a mud village.

At age thirteen, he got a job as shop boy for a willing but not very successful counterfeiter. The man's problem was that he made poor rubles. Jacob, shop boy, had an ability with metal and he also convinced himself that he was doing nothing wrong when he began to experiment with metal rubles. Formerly, the coins were of such poor quality that even children turned them down. Jake Starselsky, age thirteen, made rubles that were so good that they could be passed in a police station. Suddenly, every thief in the Ukraine was at the door trying to buy stacks of queer rubles. Shopkeepers and tradesmen accepted the bum rubles without more than a glance. It was only when the rubles hit the banks that somebody finally let out a yelp.

When banks in Kiev began turning back many thousands of bad rubles to shopkeepers who had accepted them, the wails of merchants reached the authorities. Soon, horsemen galloped up to the counterfeiter's shop and one reached down and struck the counterfeiter across the face as he stood in the doorway. The investigators thought it was impossible for the counterfeiter to stamp out anything so precise as these coins. If he would tell them how he minted the coins and who helped him, he would not be forced to serve time in prison. The counterfeiter, with deep loyalty, pointed to Jacob Starselsky, who was inside with a broom. The man in charge of the police detail got off his horse and smacked the counterfeiter and dragged him off to prison.

When Jake's mother heard of this, she went to the counterfeiting shop, where he was at work as if nothing had happened, and dragged him home to their hut. He went out and found a job in a place that made metal signs. After work, he began experimenting with placing light bulbs on the signs. One night in 1902 he flicked on the first electric light sign in Eastern Europe, on a restaurant in Kiev. He looked at how much they paid him. Rather than spit at such a miserable amount of money, he put it toward a ticket from Odessa to New York. He saved for several years. At Ellis Island, the usual immigration agent, who barely could write his own name, became infuriated with the length of "Starselsky," and announced to Jake that his new name was Jake Starr.

He took a room in a tenement on the downtown East Side and went out onto the streets of New York, where in midsummer of 1907 greenhorns were being swept up and sent to help build the Panama Canal. Jake Starr, at ninety-eight pounds, decided that there had to be something better than digging a canal and risking yellow fever. He bought a light bulb for ten cents, which was the cost of a large dinner. The bulb was good for only a couple of hundred hours. Every time he watched a light bulb drop dead, he acted as if it were a relative. Walking past a merchant's store on Delancey Street, he noticed burned-out bulbs in the garbage, picked one out and began to compare it to the one he had at home. Soon, Starr had a loft on Division Street and an assembly line of two hundred women just off the boat from Eastern Europe.

Boxes of burned-out light bulbs, picked from the garbage, sat at the end of a long table. One woman took out an old bulb, twisted the glass off the brass base and handed the base to the woman next to her, who pulled out the old filament. Another woman inserted a new filament, and another placed the bulb on a vacuum machine, which sucked the air out of the inside of the bulb. She sealed the glass by holding it to a flame that melted it closed. The new bulb was attached to the brass base again and packed in a box for resale.

Just as his counterfeit rubles excited the Ukraine, his used light bulbs scheme brought down the full might of the Edison power company. As they were not allowed to punch Jake's face, they had to pay him money to stop. Jake took the money and closed up, because he had better ideas on his mind than sitting in a workshop and recycling somebody else's invention. He started his own electric light sign-making business. "You don't get rich by the workbench," he always said. It was something he told a hundred times to a newspaper reporter named Runyon. There could be no argument. The newspapers usually were ramshackle coffins for talent.

SEVEN

THE New York newspaper world was on Park Row, a street that started at the plaza at the entrance of the Brooklyn Bridge and had only one side to it and no square corners. It branched out from Broadway and ran at a slight angle for a short distance, facing City Hall Park and City Hall itself. For years, the tallest building in Manhattan was the nine-story, red stone *New York Tribune* building on Park Row, with its clock tower that stood 285 feet in the air for all to see.

There were thirteen newspapers in the buildings along this street when Joseph Pulitzer, a tall man, as taut as wire, with a case of tuberculosis and brown eyes that were failing him by the day, came into town from St. Louis in 1883. He read a newspaper that gave one paragraph to a story about a party being planned for the opening of the Brooklyn Bridge three weeks later, on May 23. He could not wait for the chance to compete side by side with imbeciles, and he bought a paper called the *World* and ran it out of 32 Park Row. New York was a million and a half people and he tried to give it excitement. He wanted editors who could rise above the level of the public mind, yet at the same time, the excitement in him screamed that the old New York way of covering the news was abominable. Quickly, circulation of the *World* — selling for a penny, half the price of the largest papers, the *Sun* and the *Tribune* — went up to 100,000. Abruptly, the other papers cut their prices to a penny. In one day, this made the *World* appear to be a genuine contender. Advertisers in the *Sun* and the *Tribune* began to suspect that, at a penny, the papers were reaching morons unable to buy anything. The advertisers pulled ads. The price cut was a disaster for the *Sun* and the *Tribune* and made the *World* a name in

New York. Now the *World* could safely raise its price. Solomon S. Carvalho, who was then the business manager of the *World*, knew the effects of the price cut better than anyone in the city. We now are going
to watch this man closely.

Onto Park Row came William Randolph Hearst, who first turned
down the opportunity to buy the *New York Times,* as one of his advis-
ers said the price of $1,250,000 was too high. If Hearst had disregarded
the man and bought the paper, the *Times* conceivably could have become a different newspaper. Instead, Hearst bought the *Journal* for
$150,000 and published it out of the second and third floors of the *Tri-
bune* tower. His paper cost a penny and covered crime and had big
headlines, and soon the circulation was at 100,000. The Sunday *World*
cost a nickel and was at 500,000. Hearst hired the Sunday *World*'s
magazine editor, Merrill Goddard, and his entire staff, and they came
to the *Journal* and put out a magazine that featured "Are Sea Serpents
Real?" and "How It Feels to Be a Real Murderer." The Hearst circulation rose to 150,000. Then on February 10, 1896, with Pulitzer blind
and remote on a yacht somewhere, Solomon Carvalho suddenly had
the *World* drop its daily price back to a penny, causing a huge drop in
earnings, and reduced its number of pages. This was an enormous help
to the Hearst papers. Carvalho, the first fifth columnist of American
newspapers, sauntered over to the Hearst offices and was treated like
a prince and made the chief operating officer, second in importance
only to Hearst himself. It was natural that when this burglar broke his
leg, the one to profit would be Runyon, a fan of larceny.

The newsmen on Park Row first worked at tilted desks and wrote in
longhand with pencils and hats on heads. The light at first came from
wavery gaslight, and after that low electric light, much of which was
turned off because of the price of light bulbs. Only the youngest reporters were clean shaven. Most of the men dressed in dark suits, white
shirts and stiff celluloid collars. All wore high laced or button shoes,
the only types available for men at the time. Their trousers were held
up by white suspenders. They smoked pipes and cigars, but no cigarettes. Brass spittoons were placed around the floor. There was a shortage of telephones. Hearst came into these rooms late at night, ripping
off his tuxedo jacket and calmly, for such a late hour, remaking the
paper, which was dedicated to noise in the news.

With inventions, the newspaper office changed somewhat in look, in
that there were square Royal typewriters instead of pen and paper, and
the lighting was somewhat better, and there were many more phones.

The *Journal* and *American* switchboard number was Beekman 2000.
The *American*'s seventh-floor editorial room was a series of small offices thrown up haphazardly in order to keep occupants, who hated
each other, from attempting homicides. There was the centerpiece of
the city room, a horseshoe-shaped desk at which sat nine or ten copy
editors, with one man in the middle checking their work. The night
editor of the paper was Than Van Ranck, who had seen Hearst at a
society charity ball and fell on him like a flowerpot dropping from a
ledge. He wore a morning coat, whose tails stirred a breeze that caused
flimsy copy paper to blow off desks. If he heard a city-desk man mention an accident he would leap up and say, "How many dead? Where?"
He read mournfully one night the wire service story of a ferry boat that
had capsized in the Yangtze, drowning 932 Chinese. "Why couldn't it
have been the Staten Island Ferry?"

The *American*'s city room had electric light cords and fixtures dan-
gling above scarred desks. The green lampshades were suspended at
haphazard levels. Pieces of copy paper had been glued to or clipped on
to many of these shades by reporters who didn't want the light shining
in their eyes. Overhead was a maze of corroded brass pneumatic tubes
used to ship, with a rush of air, stories and headlines written by the
horseshoe copy desk. The office cat, Hypo, slept atop a filing cabinet.
The cat made his litter box wherever he was, and as a result, his smell
was over much of the office.

By morning Hearst looked over the city room and promised himself
that he would bring to this stifling garret the finest newspaper writers
in the world. While the sentiment was great, Hearst also liked people
working for him who would save him the trouble of destroying himself.
They were generally utter fools who came coated with ice. In this case,
he gave his instructions for hiring great writers to his favorite managing
editor, Colonel Caleb Van Hamm. As editor of the *World*, Van Hamm
had read several Sunday stories written for the paper by O. Henry. "I
don't know a word this man is writing," he said.

Bob Davis, a *World* editor, said softly, "God heard you say that."

"I still don't like this man O. Henry and I don't like his stories, either,"
Van Hamm said. "Get me somebody who can entertain readers. He's
fired."

By instinct, Hearst could not wait to hire Van Hamm, whose first
decision on the *American* was a vehement turndown of an idea to hire
Don Marquis as a daily columnist. Some staffers thought that Marquis's stories and cartoons about archy the cockroach and mehitabel

the cat were interesting. "I am devoted to stamping out cockroaches, not glorifying them," Van Hamm said.

From his city room, Hearst looked across at City Hall, which for so long he had wanted to own and had taken a couple of foolish shots at attaining. He had been in Congress and didn't think it was big enough for him. Now he decided he would be mayor and use that as a step to being what he really should be, a three- or four-term President or perhaps, by popular demand, a king.

The building he looked at covetously was made of marble on three sides, and brownstone on the rear. It was stated that the brownstone was done for reasons of economy, and as not all those involved in its construction were politicians, this stands a chance of being true. The back of the building was painted white, and done so well over the years that nobody could tell that it was not the same marble as the rest of the building. Just as it was impossible to tell the politicians inside City Hall from legitimate human beings. The building became blazing white in the noonday sun, then faint blue at evening, and at all hours, right until today, suggests France. It faces a plaza and park and is of two stories, with an attic and delicate tower. The front staircase of ten steps, as wide as the building, climbs from the plaza to a portico whose eight pillars make the building seem regal and remote, although it looks over a loudly breathing city.

A building dedicated to urgency has the most restful entrance to be found in the city, with double doors under the portico opening into a warm museum: a marble lobby of many archways and eaves heading into a rotunda that is hushed in the pale light of stained glass in the tower's ceiling. In the center of the rotunda are eight steps going up to a landing that is just out of reach of the sunlight coming in in oblongs through the back door of the building. From the staircase landing there rise two freestanding staircases, one curving to the left, the other to the right, each with graceful banisters that are outlined against the pale light from the stained glass ceiling. The marble staircases bend away from each other in the light, curving, curving, curving until they are directly overhead and disappearing into the second floor.

When Lincoln's body was laid out on the second floor, so many citizens were on the staircases that those below pointed at the bare undersides of the staircases and speculated on collapse. There was a fearful moan from those on the stairs each time the guards pushed more on. Hold the steps did. Over the days, the structure held the feet of an entire city without a shudder.

City Hall is a building that always has been worthy of its beginnings, which are in the struggle between thievery and somewhat honesty. About 350 years ago, the Dutch swindled tulip seeds from Constantinople, and so many plants at once pushed out of the wet earth in Holland that the Dutch had money for explorers, who went out and found and stole Manhattan. By the time the place became American, it was so big it needed a city hall. At 26 Broadway, Alexander Hamilton sat by a whale oil lamp and with scratching pen outlined the finances for the new country of America. The people running the city chose empty land a few blocks north, called the Fields, as the site for City Hall. Two architects, Macomb and Mangin, submitted fine plans, and as this phase of the game was totally honest, there was no need for delay, so in 1803 the cornerstone for the building was laid. Bureaucrats were ordered to lay out the rest of New York, starting with the new City Hall. Again, as nobody had yet figured out how to steal empty lots, they let these people sit there with their pencils and map out the whole city. What the bureaucrats put on paper is what the city is today. And the grandeur of the City Hall building shows the wisdom of giving the public something it can see and admire, in order to keep their eyes as much as possible away from the normal political activities of theft and other dishonesty. If there is a fine public building around, a politician can point to it and tell people that they are ungrateful curs.

The white marble for the building was brought in from Stockbridge, Massachusetts, and cost $43,750 more than brownstone from around New York. When the marble arrived by sloop from Sheffield, Massachusetts, the contractor used a mule to haul it from the North River. He charged the city $22 for the mule. Nobody yelled. So he put in another bill for $24 for the mule. As the workers who put the marble into a building were honest, they got paid what they deserved for being honest, $1.00 to $1.25 a day. Later, in building the Tweed courthouse directly behind City Hall, more marble was brought down from Sheffield, and the building, supposed to cost $1 million, had slight cost overruns up to $12 million. This time, however, the tradesmen knew what to do. Andrew Garvey, a plasterer, earned $133,187 for two days' work. Earned is the word, too, for he had to live with politicians for many years before participating in thievery of such magnitude. You just don't let some common shoplifter walk into a thing like this. George Miller, a carpenter, was paid $360,751 for a month's work. As the building was marble and George walked around with a mouthful of nails and nothing to drive them into, he received the pay to make up for disappointments. The politicians had such trust in George that they let him hold the money for practically an entire day before taking it from him.

In building City Hall, the contractor claimed that iron forging in New York at that time was not so advanced that a local forge could make an iron picket fence. Certainly not as good as the one that was made in Leeds, England, by a blood relative of the contractor. The fence was shipped all the way from Leeds, with costs that were good and appropriate.

For a long time City Hall had no front doors. There were two fireplaces in the lobby to warm people against the chill winter winds whipping through the opening when General Worth from Fort Worth was laid out here in 1812, the first name to rate a funeral in the building.

While the marble of City Hall was smooth and sturdy to the hand, it also was more porous than granite and thus could be affected over centuries by the salt mists coming in on the wind from the Atlantic Ocean. Those cemeteries in Queens, nearest the ocean, use Rock of Ages granite rather than marble because of the salt moisture. By the time the ocean breeze reaches Manhattan, as a whisper, much of the salt is gone, but it has taken on something more powerful than the heaviest salt, and that is the corrosive agent illusion. The least waft of air is withering to marble because the air is so laden with it. Late in the evening, when there is only lonely light and the hallways are deserted, the building's stones have neither friend nor the weight to stop illusion, which comes dancing on the slightly damp air and pierces marble instantly and with more thoroughness than anything carried by any cloud over all the ages.

The illusion forms a dampness deep in the marble and then seeps to the surface and at first is unnoticeable, then particularly in the evening a light bulb goes on in the dimness of the lobby and suddenly, in this one place, on this one drop, there is a tiny explosion at the tip of a light ray. Now, over the hours and days, more moisture gathers at the base of the droplet, turning it into a full drop too heavy to remain, and illusion falls silently from a marble arch in the middle of the busiest day. It has a stunning effect when it hits anybody on the head.

The first time Damon Runyon went to City Hall was in 1915, for a meeting with a state senator from Greenwich Village, James J. Walker, to discuss a bill that would legalize professional prizefighting in New York. They met in the lobby, standing behind a pillar for privacy. Walker, who regarded himself as a songwriter, had a hoarse voice from singing new songs through most of the night before. He never wrote the songs. As he was well known enough to get a song published, he only had to hear a tune by some busted-down guy who didn't have what to eat, and if Walker liked it, for a few dollars on the piano top he could say it was his. A guy living in a rooming house on Seventh Avenue had written something that was almost called "Will You Love Me in September as You Did in May?" He ran into Walker, who had enough sense to like the song very much, and who even may have added a syllable here and there. Walker got the song published under the name of Walker and it became close to a standard. Walker then convinces himself that he had written every American song since the national anthem. Of course he was the right guy for Runyon to approach about getting a boxing bill introduced. They spoke for about two minutes in the marble lobby when Walker said, "I hope between your Hearst papers and the Democratic Party this can get done."

"I am not a Democrat," Runyon said. "I am a Communist. I believe in sharing the wealth equally. If fight promoters make money, I am the first on line to collect."

"How is it equal if you're first on line?" Walker said.

"Because after me everybody else comes first," Runyon said.

"I don't know where we're going, but it looks like we're going to a party together," Walker said.

"I have to tell you, I don't drink anymore," Runyon said.

"That still leaves you with all the bad habits you need to overcome that weakness."

As he plotted with Walker, Runyon's work on stories about Bugs Raymond were causing immensely favorable telephone messages and mail across City Hall Park at the *American*. He was called up to see William Randolph Hearst at his home in the Clarendon House on 86th Street and Riverside Drive. Hearst had the top four floors, a private art gallery and a ballroom on the roof. Recently, he had spent four hours learning the buck-and-wing from his father-in-law while his editors waited downstairs for an urgent conference. They were in the first floor of the Clarendon, which he had taken over for meetings with his newspeople.

Hearst rose and greeted Runyon as he walked in. The truly rich always do this, as if to indicate that they regard high manners as much a part of wealth as money itself, although in this act of rising there is an element of condescension. Hearst extolled Runyon for writing positive things in a humorous manner. "We can find enough doleful things on our own each day without asking a man of your talent to do so also," he said. An aide brought Hearst a yellow apple and a knife on a pie-crust salver. As he was being served, the aide proudly told Runyon, "This salver belonged to Dolley Madison." Hearst faced Runyon and said in wonderment, "I am told that you don't drink. Can this be so?" Runyon assured him it was. "Some days, the gods do smile on us," Hearst said.

He jumped up. He had an art auction to attend. He spoke to an assistant, Joseph Willicombe. He was the usual failed editorial worker who had a great ability to say "Yes, sir!" and who wound up as clerk for the big boss. "Mr. Willicombe, it is your responsibility to see that this gentleman remains with the Hearst newspapers. I recommend the man's salary be tripled."

On the way downstairs, Willicombe tried the usual assistant's attempt to impress the boss by whittling the amount.

"That was fair of the Chief," Runyon said. "He put his finger on exactly what I'm worth. Three times the usual grunt. I better get out and earn it." He left before Willicombe could speak.

After a few of his paydays at triple the old money, Runyon got into Nat Lewis's clothes shop on Broadway and bought two suits at $25 each, thus starting what was to be the largest wardrobe in the history of the newspaper business. The purchase took hours, for he matched ties to the suits.

June 25, 1911
(Just in case. Here it is again. New address 251 West 95th Street, New York, N.Y.)
Dear mother and daddy.

I love it here. I told you when I called I knew I would. In case you didn't get the number down right, it's Cathedral 1324. I know you wrote it down but the connection seemed poor and I didn't want you to miss a number. It's busy and elegant. I especially love the shops and the houses. Mother, you would adore Arnold Constable's. That was Mrs. Abraham Lincoln's store. There is a trolley that runs on Broadway but my favorite trip is the bus on Riverside Drive that goes down and over to Fifth Avenue. I sit on the top which is open and can look right into the windows along the Drive. The houses are much bigger and more ornate than those in Denver. Daddy, you would love the subway trains. Express, local, so much switching. The apartment is very nice and I'm trying to make it cosy and warm. It's such a relief to have a whole flat. My cooking is fine. But the only meal that Alfred is always home for is breakfast and that is at lunch time. He seems to be on a whole new schedule. His column takes him out in the afternoon and evening. He gets home late and then sleeps later. I'm trying to adjust our lives. I am used to seeing him in a newspaper office rather than calling him. I tell myself I do not miss my job. When the operator at Alfred's newspaper answers the phone I admit I do have a longing. Alfred is having such great success writing about a baseball player named Raymond. He is good and nutsy. These people in New York can be vicious. Some professor at Columbia University actually wrote the paper and said Alfred was stepping over this poor alcoholic baseball player's body to get somewhere. You know Alfred and criticism. He seethed for days. He threatened to quit because the paper wanted to publish the letter. I am just going to walk up Broadway to that school. It's right near here. I am going to tell that professor what I think of him. I spend a lot of time with Irma Goldberg. Her husband [Rube] is the cartoonist. He also works odd hours and we have a grand time exploring this city. When you come I will show you all the places where the rich live.

So much love,
Ellen.

Runyon followed the rituals of baseball. Each year, as sure as a bird flies, within days of the end of the World Series, the newspapers started running pictures of baseball players relaxing from exhausting months of play by hunting in the South. The players went hunting because most didn't know how to work, and had to do something with all this free time. These photos ran right up to January, when the first stories of contracts being signed for the next season appeared. Everybody in a sports department made certain that such pictures and the stories with them were in the paper, because everybody was sure that if something ever happened to baseball, the newspapers would collapse, jobs would disappear and lives end. Thus the almost daily off-season headline: "2 MORE GIANTS COME TO TERMS."

So after the baseball season ended each year, Runyon went duck hunting at Havre de Grace, Maryland, with baseball people, and when he came home, he hung the ducks out the window when his wife wouldn't keep them in the icebox. Blood dripped from the ducks onto 95th Street.

There was a poolroom in the basement of the corner building at 95th and Broadway, and the first day Runyon went in there, one of the guys said to him, "The people in here are all right. Don't go near Tenth Avenue. They got a lot of killers there."

"Where on Tenth Avenue?" he said.

He began walking. If there are killers, he reasoned, then that means there are also a lot of crap games and, even better, loose dolls. When he got to the corner of Tenth Avenue and 47th Street, he took one look at the guys standing around and wishing mightily for trouble, and at once he felt at home. Baseball was nice, but murder was the main event.

Here, because Owney Madden is so unknown and was so important to the history of crime in America, we must pause and describe certain things about him. He was the big stick that allowed Runyon to loll with the worst murderers. In turn, Runyon made him the founder of organized crime in America. Upon hearing this phrase, people have the clear vision of some evil young Italian with overwhelming wisdom who comes stalking out of the hills of Sicily, murders everybody in Brooklyn and, at the end, sits down in a boardroom and tells other gangsters, who are dressed like bankers, that they should never sell drugs.

"We shall never sell oil," John D. Rockefeller always said.

Organized crime in America, however, was born with an English accent. Owney Madden was born on December 18, 1891, of immigrant Irish parents at 25 Somerset Street, North Leeds, at that time a dreary wool-mill city in the northern Midlands of England. He was birth number 202 for the district, as noted by registrar Isaac J. Bloomfield. His father was Francis Madden, a cloth dresser, and his mother's name was Mary Madden, formerly O'Neil. The Maddens lived in an industrial row house and the father worked as a cloth dresser in a sweatshop. In this place at these times, the word "sweatshop" was not stale and overused, for nobody ever knew how to torture worker or prisoner better than a British mill owner. The family moved to a smaller and smokier mill town called Wigan, up in the wet hills. People were awakened each day by the whine of machines starting up in the mills. That sound was a tremendous education for Madden. He never worked a day in his whole life. He attended Wigan schools, where the motto was, "A healthy mind and a healthy body." At home on the kitchen table each day was the *Yorkshire Post*, with the sports stories starting on page 3. He read everything, and used what he learned to become the proofreader of the underworld and embarrass the morons around him who could barely tell time. His interest in sports stories was to make him the closest criminal to Damon Runyon.

At Wigan, Madden took care of his father's pigeons. "He fed them, grained them, cleaned out the tiny loft and released them. As they took flight, banking in tight formation above the chimneys, against a backdrop of mist-covered moors, there was no greater expression of freedom," the *Yorkshire Post* reported. From Wigan, the Maddens went to Liverpool, which was a five-mile riverfront of sailors and dockers, of hard north-country British and the Irish immigrants they hated. Only soap had less friends. Owney worked tremendously hard at learning how to dodge anything worthwhile. He hung out in poolrooms and dressing rooms of smoky carnival halls, where his uncle was a booth fighter, the man who would stand around and fight all comers for a small purse. Owney stood on the edge of the fighting circle and shrieked and twisted and threw punches in the air as his uncle fought. Years later, Madden always was a spectacle at big fights, as he leaped out of his chair and whipped his fists as his fighter fought. Nobody ever re-called seeing him actually fight; he used a gun at those moments. In Liverpool, he also hung around music halls and later said that he had put together a smashing act with Stan Laurel, later of Laurel and Hardy. When Owney opened his nightclubs in New York, he claimed all knowledge of entertainment because of working with Laurel in Liver-pool music halls. Laurel didn't recall ever seeing Madden but knew enough not to say so.

Owney's father died and the mother sailed to America, where she moved into 352 Tenth Avenue in Manhattan with her sister. In that year, 1902, over 195,000 people left England for New York. Owney was only eleven, and he and his sister, fourteen, lived alone in Liver-pool until the mother sent tickets. Their ship, the SS *Teutonic*, was several days late in leaving. Passengers lived on the dock while young Liverpool street gangs stole luggage and purses from anyone who fell asleep. Owney stood alongside his sister, feet planted, a hand jammed in his pocket, where he had a large knife. The other hoodlums noticed the hand and remained clear of him. "His last view of England was a thicket of masts and rigging and sandstone waterfront buildings bur-nished by the setting sun," the *Yorkshire Post* noted.

The *Teutonic* was thirty-eight days at sea, which was just another Atlantic crossing. Owney and his sister joined the mother in rooms on Tenth Avenue in a neighborhood called Hell's Kitchen. His first act in his new country was to get into a doorway and hit the first drunk pass-ing by with a lead pipe. In later years, telling lies at the bar, he said he got $500 on the mugging. There was not $500 on the whole West Side of Manhattan on those nights. As his mother permitted no dishonest money in the house, Owney said that he "gave a little bit at a time to my aunt and she loaned it to my mother." He always was unable to remember how much of the mugging money he kept for himself. Schooling consisted of a stroll past St. Michael's Roman Catholic School on 34th Street, as a courtesy. He proceeded to a cellar where the Gophers, the most famous of the West Side gangs, hung out. Now, the only way to get ahead in crime is to kill somebody, the more spectacular and vicious the better. Leadership is to cut a man's lips off in front of a crowd. Once, Madden had an argument with one William Henshaw.

"I only tell a man once," Owney said.

"Me, too. I just told you I do as I please," Henshaw said.

As a gangster feels he is a tribal hero while simultaneously feeling that so many stare through him at his ruined character, the slightest challenge causes his mind to go up in flames. One night Henshaw took a girl home to upper Manhattan, then was riding the trolley car home on Ninth Avenue when Owney Madden got on and shot him in the back of the head. Madden hit the trolley bell in a salute to Henshaw's departure. "I knew no church would ring a bell for him."

Soon, Police Chief Max Schnittberger told the *New York World* that "Madden must own a cemetery." He called him Owney the Killer. Schnittberger is a strange name to see on an old New York police roster, and for good reason: he was the last German to get a job in the city that didn't call for standing behind a lathe.

Madden was the first natural leader of criminals of his time because he understood that to succeed in New York a man had to partially sacrifice one of his most precious possessions, his hatred of other races. When he saw all these Italians piling off the boats, he did not cry "Wop!" indiscriminately. Instead he made a friend of one Tony Romanello and brought him into the Winona Club as a senior criminal. The clubhouse was on West 47th Street, just off Tenth Avenue and on the second floor of a brownstone building. Madden had a bar, piano, crap game and card table. While the walls were thick, the place still was not suitable for containing the sound of gunshots, although that deterred nobody. People walking down 47th Street usually associated the sound coming from the Winona as firecrackers, although undertakers did not. The club was open to criminals of all nations. Madden was raised to think that the Poles had it right in the first place, that all Jews belonged fleeing from a cavalry charge. A young man named Little Augie Orgen changed that.

When Jack (Kid) Dropper, who might have been the first gangster ever to have a nickname, was pulled into the West Side court on 47th Street one night, his enemy Jacob (Little Augie) Orgen slipped into the courthouse lobby, where he saw Captain Cornelius Willemse, whose ambition was to live good. Little Augie and Willemse strolled the length of the lobby. Little Augie came back on the street and said to one of his men, a mental defective named Louis Kushner, who went under the alias of Louis Cohen, "You have a gun?"

"What would I do if I didn't?" Kushner said.

Little Augie told him to get into a doorway across the street so nobody would notice him. "When I wave, you come on and do the whole thing."

When Captain Willemse and a detective named LaBattaglia walked Kid Dropper out of the court building to take him to jail, strangely there was no patrol car waiting. Detective LaBattaglia shoved Dropper into a taxicab. Willemse and Detective LaBattaglia wanted to make sure the cab driver knew where to go. They stood at the driver's window and discussed routes downtown. Dropper sat alone in the rear of the cab. Standing out in the street, Little Augie waved his arm. Louis Kushner's heart leaped. He was going to do a solo! He came out of the tenement doorway across the street, ran through the stopped traffic, paused behind another taxicab, looked up quickly and saw Kid Dropper's head in the rear window of the cab in front of the courthouse. Louis Kushner came out from behind his taxicab and kept looking at Kid Dropper's head, framed in the window, as he ran right up and put the gun against the window and started firing. That took care of Kid Dropper, right in front of a crowd and with dozens of police only steps away. Kushner suddenly went crazy in his new stardom. He kept firing. Captain Willemse tackled him, and Kushner pulled the trigger once more. The shot went through Willemse's hat. Detectives came from everywhere to jump on Kushner. When they got him on his feet, in handcuffs, he said, "I need a cigarette."

When he heard about this, Owney Madden said, "The Jews are the fucking greatest. They kill in broad daylight." He went downtown and met a thin young thug on 10th Street and First Avenue named Charley Luciano, who walked him down a few blocks to Ludlow Street, where, in a poolroom doorway, was another young guy with a mean face, Meyer Lansky.

"What do you want?" Lansky said.

"To say hello to you," Madden said agreeably.

On that first day when Runyon came down to see Madden, there was initial nervousness among those on the street corner, as detectives had just been around to check on a scurrilous rumor involving the disappearance of a longtime squad room favorite, Jigger McGrath. "They got some fuckin' nerve what they're trying to say," one of the men on the street corner, Arthur Bieler, said.

What the detectives were claiming was that only two days before, Jigger McGrath, a sworn enemy of Owney Madden's, had been asked to shake hands and forget it all. This was on the corner of 47th and Twelfth Avenue, directly across the street from the shipping piers. Jigger, who didn't like to give up feuds, finally said all right, he would shake with Madden. He held out his hand and Madden took it. Madden now would not let go. McGrath tried to pull away but could not. He was concentrating on getting his hand free when Arthur Bieler came up and put a gun into his stomach and that was that. "Shake hands with the Devil!" Owney Madden said. It became Madden's slogan for years, until the remark was appropriated as a title for a gangster movie.

Now on Tenth Avenue, Bieler took Runyon down the block to the second-floor Winona clubhouse. Owney Madden had two women with him, Margie Everdeen and Freda Horner, both smiling sweetly as Runyon gave a bow from the lumbar region, an elaborate sweep of the hat as if fanning the air, and in a voice low to denote respect he said, "How do you do. It is a pleasure to meet you."

"Likewise," Freda Horner said.

"Likewise," Margie Everdeen said.

Arthur Bieler remembered for many years that he was impressed with Runyon's manners. "The guy comes from the Wild West and he acts like a footman."

"Freda is my girlfriend," Owney Madden said to Runyon.

Runyon then turned his attention to Margie Everdeen. "You would love Pueblo," Runyon said.

"Pueblo," Margie said. She said no more. Which made this one of the few times she kept her mouth shut.

Runyon had never been to the club before, but his name already had been used inside the hall. "You ought to read about this Raymond," Owney Madden said to his girlfriend one day.

"What is he?" Freda Horner asked.

"You ought to learn to read. You'd laugh your ass off."

"I should," she said. "Every time the cops write down something, I tell them, 'What's that you're puttin' down?' They always show me the paper on account of they know I don't know what's on it. They try to make me stupid."

"You should learn to read the baseball stories instead of talking,"

Owney said. "If you even tell them your last name, then you're startin'
a conversation. They get you used to talkin' with them. And it's only
about prostitution. Next thing you know, you're tellin' them about
somebody got killed." He returned to the story about Bugs Raymond
threatening McGraw. "I wish Raymond lived next door to me."

Now, with Runyon making his first appearance, six people were
playing cards, five of them outsiders and one, in shirtsleeves, the Madden dealer. Of the five players, four were tired and tense. The fifth, a
man named Nicely Hogan, who weighed about 360, was at ease and
happy. He chain-smoked cigarettes, and at the start of a new hand,
while the others picked up their cards in tight concentration, Hogan
left his cards unturned and leaned back.

"I bet I'm doin' nicely," He said to Freda Horner and Margie Everdeen. "Could one of yez get me a nice soft drink?"

"What kind?"

"Two bourbons and a big cold beer in the same glass."

Margie brought him the drink.

"Margie," Nicely said.

"Yeah, Nicely?"

"How's about a nice big pipe?"

"Don' you say that so loud."

"What am I supposed to do, fuckin' whisper so you can't hear me?"

Runyon noticed that Nicely didn't have the slightest interest in his
cards and threw two of them out automatically. The dealer flicked two
cards and this time Hogan paid attention. He spoke to himself, but
loud enough to be heard in the street. "Oh boy, that's the dynamite.
Watch me now." He said he wanted to bet the New York Central Railroad on his hand. He got the others in deep enough, following which
he threw out a hand that looked like the dinner table at Buckingham
Palace. "Nicely, nicely!" he yelled.

That is a good name, Runyon said to himself. It was obvious Nicely
was the takeout man, the guy who sits there and gets fed enough cards
to win the key pots, in this case the winnings going right to Madden.
"If we let him sit there on the up for five minutes, he would lose the
clothes he got on," Madden said to Runyon. "The man can't concentrate enough to take a leak. I love it when you write about that Bugs
Raymond. This guy here, Nicely, is our Bugs Raymond. Why don't
you give him a write up?"

"Two Nicelys, not one," Runyon said.

Sometime during the night, the owner of the building, an electrician named Keating, an utterly stupid man, too, for he did not know the difference between life and death, banged on the door and shouted, "You people are going to have to move from my building. You are making too much noise!"

Arthur Bieler stepped up to him and held a gun to his head and pulled the trigger. There was a loud click.

"Is this too much noise?" Bieler said.

As Runyon stood on Tenth Avenue and waited for a cab, he began to count. Madden, Bieler, both the broads and the big fat guy, Nicely-Nicely. Five people he could use in one place. I better go back there, he told himself.

When he did, he was told that Nicely-Nicely was late because he was a witness in the West Side court for a special hearing involving a good, decent West Sider named Jackrabbit Jack Sheehan, who had a dice game on Pier 84, North River. Runyon found Nicely-Nicely having a cigarette outside the court building. "It's bullshit over nothin'," Nicely-Nicely said.

"Why are they making so much of a dice game?" Runyon asked.

"On account of the body."

They then went into court, and when called to the stand, Nicely-Nicely paraded down the center aisle like a grand marshal, paused and clapped a hand over his midsection and bowed to the judge. He sat down and the judge asked, "How much do you weigh, Mr. Hogan?"

A. Three-sixty.

Q. What is your occupation?

A. Former flyweight fighter.

Q. You had to weigh . . .

A. A hundred seven pounds.

Q. After an answer like that, I don't see how we can possibly believe anything you say.

A. Suit yourself.

Runyon had all kinds of time for things like that. Being a sportswriter was the same as being a welfare recipient, but without any supervision. Games at the Polo Grounds and at Ebbets Field in Brooklyn started at 3:15 P.M., giving Wall Street people time to rush to the ballpark by subway right after the market shut down for the day. He went straight to the Winona Club after the Giants game two days later. Sitting against the wall, head back and eyes closed, was a little man with a derby hat, hair sticking out from under the sides, and with a cat in his lap. His face had as many cuts as a butcher block. Madden identi-

fied him as Monk Eastman. "He used to run the whole Jew mob,"
Madden said. "Not anymore. Like you can see."

"Monk smokes," Freda Horner said.

"Smokes what?"

"Anything they grow in China."

"Monk smokes too fuckin' much," Owney said.

"Who took his place?" Runyon asked.

"If you're young, Meyer Lansky. If you don't like young guys, Rothstein, but he don't want to be known as a tough guy. Rothstein wants
to rob people sitting down."

"Where does he hang out?"

"He goes by Lindy's."

Rothstein had been out of town for a month. Now he sat in silence at
his regular table alongside the cashier's desk in the delicatessen, eating
an apple. Runyon walked up, introduced himself and sat down. Both
of them knew each other without giving biographies. Rothstein was
thin, elegantly dressed and had dark hair slicked back. He was raised
to be a perfectly honest businessman, but he truly loved larceny. As
he was smarter than most gamblers, he became the biggest bookmaker
in the country. Already, he had people selling a little bit of heroin and
cocaine, although not as much as he would when inspired by politicians later on. While Runyon sat there, the cashier received a phone
call for him. Rothstein, chewing his apple, leaned on the counter and
listened as a guy calling long distance from the crap game out at Mon-
tauk Point said he needed $500 desperately.

"I can't hear you," Rothstein said calmly.

"I said I need five hundred!" the guy yelled.

"I can't hear you. The connection is bad," Rothstein said.

Now the long distance operator, who had been listening to the call,
said in telephone company diction, "He say-ed that he ne-yeds fi-yev
hundred dollars."

"If you heard him so good, then you give him the money," Rothstein
said. He hung up.

He said to Runyon, "Will Raymond last out the season?"

"I doubt it," Runyon said.

"That's too bad. I could have somebody tail him and whenever he
pitches drunk I could bet an apartment house against him." Thus letting Runyon know exactly why he was interested in sports.

A couple of night later, Jake Starselsky, who weighed ninety-eight pounds and had a mustache, stood in front of Lindy's and told the owner, Leo Lindemann, and Arnold Rothstein, who reveals himself on this night as a silent partner, that a flashing sign was impractical because of the need for a human arm to make it flash. Starselsky had built the first animated sign seen in the city. All night, atop the Flatiron building at 23rd Street in Manhattan, the sign blinked on and off, screaming into the hot night sky, "Manhattan Beach Swept by Cool Breezes." Manhattan Beach being in Brooklyn. The sign blinked on command of the scrawny but attentive arm of a medical student, who sat in a shack behind the sign and kept pulling and then pushing shut the handle that made the lights blink. He had as a partner another medical student, who studied the chapter on kidneys. When the first student's arm grew tired, the partner put down his chapter on kidneys and went to work. And the first student, shaking his tired arm, picked up the kidney text. Jake told Lindemann and Rothstein how he had these two medical students he used at the Flatiron building. Lindemann agreed that it was best to put up the sign that didn't flash.

Runyon, the bystander, now had a marvelous idea. He told Starselsky he could save him money by having one big strong guy, a heavyweight fighter with an arm of oak, do the work of the two medical students. He got this idea because he already had invested $300 in a heavyweight, Conklin, who had been around at dusk in need of room rent. Starselsky saw great future business coming from Lindy's. Even now, he had a crew replacing two hundred burned-out bulbs from his Times Square signs each day. They threw the bulbs into the garbage and he cringed. He gave the two medical students the next night off. Runyon and Mushky Jackson arrived with Conklin at the Flatiron building, where Starselsky showed the fighter how to run the sign. "Use your left hand mostly," Mushky Jackson said. "You got to get speed. Pretend you're up in the gym."

Near midnight, Runyon was summoned from Lindy's to the Flatiron building. Starselsky pointed up. The sign was black and remained that way for some time. Then it began blinking again. Runyon relaxed. After a few minutes it went black again.

Up on the roof, Conklin was doing exactly what he had been told, to pretend he was in a gym. In the place where he trained, Stillman's Gym on Eighth Avenue and 55th Street, there was an automatic bell that rang every three minutes to mark the end of a round. Fighters would immediately stop what they were doing, boxing or bag punch-

ing, take a one-minute rest, then resume at the bell. Conklin, pushing
the lever with one hand, his watch in the other, was timing his job
perfectly for a fight gym, resting every three minutes.

"He makes the sky go pitch black!" Starselsky yelled.

And so the next night, the sky over Manhattan was consistently bright
with "Manhattan Beach Swept by Cool Breezes," and behind the flashing lights, one medical student pushed the lever while the other read
up on kidneys.

On Broadway now, Runyon as writer was being formed by the great
line between "citizens," a jailhouse term used to describe people who
had all their rights, such as the vote, and "Broadway guys" or "wise
guys" or underworld guys, who either had been convicted for something or certainly should have been — at best they lived on the border — and as a result had lost the right to vote, among other things.
The Broadway wise guy, being that he wasn't allowed to vote like a
citizen, thought of himself as residing outside the law. No decent outlaw would dare stop for a red light or pay for a newspaper. A citizen
could squawk and call on the services of police, but the code of an outlaw forbade him to call the police or use civil regulations under any
circumstances. Anything done to an outlaw was considered a personal
dispute:

"Give me the phone," Itzak the Thief yelled when they got the ropes
off him. Two heist guys had walked into his card joint on Allen Street
and left him trussed up in a closet.

"What do you want the phone for?" Billy (the Kid) Lustig said.

"To call the cops on these two bastards."

"Cops? What's the matter with you, you're not a citizen. You can't
call the cops," Billy said.

"What am I supposed to do?" Itzak yelled.

"Get a gun and go lookin' for them," Billy said.

And anybody who was listed officially as an outlaw was told that he
might as well live that way. Wise guys spent little time denying the
lives they lived, and Runyon found them the only people with whom
he was comfortable. In front of Lindy's each night was Billy Warren,
who ran a crap game in a storefront on 14th Street and Third Avenue.
He threw players into cabs for the ride downtown. One night, with
Runyon looking on, a police car pulled up as Warren was juggling players and two cabs. The cop walked over and demanded, "What are you
doing?" The anger and disdain arose in Runyon. Then the cop said,

"You two, get in there." The crapshooters jumped into the back seat of the patrol car and Runyon saw Warren hold out a partially closed hand to the cop, who took whatever was in it, smiled and got into the police car. "You know the address?" Warren called out. The cop nodded and drove the two players off to the crap game. This made Runyon at ease with the sight of a policeman, provided that the policeman was not a citizen. He considered only one act as being wrong, that of disrespect of him.

At Jamaica Race Track through an entire spring meeting, a manufac-turer named Dugan, whose real last name was a bit longer, had some difficulty in identifying winners and therefore began to bet more in order to catch up. One afternoon, as a horse called Fashionplate, en-thusiastically backed by Dugan, was caught in a blind switch and the rider, S. Renick, had no way out, Dugan threw his hands to the sky. "You done me out of mine factory!" In the press box, somebody said to Runyon, "Dugan just blew a pants factory." Runyon, who had just lost most of a week's salary, barely paid attention.

Dugan left the racetrack and interviewed arsonists, all of whom wanted either a piece of the insurance or front money. In the midst of negoti-ations, Horse Thief Burke had a strong opinion on a Whitney horse, Fairweather, running in the Pomanauk Handicap at Jamaica. "I get vell," Dugan said. He went for $2,500 on the horse, which collapsed in the backstretch. There went the money for a reliable arsonist. Dugan was told that arson was a three-man effort, and the one who could not be left at home was a blanket man. This is the person who stands out-side the building with a thick Indian blanket, ready to throw it over anybody running out with the seat of his pants afire. Dugan hired Zunk, a veteran of these things. Dugan would not go for an arsonist's fee, so he decided that Junior, a promising criminal handyman who also played with matches, could do the job and he himself would be the utility man. In the dark of night, Dugan led them to the pants factory, on Blake Avenue in East New York. With them they brought eleven gal-lons of gasoline in tin cans and one good box of kitchen matches.

"Make a big fire," Dugan said. He went into the factory, spilled gas-oline and then, looking around for something to start it up with, grabbed a copy of the *New York American,* put a match to it and quickly touched a pile of goods. He took off, throwing the paper down in the doorway. Junior stood in the doorway and counted the gas cans. That was his job. If he left with one gas can short, that would mean the can probably was somewhere in the fire and would be discovered in the morning by the authorities. Some rat district attorney then would regard it as evidence.

In counting the cans, Junior lost track and started over, still felt he was one shy and went back inside to get it. He emerged on the dead run with a gas can in his hand and his backside in flames. Zunk, the blanket man, was on the job. He held the blanket by his fingertips, in order to maneuver it better, and he started running as Junior came out the door, just as runners in a relay race get up to speed before the baton is passed to them. Zunk did this to stay even with the fleeing man. Now Zunk, fingertips clutching the blanket, measured Junior and draped the blanket all over him, tackling Junior, and they went down, rolling around as the fire was successfully snuffed out. The trouble was, the same thing happened to the pants factory when the firemen got at it.

We now go to the next night on the sidewalk in front of Lindy's, where a heavyweight fighter, Donato, who knew how to make friends in top circles, is standing with his cousin Lorenzo, a fire marshal of the Fire Department of the City of New York. This is a job that calls for the investigation of fires that appear to be of suspicious origin. The cousin, Lorenzo, pulls out of a bag a rolled-up half-burned newspaper. "Tell Mr. Dugan he could do a tenner based on this." He dropped it in the gutter.

Runyon looked at the newspaper used in a cheap arson. It was the *American*. Runyon's size 5½B shoe reached down into the gutter and flicked the pages until he came to his column. By Damon Runyon. He stood on his sidewalk with eyes glaring until Dugan reported for duty later on.

"You used my column! In a cheap arson!" Runyon turned his back on Dugan and went inside and never talked to him again. But as he fumed, opportunity flourished a few blocks down.

The light from the overhead lamp gleamed on a big heavy glass filled with ice cubes. There was the muffled sound of heavy traffic coming through the high windows that looked down on Broadway. Up here in the Astor Hotel bar on 45th Street one of the bartenders watched in rising excitement as a Mexican sat at a table and took the big glass of Tom Collins and swallowed all, the orange slice left sticking out of the corner of his mouth. With him were two richly dressed merchants. They chuckled appreciatively at the sight of the orange slice. The Mexican laughed heartily. The businessmen forced themselves to roar. The

Mexican, who wore a new three-piece suit and tooled leather boots, bent over a hardcover business checkbook. The businessmen leaned forward and were so close together that their heads touched. One of them helped direct the Mexican, who with determination but obvious pain filled out the check. The Mexican relaxed. He waved the pen and with a flourish signed his name to the check, as if this was the only thing he actually could write on his own. It was. He couldn't read in Mexican or English and only had this signature, which had unusual value in this manner, writing checks, in that it was impossible for anyone else to copy the signature. The businessmen took the check casually, strolled through the lounge and, at the head of the staircase leading to the Astor lobby, went high into the air and landed halfway down the staircase. The bartender watched with the eyes of a young eagle.

The bartender, who bought his drugs from Arnold Rothstein, rushed over to Lindy's, where after a conference on the sidewalk with one of Rothstein's pushers, the old killer Monk Eastman was allowed inside to sit with Rothstein and Runyon.

Rothstein listened and told the bartender nothing except a "thanks" and a promise to see him if anything developed. When the bartender left, Runyon speculated about Hipolito Villa's being a relative of the real Villa. Rothstein again said nothing. He always was a great friend of Runyon's until the time of money, and then he became cold and silent and thought deeply about himself. Of course it was understood that Runyon, as poet, was allowed to be friend or betrayer in the same hour, and it was the role of those around him, these subordinates, to accept this gracefully.

So he and Rothstein had a good Mexican standoff, although in this instance, Rothstein was about to get alongside the Mexican.

After lunch, Rothstein went to the office of his stock brokerage — a bust-them-out operation — and called upon his financial research. This consisted of a hunchback named Moe Tear Sr. — as in rip. He sat in a corner of the office behind three desks stacked as high as you get with newspapers. Rothstein originally hired Moe because of his condition. He believed that all records men should have some curvature problem so that they could remain bent over a newspaper or record sheet and never have the excuse of a back ache for leaving early.

Moe sure was hunched over, but he also loved to read. He spent an eternity on papers nobody else would look at, going from first page to last, and no newspaper or journal was too dull or trivial for him. "He reads weather reports from towns he doesn't even live in," a man working in the Rothstein office said with great admiration. Moe also followed a story for as long as it went, through the small boring details and stupid twists that on the third day cause people to stop reading, and when he came to the end he had a fair history of the particular larceny. Moe was particularly good at spotting the exact moment of theft. As it takes four to five good days to rob a man, he knew there had to be one point when the knock of opportunity sounds clear in the morning air, the door first creaks open, the scale tips and the thief is assured of scoring. Reading about how surrogate court clerk Harry Perry suffered an ankle injury during a fall on the second day of a Virginia hunt-country horse show, he noted that the accident caused Perry to remain overnight. He also read that Perry was accompanied by a real estate magnate named Arnholt. A short clip in the *Evening Journal* the next day said that a man named Disessa from Manhattan, address 114 Mulberry Street, had arrived in Virginia to assist the fallen Perry. The hunchback, Moe Tear, went from newspaper to telephone directory. Listed at 114 Mulberry was Disessa and Disessa, bankers. Marvelous knowledge. Rothstein was at the Mulberry Street bank merely to say hello a few days later.

Moe Tear became so famous that for the next half a century, stock thieves and sports fixers hired hunchbacks to read the papers for them. News pictures of big district attorneys' raids all showed detectives assisting one bent-over man into the police wagon. The caption always identified the hunchback as a "figure wizard."

In the matter of Hipolito Villa, Moe Tear read in the sports section of the *Louisville Courier* that Churchill Downs racetrack executives denied that they were sending large numbers of race horses to El Paso for Villa. This rumor had started when Matt Winn, of Churchill Downs, who also operated the Juarez racetrack, had negotiated with the Louisville and Nashville line for a private freight train. The Louisville newspaper story reported that Winn was trying to assist Abraham Gonzalez, the treasurer for Pancho Villa's revolt, in negotiating for private freight trains to carry supplies from New York to El Paso. The hunchback also read a small item in the *New York Times* that said that the National City Bank of New York had found a way to loan the Financial Division $500,000 on a shipment of cotton seized from the Mexican government by Villa's army. Rothstein read these clips with some interest. He was immediately envious of the fastidious, correct bankers. They would wade through blood for a score, and then on the way home to their estates convince themselves of their honesty and prudence.

By lunchtime the next day, Rothstein was at the Astor Hotel and in conversation with Hipolito Villa, the brother of Pancho Villa. Hipolito announced he was the superintendent of military freight for the revolutionary army. When Villa picked up his glass to start on another drink, there was a blaze of hot white diamond light and glowing gold on the one hand. Two words formed in Rothstein's mind: Swifty Morgan. He was the gruff, delightful Broadway guy who sold bum jewelry to all suckers. When Villa sat back, causing his jacket to droop open, there was displayed at the top of the belt line the handle of a pistol that was large enough to blow up a trolley car. Rothstein now thought about the possibilities of Hipolito becoming a poor sport. This was a quite reasonable thought, for while Villa was much dumber than his brother, and had many more weaknesses, he'd shot enough people to make him an important, genuine mad dog.

Hipolito had a man in El Paso, Texas, George Benton of 329 Leon Street, so wary that Benton cheerfully held $500,000 in cash and gold coins in a safe in his house. There also was $35,000 in jewelry. He kept the money with Benton because he loved his wife, Mabel. She'd had two children with him and waited through all the revolution's battles, but at the end he would kidnap the kids and leave her destitute and scrubbing floors.

Here at the Astor bar, Hipolito was proud of his big checkbook and gladly showed it to Rothstein. It was from the Guaranty Trust and showed that he had just given $5,000 to Jas. T. Leonard and Company of New York. Hipolito said this was for hats for his brother's army in the state of Chihuahua. Rothstein now saw a check for $9,275.60, to one F. A. Sommerfield. Next was a check stub showing that the same man had been paid $4,081. And a week later, $46,700.

"For bullets," Hipolito told Rothstein. He had to buy much more ammunition for his brother's army. In order to serve him, the munitions man, Sommerfield, was scheduled to return the next day. When Rothstein asked him what he was going to do until then, Hipolito raised the glass and threw the drink down. Then he announced he wanted to see a baseball game. When he was stealing at his best, Rothstein preferred to be alone, but now he knew he needed Runyon. Rothstein now introduced Hipolito to Runyon at Lindy's.

"You write about baseball," Hipolito said. "My brother took me all the way to see the Giants baseball team in San Antonio last time."

"I'll be there next time," Runyon said.

Runyon had been told he would cover spring training of the New York Giants. There were about fifty of these jobs in the United States, and thousands worked on newspapers for decades hoping to get one of them and never did. Here was Runyon, in his first few weeks on the job, being seated in the Sistine Chapel. It was just as well that Runyon was a loner because he lost most of the office as he walked out with one of the best jobs in America.

"Will the team be at El Paso?" Hipolito asked.

"If they're not, I will be," Runyon said.

"Tell them to play in El Paso. My brother loves baseball."

"Why don't you tell them yourself?" Runyon said.

At the ballpark that afternoon, Runyon went to McGraw before the game and complimented him profusely on his tactics of the day before and then introduced him to Hipolito, who promised McGraw the loosest women in the world if he would play in El Paso. This was a subject that always caused McGraw to dismiss the speaker with a scowl, even though on long road trips McGraw was an outrageous waitress chaser like anyone else. But McGraw, too, had eyes and saw the type of artillery under Hipolito's jacket. He said nothing. Runyon asked for a baseball autographed by the team. McGraw had the clubhouse boy hand Runyon a new major league baseball signed by all the Giants players. McGraw added his name and presented Hipolito with the ball. The Mexican gave him a great kiss. "My brother will be very happy."

"I might see you in March," McGraw said.

Hipolito sat behind home plate and drank big cold beers and was asleep by the sixth inning. When they got back to Lindy's, Runyon told Rothstein, "I have to write."

"Hipolito and I have business together," Rothstein said.

The business consisted of dancer Margie Norman, who, when she finished her show that night, was introduced to Hipolito at the Astor bar. She said she would have a drink and Hipolito said he would have one too. He went into his pocket to show her the Giants baseball and the movement nearly caused him to fall off the stool. Margie saw opportunity here.

Two days later, Margie Norman came up the subway steps wearing a breathtaking new mink coat. "Look what I found in the subway!" she announced.

Rothstein, who had been told by Hipolito about plans to hire freight trains, came by with a copy of the *Railroad Journal of the Southwest*, which had been on Moe Tear's desk. When Rothstein held it out to Hipolito, he saw the man flinch. Rothstein realized Hipolito couldn't read. He now tasted a certain score. But rather than fleece Hipolito directly, what with that gun of his, Rothstein had a conference with the arms salesman, Sommerfield, who said that because of the war in Europe, the cost of such a simple item as bullets had jumped from $25 per thousand to $45 per thousand.

"They now cost fifty-five per thousand," Rothstein said.

"What do you mean by that?" Sommerfield said.

"Your partner's share." Rothstein explained why he should be a hidden partner. "Because you are stealing on my street," he said. "I own Broadway and anybody who doesn't think so winds up in the gutter."

Only days afterward, a check for $80,000 was paid to Sommerfield, whose ammunition suddenly had become more expensive even than in time of normal world war. There were other arms merchants, from such as Winchester and Remington, who arrived at the hotel and found they had to be interviewed by Rothstein first. While Hipolito drank, Arnold bought so many makes of rifles that Hipolito, as dumb as he was, would have known that this would drive his quartermasters insane. Hipolito entered the business discussions only once. That was to rip a check out of the book and stuff it into his pocket. "For love!" he announced.

All of which reinforced Runyon's love of his street. This street was the one most magnificent place in the world. Hadn't Pancho Villa sent his brother up here? Where else would he go? A Mexican thief had to go where other thieves congregate, right here on Broadway.

EIGHT

THE GIANTS' manager, John McGraw, owned a share of the team and would have been wealthy except that he gambled so much there was a price sometimes on whether he knew his last name. Yet he was the first to realize California's size. In 1910 he contracted for the Giants' spring training to be in Los Angeles, at Chute Park, the home of the Los Angeles Pacific Coast League team. The Santa Fe Railroad promised special rates from Chicago, where the players gathered for the ride to the West Coast. The low fares were important, because baseball teams also had to pay carfare and all the other bills of newspaper sportswriters. If they didn't, many of the newspapers wouldn't send writers and there would be no publicity. It was the same with politicians and reporters. "The man with the most room on his train gets the most stories in the papers," Jim Farley decided in his first attempt at being a political manager. "We take even copyboys on my train." His client, Franklin Roosevelt, did well. Railroad promotional literature advertised the Giants' training as a scenic wonder, along with Yellowstone. McGraw expected great cash crowds in Los Angeles, Oakland and San Francisco. However, it rained over the length of California for most of the three weeks the Giants were there. Breaking camp, the team traveled to San Antonio, but upon arrival late at night found that no hotel reservations had been made, and therefore the players had to sleep on pool tables.

The next year, 1911, McGraw took no chances; as long as he had to open out of town, he decided to go all the way. He went to Marlin, Texas, population 4,000, sitting on flat farmland one hundred miles south of Dallas. Marlin had mineral baths fed by underground springs, which was the extent of liquid allowed to his players. The hotel had poor food, which was fine because these slob players had eaten too much all winter anyway. The ballpark, a mile walk from the hotel, had a fence that was in disrepair, rickety bleachers and a field that looked like it had been hoed. The Giants' groundkeeper, John Murphy, said, "It's lucky they sent me down ahead. The grounds had been given up to steers, stray pigs and horses, so I had my work laid out to fix things right."

A couple of days before Runyon arrived, Sid Mercer, a sportswriter on the *New York Globe*, later to move to the Hearst papers, an important fact to know about in those days, reported, "Tuesday night, a Texan used his artillery on three colored persons. The white went on his way unharmed and the colored gentlemen were taken to the hospital for repairs."

Runyon tried to settle on pitcher Christy Mathewson, who felt that "any man who is unfaithful to his wife would cheat at baseball."

"Do you mind whorehouses?" Runyon asked.

"I wish you would call them by a better word. Prostitution. Or bawdy house. I believe that God punishes a man who goes there. But it is more of a secret sin and nobody actually gets hurt except the man patronizing such a place. I don't believe he is placing his wife and children in jeopardy. I will discuss baseball with a man who frequents a bawdy house. I will not talk to a man who goes out with another woman."

The *New York American* arrived by mail, with the first of many truly great Hearst editorials on Pancho Villa, who was involved in a revolt against the Mexican government. Villa was poor and uneducated, and Hearst had about as much in common with him as he did with a beggar. But the Mexican government, distant and arrogant, was in decay, and if anybody was going to profit from this, then Hearst wanted to be alongside him.

> The one man in this Mexican crisis and conflict who had appeared to tower above all others in personal power and capacity, in the magnetism to lead, the mastery to command and the ability to execute is Francisco Villa. . . .
>
> A strong hand is needed, a determined purpose, a masterful mind, an experience gained from personal contact with the mass, a sympathetic understanding of the people's aims and needs. . . .
>
> If Villa is made President, he will remain as President, and establish a stable and reliable government.

Runyon ripped out the editorial and put it on the dresser. This meant he had to get down to Juarez and give this to Hipolito Villa personally, and discuss it with Pancho Villa, either at a racetrack or a cockfight — a good cockfight, with bloody feathers flying all over the place and men with money in their hands and guns on their belts! Anything to get away from Christy Mathewson talking about celibacy on the road.

The reason for the sudden editorials on Villa was because Mrs. Phoebe Hearst, mother of William Randolph Hearst, owned a one-million-acre ranch called Babícora in the state of Chihuahua. Also in the area were sweeping lands owned by the family of William Buckley. The rich truly love the land.

Hearst had a man in Mexico, Jack Follansbee, who went to Harvard with the Chief, as he said over each drink. It was important for him to say this, as otherwise he would have been tagged a common drunk instead of a drunk who was a friend of Hearst's. The Chief always had people such as Follansbee to investigate matters for him; he once had a reporter named Maines and the writer Adela Rogers St. John look at Huey Long as a possible presidential candidate. Follansbee's assignment was to report on Mexico, so he met Villa in the Hearst hacienda at Babícora. Villa, who had dark Indian skin, was rebelling against a Mexican government that was as white as you can get and that treated him like an ignorant dog. Follansbee talked and toasted. Villa hated drink and only on a unique occasion, a toast to a young woman, would he take as much as a sip or two of wine. As he was wary of someone poisoning him, with good reason, as we will see, he snatched food from Follansbee's plate as they talked. Villa was astounded to hear that Mrs. Hearst kept sixty thousand head of cattle right out in the fields. But as Villa mostly smiled, Follansbee was certain that he was a close friend, and the next morning informed Hearst of this by dispatch. There then appeared in all Hearst papers the highly favorable editorials.

In Juarez, after he had the Hearst editorial read to him, Villa took the six-cent trolley car over the bridge from Juarez to El Paso and went to the Elite Confectionary, where he had an ice cream sundae and told reporters, "Señor Hearst is the only American who can see past his own border. Hearst, not Wilson, should be President of the United States." He could not write himself, but he watched to make certain that these reporters were taking down notes. One reporter, from the Associated Press, was the most important to Villa. His words went all over the world — and to Mr. Hearst, which was more important right now than the whole world.

VILLA BORN TO COMMAND!
Hearst Reportage Reveals Villa Ancestors Saved Entire Tribes with Wily Tactics.
THEREFORE, VILLA SHOULD LEAD MEXICO NOW!

When Runyon received this article in the mail, he packed a suit-case for the train to El Paso. He checked into the Hotel del Norte, which had one of the most magnificent bars in the universe, a great circle of dark wood that was under a stained glass ceiling two stories high. He went up to the bar and placed one foot up on the rail, just for old-time form, and immediately felt his insides leap at the thought of a great big drink of whisky. "Like drinking in an arena," he said. "You could hold a championship match here."

The Hotel del Norte had drawn all those people who always show up for the riot season. Upstairs in the hotel was a reporter named Johnny Roberts, who sat in a room with a typewriter and a bottle of Scotch and wrote front-line reports of the blood spilled during the Mexican revolution led by Villa. Roberts, who never left his hotel room, killed as many with his typewriter as Villa did with a gun.

And Villa did kill. Only a couple of days before this, Villa had marched seventy-five Mexican government people through the streets of Juarez to the town cemetery. They had been convicted of a most heinous crime: failure to join the revolution. In El Paso, people got on rooftops — except for Roberts, who slept through it — and looked across the river in order to see the execution. The six-cent trolley ride across the bridge from El Paso to Juarez was suspended for the moment, although people fleeing Juarez and possible execution walked across the Rio Grande, which was about 150 yards wide, with the water ankle-deep and brown. Women merely held up their skirts and waded across, their ankles splashing the brown water.

At the Juarez cemetery, Pancho Villa, in three-piece suit and se-rape, was walking back and forth in great agitation as priests took long moments hearing last confessions of the condemned men against the wall. One prisoner fell to his knees and moved across the dirt on his knees and held his hands in prayer, begging Villa for his life. Villa whipped out a pistol and shot the man dead. Villa kept firing. He waved to the priests to run and emptied his pistol into the prisoners. Then he held out his hand and a soldier put another in his hand and he emptied that one. The hand went out again and was given another gun. Prisoners toppled and ducked and screamed and flipped and jerked dead. Villa kept firing as the pile in front of him turned red.

Runyon was listening to tales of this when into the hotel bar strolled a guy from El Paso, Sam Dreben, who billed himself as the Fighting Jew. Dreben's reputation as a machine gun expert was such that a general at Fort Bliss named Pershing became friendly with him. Dreben, who was short, rotund and had a nose "as large as Bugler Dugan's horn," loved action so much that he fought for a couple of the sides in the Mexican revolt. At the moment loyal to Villa, he taught Villa's men how to fire a machine gun and showed them how to set up an entirely new idea in fighting, a machine gun nest. Though Pershing regarded Mexicans as people the color of a saddle and with as much feeling and brains, he excused Sam Dreben's tutoring as the work of one of those people who liked to be in shootouts and was with Villa only until such time as somebody could show him more action, like a world war. Pershing regarded Villa as a common murderer, and could not wait to attack him. Only these Hearst newspaper editorials were preventing it now.

A bellhop came running in to announce that there was trouble at the Shelton Hotel with Pancho Villa. Dreben and Runyon walked up to the hotel and found Villa, in a three-piece suit, a gun showing from under the jacket, screaming at the hotel clerk that he wanted the room numbers of two men. Standing alongside Villa at the desk was a huge man, Bill Greet, the police chief of El Paso.

"If you don't let me go up to their rooms and kill them, I will kill you," Villa said to the hotel clerk.

Greet put two big hands on Villa's shoulders and passed him over like a package to two plainclothes policemen. A large crowd followed the policemen as they took Villa to the bridge over the river to Juarez. Halfway across they let go of him, and he walked a few feet and swept his hand through the air. "I kill anybody who comes here!"

Runyon began to wonder if it was better to get killed here on the bridge or go back to the Giants' camp and listen to Christy Mathewson talk about celibacy on the road. The next day, he crossed the bridge to Juarez and went to the offices of the Financial Division of the North, which was run by the second in charge of the revolution, Abraham Gonzalez, an ideologue who could count. The Financial Division of the North collected taxes and supervised railroad train and bank robberies and the melting of jewelry of the rich to support the revolutionary government. As Villa was a conqueror one day and a fugitive the next,

Gonzalez often thought the addition he was doing would be his last. From 1914 to 1916 he handled some $25 million, which was used to run the state of Chihuahua and also Villa's armed revolt. While writers such as Lincoln Steffens praised Villa as a political genius, Gonzalez understood that all of Pancho's success was based on killing. "I will die on the firing line," Gonzalez said. At the same time, he never forgave an inequity and kept the anger high, to the point of being uncontrollable, in Villa, and thus assured death everywhere.

Gonzalez was delighted to meet Runyon and said Villa had the autographed baseball in his private railroad car, the General Villa. Gonzalez mentioned that he had attended Notre Dame, which then was a small midwestern school. Gonzalez was immensely flattered when Runyon asked why Notre Dame had scored 116 points in football against St. Viator. Gonzalez looked eagerly at the actual clips from New York on the Hearst editorials; they had only the San Antonio papers here in Juarez, he said, and the New York masthead on the clips would impress Villa, who although he could not read, certainly knew "New York" when he saw it.

Gonzalez took Runyon over to the house where Villa and his brother Hipolito were staying. A young woman was outside, trying to compose herself. A soldier told Gonzalez that there had been a problem, that the woman had been abused by soldiers and that when one of the soldiers broke in to try to explain what had happened, Villa, while talking to the woman, picked up his gun and shot the soldier dead in the living room. This was why the woman was so upset.

Villa, who had just finished a morning bath, sat wrapped in a towel, wearing a small sombrero with a sweat-darkened brim, while his horse ate oats that had been put in the bathtub after the water was emptied. Villa was built like a cement block and had a large floppy mustache and yellow uneven teeth. Gonzalez was starting introductions when the woman outside commenced shrieking. Gonzalez told Runyon that they would see Villa at the racetrack.

At the Financial Division of the North, Gonzalez waved to a battered car, whose driver, dressed in sombrero and gun belts, threw out a cigarette and started the engine. A young blond girl of a little bit over twelve, but not much more, walked barefoot up the stone steps as they were leaving. She carried a package and smiled dazzlingly at Gonzalez. He nodded. Runyon tried exceedingly hard not to look at her, but found he was following her out of the corner of his left eye. The girl went up those steps with her small young tail swinging and disappeared into the building. "Nice young kid," Runyon grunted. He timed it so he said that as he was sitting down, thus providing the nonchalance of an innocent conversation item. "Nice young kid."

The car exploded and lurched forward, and Gonzalez said something but Runyon couldn't hear it.

"We're going to the racetrack," Gonzalez told the driver.

The track was ten miles out on a rutted dirt road. They walked through the entrance and into stands that stood facing the Sierra Madre, which pierced the bright blue afternoon sky, the mountain shoulders decorated with clouds. There was a crowd around a box in the center of the stands. Soon Villa, wearing a three-piece suit and a business shirt with the collar button ripped off, arrived. When Hipolito saw Runyon, he jumped up with his arms out. "The béisbol!" He threw his arms around Runyon and kissed him. Then Villa himself rose and wrapped his arms around Runyon.

Sitting with Villa was the famous Colonel Phillip T. Chinn of Lexington, Kentucky, who wore a white suit and a string tie, and Pat Nablekamp, a Kentucky horse trainer. Chinn was talkative and Nablekamp was taciturn. Villa insisted that Runyon sit next to him. He apologized for what had happened back at his house, but said that it was inhuman to put an accused man through the torture of a court-martial, and therefore he had done the soldier a great justice by killing him without any attendant suffering. When Gonzalez mentioned that Runyon had brought the actual news clips from New York, Villa was gleeful. "Get them here!" Villa said. A Mexican with a gun belt was dispatched.

Villa now said, "I have only seen one thing from New York. Someone showed me the pictures in one of your magazines of the man and the woman walking the dog in the park. Was that a true picture?"

"He does have to go to the bathroom," Runyon said.

"These dogs in New York have a better life than thousands of men, eh?" When Runyon didn't answer, for the simple reason that he had a hunting dog at home in his apartment on the West Side of Manhattan, Villa said, "If I am in this New York and I see this, I shoot the man and woman. Then I eat the fucking dog." Villa roared with laughter. Gun belts jingled as everybody else around the box laughed loudly.

Villa, a peon born as Doroteo Orango, was flogged by a nobleman, and the son of the nobleman raped Doroteo's sister. When he went to get even, he was infuriated to find the son standing in front of the hacienda. He had wanted to kill the son in his bed. He emptied his gun into the son, who was dead before he hit the ground. Doroteo also was

angered to the point of blindness that the shots had alerted the place
and now he could not go in and kill the nobleman. He rode off and
changed his name to Pancho Villa. From then on, Mexican authorities
had to contend with him. Here at the track, Runyon measured Villa
against Arthur Bieler and Owney Madden. No contest. They do one at
a time, and once in a while. He made Villa for a mass murderer.

"What brings you down?" Runyon asked Chinn.

"I have some private business with the general," Chinn said. The
colonel's hair was slicked straight back and he wore thick glasses.

"He has a horse that cannot lose," Villa said.

Chinn seemed perfectly at ease. As this was how he made his living,
and he was still alive, Runyon decided not to worry about him.

After an hour, he went down to the betting windows and tried a horse,
lost, wandered around, and when he came back, here was the little girl
standing at the box, the sunlight splashing on her light hair, framed by
the Sierra Madre. Villa was looking at the Hearst *American* clips, with
his name splashed across the page. He was pointing to the dateline on
the top of the page. "New York!" he yelled to Runyon.

"Didn't we see you before?" Runyon said to the girl.

She nodded.

"She's the messenger," Gonzalez said. He introduced her as Patrice. The girl said nothing, but Gonzalez said that she understood most
of what she heard in English. He pointed to the light hair, which indicated the inclusion in her family tree of one of the Mormon missionar-
ies who were all over Mexico, and for real, in those years.

"That's quite a job. Do you like it?"

Her large shining brown eyes now looked directly at him. She said
nothing and kept looking straight at him. Villa, finished with the clips,
gave them to Gonzalez, who held them out to the girl. Wordlessly, she
took them and walked toward the exit. Runyon followed her until he
could not see her any longer.

That night, at the bar of the Hotel del Norte, Colonel Chinn was at
the top of his career. He was going to fleece an international killer.
After dinner, he, Nablekamp and Runyon walked across the bridge and
went to see the dance bars in Juarez, which entertained swarms of swills,
forgers and crooks of low estimate. Already, the city had been labeled
as essentially a city of dope fiends and vagabond soldiers. At one corner
there was a crowd around a man dead on his back on the sidewalk.

"The assistant to General Villa, Fierro, was having an argument," a
man in the crowd explained. "They were fighting over which way a

man falls when he is shot. Fierro said he falls on his face and his friend said the man falls on his back. This man here was walking by so Fierro shot this man. You see that Fierro was right. The man is on his back."

Colonel Phillip T. Chinn listened in highly meaningful silence.

At the stable area the next morning, Chinn and Nablekamp had their unbeatable horse out in the shedrow. Birds chirped in the rafters and the stable dog slept in the sun's rays striking the raked dirt. The ammonia smell coming from the wet straw in the stalls caused Runyon's eyes to open wide at this unaccustomed hour.

There was a jingling at the end of the shedrow and two of Villa's gunmen appeared, and now Villa, in the same three-piece suit and with the same ripped collar button, walked down. He greeted everybody effusively.

"Let me see the horse that cannot lose," Villa said.

Nablekamp had a groom bring the horse out of the stall. Villa inspected him. "The horse was born to win today," Chinn said.

"Then I will keep my word and bet five thousand dollars for you," Villa said. He turned to Runyon. "I will bet on the horse for you, too."

Runyon now kept his own counsel. Quite a bit. Nablekamp patted the horse's nose affectionately.

Villa said, "Remember one thing. The horse must not lose."

Colonel Chinn suddenly put his ear to the horse's side. He squinted and listened. Then he shook his head. "This horse can't run. He got a bad colic."

That afternoon, Villa's box was particularly crowded, with spies from Germany, obscure officials from Washington and rich people from Mexico City, along with several dark-haired women, one of whom might have been one of Villa's wives. All were there because Pancho was at the moment ahead in the big sport, revolution, and he was busy laughing with them and sweeping his hand out at the mountains, which he claimed he owned to the white tops. Runyon noticed a comb at his feet, light brown, a woman's comb. Had he seen this earlier, had he seen that the banshee was all the way down here at the racetrack, he would have claimed illness and left. The comb meant that fate was in the hands of somebody right in this box. He examined the laughing women. There also were a couple of fat touts, who read the race program, puffed on cigarettes and made emphatic decisions on the races. Villa, however, paid no attention until the feature race. "This is the race I was supposed to win. The horse took sick. What is going to happen? I should have spoken to the jockeys."

In unison, the touts thrust programs in front of him and pointed to the number 3 horse, Tear Out. The program was printed in Spanish but the horses were owned and named by Americans. Villa pointed out the horse to Runyon but immediately became busy talking to the German spy. The Germans wanted to pay Villa money to attack the United States and keep the country out of the war against Germany. Each time a German spy would mention a war with America, Villa would smile and grunt, as if he couldn't wait to attack the gringos. Then Abraham Gonzalez would discuss finances and soon somewhere in the world a German would drop a big good check into bank accounts of the Financial Division of the North.

Runyon showed the little girl the number 3 horse on the program and handed her $20. She gripped the program with her thumb over the name and went down to the betting windows under the grandstand. A metal door in the wall opened slightly and a nasty little face peered out. He was smoking a cigarette. There was a splash of color somewhere in the darkness. Just as quickly, the door shut. Instead of getting on line, the girl, whose name was Patrice, waited by the door. When the betting lines shortened considerably, the door flew open and four little jockeys in riding silks tumbled out and got on line. The last one kept an arm out so people wouldn't crowd behind him to see over his shoulder. Patrice ran over the cement, which was harsh on her bare feet, and jumped in front of the last jockey, who, having cleared the crowd from behind him, now put his hands on her shoulders. "Cinco," the jockey said. Patrice now got to the window and put her bill down. "Cinco!" The bet seller was pulling bills out of his own pocket and betting on number 5. The jockey behind Patrice complained that he would be late to ride in the race. The bet seller looked up angrily and said in Spanish, "What about me?" The jockey pushed ahead of Patrice and put a stack of money on the counter, which the bet taker counted and punched out tickets. Now he took the twenty from Patrice. He had so much money in front of him that he didn't know to whom it belonged. He threw his hands up. "What does it matter? We all win." He gave her the $20 win ticket on number 5.

The horses lined up at a web barrier that was strung across the track in front of the stands. The barrier was yanked up and the number 3 horse, Tear Out, sped away from the others. As the race went on, Patrice walked through the stands back to Villa's box. She stood in the aisle as Tear Out rushed around the turn and into the backstretch, where he seemed to be running beautifully until this little jockey on his back pulled hard on the reins and caused him to imitate an old lady walking home from the store.

"You are winning from here to the mountain!" the Mexican tout exulted. He watched with naked eye and thus was unable to make out the horse's stride.

"I'm dead," Runyon said. He put his field glasses down.

The horse Tear Out attempted to bend down and rub feet that were tired from acting as brakes. At the same time, horse number 5, Climbing, an improbable 20-to-1 shot, rushed past and won. He did this easily, for no other horse appeared to try. One horse, Any Port, gave a great burst of speed and the jockey stopped him and jumped off and said the horse had broken a leg.

The number 5 for Climbing was put up on the board as the winner. When Patrice collected, the jockeys were happily chattering on line behind her.

"What's this?" Runyon said when she handed him a big roll of bills.

"You won," Patrice said.

"I didn't bet that horse," Runyon said.

"I did," Patrice said.

"You changed my bet?"

"Yes."

"What made you do that?" When she didn't answer, he said to Hipolito, "Did you gag the race?"

"I swear on my mother's grave. I swear on the mountains you are looking at. I swear on my life and on my children's head."

There were so many bills that Runyon stopped trying to count. "What made you bet on this horse?" Runyon said to Patrice.

She pointed to the sky.

He rejected this notion of a miracle. If this were happening to somebody else, he would sneer and file the scene away. But how could he have that comb at his feet and not hold a deep belief in the power of mystery? Or look at these mountains rising in the near distance and not understand hidden power? He believed that you make your own breaks. Yet how could he argue against the presence of the comb, followed by the amazing winning bet by the little girl? That he wanted to place some unnatural powers in her as an excuse for having her alongside him had nothing to do with it, he assured himself. He only wanted to bring this little doll up to New York so she could kill bookmakers.

Villa interrupted his dreaming. "You smoke a lot?"

"Sure do."

"What do you light them with?"

"Matches."

"You should have something better than a match," Villa said.

Villa and Gonzalez had to leave for the railroad car to conduct the business of the revolution. Hipolito drove Runyon, the two fat touts and little Patrice into town. When Patrice hopped out and started walking, Runyon said goodbye to Hipolito and caught up to her. Suddenly at his side was one of the fat touts, who had been assigned to walk with them.

"Where are you going?" Runyon asked her.

She pointed to a hut on the street with a crowded entranceway leading through a curtain and into a noisy black hole. Two men in short-sleeved shirts stood outside the doorway, clapping their hands jovially, steering people inside. Most seemed to be American soldiers from the other side of the river, El Paso. The place inside was decorated with mortal sin, and the only light came from men lighting cigarettes. Patrice, who knew the place as well as if she lived in it, went straight to the foot of the little bandstand, where she mimicked the older, half-undressed dancing girls. Her bare feet thumped on the floor. Runyon went to the dice table and lost a couple of times, but now he threw again. His point was nine. He called for Patrice and held the dice out. "Blow on them for me, Lady Luck." She blew. A large man in a sparkling white shirt jumped up from a chair and pointed excitedly to a large sign on the wall. He yelled at the fat tout in Spanish and pushed Patrice away from the table. The man in the white shirt was gesturing wildly.

Runyon looked at Patrice. "What does that say?" She was embarrassed and smiled and twisted.

"She can't read," the guy in the white shirt said in English. "That sign says that General Villa will have anybody shot who allows children near the gambling tables." He indicated the tout. "This fool knows that he would be the first to be shot. I would be the second."

Runyon felt he had been cheated, that surely the little girl, particularly here with her own, would have pulled luck out of the air for him. Outside, he presented her with a large sheaf of bills. Then he asked her if she could read or write anything in Spanish or English, and she said no. He asked her if she wanted to learn. "I want to dance," she said, pointing back toward the little hellhole. "Well, if you learn to read and write, I'll make you a dancer in New York," he said. Even somebody with magic from the mountains couldn't be illiterate and still

beat bookmakers in New York. He told Patrice that the fat tout here
would have a message for her. He held out his hand and Patrice shook
it solemnly and walked off down a side street.

At the Hotel del Norte, the manager told him the best school in El
Paso for a Mexican girl was the Sacred Heart, a Catholic school on South
Oregon Street. The few Mexicans with money sent their children there.
It was just before dinnertime when Runyon, with his tout as escort,
arrived at the school. "Sister, I have what is known at the racetracks as
a first-time starter. A true maiden." He put $20 on the desk as special
tuition in advance, saying that as the girl had to learn twice as fast to
catch up, he would pay double. This caused the nun to laugh rather
than ask him a lot of questions. He put a hand on the tout's shoulder
and said to the nun, "Her first name is Patrice. He will bring her here."

Runyon packed and went to the station for a night train back to Marlin, and shortly thereafter, New York. In the office one day, he received a package mailed from El Paso. Inside was a heavy gold oval
lighter with a large ruby. On the bottom was an inscription:

> Damon Runyon
> Amigo Mío
> Salud
> Pancho Villa

Then, on another day sometime later, he went through the mail and
came upon a small brown envelope with a Mexican stamp on it. It was
addressed in the beginnings of a high wide flourishing handwriting.
The one-page letter, on ruled school paper, said:

> Los Cabollos run slow.
> You are Los Caballero.
> Carissima Mía. Patrice.

Horses run slow. Look at this child, he said to himself. She goes to the
humor on the first day they put a pen in her hand. Then I am a great
man. Of course it was flattery, and of course he believed that she meant
it. Carissima mía. He sat at the ledge and looked at the letter again and
again.

NINE

At THAT TIME, the newsmen used a black pencil with soft lead and a thin cotton string sticking out of the pencil's innards just above the point. If you needed a point, you pulled the string and unraveled some of the black covering. The outside coiled off like a potato skin. A real newspaperman had a pencil sticking behind his ear, with the white string hanging down the side. The Hearst papers favored this type of pencil instead of the ones used by real human beings, the yellow wood pencils you put in a sharpener, because the editor, Arthur Brisbane, had a cousin in the pencil business. Brisbane's cousin promised the purchasing department that with this pencil there would be no wasted time with people working the pencil sharpener, or copyboys emptying the thing while right on edition. Brisbane's cousin pointed out that with his string pencil, workers remained seated and still got a new pencil point. The purchasing agent said he had to think. Even though Brisbane was his cousin, the pencil man could not disregard custom. He gave the purchasing agent money. The purchasing agent now became ecstatic over the new pencil. One day, Brisbane, stumping through the editorial room, noticed the new pencils all over his city room. He sent for the purchasing agent. The purchasing agent, who was not totally stupid, arrived with one hand inside his jacket, on the envelope of money for Brisbane. Thereafter, he became the only man in the building allowed to interrupt Brisbane while he was writing. The pencils survived to become Japanese-made.

The offices of the morning *American* and evening *Journal* were open around the clock, seven days a week, and were better bunkers than anything on the Western Front. The copyboy answering the city-desk phone could announce that the reporter was "on the edition" or "right on deadline," and unable to come to the phone to discuss any false promises made to loan companies or women. In turn, reporters calling in to the office, always troubled that they would be told that the editor was looking for them, perhaps to fire them, became confident the moment the operator spoke. Newspaper operators, voices harsh with smoke, gave the instant, unmistakable feeling of city-room warmth. Their knowledge of the city and the whereabouts of editors, reporters and public figures was far more complete than any record files, and while this was fine, it was the feeling of security their voices gave that was perhaps the most important working condition on a paper.

Runyon typed with a hat on, a cigarette burning on the ledge and the lighter from Pancho Villa next to the cigarette for all to see. He understood his business as being one in which those who shower the editor with the most praise usually are regarded as the finest talent on the sheet. His policy, "I never bite the hand that feeds me," showed that he understood that with one show of bared teeth, a career of decades could be dashed of a morning. He also knew that traditionally the newsroom's reaction to any threat of individual talent was to band together in treachery. At this time, he tried to appear as benign and oppressed as the others by staying in the city room in the same conditions as everyone else. He sat at a Royal typewriter that sounded like Sam Dreben's machine gun. He always said that all writing is better done while looking at a blank wall. As he typed and smoked, Hypo, the office cat, stepped around the cigarette and watched the typewriter carriage move. His scratching announced his use of copy paper as a litter box. With the closest window on the other side of the room, the cigarette smoke stayed in the room as if it came as part of the air. In the summer, fans caused a slight movement of hot air but little more; the most nonchalant worker on a typewriter soon had his underarms dark with sweat. Yellow flypaper strung from the ceiling, leaving those searching for a word with dead flies for inspiration.

The quality of the newspaper meant nothing, for, just like actors in a bad play, it was not the newspapermen's personal responsibility and did not reflect on their ability. Reporters on the outrageous papers, Hearst's being only one of them, had the most talent and swagger. Those who climbed staircases to the most responsible newspapers usually had supplicant in their blood and great uncertainty as to how to make the English sentence move. For protection, they clutched the surest and most dreadfully boring way to write and insisted they were being responsible. Many of the misbehavers at Hearst boasted that soon they would sit in splendor on an island in Greece, or a boulevard in Paris, and produce great work. Hearst, like all newspaper publishers, easily controlled writers with talent by keeping them in need. Runyon, who felt his own freedom depended upon his ability to put enough money home to silence wife and children, never had quite enough left over to pay for his own high living. The more newspaper work he did, the less chance it seemed that he ever would turn the next page he typed into the first page of a book.

So in his case, Runyon sat at this ledge from 1914 until 1928 and produced nothing but stories that were under somebody's foot on the subway by 10 A.M. the next day. He thrilled at the very idea of writing columns that had "a dagger in every sentence," but he never wavered in his rule: "I never bite the hand that feeds me." Believing that McGraw, the manager of the Giants, sold papers, he extolled him, although always wishing he could write something that would cause the man to scream in agony.

A good part of McGraw's popularity in New York came from saloon attendance. He truly believed he was an Irish brawler, but won no fights until he discovered the Lambs, a club for actors on West 44th Street. There he found a great truth: tenors can't fight. In the bar well after closing hours one night, an actor named William Boyd, while complaining on behalf of the cleaning women about McGraw's language, hit McGraw over the head with a water pitcher. Down went McGraw. A musical comedy star, John C. Slavin, and Winfield Liggitt, a retired naval officer who loved actors, got McGraw home to Broadway and 109th Street at 8 A.M. Slavin helped McGraw out of the cab, then was turning to get back into it when McGraw sly-rapped him. Slavin hit the sidewalk hard and was taken to St. Luke's Hospital with a fracture at the base of his skull. "There is nothing to indicate foul play in connection with this case," the sergeant in charge said. McGraw remained home in bed. He was visited by Runyon and a lawyer, Bill Fallon, known as the Great Mouthpiece. Fallon wrapped McGraw's head in a foot of bandages and left instructions for McGraw to sink into a coma if anybody tried to see him. When an assistant district attorney and a man from the medical examiner's office finally were allowed up, they asked for autographs.

Runyon sat at his ledge and typed articles that worried that the Giants would fall apart, as would the entire city, if this poor, honest, victimized man McGraw did not soon arise from his sickbed and command the team. He saw nothing the matter with this type of coverage. Had not Benjamin Franklin, the nation's first news columnist, caused people to applaud in the streets over his story of a pregnant girl defending herself in court and getting acquitted? The thing had never happened.

Runyon's seat at the *American* usually was a few yards over from the financial writer B. A. Forbes, who founded a family enterprise with a financial column that once noted, "NOW is the TIME to rush to a stockbroker of the alertness of JOHN C. COLEMAN at 65 Broad Street and BUY the stock that is burning hot. That stock is ST. LOUIS PRODUCTS, INC. This stock is a QUICK EARNER and also a BLUE CHIP to leave to the children."

Behind a pole was Harry Acton, who covered shipping news by noting, "As we neared Southampton and I reflected on this bully trip, I thought of how stewards on the Mauritania extend a helping hand all across the ocean and do not expect you to place something in that hand on each occasion. Everybody with taste and a zest for life should travel on this ship." Acton was known as John Paul Jones, for the amount of time he spent at sea, on the arm, raising his champagne to the setting sun.

Runyon often sat next to Arthur (Bugs) Baer, who had arrived in New York with one suitcase and was so careful with his money that he still sent his laundry home to his mother. Sometimes Runyon, after finishing his work, would lean back and tell Baer stories of lynchings in Pueblo. Baer always half wondered about these sudden bursts of warmth from a man who usually viewed other newsmen as underlings. He noticed that Runyon usually was there on nights when he had turned in a long story, giving the appearance that he was on duty until the last moment in order to assist in any editing. Of this Baer was suspicious. "Damon will throw a drowning man both ends of the rope," he always said.

It was perceptive rather than humorous. One night, close to the edition time, an office boy brought back a proof of one of Runyon's stories that had penciled brackets around the last three inches, indicating the story was too long to fit in the paper. Runyon looked at the proof. "I guess there's always something you can take out of a story. Let me help them out on this." He went down to the composing room, which was strangely silent. The clicking sound of brass matrixes came from only one Linotype machine. "Dinner hour," the foreman said. "If you're looking to take words out, we can't do it until the next edition. Why don't you just leave out your last couple of paragraphs?"

As described in the letters of a compositor, Martin Dempsey Sr., to the journal of the International Typographical Union in Colorado

Springs, Runyon answered with cold silence. He went to the sports page, which was ready to be rushed to printing except for the three-inch clump of type that had been placed atop his story. Runyon read the story alongside his, a report on the Yankees by Bill Slocum. He showed the foreman a spot about three inches from the bottom of that story. "Cut the tail off the comma and make it a period." The foreman used a small sharp knife and snapped the tail off the comma, thus leaving a period. "Take out everything after the period," Runyon said. The compositor lifted three inches of type out of Slocum's story. This left a space at the bottom of that column, which Runyon now had the compositor fill by inserting, in wraparound fashion, those paragraphs they had dared consider leaving out of Runyon's story.

One day the copyboy told him a prizefighter from Denver was outside to see him. Runyon went into the hallway and found this large, loose, black-haired young guy. Runyon never remembered seeing him before. The fighter had a hand filled with old news clippings.

"Mr. Runyon, I used to sell the paper you wrote in, in Denver. I'm Jack Dempsey. Gene Fowler said you might remember him." By now Fowler was working at the *Denver Post* as a young reporter. He had met Runyon exactly twice in his life, which he felt was surely once more than needed for a lifelong impression. Naturally, Fowler meant the impression he made on Runyon. So with a wave of the hand Fowler had told Dempsey to make sure he saw Runyon in New York.

Runyon looked through clips from Butte and Casper, Wyoming, and Salt Lake City about Dempsey's twenty-six knockouts.

"The one I'm proudest of is this one," Dempsey said, giving him a Montana clip of his knockout of the Boston Bearcat.

"I'll tell you one thing about this town," Runyon said. "Keep everything to yourself. Never let anyone around here know what you're feeling inside, because they don't care and don't have time and they hold it against you if you dare try and let them know how you feel."

"Mr. Runyon, I'm here to fight with my fists, not my mouth. The only way I know how to deal with people is by being honest with them."

"It's time you learned the other way," Runyon said.

At this time, Runyon did not run boxing, as he most certainly did in later years, and Dempsey had difficulty getting a fight in New York. Runyon also had a pregnant wife at home. Rules for behavior were simple: just because his wife is on the sidelines doesn't mean a real guy has to suspend his life, too. His girlfriend, Margie Everdeen, kept him out so late so often that he had little energy for any cause other than his own. He did put a note in his boxing roundup about this new heavyweight from Colorado, but didn't do much else. Shortly after that, he reluctantly took a call from Dempsey, who reported that he had a match at the Fairmont Athletic Club against heavyweight Andre Anderson.

"He's way too big for you," Runyon said.

"I'm way too hungry to worry about that," Dempsey said.

Later in the day, Runyon was crossing City Hall Park when he met Ned Brown, the boxing writer for the *New York World*. Brown was a tiny man with merry blue eyes who had been in medical school when he began hanging around Park Row newspaper saloons. He decided that he could become famous with the assistance of a printing press. He looked up from a drink one day and said, "Civis Romanus est." Brown gave up medical school for a job at the *World*, where he solved a murder by finding a man's foot in a trash can, noticing that the sole was a wrinkled prune and declaring that the victim had been in a Turkish bath. Police checked the baths and found the man's body. Brown hit the bar and the only medicine he ever saw thereafter was the odd aspirin. His lifelong endeavor became boxing. When Runyon asked him what he thought they could do for Dempsey, Brown said, "We can put handcuffs on Anderson, but that'll cost too much money. So the best thing we can do is judge the fight."

As professional boxing at this time was against the law, matches were listed as exhibitions, and the winners were decided by sportswriters in their own papers the next morning. This was often a frightfully difficult decision for a sportswriter, particularly if the managers of both fighters paid him the same amount. Brown and Runyon sat across the ring from each other and immediately felt helpless when Andre Anderson, as large and tough as a drum of wire, weighing 215, gave Dempsey, 173 pounds, a whack in the first round and Dempsey went down. When he got up, Anderson hit him again and put him down again. Dempsey had to reach inside for all his Celtic, Choctaw and Cherokee fury, get back on his feet, hurt and snarling, go into Anderson and last the round and the couple of rough ones after it. After the fifth round, he landed enough punches to make Anderson go backward and allow Ned Brown and Damon Runyon to state flatly in their stories the next day that Dempsey had won the fight, which he had not. A month later, Dempsey fought John L. Johnson at the same club. Before the fight, strolling up to ringside was a handsome, light-haired man named Jack Kearns. He was dressed like an elegant procurer, manicured carefully, and spoke in a voice perpetually on the edge of a whisper. He was a walking conspiracy. "Have you seen anybody with money today?" he always asked. This time, Kearns was just off the ocean liners, where he sat in first-class cabins and worked the card tables with Swifty Morgan, whose business was jewelry that was not legitimate, and with a card mechanic known as the Professor.

"How did it go out there?" Runyon asked.

"There is no lovelier sight than a widow out on the waves with a full purse," Kearns said.

In the fight, Johnson broke two of Dempsey's ribs. Dempsey fought to the finish, but as Runyon was not a judge, Dempsey did not win in the next day's newspapers. The fight was called a draw.

"I think he ought to go home to Denver," Runyon said. He knew he could judge fighters, and he was going to save this one some pain.

"I don't think so," Brown said.

"Neither do I." Standing behind them was Jack Kearns. He said that Dempsey obviously had been badly hurt in the first round but had the heart of a Bengal tiger. Kearns asked who Dempsey's manager was, and when Brown said that was unimportant, Kearns pursed his lips. "I can help that fella."

Later, Kearns and Dempsey gave more picturesque settings for their first meeting. Kearns liked to say Dempsey appeared in a Klondike snowstorm.

After the fight, Runyon and Brown were with their personal politician, Jimmy Walker, who by this time actually had performed a couple of positive acts. Republicans in the State Senate in Albany, crying that women needed more protection from a world of dirt, decided to come up with a Clean Books Act, which would get the sex out of everything in print, including such writers as Chaucer. The Republican sponsors of the act said they were doing this to protect women. Walker, the state senator representing Greenwich Village, rose and said, "I have never yet heard of a girl being ruined by a book."

Walker spoke with a mixture of lofty phrases — recalled from the few books he had taken the time to read, the words spoken as if he had swallowed a library — and New York sidewalk remarks interspersed with all of the sentiment that the times would take, which was a whole lot. He also needed money. Not for the greedy, miserly reasons most politicians wanted it, for country houses and secret bank accounts, but money to throw into the air with girls grabbing for it.

He was still trying to pass a law to legalize professional boxing. The agreement was that Runyon would have his hands in any worthwhile fight promotion and he, Walker, would be instantly remembered when money was counted. Walker suggested that he would be glad to stand on line as long as his place was directly behind Runyon. As Runyon and Walker saw it, there was nothing dastardly or even slightly underhanded about taking money from boxing, which had no importance to daily life, harmed no innocents and, most importantly, did not require a lot of waiting around for the cash. When the fight was over, the money was paid. That was the plan for the bright future. But on this night in the present, where dreams did not as yet pay, Walker was broke. "There isn't a good fighter we could get our hands on," he mused. Runyon sighed. "Not tonight." Then Ned Brown said, "I know you disagree with me, but I'm certain that none of these fellas around today can handle Dempsey. He is too tough. He is going to be a champion. Damn quick, too."

"Where is he?" Walker said, interested.

"The last I saw of him tonight, he was in the back of the hall, talking to Jack Kearns."

Walker held out his hands. "Forget it. Kearns has the nervous system of a bank robber. If he smells a dollar on the floor, he's right there."

Runyon said this was no real loss. He was absolutely certain that he was an expert on professional prizefighting. In that capacity, he attended the fights at St. Nicholas Arena, on West 66th Street. In the lobby he met Mushky Jackson, a loud, humorous manager of prizefighters who wore a gray fedora and had enough mustard on his tie to serve sandwiches. He garbled the language and thus appeared dumb to many except those who had enough caution to look twice. As Runyon was on safe grounds, boxing, about which he decided he knew even more once he put his foot inside the St. Nicholas Arena, he was glancing around so much that he barely noticed what Mushky was saying to him. Jackson asked him if he wanted to buy a piece of a heavyweight named Napoleon Dorval. "Heavyweight!" Runyon said. "How great can he fight?"

"Terrific," Mushky said.

He gave Jackson a $25 down payment in the lobby and they shook hands. Runyon told Jackson, "You don't have to mention this to Madden." Mushky Jackson's eyes widened. "I don't say nothin' to nobody ever lived!" He took Runyon down to the dressing room and introduced him to a large, handsome young man. "Anything goes wrong, you see him," Mushky said to Dorval. "Absolutely," Runyon said. "If you're my fighter, then you're my personal responsibility. I'm no cheap flesh peddler."

The fighter was elated. Runyon went out and sat down. Dorval was in the third fight of the night, a six-rounder against some ugly man from Trenton, New Jersey. Mushky Jackson rubbed his hand in a slow circle on Dorval's back to ease his nerves. The referee sent the fighters to their corners to wait for the bell. Jackson whipped the robe off Dorval, patted him for luck and swung through the ropes. Down in the corner, Jackson kept the robe over his arm. Dorval went out, danced, threw a few punches, then tried a tremendous left hook that missed by quite a margin. The right-hand counter by the ugly bum from Trenton did not. Mushky Jackson climbed into the ring with the robe right there on his arm. Dorval did not want Jackson to put the robe over him because he said he wanted to go for a swim.

"Where are you?" Jackson asked.

"Atlantic City."

After the fight, Runyon and a few of the reporters walked to the Silver Slipper nightclub on Columbus Circle. The doorman wore an admiral's uniform and a plaster patch over the left eye. "I guess I got here before you," he said to Runyon, who now recognized his heavyweight, Dorval.

In Lindy's the next day, Runyon heard that Owney Madden was furious that he had been left out. That the fighter had been knocked stiff only made it worse in Madden's opinion: "Supposin' the fighter turned into a champeen?"

Runyon shrugged. "At least Dorval's got a job. Heavyweights eat a lot."

A couple of nights later, the fighter was waiting outside of Lindy's when Runyon arrived. "I lost my job. I come to work tonight and the manager told me to get lost."

Runyon realized this was one of the consequences of uneasy friendships with underworld people. Nothing could pass. Somebody like Madden had to get even immediately, even with people they claimed to hold dear.

"What are you going to do with yourself?" Runyon said when he and Dorval sat down inside the restaurant.

"I don't know. Whatever you want. I'm all yours," Dorval said, picking up the menu.

TEN

HIS WIFE had her first baby, Mary Elaine, on August 24, 1914, right in their apartment. "If I'm going to die, I won't do it in a hospital," Ellen Egan Runyon said. "No hospital for me. Besides, imagine being born in a hospital!"

Runyon never thought of or mentioned the fact that his wife was pregnant, and men being what they were, he was hardly the worst of all. While at delivery time of a 76-degree day he was in the sun at the Polo Grounds, he did not dishonor his wife by becoming nervous and unable to work. He stayed through the game to the last out, and he was even dimly aware that maybe something great was taking place in his house. He spent a long time writing: "The writer of this piece is about to tell a lot of well-paid, intelligent, gentlemanly professional baseball players how they should have played the pastime up at the Polo Grounds yesterday afternoon when the N.Y. Yanks were defeated by the Chicago (Ill.) White Sox, by a score of 2–1."

The child was baptized at the Ascension Roman Catholic Church on West 107th Street in Manhattan. Baptisms are fine, for there is nothing intimate or embarrassing about them, they are held on Sunday and a man can stand around and receive friends as if he were actually a part of the whole birth. The Ascension Church congregation was made up of the Irish ascendancy, politicians, doctors and stockbrokers. There was a gold metal top on the stone fountain used for baptisms. And here, after the ceremony, into the vestibule of the church, arriving straight from a night spent standing on the sidewalk in front of Lindy's, came Champ Segal. The Champ had an amazing ability to suck in his stomach and place the radio from his hotel room between his belt and his stomach and depart. "A silvenier," he always called it.

Now, in the church vestibule, he opened his jacket and, quivering with pride, took out his baptism gift to the baby. "When she grows up she could read this real nice," he said proudly. "This shows you I could think ahead." He handed Runyon a leather-bound third-edition volume of Shakespeare. Runyon took a step backward, for he knew instantly that the book was as hot as a steam pipe. He caught his wife glaring, so he took the Champ off to one side.

"The baby here is the only person in New York who hasn't heard of the book," Runyon told the Champ.

"Why do you think I'm givin' it to her? She could keep it hid until she knows how to read it. By then, nobody knows what you're talking about, somebody's book is missing."

As the newspapers had stated so often, the Shakespeare volume, part of the collection of composer Jerome Kern, had been stolen from the Brick Row Book Shop, 42 East 50th Street. Runyon revered composers, Kern in particular, and regarded it as sacrilegious to touch anything connected in any way with such talented people. Also, the bookstore owner takes it personal. The owner said the Shakespeare book was worth $10,000 and wanted the United States Army to get it back.

"It's all right," the Champ insisted. "I got this book off a guy everybody says is a legitimate person."

Runyon said to him, "This book is very dangerous. Do you know how famous this book is? This man invented Shylock."

"I know Shakespeare was good, but I didn't know he was that big," the Champ said.

At his apartment, while others toasted the baby, Runyon sat at a portable typewriter and typed out: "Harold J. Woods, Police Commissioner, Headquarters, 240 Centre Street, New York, New York." He told the Champ to have the book delivered there forthwith, and with no return address.

Later, Ellen Runyon seemed to have completely lost the wry sense of humor supposedly as much a part of a housewife's life as a sink. She was wildly furious with him for bringing hoodlums to an event this sacred. Some weeks later, when Runyon took the baby out for the first time in his life, he got as far as the corner, turned sharply and pushed the carriage down the incline and to the poolroom. He left the carriage in the outer part, where the pool tables were, and went into the back room, where the bookmakers sat.

A guy walked into the poolroom, saw the baby in the carriage and said, "What's this?"

"Runyon's marker," somebody said.

In the back room, Runyon heard it. He always maintained, even writing it a couple of times, that on that afternoon he saw in his mind the story called "Little Miss Marker."

In growing up on the streets of a western town, the edges of Runyon's conscience had been shot away and the center of the vessel left numb. A matter that others saw as plainly carrying only the words "right" and "wrong" was at best a blur to him. He had walked into a New York newspaper enveloped with the same unsteadiness, caused by the inferiority found in all news reporters: when confronted with writing about famous names, there was a need to get one sentence or phrase into a story that would cause the subject to writhe in pain. He found that this sort of endeavor took too much time in the writing, and was always followed by a mad dash for the bar, where nasty phrases were repeated over many drinks. This offended him, for he believed in writing only for money, even ahead of vengeance. And he saw no way to make any money with people who appeared legitimate. These people claimed to live within the law, yet they were millionaires, and Runyon believed it was impossible to earn that much money in America without somehow stealing. They also constantly committed the worst of all crimes, that of being boring. Therefore, if legitimate people were worthless to him from the start, why bother to turn an original, mean-spirited phrase for any of them? He wanted phrases that would cause the reader to think only of him. Nor did he drink anymore, or enjoy just about any of the newspeople enough to chortle at the bar in their company. If he was not going to harm legitimate people, there was virtually no reason to have them in his life. His outright thieves, accustomed to being shunned, were thrilled by the least bit of attention paid to them by a respectable person. All Runyon needed to do was utter one hello to one crook, and the rest fell in love with him from one end of the street to the other. A street of burglars became Runyon's private club.

One day late in the summer of 1914, Runyon happened to go past Owney Madden's Winona Club and he took Margie Everdeen to a baseball game. He showed her to a seat and started to walk out onto the field and see all the players.

"Where are you going?" Margie said.

"I have to work."

"I thought you was takin' me to a game."

"You are at a game."

"I want to go where you go."

"I have to go and meet McGraw."

"So I'll meet him too. What am I?"

He brought Margie down to the gate and had her wait there while he asked McGraw to come over and meet this woman. McGraw began his walk graciously and smiling. Of course I'll meet the lady. Upon seeing Margie Everdeen, and figuring out what she was, he turned stiff as an usher at noon mass and, as any decent Roman Catholic would, fled into the protection of the Sixth Commandment. He grunted, tipped his cap to her and scowled at Runyon. Married man bringing a broad like this around!

"Mister McGraw," Margie said plaintively.

He turned around.

"You are some real fuck," she said.

During the game, she had a seat right behind the press box, one leg kicking nice all the way through the contest. At the end of the game, when Runyon started to write, she was understanding and quiet. Then, after watching him type for five minutes, Margie said, "You through yet?" He was halfway into the first of what was to be many takes of copy.

"How's it comin'?"

He went into his pocket and took out three dollars for cab fare and suggested she best get down to the Winona Club, as he would be some time.

As Margie was leaving, she said to an usher, "My boyfriend has to write up the whole newspaper."

During the fall of 1914, Runyon received several calls at his ledge at the newspaper from Margie Everdeen. She wanted to go to a Yale football game. Runyon had in mind the Army–Navy game, because it was at Philadelphia and they could stay over. This was impossible in New York, for the same hotel clerks that were telling him stories would be the first to run out onto the street with a tale on Runyon. "I love marching!" Margie squealed.

As they made plans for the game, a problem arose on the West Side involving James Wilson, who went under the name of Patsy Doyle. All the nice West Side guys never used their right names because they all had mothers, and why should you hurt a poor old woman never did anything wrong just because you're out stealing and shooting? Use somebody else's name and she'll never know what you do. During that fall of 1914, Patsy Doyle gave a cop a major beating and announced he was the champion of the West Side and, at the least, he was going to sleep with Owney Madden's girlfriend Freda Horner. One night, Patsy saw her on the street. Of course Freda Horner never smiled at Patsy to start him off. He took her by the arm into a saloon and bought her a drink. "He raped me into a drink!" Freda declared. Owney Madden kept his mouth shut, but the scream in his throat still could be heard. Whistling, Arthur Bieler sat down with a can of oil and cleaned his pistol.

On Friday, November 13, 1914, Freda Horner and Margie Everdeen were in the Winona when Runyon called looking for Margie. They were going to get the train to the Army–Navy game in Philadelphia. Madden took the phone. "She's doing something for me," he said, and hung up. Runyon was shocked that Madden would cut him off that way. Then he decided that as this was the first time Madden had spoken to him with viciousness in his voice, there must be a reason and he best mind his own business, which at the moment was football. He caught the train to Philadelphia.

On West 47th Street, Madden had Margie Everdeen call Patsy Doyle. "Freda is pining for you," she said to Patsy Doyle. "I have to listen to her all day and night about you."

"I know that," Patsy Doyle said proudly.

The official stenographer of the Court of General Sessions and Peace, City and County of New York, Part V, reported later that Margaret Everdeen testified that she said to Patsy Doyle, "Couldn't you meet her?"

"What's the matter with her great boyfriend Madden?"

"If you would just see her, I bet she would be real good to you," Margaret Everdeen said.

"Yeah?"

"She says to me herself that she would make you real happy."

"Tell her I might be at the bar in Nash's at nine o'clock," Patsy said.

And at Nash's that night, Patsy Doyle waited for Freda Horner. The bartender said to Patsy, "A man wants to see you."

"Who?"

"Me," Arthur Bieler said.

The bartender went under the bar, and several witnesses stated that Bieler's gun appeared, and that was all there was for Patsy Doyle.

In Philadelphia on Saturday, Runyon wrote five thousand words, which filled five full columns of a page of a standard-size newspaper. Army won the game, 20–0. Runyon seemed furious that West Point refused to send a cadet over to tell him who the players were; football jerseys were unnumbered in those years, because college faculties saw the danger of some student with a manhole cover for a head becoming a hero and thus eclipsing academic endeavor. Runyon didn't leave the press box and prowl the sidelines for names, so, he noted, "A number of rising young future army officers will probably be lost forever to football fame, as no one had the slightest idea as to the identity of the young men making the plays." Runyon accused the army of meanness in not assisting him, but he was really mad that Margie Everdeen wasn't right behind him, leg kicking.

In all the five thousand words, Runyon had only one full name:

Inside the Bellevue Stratford Hotel on Broad Street, and a magnificent place to stay it is, the most interesting scene was J. Miller Frazier, the manager, hunting for enough space to stand for a moment and rub his hands in satisfaction. Otherwise, the lobby presented a spectacle of impenetrable masses of fur overcoating. Along "Peacock Alley" the ladies sat in great covies and wondered if their escorts would ever find them again, while over the picture hung a delicate, elusive odor of perfume and face powder and so forth. Mr. Frazier is the East's finest host.

On Sunday morning, when the New York papers hit the Bellevue Stratford lobby, there came from behind the front desk a ripping sound, caused by the manager, J. Miller Frazier, as he destroyed Runyon's hotel bill. After which he had breakfast with this most valued guest. This was great with Runyon, for while he pretended that bellhops were his people, he usually situated himself closest to the money.

When Runyon called his office in New York, he was not surprised to hear that a man had been shot to death on Eighth Avenue. As he believed proper etiquette at time of homicide required him to be scarce, Runyon decided to stay in Philadelphia for the day and concentrate on forgetting the name of Margie Everdeen. He also received a phone call during breakfast.

"When you called up about Margie on Friday," Owney Madden said.

"My friend, I haven't the slightest notion of what you are talking about."

"That's good," Madden said.

"Anyone I spoke to on Friday discussed football, not any Margie."

Who, at this moment, became increasingly angry as she spoke to Thomas J. Weber, Police Department of the City of New York, second branch detective bureau, assigned to the case of the former Patsy Doyle.

"Do you know Arthur Bieler and Owney Madden?" Detective Weber asked Margaret Everdeen.

"I don't know anybody got a name like that."

"Are you sure?"

"I know who I know."

"How could you lie to a police officer like that? I know that you know them."

"You seem to know everything, then," Margie said.

"I know you've been with the two of them every day lately."

"How could you say that? Owney got pleurisy. Artie don't feel good, either. He didn't even come out of the house until last night when he hadda meet Owney."

Detective Weber testified that he walked into the next office, where Freda Horner sat alone and in fright at a scarred wood table.

"Freda, you should have told me that you were out last night with Madden and Bieler. It would've saved you hours."

"Margie told you!"

"Sure," Weber said.

"She told you that she called Patsy up and told him to meet me in the bar?"

"Yes, she did," Detective Weber said.

"She shouldn't of said that. She could get Owney in trouble, too."

"Might," Detective Weber said. He went out to a typewriter to peck out a warrant for Bieler and Madden.

M. S. Connolly, resident physician, and C. S. Faulkner, house gynecologist, Office of the General Medical Superintendent, Bellevue and Allied hospitals, Eleventh Avenue and 26th Street, New York City:

> On this day of January 11, 1915, we do respectfully certify to the Honorable James T. Malone, judge of the Court of General Sessions: Margaret Everdeen, who was committed to Bellevue Hospital on December 17, 1914, to receive treatment of syphilis has been treated, and it is our opinion that her disease is NOW in a non-infectious stage.
>
> We have examined Freda Horner and do not find that her condition of syphilis is NOW in any way infectious. There is no danger of the disease by any of her associates.

"I shoot the wrong fucking person!" Arthur Bieler said.

"Arthur, don't talk out loud!" His lawyer, Charles Sullivan, held the medical reports on the dolls. A woman arrested in these years was rushed to the hospital for an internal examination; a man was barely checked for bullet holes.

"What do I care? This broad done something to my prick!" Bieler was with his lawyers in a visiting room in the old city jail on 57th Street between Lexington and Third avenues. Madden was held in the Tombs, which was designed on the outside like an Egyptian tomb, but on the inside was nothing more than freezing cells where moisture turned into water and streamed down the walls.

Instead of shooting Patsy Doyle, I should blow this dirty Margie away," Bieler said. "That's the one I was with."

Sullivan said, "I can't defend you in a murder trial if you go around saying you did it."

"What do I care?" Bieler said. "I should of shot that Margie right in the head instead of Patsy Doyle. You better make sure they get a doctor in here to look at my prick."

"I'll give them a call," Sullivan said.

"You better give that Damon Runyon a call and tell him what you told me about that Margie and Freda. Madden got his telephone numbers."

So the first two dolls of Damon Runyon's career on Broadway come up with venereal disease. There is no evidence as to whether he went away scathed or unscathed.

The first two real good gangsters, Madden and Bieler, came up with something worse, he discovered, and that was the sin of testimony. Here in this room of municipal green plaster, with scars of white plaster showing, in the old red brick New York City Court of General Sessions and Peace, Part V, second floor, the benches were filled with people who carried truck driver's caps as they watched the witness stand. There sat a dark-haired young man, and even at age twenty-one the suggestion of a snarl always was at the base of his voice. He gave his name as Arthur Bieler, and his address as 585 Tenth Avenue. This was a building with a fire escape on the front, which was on the southwest corner of Tenth Avenue and 43rd Street. Here in the Court of General Sessions and Peace, Assistant District Attorney M. L. H. Edwards rises to question Bieler, whose case is calendar number 160555, indictment number 103194, People of the State of New York versus James Ward, alias Arthur Bieler. The charge: murder in the first degree.

The judge is Crain, the court stenographer is Peter P. McLoughlin, the date is March 17, 1915. Somewhere uptown, bagpipes sounded in the chill air and a quarter of a million Irish were gathering to march past St. Patrick's Cathedral. Bieler was a fierce German, but he knew how to celebrate and by now would have been asked a dozen times what he wanted to drink. Instead, he had to twist in agitation as this rat prosecutor cleared his throat and began the court day.

Q. Now why were you carrying a gun for that evening?

A. Because I was going to a dance that night.

Q. Do you always carry a gun when you are going to a dance?

A. Yes. Except for a dance after a wedding for somebody in the family.

Q. Now where did you go with that gun on this night?

A. First, I went to Nash's saloon on the corner of 41st Street and 8th Avenue. I walked into the saloon with the intention of getting a drink and waiting for Patsy Doyle.

Q. All right, now just describe what happened when you went in, and tell me the door you used.

A. I come in through the 41st Street entrance. I got about halfway to the bar and my back is turned from the rear entrance and I got fired at.

Q. You didn't know by whom?

A. No, sir.

Q. You were fired at?

A. Yes, sir.

Q. What made you think you were being fired at?

A. Because the man was firing point blank at me. The shot went right past my head. I heard it go right past my ear and my head.

Q. Then what did you do?

A. I seen my life was in jeopardy, and I fired back.

Q. Did you empty all the shells of your gun?

A. I don't know. I fired until I seen the man was hit; I seen the man fall, and as he was falling he raised his gun up in the air, and shot his gun up in the air.

Q. Then what did you do?

A. I walked over to him and I seen Patsy Doyle sitting down like on the floor.

Q. Did you speak to him?

A. I shook him. I said, "Patsy, speak to me."

Q. And did he speak?

A. No, sir, he did not.

Q. Then what did you do?

A. I walked over to Lexington Avenue and 51st Street and I went into a dance hall.

Q. You went to a dance there?

A. Yes, sir. It was a benefit dance.

Q. You went to the dance, and danced that evening?

A. Yes, sir.

Q. Right after killing this man?

A. Yes, sir.

Q. Whom did you meet at the dance that you know?

A. Owney Madden.

Q. What time of night did you meet him there?

A. About twenty minutes after nine or so.

Q. And what did you say to Owney Madden?

A. Hiya, Owney.

On the witness stand at the first murder trial of his life, for the shooting of Patsy Doyle, Owney forgot that he faced the electric chair and thought it was more important to come right back at this rat prosecutor asking him too many questions.

Q. You did at that time know that Doyle had been shot, did you?

A. No.

Q. When did you find out Doyle had been shot?

A. When did I find out?

Q. Yes.

A. I found out the next morning.

Q. You have told us that on Sunday morning you did not know that Doyle was dead.

A. No.

Q. You did not?

A. No.

Q. If you didn't know about Patsy Doyle being dead, then why were you so afraid of being arrested?

A. I don't know.

Q. What?

A. No — what I might as well do right here and say I am guilty of what you are framing me with and be done for it. All I am getting out of here is you standing there making a frame for my head.

Q. You ARE guilty, are you not?

A. No, I don't know I am guilty. I ain't guilty. If I was guilty I would plead guilty. I am not guilty and I don't want to testify no more. I ain't getting a fair chance from the likes of you.

THE COURT: Sit down, Mr. Madden.

COUNSEL: Now sit down and answer the question.

Owney and Arthur Bieler failed courtroom, but when they got out
of prison a few years later, they did wonderful at Prohibition.

In the spring of 1915, the sidewalk in front of Lindy's came alive with
Otto Biderman out there whirling around, his chubby hands groping
in his pockets as people handed him bets and money.

"I'm a genius," Biderman shouted.

"That's good," Runyon said.

While talking to Runyon, he tried to maintain his rhythm of hand
gestures, for he was deep into his act, which had charmed half the underworld and, he hoped, also would captivate Runyon. Biderman had
an imagination as wide as his belly, which made it some imagination,
for he had 225 pounds hanging on exactly five feet six and a half inches.

"Are you allowed out here?" Runyon asked.

"What do you think, I'm here on my own nerve?"

Of course Biderman was conducting a private raid. He was associated with a Bronx gangster, Dutch Schultz, who had not quite murdered enough people to be regarded as a force here on Owney Madden's territory. As Madden and poor Arthur Bieler were off in prison
as a result of their trials, which as previously shown did not work out
so well, some might have deemed Biderman safe. But those were the
people who did not know Madden's caretaker, Mr. George (Big Frenchy) DeMange. He was called Big Frenchy because nobody in front of
Lindy's ever had seen anybody who wasn't Jewish, Irish or, the up-
coming race, armed Italians. One night somebody said, "I bet he is
some big fucking Frenchman." The name stuck. So would his penalty
if he caught Biderman, who was unconscious of any danger as he stood
on the sidewalk and recorded each horse, the amount bet and the initial of the bettor on a small pad that had carbon paper inserts. Biderman gave the top slip to the bettor as proof of the bet and kept the
carbon. The small white pad came apart at the top as he wrote, leaving
him with a pocketful of loose carbon slips. Biderman was so happy to
meet Runyon, a known legitimate person, that when Damon started
into Lindy's, he trailed after him, dropping a betting slip on the sidewalk. As it was early in the night, hardly dinnertime, and there were
parents out with children, a little girl, age six at most, took a giant leap
and picked up the slip and gave it to Runyon.

The bet recorded on the slip was a simple $50 bet on a three-horse
parlay, the payoff for which could be in many thousands of dollars. Even
a citizen would murder Biderman if such an amount was involved in

one of their bets. A bookmaker is supposed to take a bet like this and hedge it off, which means to spread the bet to other bookmakers to lessen the impact if the horses win. "Is this yours?" Damon Runyon held out the slip.

"Can't be," Biderman said. He turned and walked away from the crowds on the sidewalk and into Lindy's. One fat sweaty hand was clamped over the betting slip.

At the table, Biderman had cheesecake and brandy, and with much noise unfolded the racing form for the Kentucky Derby, at week's end. He now called out for all the room to hear, "I make Regret a fuzzy," meaning that when he looked at the form charts, he saw an imaginary circle drawn around Regret's name with a thick pencil that left a fuzzy fringe. As Regret was a filly, and a filly never had won the Kentucky Derby, Runyon and everybody else realized that Biderman, his mouth full of cheesecake, did not know that it was biologically impossible for a filly to win a race against colts in the spring.

"The minute the filly gets in the post parade, she'll get crazy over these stallions and she'll spend the whole race trying to kiss them," Runyon said with great sagacity.

"This horse got too strong a will to get bothered by some lousy stallion," Biderman announced. "In fact, she cannot lose."

On Saturday, Runyon was covering a Yankees baseball game at the Polo Grounds for the *American:*

> A large crew of able seamen from Your Uncle Sam's trouble-tubs in the Hudson River were present, with their trousers snugly laced in the vicinity of what you might call the aft, and their flat caps aslant, while there was an additional deep sea touch to the programme in the sinking sensations enjoyed by the landlubbers in attendance over some of the baseball exhibited by the Wild Yanks. Our log of the pastime shows a score of 3 to 1 in favor of the Boston Red Sox.

Between pages, Runyon asked Leo Levitt, the telegrapher, to find out who won the Kentucky Derby. Levitt tapped out the question, and from the sports department there came the answer: "Regret wire to wire."

Biderman was in front of Lindy's that night with a crowd around him. "I'm a genius!" he screamed.

"Well, yeah," Runyon said.

"A genius with mathematical!"

In the underworld, Otto Biderman had started calling himself Abba

Dabba, and he was such a monumental liar that he had everybody believing he could figure out in his head, in moments, the exact amount being bet at a whole racetrack, and right as the money was being bet. He claimed that this gave him the power to fix the policy number, based on the total take, with a simple $2 bet. Dumb scoundrels in crime believed it implicitly. Runyon knew otherwise. "He is a non-finisher in a long-division test," Runyon said. Biderman talked so much about betting on Regret that Runyon put him in the paper as a character named Regret.

Arnold Rothstein, the gangster, called him Avisack because he won a lot of money on a horse with that name. In an autograph on a barbershop wall, Biderman wrote: "My dearest Friend's. Don't let nothing scare you're thoughts. Regards, The Fast Avisack."

Biderman was the only man on Broadway who had three nicknames, although shylocks knew him simply as "He owes." At this time, his main man Schultz was an unknown bedbug who could not hold his hands properly in a fair fight and caught beatings because of it. But Schultz also could sneak up behind somebody and stab him or shoot him. Schultz began in a saloon on Third Avenue and 149th Street in the Bronx, and couldn't wait to see his name in a newspaper. If he listened to a few bars of an aria, he became an expert on Puccini. If he opened a book, he was a literary critic. Mostly, he was a lunatic killer. He was the only man in New York whom Ray Arcel, the fight trainer considered the finest gentleman in New York sports, would not greet. "Ray Arcel would say 'Yes, ma'am' and 'No, ma'am' in a whorehouse," Runyon said. "If he doesn't talk to Schultz, that tells you all you have to know about the guy."

Runyon found, however, that whenever anybody with brains saw Biderman, or Regret, they were immediately impressed. He saw this best at the end of a long day which started at Aqueduct Racetrack when a man came pushing excitedly through the press box, clutched Biderman's hand and introduced himself. Dressed grandly in banker's blue, a pince-nez, summer spats and a collar and tie, he was E. Phocian Howard, publisher and editor of the *New York Press*, a paper of racing and stock tips. As he was a man of taste, which placed him well beyond his surroundings, and as his opinion helped turn Runyon into a major writer, we must pause here to say something about him. He took the nickname of Phoce as a sign of Ivy League clubbiness, the better to bewilder the rich suckers. He also had a great interest in literature, and here at the racetrack he began to thump his small fist on Runyon's shoulder. "Dostoyevsky dropped his left hand after jabbing. He concentrated on the rich gamblers. He makes the odd mention of riffraff and small thieves. He dismisses them with the back of his hand. Those are your people. The runner for a bookmaker. They are the source of the one thing the world needs. Laughter. That is what you can provide."

He took Runyon to the splendor of the Trustees Room, where he stopped the bartender from pouring the usual basin of brandy. "Champagne for an occasion!" Phoce said. When Runyon said he didn't drink, Phoce was immensely pleased. "How marvelous! You have nothing to prevent you from greatness. Thank heavens. If there is one thing I cannot bear hearing, it is a writer using the insufferable excuse of not being able to function without alcohol."

He toasted with champagne, and as Runyon drank coffee, Phoce gave his own pedigree. He was out of Danville, Illinois, and had a father who was a reporter for the *Chicago Tribune*. A brother, a daredevil motorcycle rider for the Sells Brothers–Otto Floto Circus in Columbus, Ohio, broke his neck and died while rehearsing a loop-the-loop. Instantly, mention of the circus where Runyon once worked caused the two to become close friends.

When Phoce was fifteen, his father, named the Washington correspondent of the *Chicago Tribune*, left his wife and other children at home in Danville and took Phoce to the capital. After two years in Washington schools, Phoce was appointed a congressional page by House Speaker Joseph Cannon. Possessing a fine curiosity, he made sure to glance at all messages, and found the subject of most was larceny, particularly those sent over from the House to Senator Wesley Jones of Washington State. Jones spoke of Prohibition as if it were the concluding paragraph of the Lord's Prayer. At the same time, Jones received many emergency phone calls and hand-delivered envelopes from New York attorneys representing shipping lines. Most dealt with hotel suites being reserved for the senator, theaters at which tickets were being left and private clubs where shipping-line owners would meet him for dinner. "He is selling the landing rights to Puget Sound!" Phoce overheard another senator say one day. Phoce regarded this as most important education.

One day, a lawyer assisting William Cromwell, a New York attorney in the ceaseless task of bribing legislators on behalf of the New Panama Canal Company, swept up all the congressional staffers he could see, including Phoce, and took them to Bowie Race Track for an afternoon's sport. Phoce had crab cakes and great big cold beer, and got a packet of money for betting. He blew the money but remembered forever the comfortable feeling of standing alongside a member of the Vanderbilt family. He asked his father about a newspaper job, particularly a sportswriting job, one that would have him at the racetrack. The father got him a job in the Washington bureau of the *New York World*. Phoce covered McKinley's assassination, his byline appearing as "Special from a World Correspondent." It took many years to gain a real byline, and he realized at the funeral that it made no sense to wait. "I knew I never would see a bigger story than this, so I decided to take my leave from journalism. Besides, I had my fill of covering death. It will happen soon enough for all of us."

When his wife died suddenly, Phoce left Washington and went into the sale of Canadian mining stocks. One engineer in the far north of Canada told him, "The only thing you'll hit at the bottom of this shaft is a dead polar bear." Business was wonderful, but he thought the cost was far too high for printing new stock certificates each time he switched the name of his mining company, which happened every few weeks. Instead, he opened the *New York Press*, and combined racing stories ("Jefferson Park Handle Indicates Prosperity!") with dispatches on how to buy good stocks, and from whom. At all times he indicated this by the placement of pictures and captions such as these in the paper:

BROKER AT PLAY
John F. Harris, senior partner in the firm of Harris and Winthrop, of the New York Stock Exchange, snapped at Belmont Park. His prognosticators back in the shop are said to be having such a terrific season that between races Harris can be seen reading prospectuses on new yachts.

MINGLING WITH DAIQUIRIS
Broker William A. Reed takes time off from a huge run in his Pine Street stock shop to visit Havana for a week. For horses and, as shown here, good cheer in the afternoon!

After Phoce finished his champagne and his life story, he drove Runyon back to Broadway from the track. He had a used Rolls Royce and a chauffeur named Ben Jones, who kept fried chicken on the front seat and handed it back to passengers in case they had no meal money left after the day's events. On this day, the racing had gone so extraordinarily bad for Phoce that he took Jones's hat, got behind the wheel and had Ben sit in the back with Runyon. "I can't pay his salary this week," Phoce said. When Phoce pulled up in front of Lindy's, he spotted Regret right away.

"How are you this evening, sir?" he said.

Regret sneered at the chauffeur. "I don't talk with help," he said. "I'm a genius."

"Could I ask at what?"

"At mathematical."

Phoce grabbed Runyon's arm. "That man is an oil well towering right out of the sidewalk in front of your eyes."

One night weeks later, Runyon was in front of Lindy's and he met a stumpy man with a worried look named Butch Tower. He was worried over two matters. The first was that as a tout he was at least not flourishing. In fact, some people were going to kill him. The second problem was a safecracking job, and for the first time in crime in New York, they were bringing a baby as a beard. Runyon asked when this event would take place. When Tower told him that it would occur in an hour, Runyon said that he would like to accompany them as observer.

There were two guys from Brooklyn with Butch Tower, who was supposed to be the best at safes. There never was such a thing as "the worst" at safecracking, although new prison wings had to be built to accommodate "great" safecrackers. Butch held the baby, which was said to be his. The baby, teething, nearly got everybody killed by biting down hard and loosening the cap of the bottle of nitroglycerine.

At this point, Runyon took leave. Not out of some cheap fear of being blown up, for this could happen to a news reporter who got too close to an oil tank fire, but simply because the coverage of crime as a sport, which is important because decent people are so excruciatingly dull, always reaches the point where the sport becomes something that is against the law. The preparations were great fun. But now it was the business of robbers and cops. Any observer who remained became a participant. Runyon was a good block away when the sidewalk underneath him almost lifted him into the air. Running out of the building was Butch Tower, clutching the baby. A couple of blocks away the police stopped him. They were looking for thugs running from a safeblowing. Butch Tower said the baby was teething and he was looking for a drugstore. One of the policemen said that, bein' he was a father himself, he began to tell Butch exactly what to get for the baby's teething. Then he directed Butch to the nearest druggist. The night gave Runyon material for about as good a short story about New York as we have. He got it the only way you can, by hanging out with people for long hours. Through so many decades in the city, only a couple of people ever came around with enough guts and energy to do a thing like this, and then at the end of the night they came up empty because they couldn't write well enough to do a travel pamphlet.

ELEVEN

AT Mrs. Hearst's ranch at Babícora in 1916, the Hearst man Follansbee had been forced to return to New York with a bad case of being overserved by butlers. Then one day the replacement, John C. Hayes of the Hearst organization, awoke to gunfire on Mrs. Hearst's great ranch. "Villa!" a ranch worker said. Villa copped the sixty thousand cattle chewing grass. He figured that Hearst would understand. Why, for Hearst to change his opinion in public after hailing Villa as the savior of Mexico, he would have to humiliate himself. I, Villa, would never do such a thing. If a man I embrace then betrays me, I would execute the man in his bed, but I would not admit to a mistake in public. Also, had he not given the Hearst sportswriter Runyon a lighter with a great ruby in it? Hayes waited for the firing to stop and fled to El Paso and sent a dispatch to the Chief. The Hearst newspapers reacted within a day:

MEXICANS PREPARE FOR WAR WITH U.S.!
Indians Revert to Cannibalism and Are Threat to Our Nation!
CAN WE BEAT THEM? WHAT'S THE ANSWER, AMERICA?

Is it not time for soldiers of the United States to do something PERMANENT? The way to IMPRESS the Mexicans is to REPRESS the Mexicans. We are GOING INTO MEXICO. And as far as we GO, we'll *stay*.

Villa answered, "What is this man Hearst crying about? I only took from his mother, not from him."

The United States had twenty thousand troops at Fort Bliss, outside

El Paso, under General John Pershing. One of the field artillery outfits at the fort rolled its pieces up to the river, then shattered the still sky to its very top by commencing to fire on the Juarez racetrack.

"They shoot at us because they lose all their fucking money here," Villa said. When a shell blew the roof off a barn on the backstretch, Villa became angry. "Fuck these people," he said.

By March of 1916, Villa, sold out by politicians and generals who originally swore to die if it would help him save the people, was out of Juarez and using robbery proceeds to buy arms at Ravel Brothers Mercantile, Boulevard Street, Columbus, New Mexico. At Columbus, population 300, there was a yellow frame railroad station of the El Paso and Southwestern Railroad. Opposite the tracks was an army encampment of 120 regulars of the Thirteenth Cavalry, commanded by Colonel Slocum. Mexicans always came into town and bought bolt goods, cooking utensils, boots and overalls. Nobody noticed when several of Pancho Villa's riders came in one day and left a large sum of money with the Ravel brothers for guns and ammunition. Some days later, at nightfall, Sam Ravel took them to the yard behind the store and told them to take a wagon that was covered with a thick tarpaulin. Villa's men dragged the wagon through an arroyo, a dry gulley, and to Palomes, Mexico, where by torchlight they found that the shipment was short by at least $2,500 worth of guns. Villa gathered his last six hundred horsemen. Colonel Slocum, who said there was a border between the countries and that alone, a line on a map, was protection enough for the United States, and Columbus in particular, took his officers thirty-two miles north to a dance at Deming, New Mexico. Lieutenant Castleman, as officer of the day, would be in charge at Columbus.

Villa and his horsemen rode with rifles, pistols, bandoliers and many five-gallon cans of kerosene. The muffled click of horses' hooves and the creak of leather were the only sounds in the night. They moved three miles through an arroyo. They saw one army sentry pacing. The rest of the encampment and the town was asleep. Out of the arroyo — some on foot, others riding — came Villa's men. It was the only time since the War of 1812 that the United States had been invaded by foreigners. The men hit encampment and town, guns firing even at shadows that moved. Buildings burst into flames. At the army encampment, Lieutenant Castleman and his men were trying frantically to break into the guardhouse, where rifles and ammunition were locked. The keys were on Colonel Slocum's belt as he whirled about the dance floor up at Deming.

Dean's Grocery went up in flames. Dean ran from his house to try and save the store. He was riddled with bullets. Miller, the druggist, took a gun and tried to protect his store. He was blown away. Castleman and his men now got into the guardhouse and brought out a machine gun, which fired one burst before jamming.

As Larry Harris of the *El Paso Times* writes in his book *Pancho Villa and the Columbus Raid:* "High above the bedlam, rose the cry, mixed with profanity: 'Donde es Sam Ravel?' "

Sam Ravel, one of the world's smartest men, was in El Paso having his teeth drilled. Even if the dentist had palsy, it was better than being in Columbus. His brother hid under cowhides at the rear of the store. When the Villistas got down to the last few hides, the Ravel family tale states, they stopped searching, which saved the brother, who was hidden under the bottom hide.

The attack lasted two hours, and eight soldiers and nine civilians were killed. Villa went back to Mexico.

On 168th Street in New York, in the Presbyterian Hospital, on the heights overlooking the Hudson, a Hearst messenger walked rapidly down a hallway, arms bulging with dispatches on Villa's raid.

In his room, Hearst, recovering from an appendectomy, had his great editor Arthur Brisbane at his bedside. "Villa has invaded the United States," Brisbane said ominously.

"He has already invaded America," Hearst said. "The day he set foot on Mother's property at Babícora was an act of war against the very heart of this nation."

The *American*'s editorial page came out with a column-and-a-half cut, running down the length of the page, showing an angry American eagle with its claws holding on to the top of a flagpole from which, all down the page, unfurled Old Glory. The editorial was printed in type that could be used for a billboard.

General Pershing has ordered General Funston to get Villa. The country can rest easy over the outcome. Funston will get Villa.

When our soldiers are through with these villains, we think it will be some time before another band of brigands will murder Americans.

In the hospital the next morning, Hearst sat on the edge of his bed and looked at the newspapers spread on the floor. Here was a Runyon baseball story on the New York Giants' spring training from Marlin, Texas. Hearst's big toe touched the story. "Why is he there?"

"Baseball sells the paper," Brisbane said.

"War is the number-one newspaper seller of all time," Hearst said. "Get Runyon to war."

The principal of Sacred Heart School, on South Oregon Street in El Paso, was in an office with a door opening on an alley running behind the school and convent. A nun was at the convent door, scraping lunch plates into buckets. The principal's starched white cap, collar and bib had rubbed her chin and cheeks pink. It was a shame, she said, that Runyon had traveled so far, what with all the trouble on the border. The pastor had decided it would be best to have only half-days for the time being. There was no way for Runyon to reach Patrice over in Juarez. The principal inquired about Runyon's interest in her.

"Any time I can get somebody to read and write, I make myself one-two to get them as a reader," he said.

"You should come tomorrow," the principal said. "We'll have her dance for you. Every time you look for her, she's dancing."

Runyon said he was due at Fort Bliss by dusk and would let the nun pass along his regards. He asked the nun for a sheet of paper and printed one word on it: "Study!" Runyon now put $25 for the next school year on the desk.

Right away in Mexico, in an early dispatch, he got to the heart of the matter:

> With Headquarters, United States Army, in the field in Mexico. (Via courier to Columbus, N.M., March 21.) March 23 — There are several varieties of hell on earth and among them must be included an infantry hike along the dusty roads of northern Mexico.
>
> Horses and mules died during the first couple of days and were left to the coyotes and buzzards that trail every column. Cavalrymen rode in saddle sore, but the men plodded along and made their camps every night, limping a little, but still afoot.
>
> Their very souls are steeped in dust in these marches. It is hot overhead. It is powdery soft under foot. The grind of the wagon wheels and the churn of the horses' hoofs have cut the dry roads to chalk.
>
> The Americans are driving forward with amazing speed, given the conditions. Villa was reported to-night in the Babicora Lake region on the ranch of Mrs. Phoebe Hearst, which he has raided several times in the past.
>
> Babicora is about fifty-five miles south of Galena, where one sec-

tion of the American expeditionary force has arrived and is pushing forward at the rate of thirty-three miles a day.

They found no Villa but had a greater victory, reclaiming the Hearst ranch. Hearst loudly supported a United States senator, Sherman of Illinois, who called for 55,000 volunteers to fight in the war in Mexico. His papers printed nothing when a total of 507 volunteers showed up at recruiting offices around the nation. Runyon reported that the Mexican villagers were acting as if the American troops didn't come to save them from themselves. Hearst glumly allowed it to be printed. But when President Woodrow Wilson said there was a conspiracy to force a war with Mexico, Hearst became furious. "How would he feel if these filthy bandits forcefully occupied his ranch!" Hearst papers ran a page 1 story by the Republican leader of the Senate, Jacob Gallinger of New Hampshire, who said, "I cannot free myself from the belief that the situation on the American side of the Rio Grande is full of peril."

In writings from the dusty Mexican fields, Runyon didn't mention that he had met Villa at a racetrack. It was bad enough that there was a war without having to drag his personal life into it. What if he had been talking to Villa at a time when he was deciding to invade the Hearst ranch?

Pershing chased Villa with troops in trucks and with the first aircraft ever used, biplanes that swooped over the hills and wastelands and looked for signs of Villa. A lieutenant, George S. Patton, traveled with troops in a car. They jumped out to look for a fight. He shot Cardenas, the man closest to Villa, in front of his wife, mother and baby. He then shot two others. He threw the bodies on the hood like deer and drove back to his camp. When he was asked how he felt about shooting Cardenas in front of his family, Patton said he had taken no notice of this. Nor was he afraid of Cardenas's bullets. "I was only afraid that he would get away." Runyon and everybody else wrote about it. Runyon had a mistake in how the fight began, and somebody on Pershing's staff wanted to ask for a correction. Patton became furious. "The story's about me. When they do one about you, then you complain." Patton spent hours with Sam Dreben and a machine gun mounted on a truck. Patton showed it to Pershing as an idea that might be good for killing Mexicans now, if they could be found, but would certainly be effective against massed troops, like Germans. The senior officers couldn't wait to fight in a big war.

At the expedition headquarters one day, Runyon was attracted by shouting of a volume unusual even for war which came from the direction of General Pershing's tent. He found four Japanese men facing a large group of soldiers. On the ground was a large dead dog. The dog's tongue was stuck out as stiff as a board and his mouth was covered with dry froth. The soldiers pointed accusatory fingers at the Japanese. They screamed that they wanted the dog back so they could bury him. "Then we'll bury you!" one of them snarled at the Japanese. When a soldier reached for the dog, one of the Japanese grabbed the dead dog's tail and pulled the body closer. A soldier kicked one of the Japanese, whose foot immediately shot back. Another soldier hit one of the Japanese right over the head. They were ready to go, and the Japanese didn't back off. A command car roared up and all hands fell to sides. Pershing stepped out. One of his aides walked rapidly over to the Japanese and told them to wait, that the general wanted to see them shortly. A soldier asked Pershing's aide about burying the dog.

"The dog is none of your business," the aide said.

"But that's our dog," the soldier said.

The aide dismissed this and told the soldiers to leave. The aide went into Pershing's tent. Runyon began talking to the Japanese and found that they helped operate an iron ore mine in Chihuahua, part of their duties being to supervise food and medical services for the workers. Villa often came by to inspect the mine, and the Japanese fed him and also helped doctors sew up any of the wounded Villa brought with him. Runyon took their names, which were Tsutomo Doyo, K. Fuzita, A. Sapo and T. Suzuki. When he asked about the dog, Tsutomo Doyo grabbed the dead dog by the tail and held him up. "It works," the Japanese said excitedly. "Only two tablets and he is dead. They want us to give Villa thirteen tablets. He will die like an entire pack of dogs."

Pershing now stepped out of his tent and seemed immensely pleased to see the Japanese. When he noticed Runyon, his face showed concern, which was one shade behind the anger he undoubtedly felt.

"I must ask you not to write this," Pershing said.

"Now that you ask, I won't do it," Runyon said. "But even if I did, your people would have censored whatever it is."

Pershing thought for a moment. "I suppose you'll do it when you get home."

"Certainly, after the action is over nobody gets hurt."

By now, half of Pershing's staff was around him, one more worried than the other. Then when Pershing's chief surgeon walked up, the

Japanese, Doyo, waved the dog happily. "We tried it out. It works just like you said."

Pershing's worried sigh could be heard for a mile. He asked Runyon to come into the tent. Then he and his staff officers and the surgeon sat down and told Runyon that as a patriot he had to forget forever what he had heard. "Sometimes, the aftermath of a battle requires more secrecy than at the outset," Pershing said. The Japanese were part of a plot to poison Villa, of course, the detailed outline of which Pershing had placed in a letter, in his own handwriting, to Washington, where it had been approved. His letter was in the records of the Punitive Expedition, in the Department of the Army in Washington. When Runyon suggested that Pershing get the letter back, Pershing's legal officer shook his head. "Any such request would start gossip immediately," he said. "It is best to leave it where it is."

In the style of Runyon's times, and in nearly every other time in the country's history of its free press, Runyon told Pershing that he was an American first and a reporter after that. The idea of the country is that he is supposed to be both at once. Reporting is an American act. Yet he said that the story never would be written. As he said this to Pershing, he heard in his heart a loud barroom snarl coming from somewhere in the parched, barren land around him: it was that of A. L. Runyan, who spelled "Custer" with an *a*.

After the meeting, Runyon spoke to the Japanese for a moment. "Look out for that fella," he said, meaning Villa. "I know he never eats off his own plate, for the same reason that you're carrying those pills around."

The four Japanese picked up fistfuls of gold coins and left for the mine in Chihuahua. The records of the Punitive Expedition show that two of them, Doyo and Suzuki, were at the mine when Villa arrived with some wounded, and they gave Villa a cup of coffee with thirteen pills in it. Villa thanked them and held the cup out for one of his men to drink. Nobody knows what happened to the man because Doyo and Suzuki fled into the night and made it across the border and flung themselves into the arms of American soldiers. The account of this went into the records of the Punitive Expedition, along with Pershing's handwritten note.

The letter stayed, and was taken out once, in the late 1950s, when a plan to poison Fidel Castro in Cuba was drawn almost to the detail from Pershing's plan to get Villa, down to the use of a food handler, in this case a spy working as a soda-fountain clerk in the Havana Hilton Hotel.

Similarly, so many years later, the spy who was to poison Castro stuck
the pill into the ice cream freezer in the Havana Hilton Hotel and waited
until called upon to make the usual late afternoon milk shake for Castro. The pill was frozen in a thick clump of ice on the side of the ice
cream container. The clerk dug at the ice. When the pill didn't come
loose, he began digging in a frenzy. This caused one of Castro's guards
to become curious. He leaned over the counter and stuck a large pistol
in the clerk's face, and this, too, was the end of another attempt by the
United States to assassinate the leader of another country.

In the matter of Pancho Villa, Runyon never wrote a line and Pershing made a point of thanking him on several occasions, and said
the usual "If I can be of help sometime." He certainly would be, and
shortly.

Runyon sent a short dispatch that noted:

> First full details of the fight between Col. W. C. Brown's command
> and a band of Villistas at Aguas Calientes, arrived here today.
> Colonel Brown's men were Negro troops of the Tenth Cavalry. About
> noon, Colonel Brown's troopers crossing a wide plain toward a ridge
> of mountains, suddenly were fired upon from behind rocks on the
> mountainside, where forty Villa followers had ambushed.
> The Americans divided, one force charging the rocks while another
> went through a pass to flank the Villistas if they retreated. One Amer-
> ican horse was shot out from under the rider. The Mexicans mounted
> and rode for the heights. Three were shot to death as the Americans
> pursued.
>
> In the Field in Mexico, March 26 (via army aeroplane to Colum-
> bus, N.M., March 27.) — Some of the infantry with the more ad-
> vanced flying columns of the punitive expedition have now covered
> over 180 miles of Mexican roads and are still moving. The foot sol-
> diers are in magnificent condition. The "doughboys" are rapidly es-
> tablishing a record that will stamp the Americans as the greatest of all
> the world's foot soldiers.
> The commanding officer of the expedition received a letter today
> from an enterprising undertaker in Lynnburg, Tenn., expressing the
> belief that General Pershing will capture Francisco Villa and request-
> ing that the body of the bandit chief be turned over to him for em-
> balming and exhibition.

Villa was never found and the Punitive Expedition was unsuccessful.
Pershing was more interested in the performance of the biplane and

Patton's mounted machine gun. President Woodrow Wilson had just said that he, Wilson, would die before allowing Americans to fight on foreign soil. Immediately, Pershing began to plan how he would use biplanes and moving machine guns when his troops were ordered to war in France.

Runyon swatted the dust from his uniforms, packed, and then, in a three-piece suit, returned to New York.

When America was on the verge of entering the war in Europe, Hearst, who had more Germans working for him than the Kaiser, became one of America's most hated men by lauding Germany in editorials. He filled newspapers with stories about the hideousness of the European war and the need to keep Americans out of it.

For assistance, Hearst looked to Irish Americans, who bought his papers in big cities and wanted to see the Germans run an Oktoberfest in Trafalgar Square. Hearst wrote, "I thought that if ever I were elected President of the United States, I would send to the Court of Saint James's an Irish-American. I offer the suggestion to somebody else, with the ardent hope that it will be acted upon." He said American diplomats in London were "more snobbish than their English butlers." Hearst had servants all over the place, but never allowed them to wear uniforms. "I have never seen the hand of England outstretched to this country unless there has been some sort of brick in its clasp. We have been favored with two distinct types of these bricks — the ordinary barnyard variety of brick, and the gold brick." When an Irish nationalist leader, Sir Roger Casement, was executed by the British for holding secret conferences with the Germans, Hearst assailed Britain and did not allow any war to stop him.

One day in the *American*'s sports department a note arrived asking Runyon to contact Brisbane right away. He called Brisbane at Hearst's headquarters at the Clarendon. As Brisbane spoke to him, he could hear Hearst talking over Brisbane's shoulder. Suddenly, Hearst took the phone. "You are the greatest feature writer in the world, and we need your talents so badly at this moment in your nation's history." Brisbane came back on. The Chief had a request. Could Damon, as the best feature writer in the paper, do a personal favor for the Chief and interview Jeremiah O'Leary? O'Leary, who had a paper organization called the American Truth Society, had just received a telegram from Woodrow Wilson, who in the middle of a presidential campaign called him "a filthy degenerate pig."

He found O'Leary one flight up on East 86th Street in the Yorkville neighborhood. O'Leary was in New York because in trying to blow up a statue of Benedict Arnold upstate, he not only failed to get the job done but antagonized the police and left the small town in anticipation of leg irons. O'Leary had been a close friend of Casement's, and he now favored American withdrawal from the war and some sort of attack on Great Britain. His American Truth Society claimed that Great Britain was responsible for all that was wrong in the world, from torture and the Black Hole of Calcutta to slavery. He wanted the Irish to help the Germans defeat the British. Runyon excused himself. Back at the paper, he sent a memo to Brisbane and Hearst in which he told them that O'Leary's stand was not only impractical but boring to a reader, and therefore Runyon would like to pass. What bothered him was that O'Leary was absolutely legitimate, which made it impossible for the body to spring upward in forming and recognizing a fine phrase. By now, he was so sure of himself that he felt Brisbane and Hearst would understand. He received an answer four days later, in an endless editorial that covered the page and called O'Leary a modern saint. In reading this, he knew his purportedly magnificent shining star at Hearst easily could be at the start of what would be, if it followed the path of so many others, a fast hard fall into a cold earth. He tried to stay calm, reminding himself of his ability to excite readers, but the realist in him said that he was in newspapers, where talent often is meaningless when placed against a difference of opinion with bosses. Which wouldn't be his first encounter with this. The problem, however, was that now there was too much money involved, his family obligations too large. He had a small fear, which lasted only a day or so but left an imprint on him for the rest of his time: yes, he had broken his law — Never bite the hand . . . There is no fear to match loss of career.

Hearst had a man writing editorials for his papers throughout the country, Phillip Francis, who ended the war before it really got going: "The Teutonic powers are winning the war. The genius of Hindenburg has triumphed. That wonderful old man, who now looms up as the greatest of living soldiers, among the greatest of soldiers living or dead, has altered the whole face of the war in eight short weeks. The Allies are beaten."

Runyon was exchanging lies with Jimmy Walker in a private third-floor dining room at Leone's Restaurant on West 48th Street. Runyon had with him a chorus girl named Charlotte Otis, who worked with Vonnie Shelton in the Ziegfeld Follies.

"Does this mean that we gotta study up German?" chorus girl Vonnie Shelton said to her date, Jimmy Walker.

"You might learn English as a base," he said.

"The Chief starts the war with Spain," Runyon said. "He starts the whole thing with Villa. And the whole country loves him for it. Now he decides that he is against a war and they call him a traitor. All he has to do is call for fifty thousand boys to be killed in France and he'll be a national saint. No wonder he's mad at me."

"I don't like no wars," Charlotte Otis said. "They got us up eleven in the mornin' rollin' bandages. I need my sleep."

Hearst became known as "the spokesman of the Kaiser." Theodore Roosevelt called him "the Hun within." Brisbane, his editor, had suggested to thirteen German-American businessmen that he wanted to purchase a paper of his own and would not refuse any assistance. They gave him $375,000, and the harshness of editorials against Britain increased. Then for Hearst, the worst thing of all now happened, which was that the Germans started to lose the war.

Runyon's son, Damon Junior, was born on June 17, 1918, also in the apartment on West 95th Street. That day, Runyon covered the game between the Cincinnati Reds and the Giants. In his notion of a family, father went out and wrote about baseball for the rent and mother did the rest. The Giants won, 2–1, which was the exact score the Yankees won by on the day his daughter was born four years before.

That night, he walked into the poolroom on the corner of Broadway and 95th, took $50 from a roll and bet it on combinations of the numbers 2 and 1. When these combinations did not hit, he went home and looked at the newest arrival and announced, "He owes me money and he's not even walking yet."

The baby was baptized at the Ascension Church. The Reverend Matthew J. Duggan pointed out that all Catholics must carry a saint's name and there was no Saint Damon. The closest was Saint Damian.

Ellen Egan was wildly upset: "Damian of the lepers!"

Runyon said, "I make myself even money against a bum ticker. That typhoid is tough, isn't it? Well, I still make myself two-to-one in that match. I am three-to-one over tuberculosis. I am five-to-one over diphtheria. And I figure I must be, standing right here, a twenty-to-one favorite over leprosy. Any son of my mine won't have trouble with it. On with the show! Mother, will you please hand Saint Damian to his godparents and we shall begin this service." When they left church, they still called him Damon Junior.

Deep in the summer, Hearst asked to see Runyon at the Clarendon.
The sitting room was one quarter of a city street long, and Hearst usually walked in late, sat in silence, crossing legs, inspecting a hand, calling for a butler to spray disinfectant on the telephone, waiting for the
visitor to become intimidated. Not this time. He had arisen to the news
that victory was so near that General Pershing had begun assembling
an army of occupation for Germany. While dressing, Hearst was reminded that not only did Runyon know Pershing, but he also was close
to Eddie Rickenbacker, from Rickenbacker's auto-racing days. So Hearst
walked in with long strides and voice booming. "You can be of immeas-
urable assistance to America!" Since the Germans were losing the war,
Hearst now referred to them as the Hun and was dedicated to their
total destruction. He saw Runyon contributing to America's victory by
writing stories that would cause a prolonged cry for German blood.

Runyon mentioned the World Series. Hearst said, "You name your
replacement. It doesn't matter where he comes from. Bring the man
to me and he will cover the World Series for all our papers."

This eased all of Runyon's anxiety. Of course he would go to France
and write about the doughboys. "Don't forget Pershing," Hearst said.
"Let's enshrine him." Privates were nice, but he needed the general.
Hearst left for an art gallery, where he was going to offer $350,000 for
Van Dyck's portrait of Queen Henrietta Maria. He often didn't understand which was more important, a great news event or the chance to
spend a galleonful of money.

Runyon called Gene Fowler in Denver and told him he had a job.
As he blew the Hearst expense money on going-away parties, Fowler
started for New York on a free ticket given to him by a Denver undertaker who had to ship a body east. The law required two tickets for the
shipment of a corpse, one for the deceased, the other for an escort.
Fowler was to accompany the body of a fine old dead woman from
Denver to her family's undertaker in Gansvoort, New York, outside of
Albany. He lost the dead body when he got off the train in Chicago.
He said he had been arrested for being a spy. Fowler said agents tried
to break him by putting him in jail on Harrison Street, which was named
after William Harrison Dempsey, who had sold newspapers with Fowler in Denver. Fowler said that Charles MacArthur and Ben Hecht,
then on Chicago newspapers, came down to the jail and got him out.
He sent his "Mother is well. Be with you soon" telegram to the dead
woman's family and boarded a Hudson River day liner and sailed into
New York like a Greek immigrant. "The Hudson became a silver slash

across the July-green breast of the storied land," he later wrote. "Three
hundred years of history sailed with me!"

Fowler wore a pince-nez he didn't need and a flowing tie, and used
a walking stick. When he was settled in New York, Runyon took him
to Hearst's assistant, Joseph Willicombe. Runyon told Fowler to ask
for $60 a week. Fowler looked at Hearst's assistant, called him Joe, and
asked for $100 a week. Why, Willicombe said, at such a price, Mr.
Hearst himself would have to interview Fowler. "I shall be available,"
Fowler said.

Runyon was silently furious. Outside, he told Fowler, "Fella, cool
off your soup before you burn your tongue." He told Fowler that he
had started at $40 a week. And, by the way, Fowler shouldn't go around
calling important people such as Willicombe by their first names.

Fowler and Runyon went into the bar of the Knickerbocker Hotel,
which was famous for having both Caruso living upstairs and the most
expensive glass of beer in town. "Barney Oldfield just went for a drive
and he hit a road grader," Fowler said. "His wife has a broken jaw. Do
you know why Barney Oldfield can't drive in traffic? He said he couldn't
think clearly at under a hundred miles an hour."

"What is that supposed to mean?" Runyon said.

"I cannot think clearly on less than a hundred dollars a week."

Fowler stayed at the bar. Fowler's wife Agnes, who had arrived by
train, was living in a $3-a-day hotel room on West 48th Street that had
"the decor of an alms house." When she complained, he told her to go
over to the Astor and see if they had a room. The Astor had the room
but Agnes Fowler didn't have the money. She wound up staying with
Ellen Runyon. Fowler and Runyon did not come home for a couple of
nights. Runyon attended crap games, and Fowler fell in love with his
first chorus girl in New York.

When Fowler went to see Hearst a few days later, he did not tell
Runyon. This was not an act of disloyalty; there would be plenty of
time for both to practice that. Fowler just had more confidence in himself than Runyon did. At the Clarendon, Fowler said to Hearst, "My
favorite story is a landslide that kills many people in a humorous manner." Hearst said that at his castle at San Simeon the mousetraps were
constructed so that they did not kill the mice. They were taken by servants each day to the beach six miles away and let loose. He asked
Fowler if he drank. "Not any more than I ever did," Fowler said. That
took care of the business. No grubby talk of work hours and pay — that
he had the hundred dollars went without saying. The occasion was far

too important. For a newspaperman, New York was the only place in the world to work, and anybody who spent his life elsewhere was a person without a dream. Later he wrote it out: "The building of castles in the air made architects of us all."

Because Fowler wanted to celebrate, he and Runyon took their wives to the Club Alamo, on West 125th Street between Seventh and Eighth avenues, in Harlem. The club had everything Runyon wanted: it was in a basement that was flooded with sin, yet it also attempted to guarantee personal safety. As people came in, the maître d' said firmly, "Ladies, check your coats, please. Gentlemen, check your guns, please. This establishment obeys the Sullivan law." The bartender held out a metal box filled with cracked ice. Patrons were told to plunge their pistols into the ice, where they would remain well hidden.

The act at the Alamo was Durante and Jackson. Jimmy Durante was a small man with hair disappearing quickly. He had perhaps the largest nose in the city and an off-key truck horn for a singing voice. In a bad world he stayed good. His heart was in his voice and his body movements. When he got behind a piano or went on a stage, he was a man who put love and warmth into a room. He was a barber's son from 90 Catherine Street in lower Manhattan, which was a walk across a street, only a few yards, from the back entrance to Hearst's new *Journal* and *American* building. Jimmy started as a singing waiter in Coney Island and, through all the years, was a victim of his own sensitivity. When he liked a horse, he could not bring himself to bet against the animal. If a steerer for a crap game even nodded to him, Durante felt he would be hurting the guy's feelings if he walked by. This led to hundreds of nights of dice playing, when all he had wanted to do was buy the first edition of the morning papers.

Eddie Jackson's act was to wear a high silk hat and cakewalk across the stage. He was a peddler's son from Brooklyn who said he was a graduate of P.S. 55, although the records for this must have been misplaced. He worked in a bookbindery in the Bush Terminal industrial buildings on the Brooklyn waterfront. One of those on the payroll was Alphonse Capone. At his early age he did not like work, and his ardor would diminish even more over the years. Later, when Eddie Jackson was dancing in night joints, paper airplanes made out of hundred dollar bills would come sailing at him out of the smoke and darkness. Then he would hear Al Capone's roar from a front table.

The act at the Alamo began with Jackson sprawled on a chair and pretending to be smoking opium. He used a broom handle with a tin cup at the end as if he were cooking opium. There wasn't a patron in the joint who had to ask what they were pretending to do. When Jackson took small balls of wax and said he was making "toys," everybody laughed. Jackson borrowed a hairpin from a chorus girl, put the wax balls on it and announced, "Yen-hock." All knew this was the way you cooked opium beads. Durante came out in a raccoon coat and a hat pulled down over his forehead. "Take off your hat and coat and stay awhile," Jackson called. Durante pulled off the raccoon coat, and under it was another fur coat. When he took this off, there was another coat. When this one was pulled off, there was still another coat. Durante got that one off and now was in a full dress coat, which he tugged off and showed that he still had on a dinner jacket.

"Did you expect a storm?" Jackson called from a chair.

"I didn't expect it. I brung it with me."

After the show, Durante and his new wife Jeanne, a singer, joined the Runyons. Jeanne complained that while she had offers of work, Jimmy wouldn't let her. Ellen took her side. "Why can't she have a career?" Runyon and Durante grimaced. "I gave up a chance to be a major newspaperwoman to come here with you," Ellen said to Damon. "I don't see where it got me. All I do is sit home and talk to the first person I see on the street. I don't see why Jeanne is supposed to do that, too. She could work right alongside you. I think that's splendid."

"Ellen, you are makin' a homicide out of me," Durante said. "I try to tell Jeanne the truth. You'll have me committin' subterfuses."

Runyon said to Ellen, "A guy can't have his wife working — and in the same joint? Impossible." Jeanne then began to bother Durante about his getting home to Flushing. Durante only misstated his hours to Jeanne. Little lies, he called them. What was he going to tell her, that he could not stay away from a crap game or a broad who drank gin?

"That was the night me and Damon knew we was in trouble," Durante recalled. "We put our wives on a pedasill but it wasn't enough."

Ellen saw few nights out after that.

Runyon was in France by September, and in early November of 1918, writing of the First Army, he noted:

These have been big days for America. They have been big days for all the Allies' arms. So fast did the Germans fall back before Liggett's columns on Saturday, the leathery doughboys finally grew leg weary from pushing over the grassy ground, made slushy by the rain.

One division commander had a happy inspiration. Up came a strong battery of muddy motor trucks, driven by almond-eyed French Cochin Chinamen and devil-may-care American chauffeurs. The tired foot soldiers were loaded in, bag and baggage. They were packed in with rifles and rig and soon found themselves much like the passengers on a Bronx subway express during the rush hour.

The brilliant Pershing once chased Villa 500 miles with his infantry in motor trucks. Gallieni saved Paris by hustling all hands out in taxi-cabs. But probably never before was a whole army pursued by another army under gasoline power. . . .

In the morning, a negro private with an artillery outfit was working one of the American guns which was throwing chunks of metal into the German lines this afternoon beyond Buzaney. He worked with dedication and swift, deadly efficiency. Every time he pulled the lanyard he was heard to say something that was lost in the roar of the gun. A curious chap got over close enough to catch the negro's words, and this is what he was saying with each shot:

"Mistah Kaiser, count youah men!"

Which made Runyon one of only a few reporters to mention blacks as American fighting men in dispatches. Otherwise, papers carried the fact that they simply were in France, just like trucks. Here was a slight chance for greatness, but he allowed it to pass and for most of his life was just another old white from out west, looking at blacks as the successors to the Indians he truly hated.

When the war was over, Hearst threatened to end New York Mayor John F. Hylan's life if he didn't get appointed to the official city delegation welcoming the troops home. Then soldiers on the SS *Patria*, sailing from Marseilles to New York, signed a resolution that said, "We register our unqualified disapproval of the designation of William Randolph Hearst . . . because of the conviction that he has proved himself to be un-American, pro-German and inhumanitarian and therefore totally unfit . . ." They prepared to protest upon disembarking at New York.

"They will castrate me on the pier," Hearst moaned. His man Willicombe sent a dispatch to Runyon, who went to see Pershing. Runyon brought up the troops on the *Patria*. Pershing said, "The commanding officer of the *Patria* is Colonel Patton." No further conversation was needed.

Aboard the troopship, outside New York harbor, Patton assembled his officers. "Whatever your opinion, you ought to be gentlemen enough to appreciate what Hearst is doing for returning soldiers and not criticize him." Patton let that sink in. He said, "Gentlemen, I do not shoot at a printing press."

When the *Patria* sailed into the harbor, here was Hearst on a tender, flapping his arms at the ship and beaming when all those olive-drab arms seemed to wave as one. Hearst was so dumbstruck with ego that he didn't notice that the soldiers were waving excitedly at the crowd along the Brooklyn shorefront. At the dock, he linked arms with Fowler and skipped off the pier to the car like a schoolboy. Runyon was still in Europe, but Hearst went back to the Clarendon and ordered Willicombe to make out a contract giving Runyon $25,000 a year, which made him the highest paid newspaper writer in the nation.

At Christmas of 1918, Ellen Egan Runyon alighted from a cab in front of the Fowlers' apartment house in a black sealskin coat, a dark hat worn low on her head, which was then the style, and a pair of red galoshes, which were unbuckled and rang like little bells. She had trim legs and ankles, and loved to buy shoes from I. Miller, where the Broadway actresses went. She had in the cab all these presents, which in his last letter Runyon had asked her to distribute. "Alfred has the damndest assortment of friends," she said to Agnes. "He wants me to get presents to each and every one, but doesn't let me know until the very last minute, never a hint of what to get for whom. How can I know what to choose for some bum with tin ears? Or for that waiter at Haan's who used to be a lookout man for Canfield? If Alfred should die — God forbid! — I wouldn't know a soul at his funeral. Well, I can't stay for but a minute."

She kissed Agnes on the cheek and entered the apartment, and the moment she did, she sensed the turmoil in the house, which was caused by the ceaseless drinking of Gene. Ellen threw off her coat and galoshes and began to tour the living room, regrouping bric-a-brac, centering a Grecian urn. She wore a dress of dark red, hand-twilled silk and made a swishing sound as she moved, for she always wore silk petticoats. She had on her own mixture of perfume. She had a cut-glass bottle at home into which she kept pouring half of various smaller perfume bottles until she had five or six kinds in her bottle, and this became her "extra special brand." Otherwise, she tried to save a quarter wherever she shopped. Upon finding earmuffs on sale at Sterns, she bought a dozen pair, although her husband said he would not wear earmuffs, even if dead. One set was given to the cartoonist Rube Goldberg.

On this December day, she stayed for several hours. She did not send the cab away. She sat in the Fowler house and replaced the alcoholic's tension with her swirl of activity and gaiety, and reminiscences of their growing up in Denver. But after a while, Ellen began to describe the loneliness of her life with a man who slept until noon, read the papers and had a wife and children who knew enough never to interrupt him. After breakfast, he would retreat to the bedroom and bathroom, dress for the day and leave for a ball game or whatever the city had to offer, which was everything he needed. He would return with the start of the new day. At the Fowlers', Ellen said, thinking of when he would return from France and take up his old schedule, "How can a man spend all that time in the bathroom?" Then her tone changed and was full of Christmas gaiety again and the moment passed, but it was obvious to Agnes Fowler that the marriage was passing, too. One week later, during a visit, she found Ellen going into her clothes closet for a nip.

Runyon came home in March of 1919 on the liner *Leviathan*. All across the sea he pondered the future, which did not include the writing of anything except presidential speeches for Eddie Rickenbacker. Certainly, he was going to make Rickenbacker the President. It would be extraordinarily easy, too. Runyon had the father who went before him dancing in his head, hands clutching wonderful business deals. The first thing he and his partners were going to do was form a corporation that would make millions for everybody, after which they would use some of the proceeds to put Rickenbacker in the White House. In a letter to Fowler written on the ship, Runyon said, "I then can be assigned to some embassy in a warm country. Not too busy a one, either, as I intend to spend the long days writing. I am willing to emerge on local holidays and pat some bare-foot child on the head." The corporation Runyon dreamed about consisted of himself, Rickenbacker, General Pershing and Enrico Caruso. He thought anything with Caruso's name on it would sell anywhere on earth. At this time he was unsure as to whether the product manufactured should be a car with the name Caruso-Rickenbacker-Pershing or war equipment for South American countries.

He was so excited about his plan that he could barely remain at home for an obligatory day with his wife and babies before running down to Broadway to find Caruso. He dropped in at Lindy's to say hello and that he was heading for the Knickerbocker Hotel when he was brought into a sidewalk conference of great importance. Joe Gould, a fight manager and an associate of Owney Madden's, who at this time was still in

Sing Sing for murder, had been commissioned a captain in the army as a purchasing agent and he had taken kickbacks. This offended the patriotism of the prizefight people. A half dozen of them now stood on the sidewalk and formed a jury. Runyon was asked to preside. He pointed at Sam Taub, a fight announcer, and named him jury foreman.

"Mr. Foreman, the verdict, please," Runyon said.

"He never should of done it in time of war," Taub said.

Runyon went to the Knickerbocker to see Caruso, who was with Tommy Francis. Caruso lived in a suite at the hotel, an ornate red stone structure on the southeast corner of Times Square and 42nd Street. For Caruso's major social events, the hotel provided gold plates. Even this was not near the opulence in which Caruso usually lived: a castle made of stone in Italy, which was set in a park with gardens, vineyards, tennis courts and, on the first floor alone, two salons, a chapel, a forty-foot-long drawing room, kitchens, a baggage room and a servants' wing.

"We have to do a business together," Caruso now said.

"That's what brings me here," Runyon said.

"First, I have to take care of myself," Caruso said. He began treating his throat.

Caruso used boiled water and crystals to gargle for five minutes. Then out of a vaporizer came steam made of water, bicarbonate of soda and glycerin, of such strength that it caused Caruso to choke. After many minutes of this, he swabbed his throat with gelatin on long sticks with cotton tips and finished it off with great glassfuls of iced water.

"I must protect my throat," Caruso said, reaching for his pack of cigarettes and lighting the first of what would be half a pack before he was through talking with Runyon. For years afterward, as he lit a cigarette, Runyon would say, "They never hurt Caruso's throat, and that was quite a delicate throat." Caruso now brought up his immediate business. He wanted Runyon to help get a horse named after him. He walked about the living room in his silk robe, waving his cigarette as he dictated to a secretary a letter to the Jockey Club, the group of rich men who controlled all of racing, from the names of the horses to the amounts of purses.

"I hereby agree on this day, March 21, 1919, to have the colt Airnat, by Van Tromp out of Gano Belle, called Enrico Caruso." He asked Runyon, "What you think?"

"They have to do it. You're Caruso."

Even Rickenbacker's presidency was postponed as Runyon spent a couple of days going between Caruso's suite and the Jockey Club offices, and when he delivered papers showing that the horse, owned by a combination of hoodlums, now was officially known as Enrico Caruso, the singer erupted in joy.

Tommy Francis, his cigar smoke turning the room blue, announced that they had found a race for the horse that was so sure that they all should be arrested for taking the money. "The horse cannot lose. Do you hear me? He cannot lose."

Caruso hugged Tommy Francis. "Tommy, you make-a me so happy!"

The race was at Lincoln Downs in Pawtucket, Rhode Island, a trip that was out of the question for the great Caruso, who had rehearsals. At breakfast, he sent Tommy Francis down to the lobby to bet with bookmakers. He continued doing this all morning, as a convention of bookmakers in the hotel lobby begged for Caruso's bets on this extraordinary hot horse. When it was time to leave for rehearsal, Tommy Francis put an arm around Caruso's back, lovingly and also for safety: there was no way for Caruso to reach out and grab some woman's backside. Tommy Francis squired the world's greatest singer through the lobby and off to the rehearsal hall.

From which, at 3:44 P.M., there came a roar usually emitted by an opera singer as a sword goes through him in the final act. Up in the bare rehearsal hall, Tommy Francis was trying to calm the singer. "He got bumped at the start. He would've won from here to the Pacific Ocean."

At Lindy's, Damon Runyon drank coffee with a straight face and with one hand clapped to his side against the greatest pain of all, losing.

The horse Enrico Caruso ran in sixteen races in the next year and a half and finished second on three occasions, third on two others and then, almost at the end of 1920, finally won a cheap race, but by then Caruso wasn't around and neither was anybody else.

Eddie Rickenbacker had tried one political speech, an ode to America written by Runyon, and Rickenbacker was so nervous that he read the speech as if it were a composition in high school. He nearly killed half the audience. When Rickenbacker finished, Runyon's thoughts about controlling the country were scaled down to worrying about his next column, which was, he reminded himself, the only way he could pay the rent.

TWELVE

THE ROARING TWENTIES in New York began with C. Bertall Phillips, who had a paid job as a fund raiser for the New York Anti-Saloon League, standing in an office with this check fluttering in his fingers.

"What's that?" William Anderson said.

"Mr. Rockefeller surprised me," Phillips said. "This check is even larger than I expected."

Anderson, a big, dark-haired man who was in from the Midwest, was the superintendent of the New York Anti-Saloon League. He was purportedly as honest as a row of corn. He also choked when he saw that the check from John D. Rockefeller Sr. was for $75,000. This meant that Phillips, this cheap beggar, this birdbrain little fund raiser, was in for a $10,000 commission!

Anderson brought Phillips into his rear office in suite 672 at 370 Seventh Avenue and took half the commission off him. Phillips swore to himself that he would get even.

On January 22, 1919, the New York State Assembly voted 89–55 to ratify an amendment to the Constitution of the United States that would prohibit drinking. When the bill reached the State Senate, James J. Walker (D., Manhattan) voted to adjourn. William Anderson sat in a front seat in the gallery. He led a committee of thousands of wintry little farmland Protestant ministers, and he had Rockefeller's money in his pocket. Few cared to fight him, and the national amendment passed. "This is a law that is born in hypocrisy and will die the same way," Walker said. He had no help. Runyon at this time still was in France writing about American troops. He was scheduled to come back on the *Leviathan*. Hearst said Prohibition would save the country. There would be a one-year wait, as specified in the law, before whisky became a crime.

By following the money, Prohibition is self-explanatory. North for the money came Bishop James C. Cannon Jr. of the Southern Methodist Church, where salaries of bishops were $1,500, with up to $1,200 additional to pay for clerical help, office expenses and all traveling expenses while on church duty. We tell you of Bishop Cannon because he figures prominently in the era that made Runyon and Broadway so famous. In the South, the bishop's salary could be easily augmented by the duping of large congregations of people. Decent Southern Methodists and Southern Baptists, in the name of Christ, sat like ivy plants as their ministers told them that they couldn't drink, smoke, play cards, go to the theater and watch Sunday ball games, and that they had to forward all loose money to them. Bishop James Cannon announced that Madame Curie was a slut. "She belongs from now on in the same class with Byron and George Eliot and George Sand." Most of his parishioners didn't know what the word "radium" was about. Cannon also was president of the Female Institute of Blackstone, a school in a tobacco town in Nottoway County, Virginia. The school motto was, "Thorough instruction under positive Christian influences at lowest possible cost." To this, Cannon added a motto of his own: "No young ladies are wanted as students at the institute who are not willing to accept the guidance of principal as that of an older friend, who is planning to give them such training as will develop them into helpful and attractive women." He also said, "Dancing is a temptation to the flesh! The tango and turkey trot are shameless and shamelessly suggestive!" It was noted by some that when the bishop greeted a woman under sixty, he turned it into Greco-Roman wrestling.

During a wartime shortage, he swung 625 barrels of flour from the school into the black market. When questioned, he roared. "I wouldn't do this because I am an American." Everybody agreed and nobody worried that the Bishop's records had gone up in a fire. His Virginia tax returns showed an income of $1,800 and $3,000 in exemptions. He said that proved he was honest. He grew a beard because he said he couldn't spare ten minutes a day for shaving. He took young Blackstone women with him on trips as secretaries, in order to work as he rode. One young woman said that he made her ride to Roanoke and then miss the last train back to school. He threw her to the floor in an empty house for which he had keys. When she complained, the county prosecutor said she was a dirty filthy hussy and that he was going to arrest her for a high crime. Bishop-tempting!

Cannon announced that the Devil, with his world capital in New York, was on a mission to destroy him personally. He asked for prayers and remuneration to fight the Devil. When he was asked to fill in at a Prohibition rally at Indianapolis, he said, "Renumeration." He was informed, "Oh, we have no financial trouble these days. John D. Rockefeller believes firmly that if we had Prohibition, employees would work harder."

Cannon went to Indianapolis and told the crowd that an inebriated man on a railroad train tried to slash his throat with a knife. He sent clippings of everything he did to the Rockefellers in New York. He became Prohibition's fiercest southern advocate and superintendent of the Virginia Anti-Saloon League. He then went to New York to visit the Rockefellers, after which he went down to Anderson's offices on Seventh Avenue and said that Rockefeller had ordered him to move in. Anderson wanted to argue, but had the terrifying vision of the entire Rockefeller family going insane at the sight of people fighting about their cash, and throwing them all out of the office with nothing.

"How can we work with you?" Anderson said reluctantly.

"Show me how to withdraw money out of the bank," Cannon said.

He stayed at the McAlpin Hotel, which was a block from Penn Station and also was quite crowded on many afternoons with responsible, very high class women emerging from shopping directly across the street at either Macy's or Gimbel's. When he looked over the lobby, filled with women, young ones, too, the bishop went mad.

We now go to the affliction that for so many years was kept in the alleyways. The city's drug panic of 1919 started in another place, this time with an epidemic of influenza. In November of 1918, there were 130,606 cases and 10,972 influenza deaths, and 11,730 cases of pneumonia and 10,288 deaths. When influenza tore at the city, the commissioner of health was Dr. Royal Copeland, who had snared the job by walking into Mayor Hylan's office and saying, "I know how to keep you alive longer than anybody in the city."

"God sent you to me!" Hylan said. He appointed Copeland right there. The day after he got the job, Copeland contracted to write a column for the Hearst afternoon paper, the *Journal*. He invited any obese women to a clinic on the roof of the Health Department building. There, with cameramen crouching for great shooting angles, a thousand fat ladies did knee bends. The photos ran all over the world and made Copeland famous. Soon, he visited his first Democratic clubhouse and spoke for an hour.

At the height of the influenza epidemic, Louis Harris, a doctor who was chief of the city's Bureau of Preventable Diseases, went around New York and found that groups of doctors and nurses were shoving one another to enter houses where the sick inside had cash money. People without money were putting bodies out on the stoop as if they were leaving empty milk bottles. Harris announced, "The socialization of the medical and nursing professions to place them under government control should no longer be deferred."

Mayor Hylan was given a sheet of paper to read that said, "Nowhere does it say that a doctor has to starve."

Copeland said, "This epidemic can only be stopped by the public volunteers in the hospitals."

"When he went to medical school, he failed stethoscope," Esdail (Doc) Cohen of the *New York World* said.

November, a month of dangerous breath, finally ended, and influenza, and the far more sinister threat of socialized medicine, waned. Only a little more than four months later, on April 8, 1919, the first federal drug agents in the nation raided six physicians and four druggists who were prescribing opium, cocaine and heroin to people purportedly in need of hop as medicine. That weekend in New York, some two thousand addicts walked into Bellevue Hospital on First Avenue and begged for help. By Monday, the hospital opened a drug treatment center, alarming doctors, who saw it as another attempt to establish socialized medicine. If you have a center for drugs, they said, then you could have a center for gall bladders, and then sprains — and then you have socialized medicine. "These people don't need their own place. They don't have tuberculosis," one doctor complained.

When older doctors decided that Harris intended to use the emergency to put over socialized medicine, they stood up and fought like the gentlemen they were. Harris said that drug taking was a disease and he wanted to establish treatment centers. Immediately, the Committee for Responsible Medicine put out a statement: "Those apparently responsible people who call drugs an illness could be secret addicts."

At Bellevue on that weekend in April, the two thousand addicts were treated with three grains of opium a day for the first three days and then, to start withdrawal, a capsule consisting of rhubarb, ipecac, strychnine, atropine and two grains of calomel, along with three one-grain doses of opium or cocaine. On the fifth day of the treatment, drugs were cut down, and this continued until the patient was on 1/200 grain, with 1/250 grain prescribed for women.

Arnold Rothstein, the Broadway gangster who always heard the first moan of human weakness and rapidly calculated how he could earn money on it, sat on a bench in the waiting room at Bellevue and ate an apple and observed the derelicts writhing in the hallway outside the emergency room. Runyon had walked down from Lindy's with him.

"How long does it take these people to get over it?" Rothstein wondered.

"In China, they can wait a thousand years for anything," Runyon said. "They kill a hophead right away."

"Nobody here wants to be treated," Rothstein decided. "They just want some drugs."

"Anyway, this is no business of mine," Runyon said.

"You're not putting it in the paper?" Rothstein said.

"They don't want to hear anything about drugs. They say it's too small and lousy for them."

As there was no place for drug addicts to go after they were detoxified, the state planned to open a long-term treatment center at Mount Lebanon Shaker Village in upstate New York. Which only made doctors more uneasy. "These people should get treatment all right," a Bellevue doctor announced. "They should get treated to jail."

Dr. Royal Copeland, the New York City health commissioner, reported, "Over 95 percent of all drug addicts have shown, by their acts, a non-appreciation of the service, and have repeatedly attempted to be discharged before the end of their treatment. It is, therefore, recommended that the Department of Health discontinue any sort of drug treatment program."

Arnold Rothstein sat through the Broadway nights without alcohol, coffee or food; only an apple. When he found out that the drugs were merely a political worry for medical authorities, he decided whatever he did with drugs would not be so morally intolerable. Rothstein decided to provide an orderly distribution of drugs by a professional criminal, himself. He told Frank Costello, "There can't be so much wrong with them. Nobody cares."

"What could they be mad at?" Costello said.

"The only trouble I can see is if somebody sold hop to the Negroes."

"They would go crazy," Costello said.

"We can only sell to the whites," Rothstein said.

Rothstein was the nation's first major underworld distributor of drugs. The first federal drug agent in New York, Max Roder, always said the biggest name he had on his list as a dealer was Arnold Rothstein. "Every time you mentioned his name in the office, five people on his payroll went to the phone to call him up."

The Roaring Twenties, brought on by Prohibition, and the Golden Age of Sport that was supposed to go with it, actually started in July of 1919, in Toledo, Ohio, where people were so impatient to end sin that they installed temperance ahead of time and at the exact moment of the heavyweight championship fight between Jack Dempsey and Jess Willard. "We're going to need plenty of champagne the second the fight ends," Kearns told the manager of the Hotel Secor. "You can call it medicine and be telling the whole truth." And out at the Dempsey training camp, a busted-down place called Point Place, on Lake Maumee, Kearns watched as trainer Jimmy DeForest set up the outdoor ring and two workmen unloaded cases of whisky and beer from a truck. Kearns considered both jobs of equal importance at this moment. There was no use in staging a fight if you didn't have sportswriters drunk for a week before it.

One of the first announcements made by Tex Rickard, promoter of the fight, was that both Dempsey and Willard would appear in the ring bare-handed. Willard himself had been demanding this. For some reason, he didn't trust Dempsey's corner, particularly when it came to taping Dempsey's hands. All wrapping of the hands with tape and gauze would be done in public, as would the donning of gloves. "This keeps the people who buy tickets happy," Rickard said. "All I care about is that we all get the same honest chance," Kearns said. "If taking the time in the ring to bandage your hands in public helps promote honest chances, me and Dempsey are all for it." Willard said he would insist on only a thin layer of cotton bandage, and with just enough tape to keep it in place.

Kearns then spent much time fussing over the schedule of Anthony Drexel Biddle, the Philadelphia millionaire, who was to be a judge at the fight. Biddle, a Marine major, had asked if he could stage a bayonet drill in the ring before the fight in order to promote the Marine Corps.

"He wants to do it for the country. So we have to let him," Kearns said. He got his way.

Later that day, Kearns acted as if the important business of the fight, the agreement to tape hands in the ring, in front of the crowd, had never been mentioned. Kearns said, "The fight don't go one round. I just hope he don't kill Willard." Kearns said this in the presence of Al Capone and a crowd of hoodlums who idolized Dempsey and hung around the training camp at Point Place. One such person from Brooklyn, Frankie (Yale) Uale, was disappointed to hear Kearns speak like this. He wanted to see a man die in the ring.

Runyon decided that Kearns and these gorillas had something on the game. "All I can tell you is that I am betting $10,000 that Jack knocks him out in a round," Kearns told him. Runyon started betting with both hands on a first-round knockout. In these times, all newspaper people bet openly on things they were covering. In Toledo, Ring Lardner wrote that he was betting $500, just about a fortune, on Willard to destroy the smaller Dempsey. Because these newspaper people bet money and established a conflict of interest, and had personal venom and exhilaration through each second of the contest they covered, stories were horribly biased and always a thrill to read.

Promoter Rickard then announced that he had established a special ladies' section for the fight, so that women could be encouraged to witness the most exciting sight of men crushing each other's brains while at the same time be protected from the improper language of excited male spectators. Rickard was so worried about ladies being embarrassed that he was considered prissy, a reputation that helped him greatly later on, when he was acquitted in New York of the charge of molesting small girls.

Smack in the middle of a heavyweight championship fight week, with a gangster at your elbow, with all lips full of lies, with women squealing, with all drinks even more delightful because they were the first illegal alcohol served in the nation, here in the center of all this excitement was E. Phocian Howard. His enthusiasm for discussing literary effort with Runyon, however, at first became subordinate while E. Phocian handled such petty trifles as tending to his rent payment. He had taken a suite in New York at the Plaza Hotel, where he resided with his mother. As a bill payer at this time, he was writing a column of hot tips on agriculture stocks for his paper, the *New York Press*. The publication had enough horse race news to satisfy Kentucky, but Phoce knew the moment recommended that his special inside column on ag-

riculture betting — by "Argus" — have some Midwest thump to it.
He also had to get the thing done in record time, as he wanted to lead
the revelry.

"Be a dear fellow," Phoce said, holding out some farm charts to Runyon. "Do three great paragraphs on wheat for me. Just say wheat is as
hot as a smoking gun. Your stuff will directly follow two big paragraphs
on corn being dead as a whore."

Runyon went to his room and wrote:

> "Never sneer lightly at wheat," is the creed of all students of sea-
> sonal market moves. Do not pay too much attention to these loud-
> mouths who insist that the price of wheat depends upon the inexora-
> ble law of supply and demand with which the government cannot
> interfere. The calendar players have just thrown out their calendars
> and are buying wheat months ahead of those late Fall months when
> the boobs and suckers come around to buy on schedule. The money
> cry for this week is: Get onto wheat! Go for the whole chunk on wheat!
> With corn going under for the third time, the smart boys in Flanders
> and Company, 24 Wall, are sending people sprinting to the bank!

"Oh, this is marvelous. Everything will be all right," Phoce Howard
said. He handed it to a Western Union operator and reached for a glass.
He now could return to his foremost thrill, managing a literary contender.

Two nights before the Dempsey–Willard fight, at the start of the
evening activities, featured by a full gaming room with roulette, craps
and blackjack, Phoce thought that Runyon spent too much time with
Ring Lardner. All of it strained, as Lardner and Runyon were in about
the same situation as Dempsey and Willard. Phoce took Runyon aside.
"I put you at even weight with O. Henry. Forget this man Lardner.
All he does it cater to rich fools. You have the characters that will last
forever."

When Runyon became so inspired that he said he was going right up
to his room and stay there writing, Phoce became nervous. "You can't
do it just like that. Kearns is on the way over here," he said. "You have
to stay close to the boys here and find out what they're doing with the
fight. We have money put up on this thing."

Which was all Runyon had to hear. He would let anybody distract
him from creative writing. Newspaper writing was defensive, reacting
to something live in front of you, and with a score sheet or a police
report or a court transcript to further verify it. Deliver it in writing in

order to pay the rent. A grocer with a typewriter. The writing was done in a certain amount of words and time. Always time, and that time being today. As a newspaper columnist, he could choose any event or conversation and do what he wanted with the subject. On his terms, it was one of the fairest of jobs the land could provide. It required no heavy lifting and was marvelous for the ego. Fiction writing, however, was aggressive. You must reach out and clutch the dust in the air and turn it into a solid form, a detailed picture of something that never really occurred, a conversation you might have heard in another form, but one that must be changed in order to fit the story you tell now. There is no scheduled event to describe. The idea for each sentence must start with the writer. Even the names and addresses must come from a thought. Most writers never summon the discipline to sit down and simply start on their own. Those who do get the discipline spend many years trying for it. The ones who sit in fanatical hope of being disturbed never make it. Those with a chance reach a point in concentration where even the suggestion of having dinner with somebody in two weeks is bitterly resented as an intrusion. And when Phoce Howard just suggested that Runyon stay around the fight boys rather than go upstairs and type alone, Runyon couldn't wait to say yes. It still was several years before he got the spirit to sit by himself, with no notes and no scorecard, and make up stories again.

Two days before the fight, Kearns locked up the Dempsey camp and announced that no visitors were allowed. Then he received a call concerning S. M. Vanclain, president of the Baldwin locomotive works, who had arrived in Toledo with a large, jovial crowd and wanted to see Dempsey in person. Kearns at first was adamantly against this, but changed his mind when Vanclain's secretary got on the phone and mentioned money. The invitation was issued, and at the camp Kearns enthusiastically greeted Vanclain and his party and led them into a room where Dempsey was lounging. Kearns took Vanclain's secretary off to the side and concluded business. Immediately, Dempsey jumped up and walked out. He was nervous and suspicious of strangers before a fight.

"Thank you, gentlemen," Kearns told the locomotive people. He showed them to the door. He had their money in his pocket — over the years he would say it was anything from $1,000 to $10,000 — and there it would remain. Dempsey was guaranteed only $27,000 for the fight, but Kearns felt that Dempsey shouldn't share in any larceny he wasn't smart enough to dream up on his own.

The fight was scheduled for 3:30 P.M. on the Fourth of July. The temperature that morning was anything you said it was. The blazing midwestern sun had the land broiling by noon. Kearns arrived at Dempsey's dressing room with two witnesses from the Ohio Boxing Commission. Both witnesses were supposed to oversee the hand bandages and gloves used by Dempsey. They were good Toledo Republicans, Bill Jackson was mayor. The moment they walked in, Kearns introduced them to a big young gorilla named Al Brown.

"Could I see you fellas for a minute?" Brown said. He took them into the shower room and handed them money. Later, when Kearns was asked if the two inspectors knew that Brown was Capone, in from Brooklyn, he said, "Why, certainly. They were politicians. They weren't going to take money off a complete stranger."

Promoter Rickard now came to the dressing room and said, "You're going to have to tape your hands in the dressing rooms. Biddle got a squad out there in boots, and they're rippin' up the canvas so bad we're goin' to have to put a new one down. Then we're goin' to have to put on the show right away on account of people are faintin' in this heat."

Kearns said that this was fine with him. When Willard heard this he started to complain, but here was Kearns in his dressing room already, to observe the bandaging of Willard's hands. After that, he returned to Dempsey's dressing room with Willard's chief second, Walter Moynahan, who would witness the taping of Dempsey's hands. Or try to. The moment Moynahan walked in, he tried to push past one of Capone's young gorillas so he could see what was going on. "If you touch me, I'll kill you," the gangster said. Moynahan stayed in the back of the crowd of gunmen and tried to see over their shoulders. He could not. At first, Kearns flamboyantly waved the roll of gauze around as he spun a couple of layers onto Dempsey's tanned hands. Then Kearns crouched and kept his back to everybody. It is here that a historical argument takes place. Manager Kearns, writing for money many years later, stated that he had plaster of Paris in a talcum powder can and that he sprinkled Dempsey's tape with it, then soaked the bandages, all the while claiming he wanted his man's hands cool in the fierce heat. It was 101 degrees under an umbrella. As Kearns told the story, he was a genius. But E. Phocian Howard recalled that, as with nearly all larceny, it was done crudely. Moynahan was afraid to push the gangsters, and some remember Kearns using something metallic looking, heavy tinfoil, which when wrapped around a hand and put in a glove can be halfway to a pile driver. Most everybody else, including Phoce Howard, insisted that a couple of pieces of lead pipe, cut to fit, were included in the bandaging around Dempsey's hands. As proof, Phoce noted that as the metal was in the palms and therefore put great and dangerous pressure from behind on Dempsey's knuckles, only highly irresponsible people, who didn't care if Dempsey broke both his hands, would do such a thing. Among people that uncaring would be gangsters betting on a one-round knockout. Phoce certainly was, and so was Runyon. As this was boxing, there was no such thing as honesty, and therefore no invisible line to observe.

Dempsey was sent out to the ring with a couple of lead pipes, or thereabouts, inside his gloves. At 245, Willard was 58 pounds heavier, which meant nothing when Dempsey, 187, hit Willard with a left hook and a short right hand. The right hand broke Willard's cheekbone and put him on his back. Dempsey stood right over him. He had no belief in neutral corners. When you are cheating before the fight even starts, why become fair while it is actually going on? When Willard started to get up, the entire left side of his face sagging horribly from the broken cheekbone, Dempsey punched and Willard went back down. His right eye bulged. He took a six count. He was down seven times in that first round. On the last knockdown, in the final moments of the round, Willard was still on the floor at the count of seven. There was no way that Willard was not going to get up. Kearns climbed the ring steps and began howling in victory. At ringside, gangsters in their undershirts were pounding each other. Willard was on the floor covered with blood when the count reached nine and the referee waved his hands, apparently to indicate the fight was over. Kearns jumped into the ring and held up Dempsey's hand. At ringside, Runyon threw his straw hat into the air because he thought he had won all his bets, and also because he liked Dempsey. But the referee now rushed around the ring, restoring order and announcing that the bell had rung at the count of nine. The fight was to go on. Runyon slapped his hat back on his head so hard that the straw brim broke. He despised the referee; no wise guy can handle defeat by a dumb sucker's honesty.

"The referee ought to be beat to death," Capone said at ringside.

In the next round, Dempsey threw a right hand into Willard's side and the ribs caved in. Nobody had ever seen damage like that done before by a prizefighter, and for good reason. Until Kearns came around, no prizefighter ever had gone into the ring with his hands full of water pipes.

Runyon wrote about Willard's corner, where "a dark spot which was

slowly widening on the brown canvas . . . was replaced by the drip-
drip-drip-drip of blood from the man's wounds."

Many hours after the fight, at the party in a suite of the Hotel Secor,
Kearns handed Runyon coffee and poured champagne for a broad and
a guy with her. Kearns knew neither of them. The windows were open
but only heated air came in from the terrible Ohio summer. People
were sopping wet and standing so close together they could not fan
themselves, but none left. Not while Dempsey, fierce, dark-haired, so
young, was against the wall. The legend was formed forever right in a
steaming room. Kearns, however, was vitally interested in the couple
next to him. The younger woman was beautiful, but the hell with that,
there are a lot of beautiful broads. The guy was ugly and old, but with
plenty of money. He got some nerve thinking he can be at a private
party for a new heavyweight champion of the world and not show us
his money, Kearns thought.

Kearns called for the services of the nearest thief, who in this instance was Swifty Morgan. He was a man whose hand slowed only when
it was on his own money. He sold ties and swag jewelry, and if that
didn't work for him he went to cards or dice. He was short, rotund,
with a goatee and an insulting manner that caused suckers to love him.

"What are you bothering me for?" Swifty said in his rasping voice.

"I want you to meet my dear friend," Kearns said, arm around the
sucker's shoulder.

"What do I want to meet this bum for?" Swifty said.

The man wanted so much for Swifty Morgan to like him, for Swifty
was a true big shot. Why, he had been absolutely irritated when Kearns
had disturbed him.

Swifty put a hand in his pocket and brought something out inside his
fist. "Here," he said to the guy. "Let me see if you got any class." He
put a gold necklace into the guy's hand. "Go ahead, show me what
you're made out of. I can't show you a selection because this is the last
thing I got."

The man smiled thinly. "Well, how much are they?"

"If you got to ask, you're not ready to hang around with us. The girl
here ought to take a walk. You ain't got the taste of a goldfish." He put
the necklace back in his pocket and complained to Kearns, "Why do
you make me stop what I'm doing and come over here for nothing?"

Kearns apologized so profusely that the businessman, terrified that
he might be asked to leave the party, took out his billfold.

"Seven hundred and fifty," Swifty said.

"That's not much."

As the man paid, Swifty was delighted to notice that there was more where that came from. He handed him the necklace.

"Here, darling, I want this to be yours," the businessman said.

The girl took the necklace as quickly as if she were saving it from a fire.

"I like you," Kearns told the guy. "You got some class. Dempsey thinks you're a helluva guy, too."

"Does he?"

"You couldn't see that when you met him?"

The girl went into the bedroom and looked in the mirror at herself wearing her new necklace. She truly liked what she saw.

Swifty watched from the doorway. "You know this guy?"

"He is a dear old friend of mine," the girl said.

"For how long?" Swifty asked.

"Since Monday."

"First of all, keep the necklace out of your dresser, because when it turns green, it'll louse up all your clothes." He looked at the earrings she was wearing. "Just give me them." When she hesitated, he said, "Stop worrying. You're in on the play."

He walked up to the sucker. "You're in love with this girl, right? How could you not be?"

"Yes."

"Well, she ain't even got earrings to go with the necklace." Swifty turned and waved to Dempsey. "Jack, this bum don't want to buy the girl a present."

Dempsey shook a big fist at the guy. "Pardner, we always come around to the aid of any lady who gets mistreated."

The guy was so thrilled he nearly collapsed. Dempsey spoke to him!

"Here!" Swifty said. He shoved the earrings into the guy's hand. "Before you ask, just give me five hundred."

The guy lovingly handed the girl the earrings. Later, Kearns held out some money to Runyon. "Here's your piece." Runyon refused the cash. Kearns said, "Come on. You just went broke on the fight." Runyon said, "I am a Communist. If I help somebody make some money, then I'll take what's rightfully mine. If I didn't earn it, I don't want it. That score is yours and Swifty's."

Hearing this, the young woman, returning as if something had been forgotten, which it had, said, "Where's mine?"

Runyon was enthralled. Kearns had just clapped both hands onto the heavyweight championship and yet he could take the time to rob a sucker. A true thief, Runyon thought. He will take anything, from newsstand change to a bank vault. On the train back to New York, in a club car filled with excited talk about Dempsey's power — they made him either a leopard or a bear — he and Phoce Howard discussed Kearns. Phoce extolled bravery and larceny equally, and influenced Runyon to such a point that Runyon cared only if a person was entertaining for him as a writer, and thus for readers. What the subject did was of no concern. The cops and robbers started out almost equal in Runyon's estimate, but as the cops proved to be not as entertaining, they were dropped in favor of the gangsters. Runyon knew that Phoce Howard was right. Dempsey was a terrific fellow, loyal to the bones to Runyon. But Dempsey was in the business of going to bed early. Who needs that? "Kearns is the greatest!" he announced on the train.

THIRTEEN

O N THE freezing night of January 16, 1920, with Prohibition to start at midnight in New York, there were 10,343 licensed premises in the city. About a month later, there were more than 15,000 speakeasies, and the number rose every day. The theater in the twenties used the term "on Broadway," but this also had a separate meaning. Runyon's Broadway was the Big Street, the Great White Way, and it consisted of a couple of hundred saloons in cellars of old buildings which had a pool of about five thousand customers and were mostly populated by marauding press agents, who had to make the time and place famous in order to eat, and gangsters who needed a place to sit at night, as their own homes usually were hovels and decent people refused to have them in. Vincent Coll, who was called Mad Dog and had gangsters terrified, slept on the couch in his mother's apartment on Brook Avenue in the Bronx. A table in a nightclub, even if the club was an airless cellar, amounted to grandeur. The gangsters who enjoyed these clubs once in a while did what they were supposed to do, which is shoot each other.

"It was the time when the country took a last vacation from fear," Gene Fowler said wistfully. When only four and a half blocks from the big lighted street, longshoreman Gus Barrett worked two hours and then was told to go home. This was the third time in a week that this had happened. As he figured out that he wouldn't bring home $10 for the week, he exploded. The other workers, who were making $12 to $15 for a fifty-hour week, were silent out of fear of being sent home themselves. Prohibition, then, was a time when hundreds danced wildly while tens of thousands stared at the floor and tried to find a slice of bread.

The first expression used to describe the 1920s was Runyon's "Roaring Forties," and it had to do with the streets from 42nd to 49th running off Broadway. In 1922, F. Scott Fitzgerald called it the Jazz Age. He based this on the absolutely marvelous atmosphere lived in by 325 Princeton graduates following World War I. The nightclubs were fabulous and the conversation was exhilarating and the money inconsequential to the rich patrons. It was not until 1939 that somebody in need of a title looked back and said expansively that, why, it had been the Roaring Twenties. By this time, however, lives were being lived in another time, described by one word, Depression, and lies about another period were accepted gladly, as they were amusing, far better than no lies at all.

What actually happened in the twenties in New York was best told in official writing done in the rolling penmanship once called the Palmer method. This is from the police blotter of the 103rd Precinct, on 168th Street, Jamaica, Queens.

Saturday, July 24, 1925
    10:05 a.m.   Lt. Delaney relieved from desk duty.
    10:05 a.m.   Sgt. Dannheuser on desk duty.
    10:35 a.m.   Complaint against Ptl.
    Arthur Hadley, 50 Willett St. present complains that while his wife Margaret was waiting for an auto, soon after 8 a.m. at Rocky Hill Road and Hillside ave., on July 5, patrolman on duty at that time in the booth at that location put his arm around her waist and said, "What I could do to you in the dark." Hadley was told that his wife would be told when to report to the office of the 8th Div.

Saturday, August 1, 1925
    5:30   Lt. Downs relieved from desk duty.
    5:30   Lt. Dannhauser on desk duty.
    6:00 a.m.   Open door
    Ptl McAllister reports that at 4:30 a.m. he found front door of automobile sales room unlocked at 129–29 Hillside Avenue. Notified owner, Edward Fausner, who searched premises with the officer and locked the premises.

When Prohibition began, Tutie Somese, age ten, started the day by shaking the ashes out of the furnace of his father's saloon on 86th Street in the Ozone Park neighborhood of Queens County, New York City. After he filled a bucket with the hot white ashes, he carried them outside and spread them over the path alongside the saloon. Inside, his

father was serving as usual the cops and firemen who were getting off
the night shift and the daily half-dozen others who took a drink during
daylight hours. Tutie got his books and walked to P.S. 58. When he
came back at noon for lunch, Patrolman Harry Young, 102nd Precinct,
came in, in uniform and on duty, and had a couple of beers. People
from the Lawrence and Grosjean factory, which made kitchen utensils,
stopped for beer and free lunch. Tutie's father told him to make sure
he came straight home after school. When Tutie arrived home, he found
his uncle at the silver meat grinder clamped to the table, usually used
for turning out chopped meat, now grinding malt leaves into powder.
His father and mother were wrestling with huge jugs at the kitchen
door.

On the stove, filled to the brim, steam rising as the liquid started to
bubble, were new pots from Lawrence and Grosjean, huge pots for
industrial cooking, pots you could fit a horse in, or cook macaroni for a
neighborhood. In the pots were malt, water and yeast, Tutie recalled.
Tutie's mother stretched a cheesecloth and the father tipped each huge
pot until the liquid ran through the cloth and into the large jugs. His
father poured the hot liquid back into another pot and boiled that with
ground hops. "It looked like nuts," Tutie said. By five o'clock that night,
they were pouring the liquid back into the big jugs. Officer Harry Young
helped them carry the jugs to a shed behind the house. They were left
there for five days. After which, he remembers, they put sugar into
the mixture and sat there jamming corks into the bottles. The biggest
problem with making the beer was that in the first weeks they never
had enough corks. But once his father was able to get that fixed, things
ran smoothly. There always was a pot on the stove, cooking beer instead of macaroni, and out in the back, a line of bottles and boxes of
corks that fit the bottles in the shed.

"The hell with bottling it. From now on, we put it in kegs," Tutie's
father said. The bar never closed one day, from the start of Prohibition
to the end, and the people in Ozone Park patronized the place as if
nothing had ever happened. Which, in Ozone Park, it sure did not.

When Prohibition was supposed to be a worldwide movement, John
(Red) Dorrian and John Mulcahy were among those disembarking in
New York from a steamship from Liverpool. Nobody had told them
that you couldn't drink in New York. This was for the simple reason
that you *could* drink in New York, with no impediment other than the
inability to swallow any more. Both arrived in the aftermath of an explosion in Belfast, caused by a bomb placed underneath the main street,

the Royal Avenue. They recited the act of contrition after placing the bomb, which caused a police officer, standing on a manhole cover, to rise into the sky like a statue on a pedestal. When they reached New York, Mulcahy went to Brooklyn, and Red over to the East Side of Manhattan.

In Brooklyn, Mulcahy moved in with cousins at 378 Seventh Avenue, between 11th and 12th streets, a four-story building with a pub in the ground-floor storefront, which, the moment Mulcahy saw it, he swore to stay out of until he had his life properly straightened in this new country. On his first full night in Brooklyn, he sat upstairs and listened to the radio of the man in the next apartment, who left the door open for others to listen. At 9:45 P.M. on station WLWL there came "The Hour of Irish Songs and Music," with Nell O'Brien, soprano; Bryan Kilpatrick, tenor; and the Emerald Instrumental Trio; all accompanied by static. Midway through the show, when Kilpatrick was singing "Come Back, Paddy Reilly," Mulcahy was in tears of gratitude and warmth. "You don't have anything to miss if you bring your native land over here with you," he exulted. He was so happy that he nearly went downstairs for a wee drink.

The next night, the radio was on again. At 5 P.M. there was "The Hofbrau Orchestra" and then at 6, "Dinner Music." Mulcahy had never heard one of the tunes. At 7 P.M. Warren Scofield, baritone, sang for fifteen of the longest minutes Mulcahy had ever experienced. As he listened, he sat and looked out at the scar in the plaster and at the bare bulb in the hallway and at the leading edge of the neighbor's open door. And Warren Scofield, baritone, droned on. At 7:15 there was a "Columbia University Lecture," this one by Harold Jacoby, on astrology. "Mother of God, I didn't have to come this far to hear about the Big Dipper," Mulcahy called out to the guy who owned the radio. "Can't you be a good fellow and change the damned thing?"

The man called out, "Why, certainly." He then switched to station WJZ. It was carrying a live report on the Erie Canal Centennial Dinner at Buffalo.

The next day, on his way home from looking for a job, Mulcahy read the radio listings in his paper, the *American*. These included: Male Quartet; Dinner Recital; Marvion Huse, speaker; Grace Stevenson, harpist; Time Signals; "Timely Topics" by Reverend James M. Gillis, O.S.F.; Clyde Monroe, Inspirational Message; "Mushing to the Yukon" by Frederick H. Chase; Weather Forecasts; Advanced German Lesson by W. J. Harrison-Berlitz; Christian Science Lecture; News.

He looked forward to that, and asked the man next door to put it on. Station WOR at 7:25 P.M. Here now came the news. It was about a traffic accident on Market Street in Newark. Then there was a report from the Essex County sanitation commissioner. "Where the hell is that? I thought this was Kings County," Mulcahy said to the man.

"Newark. This is a Jersey station," the guy yelled.

When he had the last of his money on the bar, and had that first big cold beer in his hand downstairs, Mulcahy, by way of making conversation, noticing the window had no sign on it, asked the proprietor, "Why don't you put a sign in the window?"

"What's the matter with you? This is Prohibition," said the proprietor, Willie Sutton, who in off hours from the saloon was a robber.

"What's Prohibition?" Mulcahy said.

"There's a law against drinking."

"Well, I'm doing all right now," Mulcahy said.

"Yeah, but that's why we call this a speakeasy," Sutton said.

"What does that mean?"

"That you can't be yelling. It tips off the police."

"The police come in to stop a man from drinking?"

"Never. But it's a little exciting to call the place a speakeasy."

The place never closed through all Prohibition.

Over in Manhattan, Red Dorrian had with him a note of introduction to John Kaiser, a detective first grade in the 17th Precinct on Manhattan's midtown East Side. Kaiser had family on the Crumlin Road in Belfast. A first grade detective in the 17th Precinct, the diamond tray of law enforcement, was a better job than President of the United States. There was no Congress to dare check on what the detective was doing. Red Dorrian climbed the flight of stairs, with pale green walls and the municipal smell of a precinct, and stopped at the wooden gate leading into the detective's office. When he asked for Kaiser, a big guy with a crew cut yelled, "Will you listen to this just off the boat?" Kaiser read the note and asked Dorrian what he was going to do here in New York.

"Open a pub," Red said.

"Didn't you ever hear of Prohibition?" Kaiser said.

"What's that?" Dorrian said.

"That means you can't sell alcohol."

"Do they give it away here?"

"No. They sell it in a place with no sign on the outside."

"I won't have a sign," Dorrian said.

"Good. Tell me where it is."

Dorrian gave him an address, 235 East 48th Street, the basement of a brownstone a cousin had rented for him.

"When you open the place, put a little sign on the outside bell saying, 'The Pope Has Blessed This Place.' Nobody will bother you. I am the pope around here."

Dorrian went to his place on 48th Street and immediately began to make whisky. He got out some barrels, with alcohol, charcoal, distilled water and glycerin. He forgot to cover the barrels, which allowed the fumes to overcome anyone walking in. The second time, he covered the barrels with potato sacks. He bought his beer from a gangster named Levy, who had the East Side up to 125th Street, where Dutch Schultz took over. He wanted to buy the beer from the West Side, where Owney Madden made the best in town, but Prohibition gangsters had agreed on territories and Madden would not come to the East Side.

When a beer delivery was made, the truck driver told Dorrian, "The rule is, if it hits the sidewalk, you pay a dollar a barrel."

"Who to?"

"The cop on the beat."

"I'll lift the barrels myself in my wee fingers," Red said.

Red Dorrian had a friend in Belfast who had done handsomely by serving homosexuals in a shabeen, a private drinking club housed in a shed. When Dorrian heard that there was no gay speakeasy in New York, he immediately corrected the situation. Two months later, Kaiser walked into the place and noticed that he was in an all-male bar, with men dancing with each other in a space at the rear.

"You got queers in here!" he yelled at Red.

"And that's all I'll ever have," Red said.

Kaiser's partner said to him, "Is Red a queer, too?"

"Certainly not. He's a Catholic."

Even with a place this disreputable, with a lot of outright homosexuals getting drunk and even holding hands at the bar, Red Dorrian, too, never was closed for a moment during all of Prohibition.

For enforcement during Prohibition in New York, there was a federal agency that, in all but a couple of cases, operated on the principles of a collection firm: if you paid, they went away. But in some loud, known Broadway clubs, and usually only those where the owners just brazened it out and paid nobody, there were raids by Prohibition agents. Two agents, Izzy Einstein and Moe Smith, originally came from mail routes in the post office and became famous for operating in disguises and closing places in Brooklyn, where Einstein pretended to be a judge, and in West Point, where he pretended he was a sergeant. Then the two agents went to Harlem with their faces and hands covered with shoe polish. They nearly were killed by decent people outraged at the shoe polish on their faces. Izzy turned into a megalomaniac, and with Moe Smith following him he busted into hundreds of speakeasies and made wholesale arrests. When people in his office told him that it would be better for everybody if he stopped this, Izzy said he was doing the work of the federal government. He then got himself elected to the Lambs Club and, finding his way to the bar, raided the place. Afterward, everything worked at magnificent speed. Izzy and Moe had the guns and badges taken off them and were told to go back and deliver the mail.

The only thing Prohibition proved was that there can be no way to stop people from doing what they want to do, that no cheap lawyer can come down from his grubby office upstairs over a drugstore and, through emptying wastebaskets at a Democratic club, get elected to a legislative body and then dare try to affect the personal lives of people. Yet, if given a second chance, the same cheap politicians would have voted for it immediately because of the shrieks of the wintry people who demanded it. No imaginative leap is required to understand how government later involved itself in something else it could not control, abortion.

A morning mist rose from the river outside the window as DeWitt Crane, commissioner of the New York State Parole Board, said to Owney Madden, "Now you understand that you are under oath."

"Yes, sir."

"And you swear that you will restrict your activities only to lawful employment in this laundry? And furthermore, you will at all times remain away from any persons listed as being known criminals?"

"You have my sworn word."

"Now you have served seven years for murder. Do you understand that one violation can place you back here for the rest of your sentence?"

"Of course. I wouldn't go near one of these undesirables."

Three weeks later, on a bright February day in 1923, Owney Madden walked out of the gatehouse at Sing Sing and into the parking lot, where Joe Gould sat at the wheel of a big green Packard car. In the back seat was Arthur Bieler, who by now was finished with his sentence for murder, and one Tom Robinson, whose record was spotless — not one decent act had ever been recorded. After backslaps, Madden got into the front seat.

Bieler handed him an opened bottle of beer. "This is what Schultz puts out," he said.

Madden took a swig of the beer. His face became contorted and he leaned out the window and spit it out at the prison. To reach Route 9, the highway to New York, Gould drove up a street running along the always popular north wall of the prison. Madden threw the Schultz bottle at the wall, causing it to shatter.

Next he was handed a bottle of beer made by a man named Levy in East Harlem. After a long swig, he shrugged. "These people don't know the first thing about beer. Get me home."

On the way down to New York, Madden spoke with great excitement about opening a brewery. Bieler mentioned that a guy from Chelsea, O'Hare, had been trying to front for Dutch Schultz in that neighborhood.

"How could he do that to me?" Madden said.

"Because he don't know you," Bieler said. "He was only sixteen years old when you went away."

"Then the man lived a short life," Madden said.

"You going to whack him?" Bieler said.

"I can't. I'm on parole. You'll have to do it."

Some weeks later, police found the body of Eugene O'Hare, twenty-four, in an empty lot on West 18th Street. He had been shot several times.

It took Madden quite some time, almost a whole year, until he had a huge brewery, a fleet of trucks and control of the West Side of New York. Then he took friends, including Runyon, to see his new business.

Tenth Avenue always was comfortable as a free bed for anybody on the far side of the law. But by now the street was ecstatic with the unusual condition of people everywhere else wanting to see a law, Prohibition, repealed while people on the West Side wanted the law to last forever. As all crimes committed on the West Side were done in the name of Prohibition, they were largely ignored by the rest of the city. Any gunning down of some dirty rat bastard was considered a private matter on the West Side which affected no one, and people were able to blame it on Prohibition.

In Chelsea, an Irish neighborhood, where the notion of any authority removing drink from their hands could cause immediate resistance, virtually all laws were going unheeded. Because of this, Owney Madden was the hero of the area. He now had this great building with the Phoenix Cereal sign, on Tenth Avenue between 26th and 27th streets. It was filled with brewery workers who made the town's newest and best beer, Madden's Star. Madden, with proper upbringing at a workingman's table and around the pubs of the British Midlands, knew that you best honor a workingman's palate when you serve him a pint. Other bootleggers, such as Dutch Schultz, made colored water and had to threaten to maim or murder speakeasy owners who didn't take it. Madden Star Brewery customers only called for more. His best brand, Madden's Number 1, was so creamy that it was said to be English in texture.

Runyon was with Madden and Bieler on Tenth Avenue one night when a factory door in the large Phoenix Cereal building opened and a haggard man, face red from the heat inside, came out for air.

"That's Heinz O. Seibert," Owney Madden said. "We call him Heinz the German."

"That is because he is a German," Arthur Bieler said.

"Did he fight with the Kaiser?" Runyon said.

"He fought against the Kaiser," Madden said. "When the Kaiser told people not to steal, Heinz opposed him."

"Mannheim Prison," Bieler said. "He was a brewer before that. He is the first German lammister I ever met. So he can't say nothin' even if they torture him."

On this night, Runyon saw fourteen trucks parked on Tenth Avenue, each filled with 120 half-barrels of Madden's Number 1. There are 180 ten-ounce glasses of beer in a half-barrel.

Madden explained that they were waiting for four more trucks to be loaded inside, and then all the trucks would leave in a caravan to deliver beer all over the West Side, which was Madden's territory. When Runyon asked him if having his name emblazoned on a bottle of beer wasn't a parole violation, Madden was puzzled. "My beer is the most popular in the whole city. I'm glad to put my name on it."

He told Runyon that on the night before this, Prohibition agents had pulled up, counted Owney's trucks and withdrew to plan a raid. "We always got our defenses up," Owney said proudly. Upon their return, the agents noticed light gleaming from the cracks of two old wood doors leading into the brewery building. A lone man up at the corner spotted the Prohibition agents and promptly disappeared. He was George Raft, still a neighborhood dancer. When fifty agents returned later in a full convoy, they found the trucks still on Tenth Avenue. Then they joyously piled onto a battering-ram truck and rode it right at the two old wood doors leading into the brewery. They did not notice that this time no light gleamed through the doors. But they did notice the triple steel doors now protecting the brewery when the front of the truck crumpled on impact and agents rocketed out of the truck.

As Madden finished conducting his tour, he introduced a dark-haired guy lounging at a loading dock. He gave his name as Jack Diamond. "We call him Legsy," Madden said. "On account of you never saw anybody run away as fast with some girl's purse."

By now, Madden was living in seven rooms in the Maurice apartments, on West 58th Street between Sixth and Seventh avenues. He also had a penthouse atop the London Terrace apartments, on 23rd Street and Ninth Avenue, which is where he and Runyon went after the brewery tour. Madden led him down a hallway, not opening any doors, and directly to the penthouse terrace, which looked out onto the brewery.

"It's really better than killing somebody," he told Runyon.

A voice called from inside. "I'm thirsty."

"Just gargle," another voice, familiar to Runyon, called.

Madden opened the door to a bedroom. Here was Ray Arcel, in bed, and Charley (Phil) Rosenberg, a prizefighter, in the bathroom running the water.

Rosenberg weighed about 155 pounds. Madden and Champ Segal had matched him with the bantamweight champion, Eddie (Cannonball) Martin, for March 15, 1925, which was nine weeks away. As the bantamweight limit was 118 pounds, Rosenberg had to remain more than somewhat aware of what he was eating. He and Arcel had gone to Hot Springs, Arkansas, but the manager on paper, Champ Segal, never sent them expenses. "He's supposed to starve to death. What does he need money for?" the Champ reasoned. When Arcel and Charley Phil returned, they moved into the London Terrace apartment.

A woman appeared at the door to another bedroom. "Charley, you want something to eat?"

"He can't," Ray Arcel said.

"I didn't ast you. I ast my Charley if he wanted something to eat."

"You want cake, Charley?" the woman said. "You got to have some pleasure."

Arcel introduced her as Charley Phil's mother. At home on 116th Street in Harlem, she used to put meat loaf on the kitchen table and tell Charley to grab some whenever he passed the doorway. When Arcel and Charley Phil moved into the London Terrace apartment, to get away from her food, she came, too. Charley Phil's diet was one egg and one cup of tea for breakfast, and for lunch, nothing. At dinner, he had a small piece of steak, lettuce and tomatoes, and a cup of tea. For a snack later in the evening, he was allowed a spoonful of Jell-O.

In the weeks that followed, Runyon, calling from California, kept asking about Charley Phil's weight, and on March 14, Arcel called and told him, "He's at one-twenty." On the morning of the fight, Arcel took Charley Phil into a drugstore in the London Terrace building and weighed him. Charley Phil was 116, two pounds under the bantamweight limit. "You'll get sick!" his mother said. At the weigh-in, when the boxing commissioner called out Charley Phil's weight, Champ Segal yelled at Arcel, "You made him too weak!" Runyon, who was with the baseball teams, was told of this by Segal during the day. Madden was betting against Rosenberg too, Segal said. Oh, Champ was betting against Rosenberg, don't worry about that. It was not that Champ wasn't loyal to Charley Phil; he just didn't think he could win. Runyon became the center of attention on Hollywood Boulevard when he bet a thousand on Martin to win the fight.

That night, Arcel told the fighter, "Only you and I know that the human body doesn't need any food."

From the tenth to the fifteenth rounds, when reserves of strength counted most, Charley Phil Rosenberg half slaughtered Eddie Martin and won the championship. And the next day, a jubilant Champ Segal told Runyon on the phone, "How do you like what our boy did? Didn't I tell you how game Charley is?"

People in the Roaring Twenties would have gone to speakeasies even if the places were pouring poison because there was, as Mulcahy from Brooklyn, living atop Willie Sutton's speakeasy, soon learned, nothing else for most men to do. The male gender is stressed here because women, with children and household work, had more than enough to do to fill most of the hours of the day, and also could talk about all this with other women who spent their days in similar fashion. The American washline, with a woman in the next window running hers at the same time and talking all the way through it, was a method of remaining somewhat sane. The male in this era went to work and then sat around and demanded. As there was nothing past scratchy radio, and the movies still were sparse, the ability to talk, to tell a story coherently, established a person in a new constellation of those admired by others. Newspaper writers, particularly the good sportswriters, concentrated on getting anecdotes into their stories, for they formed the word of mouth in the neighborhoods, on the stoops and bar stools, especially the bar stools, of the city. It was this need to talk, to hear stories, much more than the need to drink, that filled the speakeasies and saloons. Two hundred thousand alcoholism counselors later, you find that all you ever needed was a storyteller.

The first World Series game ever played in Yankee Stadium started at 2 P.M. on October 10, 1923. It ended at 4:07 P.M. For Runyon, who made the day for the sport of baseball, it began when he sat down at a bench in the press box at 1 P.M. He had on his Nat Lewis suit and a floppy Panama hat. A cigarette hung from his mouth. He unzipped his red-and-white-striped typewriter case and put sheets of copy paper, which was newsprint paper cut to typing size, into the portable. He sat silently, sucked on his cigarette and stared at the field below. The starting pitchers, Waite Hoyt of the Yankees and John Watson of the Giants, were in front of the stands, throwing easily at the start of their warm-up. The four umpires appeared on the top step of the Yankee dugout, causing the first sound of the day, boos, to blow out of the gleaming new stands. The umpires walked through this traditional greeting and gathered in a solemn huddle at home plate. Now, at this most wonderful moment of American life, with Hoyt and Watson throwing a little harder, Hoyt coming down with that first curve, and with the umpires talking, the smacking sound of the ball hitting the catcher's glove amidst booing for the umpires, while outside, people were coming off the el trains, necks turning to see the stands and the flags flying on the grandstand roof, and, once inside the ballpark, bending down as they went up the ramps to get that first breathtaking look at the field, now from the Broadway wise guys gathered at the rear of the brand-new mezzanine, there rose Mendel Yudelowitz's cry, "Who vins the game?"

Runyon composed sentences as quickly as he typed: "The umpires, four solemn looking gentlemen in dark, funeral blue uniforms with little blue caps, held a meeting at home plate just before game time. They were 'Billy' Evans of the American League, who can wear an umpire's uniform in such fashion that he looks trim and neat, 'Dick' Nallin, of the same league, and 'Bill' Hart, and 'Hank' O'Dea, a dour looking man of the National League."

Through the rest of the game, he typed after each batter and between innings. He gave almost every step of the game, and upon filling a page of paper, he handed it to the telegrapher, who tapped out the Morse code to the newspaper sports department, where another telegrapher typed as he listened to the bug.

As the first part of Runyon's World Series story on Casey Stengel came in, the desk man read it, fitted it into a cylinder, which he stuffed into a pneumatic tube, air whistling, and sent it on its way to the composing room. The story was in chronological order until the Giants came up in the ninth. In the roar and delicious excitement, all that he had written, from the first appearance of the umpires onward, maybe six thousand words in all, was to be set in type and used as the last half of his story.

Baseball has lasted for so long because the size of the playing field and the rules of play, three strikes and you're out, never changed. And all around a game, there is the most fanatical energy put into preserving its record. At the ballpark, all during the game, a guy in a topcoat who worked for the Yankees sat with a sheet of paper in front of him divided into two columns, and he kept counting the pitches. He had lines of ones in each column, and whenever he had five of them together he crossed them out and placed a 5. He made a mark for each pitch thrown and the result of it: ball, strike, hit, foul, out. At the end of the game, the guy made his last cross-out, and now he made out an orderly sheet, with carbons for everyone. The sheet said there had been 246 pitches in the course of the game, with 94 of them called balls and 50 called strikes by umpire Evans. There were 133 pitches by the Giants' pitchers and 116 by the Yankees'. There were 29 foul balls and 9 fouls that were caught for outs. There were 24 infield outs and 18 made by outfielders. There were a total of 20 hits, including one by the thirty-two-year-old Giants outfielder Casey Stengel, a line drive in the ninth inning of a tie game which went between the right and center fielders and skipped off the bleachers wall. When nobody got near the ball right away, Stengel could taste money on his tongue and ran for home and did not stop until there. He had an inside-the-park home run in a World Series, which was a nice thing. But then, as Runyon started typing, he had fame that would last him through what turned into three careers before the undertaker tagged him out.

This is the way old "Casey" Stengel ran yesterday afternoon, running his home run home.

This is the way old "Casey" Stengel ran running his home run home to a Giant victory by a score of 5–4 in the first game of the World Series of 1923.

This is the way old "Casey" Stengel ran, running his home run home, when two were out in the ninth inning and the score was tied and the ball was still bouncing inside the Yankee yard.

This is the way —

His mouth wide open.

His warped old legs bending beneath him at every stride.

His arms flying back and forth like those of a man swimming with a crawl stroke.

His flanks heaving, his breath whistling, his head far back.

Yankee infielders, passed by old "Casey" Stengel as he was running his home run home, say "Casey" was muttering to himself, adjuring himself to greater speed as a jockey mutters to his horse in a race, that he was saying: Go on, Casey! Go on!

People generally laugh when they see old "Casey" Stengel run, but they were not laughing while he was running his home run home yesterday afternoon. People — 60,000 of 'em, men and women — were standing in the Yankee stands and bleachers up there in the Bronx roaring sympathetically, whether they were for or against the Giants.

"Come on, Casey!"

The warped old legs, twisted and bent by many a year of baseball campaigning, just barely held out under "Casey" Stengel until he reached the home plate, running his home run home.

Then they collapsed.

They gave out just as old "Casey" slid over the plate in his awkward fashion, with Wally Schang helpless and late, reaching for him with the ball. "Billy" Evans, the American League umpire, poised over him in a set pose, arms spread to indicate that old "Casey" was safe.

He typed and lit cigarettes and handed copy paper to the telegrapher and he finished in the cold and gathering darkness, the last person in the ballpark, still writing. He covered his typewriter with the red-and-white-striped case. A man from the Yankees' office offered to store it overnight. Runyon stared at him. "I would much prefer to leave my prick."

He left Yankee Stadium and took the subway downtown. In the fall night, he walked past City Hall and the *World* building on his way to the *American* offices on William Street. In a small cubicle just to the left of the entrance of the *World* building, there was a small counter that was supposedly a drugstore, Perry's, but it was called the Pot of Glue and it dispensed Brown Ruin, which was just off a speedboat and could raise the hair of anything on two or four feet. The place became the meetinghouse for the most successful group of literary people the

city ever had. In lore and books, the Algonquin Round Table was considered the very top of intellectual activity, but the Algonquin had Ring
Lardner and George S. Kaufman and after that a collection of over-
rated misfits and half-talents, such as Robert Benchley, and I never did
quite understand what it was he actually did, and Wolcott Gibbs, who
wrote nothing more than reviews, and a half-poetess, Dorothy Parker.
Their fame would extend all the way to Connecticut. Meanwhile,
banging away at the Pot of Glue on Park Row were O. Henry, Gene
Fowler, Don Marquis, Nunnally Johnson and Runyon.

"Let me ask you this," said rewrite man James Cain of the *World*
one day in Perry's. The place fell silent as he took a large swallow of
the drink of the month. Upstairs in the *World* city room, James M.
Cain, rewrite, between stories of women leaping from windows, had
been attempting two fiction projects. Now, with plenty of whisky in
him, he completed his question. "If you were a newsboy and you were
bringing home money to your poor sick mother, what would you rather
have for a headline, a big day by Babe Ruth or a big speech by the
President of the United States?"

During the laughter, Cain then said, "Does anybody know why the
postman always rings twice?"

When nobody answered, he said, "Well, I do."

"Why?"

"You'll read it," Cain said. "Do you know anything about double
indemnity?" Before anybody answered, he said, "I know it makes a
good plot. Good day." He put down his glass and went back up to the
typewriter. As talk of writing usually runs five years before the job is
completed, Cain was missing for quite a while. But he turned out *The
Postman Always Rings Twice* and *Double Indemnity* and left the newspaper business forever.

When Runyon reached the *American*, he stopped at the wood cub-
byholes, and he went to the *R* and pulled out the proofs for his story.
He took the proofs to his ledge and with one of the string pencils began
to mark the typographic errors and do some editing. He read for some
time. After which he held up the proofs and, his back to the city room,
bawled, "Boy! Oh, boy!" He left when he was sure that his entire story
made it, and no walk to the composing room to cut somebody else's
was required.

Another Runyon sports story lasted by word of mouth as long as if it
had been issued on a bronze plaque. This occurred on a Sunday in
October of 1926, when the seventh game of the World Series between

the St. Louis Cardinals and the Yankees was played at Yankee Stadium. The thirty-nine-year-old Grover Cleveland Alexander had won two games for the Cardinals and, with an arm numb from all that pitching at his age, expected that he wouldn't be needed in the seventh game except to sit in a jacket on the bench. He prepared for this by spending most of Saturday night at the bar in Billy LaHiff's Tavern on West 48th Street. On Sunday morning, he returned to LaHiff's and told the porter that he wanted coffee, and when the porter produced coffee, Alexander threw it at him. He caused such a commotion that Billy LaHiff had to run down.

Alexander made LaHiff sit with him and he began drinking. Was he going to attend the game? "What am I, some fan?" Alexander said. "I've done my job. Let them take it from here." He said he was going to spend the day as he should. Right after serving one great big good drink, LaHiff excused himself and went to the phone and called Runyon at home, which he did out of loyalty but also because he understood that Runyon was the only writer in the city who would think that Alexander sitting in the bar was a fine story, perhaps as good as the game itself. Runyon rushed down to the tavern by cab, paid his respects to Alexander and took a cab up to the stadium. He had the scene of Alexander in his pocket and intended to use it in his story. At the time the first pitch was thrown, Alexander was sitting on a stool, barside, LaHiff's Tavern, West 48th Street, New York City. This was a considerable distance away from Yankee Stadium, which was up the length of Manhattan and across a river to East 161st Street in the Bronx.

At this point, both Runyon and Alexander had great luck.

In an early inning, Jesse Haines, pitching for the Cardinals, came back to the dugout and began inspecting the index finger on his throwing hand. There was a red lump on it. "It's nothing," O'Farrell, the catcher, said. Haines shrugged. Manager Rogers Hornsby walked over and looked at it. Then he looked up and down the bench. "Where is Grover?" Hornsby asked. Somebody knew and a call was made to LaHiff's.

"They want you," LaHiff said to Alexander.

"For what?"

"Hornsby says he might need you."

"They're crazy."

Alexander took the phone, listened and decided he would have to go to the ballpark. "I'll sit in the effin' bullpen and have to watch the whole game from there," he muttered.

By the seventh inning, the Cardinals were ahead, 3–2, and Alexander was in the left field bullpen. The Yankees were up with two out when Haines, the St. Louis pitcher, felt the finger split on a waste pitch, which was a fourth ball to Lou Gehrig. This loaded the bases. The next Yankee hitter was Poosh 'Em Up Tony Lazzeri. While the nickname once had been a slur, it now was a threat. In all the years of the sport there were only one or two second basemen who could hit the ball as frequently and as far as Lazzeri. He batted sixth in a lineup that included Babe Ruth, hitting third, and Lou Gehrig, fourth. While Haines shook his finger, the Cardinals' manager, Hornsby, walked out of the dugout, looked at the open split on Haines's finger and then turned to left field and held his right arm high in the air. A right hander. Alexander. It was the start of a great American sports story, and was told with an anecdote by Runyon:

> Old Grover Cleveland Alexander, with his cap perched high above his ear, shambled in out of a fog into the seventh game of the World Series of 1926 up at the Yankee Stadium yesterday just in time to fan Poosh 'Em Up Tony Lazzeri with the bases full, and to hold a one-run lead that made the St. Louis Cardinals champions of all the baseball world.
>
> It was fortunate for the Cardinals that they located old Grover Cleveland Alexander at the moment Haines' finger began to pain him. Some say Grover had been heating himself up under the bleachers.
>
> Others claim that he was found in his favorite chair down at the Tavern, discoursing over his two previous victories in the series with Mine Host Will LaHiff and that the Cardinals chipped in towards a taxi to send for Grover.
>
> They sent word by the taxi jockey that his presence was urgently requested at the baseball orchard and that it might be worth $2,000 to him to make the trip. Old Grover sighed and accompanied the taxi back to the Yankee Stadium, but it is said he insisted that Mr. LaHiff go with him.
>
> He did not care to take such a long ride without somebody to talk to. I do not vouch for this report, you understand. All I know is that Old Grover Cleveland Alexander may usually be found at the Tavern when he is in New York and that he appeared out of the fog that hung over the Yankee yard in the seventh inning.
>
> Mr. LaHiff waited for him in the taxicab outside. He knew Grover

would not be long. Meanwhile, poor Lazzeri was waiting at the plate, mind filled with foreboding as he watched Grover Cleveland Alexander shambling in out of the fog, walking first on one foot and then on the other.

He then looked down at catcher O'Farrell and pitched what the umpire called a ball to Tony Lazzeri. The next Mr. Hildbrand, umpire, said was a strike. Then Tony fouled one into the stand that caused the clients to jump. It was the second strike.

On the next pitch Poosh 'Em Up Tony shattered the air with the force of his blow and everybody got right up and yelled for the Grover.

It all came together here. Here was a story naming the very bar stool on which Alexander sat while he got drunk, and of course LaHiff's Tavern never was closed for an hour of a day of a week throughout the entire Prohibition. And Alexander filled the need for stories that could keep men talking on stoops and bar stools for the entire winter.

With the Roaring Twenties came another marvelous illusion, the Golden Age of Sport, which consisted of a lot of preposterously small men who were called great stars and yet didn't seem strong enough to carry luggage at a hotel. The Golden Age began as we have told you, with Dempsey winning the title in 1919.

On May 18, 1920, Man o' War was standing sideways in the saddling enclosure at Pimlico Race Course in the noise and the late afternoon sun just before the running of the Preakness Stakes. When the jockey's valet came out with the saddle over his arm, the trainer, Louis Feustel, said, "I'll turn him straight." The horse's reaction tells you as much about his condition as a look into a man's eyes tells you what he was up to the night before. If the horse is in top condition, he handles easily and moves with little urging. If you have to place both hands on the horse's flank and push as if he's a garage door, forget about it. Man o' War was sixteen hands high, weighed over 1,100 pounds and had a girth of seventy-two inches. Feustel placed the tip of his index finger into Man o' War's side. The horse moved. Feustel's finger remained on the horse's side, pressing, but only slightly, and the horse swung all the way around so that he no longer was standing sideways.

"He's as fit as human hands can make him," Feustel said to the jockey, Clarence Kummer.

In the crowd outside the fence at the saddling enclosure, watching the animals, was a young hustler whose true name belonged in the Kiev phone book, but had been simplified to Eddie Burke, later to be refined to Horse Thief Eddie Burke. This occurred when he tried to walk off the grounds of Bowie Race Track with a stray rope he found on the ground, on the other end of which was a racehorse. Right now, he had decided to become a handicapping genius.

"Look at how nervous the horse is, all you have to do is touch him and he jumps around," Burke said, watching Man o' War. "He'll see his own shadow and drop dead." Burke looked around at the mutuel board. "Let's get a price horse against him."

"Upset is two-to-one," somebody said.

"Too short," Burke said. He watched jockey Earle Sande walking up to ride King Thrush, now 9-to-1. "We go naked on this one." He waved his hand in disdain at Man o' War. Horse Thief Burke walked into the crowded grandstand to find some money. Pimlico believed in supply and demand. It always had the most touts and also the most helpless suckers of any track in America. Somewhere on the grounds was a man who would listen to Horse Thief.

As Man o' War was being saddled, August Belmont II, the owner and breeder of the horse, was quietly off to the side. His father, after getting rich by building the subways in New York, had established Nursery Stud Farms in Babylon, Long Island, and father and son had spent glorious hours planning breeding lines. Their eyes misty with power, they drew graphs with lines zigging out of the pack, those great outcropping lines that would have stable managers bringing mares to stallion barns for the perfect mating. "We are not in this sport for winning races," Belmont had said. "We are in it for the improvement of the breed to the point that it cannot be improved anymore, thereby giving us the master thoroughbred racehorse."

For his own tastes, old Belmont usually could be found off somewhere making a maid giggle. His son adored women from diners in Commerce, Oklahoma, who wanted to be actresses.

Rules for breeding in America had been established in 1891 by Pierre Lorillard, who had large farms that grew tobacco, which at the time everybody thought helped exercise the lungs. He gave a dinner at which men could sit and talk of breeding to get a master stable of racehorses. Lorillard matched the stallion Fair Play with a mare sired by Rock Sand. The sire is the only thing the breeders, all male, ever considered. There was no way to consider a mare's own worth in breeding, for its value was fixed by the name of its sire. August Belmont bought a "stand," as an assignation is called, by Fair Play, and he brought around the mare, named Mahuba. Their offspring was this red-coated horse Man o' War.

Horses are far dumber than dumb dogs and certainly don't have the brains of an alley cat. Only the rare horse can show more animation than a blank stare. This one looked down at people with a fierce, unmoving eye and caused them to tremble.

A band in the infield played "Maryland! My Maryland," and the horses walked out into the sun on the neatly raked track. At the starting gate, Man o' War threw his head around and caused Kummer to tug on the reins. Watching from the old Pimlico stands, Horse Thief Eddie Burke announced, "He's so nervous he won't be able to make it around the track." By now he had suckers, and one of them raced to make another bet for him on King Thrush.

Man o' War stood still long enough to have all four feet on the ground at the time the web barrier shot up into the sky. He then detonated. The horse took great even strides as he went past the grandstand on a lead that lengthened each time his forward foot reached out for more track. King Thrush tried running with him all that way, then started running with a stride associated with old people climbing a steep flight of stairs.

Clarence Kummer knew he was having the fastest ride of his life. As Man o' War came through the stretch, the crowd was in tears at the sight. In the cheering at the end of the race, Horse Thief Eddie Burke raced upstairs to the press box, where he pounced on the man who was going to bring him to New York as a special turf adviser.

"How did you like that?" Runyon said.

"I knew he was great," Burke said.

Horse Thief Eddie Burke was auditioning for the position of walk-around guy for Runyon. This is a role of colossal importance, and it goes far beyond the duties of some common valet, and is filled with hazardous moments, for while a valet can insult his master, this is usually done in private, but a walkaround guy can humiliate his boss in the middle of a crowded arena. It is always assumed that the walkaround guy is honest as far as the boss is concerned, for the boss does not want the lines of his suit ruined by any bulges and has the walkaround guy carry the money. Beyond this, it is up to the walkaround guy to ensure that the big guy is never inconvenienced, never hears anything bad, and thus is always in excellent humor.

Horse Thief Burke was a modified "up-up man" — the person who runs into a crowded hall before his client and starts calling out, "Everybody up for the mayor!" He could chant no such thing upon arriving at a crap game in a cheap hotel room, but at later dates, at such huge movie hits as *Little Miss Marker* and *The Big Street*, he could perform this role loudly and admirably, causing Radio City Music Hall to rise in cheers. Here at the racetrack, Horse Thief Burke performed another vital role, that of official rooter. This is a full step beyond the more passive job of agreeing with anything the boss says. That is known as being the "ditto" of the entourage. But this is a task that can be accomplished with merely a nod of the head and an agreeing smile. Being official rooter demanded some energy and timing. Burke had to stand and root for anything that Runyon wanted to see win, and this required a knowledge of all sports at all times. Runyon professed a liking for "chalk horses," meaning the favorites, but at race time he always was putting money on some hopeless 30-to-1 shot. Horse Thief Eddie Burke then would take a deep breath and begin a holler for the slow animal. "Runyon loses his money, I lose my vocal cords," he said.

On this day in May at Pimlico, Man o' War won in the record time of 1:51⅖. In a sport dedicated to Belmont's "improvement of the breed," this race seemed to place the thoroughbred a great step ahead. But horses by then were so inbred that they were Siamese cats with jockeys. Through the next three quarters of a century, no horse ran an instant faster than Man o' War.

FOURTEEN

AMONG humans in the 1920s, the Golden Age of Sport, the mile was being run in four minutes and eight seconds, and not one person ever suggested, even at a wild moment, that someday clockings would be at 3:46. British runner Harold Abrahams, whose race in the 1924 Olympics would inspire movies, became immortal with a 10.6 second clocking for the 100 meter dash. Many decades later, in the 1980s, a woman named Florence Griffith Joyner did it in 10.49 seconds; Carl Lewis, 9.92. In the 1924 Olympics, swimming champion Johnny Weissmuller did the 100 meter freestyle in 59 seconds. In 1986 Kristin Otto swims the 100 in 54.73 seconds, about 5 seconds faster than Weissmuller. All men swim it in 48.6 seconds and that is 13 seconds faster than Weissmuller. The runner Paavo Nurmi did the 1,500 meters in 3:52.6. Paula Ivan of Rumania did it in 3:53.9 the other day. And Sebastian Coe won the Olympics in 1984 with a 3:32.53. Therefore, Nurmi the Hero really was taking a brisk walk. Everybody began running the 1,500 meters in 3:30 and less.

Maybe the athletes simply grew and were able to do more — Christy Mathewson was just six feet tall, while many pitchers today are six foot five. The Notre Dame backfield called the Four Horsemen consisted of Harry Stuhldreher, 154 pounds; Elmer Layden, 164 pounds; Jim Crowley, 160 pounds; and Don Miller, 162 pounds. In recent years, the average weight of any college backfield was 210, and its speed has increased likewise. But when Notre Dame came to New York and played Army in 1924, Grantland Rice of the *New York Herald Tribune* wrote a lead paragraph that people around newspapers memorized: "Outlined against a blue-gray October sky, the Four Horsemen rode again. In dramatic lore they are known as Famine, Pestilence, Destruction, and Death. These are only aliases. Their real names are Stuhldreher, Miller, Crowley, and Layden."

It was hyperbole about college midgets, but everybody read it with tears because it was written by Rice, who, while mawkish with words, had a part of him inside that was polished metal. In World War I, he had been assigned to some military writing project in France, but he got out of that, walked to the front and found the nearest trench. Afterward, the only stories he told were of injuries to others. As Rice came from a little money in Georgia, he had left an accountant with $75,000. When he got home, he found the accountant had embezzled all his money. "It's my fault for putting him in such temptation," Rice said. For the next fifty years his sports columns gave athletes a purity that only Rice himself had. He described bums that you wouldn't want to meet as being noble warriors. He even maintained that jockeys were as honest as he was. He was the only person using a typewriter whom Runyon could not find a way to despise. "If Rice says it is all right, then even I can't make it wrong," he said.

When Rice played golf with Warren Harding, however, he stood off on the side of the fairway and writhed about the situation Harding was in, being that he was being charged with giving away the United States Navy's oil reserves at Teapot Dome, Wyoming, to Payne Whitney. Rice's deep love for the word "innocent" was being tortured by facts. There was no way he could use that word on Payne Whitney. Therefore, neither could he describe his golfing partner for the day, Harding, as the new John the Baptist. He decided Harding was a poor unfortunate. In writing about his athletes, however, Rice began to call it the Golden Age of Sport, which it certainly was for him. He was home from a war alive, and he loved everybody and they loved him, and he drank more whisky with a fine rug under his feet than anybody.

The names of the twenties who were supposedly such legends included Bobby Jones, the golfer, and Runyon hated golf unless it was being played by gangsters, so he never did see Jones play. The greatest heavyweight champion, Jack Dempsey, had five title fights and lost two of them. He defeated one journeyman, Bill Brennan, and two preposterous stiffs: Georges Carpentier, who at 164 pounds shouldn't have been allowed in the ring, and Angel Luis Firpo, absolutely unqualified for a championship fight. He was a dumb slob who got lucky with one punch that had Dempsey through the ropes for a few moments. The newspapers, which gave the promoters what they wanted, said Firpo was "the Wild Bull of the Pampas." In this era there also was Ruth,

who was more than real, Gehrig and Earl Sande, the jockey. Runyon
wrote verse about him, "A Handy Guy like Sande," which appeared
first when Sande took a fall at Saratoga and looked like he was dead.
That day, Runyon started the report with:

> Maybe there'll be another,
>   Heady an' game an 'true —
> Maybe they'll find his brother
>   At drivin' them horses through.
> Maybe — but, say, I doubt it.
>   Never his like again —
> Never a handy
> Guy like Sande
>   Bootin' them babies in.

Of course Sande got up as soon as he could because despite all his
victories he needed success every day to keep up with his living. The
era went on whenever he appeared. In 1935, Sande was at Churchill
Downs, in the red spots and white silks of Belair Stud Farm. Before
the race, trainer James E. (Sunny Jim) Fitzsimmons, who, poetry and
all, still regarded a jockey as something you put on the horse like a
saddle, gave the same instructions to Sande that he gave to all riders:
"Do not impede the animal."

The horse was Gallant Fox, and he could have won with a full safe
on his back. Win the horse did, with Sande on him, and when Earl
raised his baton in salute in the winner's circle and then hopped off the
animal, Runyon went right to the old poem and brought out the up-
date, which became the version that was considered the most famous
of all sportswriting in his time. Everybody assumed that Runyon wrote
the poem on a deadline in the Churchill Downs press box. What he
did was rework the verses he had written six years earlier in Saratoga.
This time he began with:

> Say, have they turned back the pages
>   Back to the past once more?
> Back to the racin' ages
>   An' a Derby out of the yore?
> Say, don't tell me I'm daffy,
>   Ain't that the same ol' grin?
> Why it's that handy
> Guy named Sande,
>   Bootin' a winner in.

The poem lasted a lifetime. Sande believed it all so much he regarded himself as invincible, even against whisky, which he was not. He wound up in one room over a saloon at the Westbury, Long Island, railroad station, with a half-empty bottle of Scotch, a can of Bumble Bee salmon and a fistful of wrinkled ties on the dresser. Under his window was a car that had not started in a couple of years. He was angry and drunk and yet carried himself with Turf and Field Club manners. Bald, with his blue eyes now set in creases, he remembered singing in a place called the Stork Club as if it were real. He stood in his empty room, eyes closed, and burst into opera.

During the twenties, two athletes did change the national habits. One was Red Grange, the football player, and the other Big Bill Tilden, the tennis player. Runyon never went near Tilden because he was at least a homosexual. Runyon thought killers were more wholesome, and so did everybody else who wasn't a homosexual. Yet along came this man with the temperament of a diva who often liked to talk and swing his body like a woman, yet took a game considered for rich weaklings or girls and soon had it accepted as a virile man's competitive sport. Grantland Rice established the tone followed by all newspaper sportswriters of the time. He decreed that Tilden was an all-time American great and left no room for any other opinion. Yet Tilden did nothing to hide his behavior; at day's end he could be found strolling in Station Square in Forest Hills with two young, adoring ball boys.

After Tilden, who founded tennis, the only one to leave any legacy was Red Grange. Until he came out of the University of Illinois, pro football had been a sport of college players who were vaguely disreputable because they were taking money and thus removing the thrill, the charm, from a sport of madly cheering girlfriends and alumni tearing down the goal posts. After playing his last game for Illinois, Grange contemptuously broke the amateur code by signing with the Chicago Bears. He hired an agent, C. C. (Cash and Carry) Pyle, who despised anything that was not good for Pyle, and maybe even Grange. He got $25,000 for Grange in the game that made pro football. It was in New York, of course, for nothing could begin anywhere else.

He drew 60,000 to watch him play for the Chicago Bears against the New York Giants at the Polo Grounds on a Sunday afternoon in November of 1925. Until then, pro football had been a game played at a strange, sinful time, Sunday afternoons, with out-of-shape men who practiced once or twice a week, performing before crowds of 2,500 to 3,000. Newspapers gave pro football only a couple of paragraphs. You had a country of people who never got as far as high school and were in love with tales of ivy walls. Sportswriters, who either never got to college or never got out of it, wrote about Yale and Harvard at football. It turned out that Runyon bet right down to the shoes on college football, and detested every moment of it because it appeared to be totally honest and he would have preferred it to be fixed.

In the game in New York, Grange played until halfway through the second quarter. He had been knocked around on the muddy field and found no room to run. He played defense with the aloofness of a man standing with his newspaper on a crowded bus. He made one tackle when the runner banged right into him, and batted down a couple of forward passes. Otherwise, he remained clear of all action. As the Bears had been playing two and three times a week in places like Decatur, Illinois, with Grange as the attraction, his manager, Cash and Carry Pyle, had insisted that the halfback play only enough in each to appease the crowd. "He is getting too much money to take undue chances," one newspaper story agreed.

Pacing behind the Chicago bench, Cash and Carry Pyle complained to Paddy Driscoll, the Bears' coach, "Red sure could use some of these open Illinois formations that Bob Zuppke had for him."

Driscoll, feet in the cold mud, said over his shoulder, "Let Zuppke give you the twenty-five thousand."

At the start of the final quarter Grange was still sitting on the bench. Then George Halas, right end and owner, Chicago Bears, heard the first scream from the stands.

"I'm getting robbed!"

Halas knew this was catching. We will have people running onto the field to beat us up in a couple of minutes, he thought. He waved and Red Grange came on. Grange was five foot ten and weighed 164 pounds. He could start racing to the right, then cut to his left in one astonishing moment and run away with a body that shook all over.

Now with Grange on the field, Halas immediately had his play called. Grange made six. On the next play, Grange tried to make it around end, but nobody blocked for him and the Giants tackled him for a two-yard loss. Halas was angry about the blocking, but he knew there wasn't much that could be done. He had men on the field who were making $75 for the game and were supposed to block for Grange, who was getting $25,000. That does not happen so easily when players feel somebody is getting too much, and it does not happen at all when Grange arrives with a man like C. C. Pyle, who, looking at the other players, said in disdain, "I hope they know enough to all fall down at once when Red gets into the open field. That's all they're paying to see anyway. They don't care to see another living human on this football field." The $75 men tumbled into the mud and watched, out of harm's way, as the Giants' tacklers, also making about the same, came stomping through the mud and tried to kill Grange. He lost two yards. "The crowd applauded him whether he gained or lost, just as it applauds Babe Ruth hitting a home run or striking out," Runyon's story said.

Moments later, the Giants, trying to get out of their end of the field, gambled with a pass. Playing defensive halfback, Grange snatched the ball and had nobody between him and the goal line. He brought his knees high with each stride and his hips swayed and he was all alone and the whole stadium was on its feet. The people had seen what they had paid for, Red Grange scoring a touchdown.

In the noise and excitement, Tim Mara, a bookmaker sitting in the stands, and down on the field George Halas, right end, both had the same notion, that perhaps someday all their Sundays would be like this.

Outside of the horse Man o' War, and Tilden and Grange, because they each founded sports, just about all sports records aren't worth a glance because over half the athletes able to play the sport were kept out.

Madden opened a club in Harlem, the Cotton Club, a dump that had been owned by Jack Johnson, the black heavyweight champion. Owney hired decorators an turned the place into what he thought was nighttime elegance, an arena where whites from downtown could come uptown and simultaneously experience the jungle and be protected from it. He hired a band led by Duke Ellington and advertised it as "Jungle Music." Madden had hoodlums to keep anybody black out of the club. If there was anything he wanted to do more than have somebody shot, it was to be the emcee at his own nightclub. He had an elocution teacher come to the house twice a week in an attempt to put tones into his northern English accent that would be familiar to nightclub patrons. The teacher spent many hours trying to get Owney to soften his accent. One night Owney took the floor at the Cotton Club and announced: "Ladies and Gentlemen. If you will hold everything for a wee minute, I am going to give you a chack-up on the new acts . . ." A waiter rattled dishes as Owney Madden spoke. Owney snarled, "Eejit!"

At Runyon's table they argued baseball. Overhearing this, a busboy walked back and forth many times before summoning the courage to approach Runyon. He said the best baseball pitcher alive was right down the street, at the Club Interlude. The busboy said the pitcher was named Smokey Joe Williams, and Runyon said that certainly he had heard of the man. "He deserves a story about him in a white paper," the busboy said. "I could take you down there."

Runyon said, very softly, "I have a young lady with me and I can't be bar hoppin' with her."

"It's just a neighborhood bar," the busboy said. "Ain't nothin' ever happen in it."

Runyon said, "I'll see him. Some other time. But I'll see him." He reached out and put a few bills into the busboy's breast pocket.

At the Club Interlude, on 133rd and Lenox, the bartender was Smokey Joe Williams. His mother was part Indian and his facial structure was Indian. He was six foot five and had a right arm that was thick from use and had the reach of a tollgate. He worked the bar when he wasn't pitching baseball. Smokey Joe had started out as a baseball player with the Lincoln Giants, who played in a lot at 136th and Fifth Avenue in Harlem, with crowds standing along the foul lines. Smokey Joe, pitcher for the Giants, was paid $20 a game. After this, he went with the Homestead Greys out of Pittsburgh, in the Negro League, where he became known as the best pitcher of his color alive. The catcher was Josh Gibson. Cool Papa Bell was at first base.

One day that summer, Runyon was at Yankee Stadium talking to Paul Krichell. He had eyes that could take one look at a muscle and tell how fast it could throw, how fast it could swing, how much it could assist in the building of this sports dynasty called the Yankees. Runyon asked about Smokey Joe Williams, and Krichell said he was going to see him pitch in a week, in a semipro game out at Dexter Park in Queens. Krichell was interested in a white player out there, and he wanted to see him bat against Williams. He made a date with Runyon, and they met for breakfast one Sunday morning at Lindy's, and then Krichell drove to Queens.

Driving from Pittsburgh after a Saturday night game, the Greys had pulled up to the lone light on a street called Elderts Lane in the Woodhaven section of Queens. A night watchman stood at the gate leading into Dexter Park, the semipro baseball field where a team called the Bushwicks played. The Homestead Greys' manager asked the night guard to open the gate so the players could go inside and stretch out on the benches in the dressing room. They had a doubleheader against the Bushwicks scheduled for 1:05 P.M. on Sunday.

"I can't let nobody come in," the guard said. "They're liable to steal the field."

They remained in the bus trying to sleep. At 10 A.M., the ballpark owner, Max Rosner, arrived and the players went into the dressing room under the stands and dozed before the doubleheader. The Homestead Greys always were a big draw, and the local gamblers automatically made them 13-to-5 favorites. There were two things you grew up with in the section of the city known as City Line because it was directly on the line dividing busy Brooklyn and dozing Queens: Sunday dinner at noon, Homestead Greys 13-to-5 over the Bushwicks.

Runyon and Krichell walked into the stands behind first base, which was the Homestead dugout. Runyon, head down as he walked down an aisle, was confused by the row of white-and-brown, white-and-black, and pointy yellow shoes. He looked up and was startled by the first black crowd he had ever seen. They took up most of the seats behind first base and all the seats along the right field line. The whites sat behind home plate and along the third base and left field line. It was Queens, and there was no such thing as segregation, except there was. Krichell and Runyon went to a box behind home plate, and Krichell hunched forward with his face against the foul screen and concentrated.

On this Sunday, Williams started the first game for the Greys. He had just gone twelve innings against the Kansas City Monarchs and pitcher Chet Brewer. Williams struck out twenty-seven batters and gave up only one hit. He got rid of the first two batters with his fastball. Cuccinello, the player being watched by Krichell, was the third Bushwicks batter. Williams put his arms over his head, brought a leg up and threw a fastball that Cuccinello tried to watch as it went past. He did this because he could not get his bat around fast enough to swing. It was a clean strike. Krichell's face showed nothing. Not a finger moved. Right away Williams threw again, this time another fastball right down the pipe, but simply too fast for Cuccinello to swing at. Two strikes and no balls. Cuccinello swiveled his feet. There was the inevitable waste pitch coming, and just in case it was near the strike zone he had to be ready to chop at it. Williams wound up again and threw the fastest pitch Runyon believed he ever had seen. It came right down the middle, belt high, and Cuccinello did not swing. The crowd booed as he took a called third strike. Krichell smiled. "He couldn't swing. The pitch froze the man. Nothing against Cuccinello. Most everybody up in the leagues would be called out on strikes, too."

Williams did not allow any runs, and decided to come out after the sixth inning with the Greys well ahead.

The Homestead Greys won both games against the Bushwicks. In one of them, Gibson, the ferocious catcher, hit a ball into the cemetery in left field, and the usual argument over its length began. Nobody ever had measured the distance to left field because there was no fence, just clipped outfield grass that began to slope upwards and, with the ballpark appearing to be miles away, the outfield grass became a cemetery. The left field could have been five hundred or six hundred feet. It truly stretched to eternity. One thing was certain: Gibson was the only one ever to hit a ball into the cemetery.

During the second game, Runyon and Krichell walked back to the Greys' dressing room and asked for Williams, who came out and stood with them under the stands, with silver foil from gum dropping through the spaces under the seats.

"How much do you get for a game like this?" Runyon asked him.

"Twenty-five dollars."

Runyon winced. He told himself he was going to write a column about this guy and try to do something to help. Why, this was another Walter Johnson, at least.

"I figured I'd like to meet you," Krichell said. "I've heard about you all my life. I just had a look at that fastball of yours and now I know why. How old are you now, anyway?"

"Fifty-four."

"I'm sure sorry I didn't see you long before this," Krichell said.

"You could come in for a drink where I'm workin', but the place is all colored," Williams said.

Runyon and Krichell left the park. Runyon went to the office the next day and tried to write about the black pitcher, but he couldn't make it work. He could write about a black fighter all right, or a track runner, but the idea of a black baseball player was too alien to him and, he figured, to his readers. So he did not write about the best pitcher he ever saw. In the end that was his loss, and he left several rueful letters to his son admitting this.

Fowler had a child, Eugene Junior, whom he would push by carriage to Sweden if the kid wanted it. He had Runyon out with either Mary

or Damon Junior, and while they favored Riverside Drive, particularly
in any winter snow when they would pull sleds and imagine they were
in Colorado, Fowler also had ways of directing the march to Cannon's
Bar on Broadway and 108th Street. They would push the carriages just
inside the door, and Runyon would sit in a booth and read race entries,
and Fowler would put one foot up at the bar and tell delightful stories
about the children. Agnes Fowler and Ellen Runyon were at first surprised that the two men would even deign to push baby carriages, but
late one afternoon, upon inspection of Fowler's breath, and seeing
Runyon's racing page marked with pencil at too many races, the two
women understood their husbands' interest in the children.

Mary Runyon started school and attended church at Ascension on
108th Street. By now, the Runyons lived at 102nd and Riverside Drive.
They had moved into a seven-room apartment when he received the
new contract from Hearst after the World War. The apartment looked
over the trees on Riverside Drive, out to the Hudson River and straight
across to the Palisades of New Jersey.

When Mary Runyon was in Ascension school and church, a scolding
nun came down the aisle at the least noise during the nine o'clock children's mass on Sunday. If a baby did so much as gurgle during one of
the masses for adults, the mother would get up and take the baby out
of the sanctuary in embarrassment. The church imposed the same
dreadful silence as Mary Runyon and her brother Damon lived with
each morning. For bringing home this kind of money, the father demanded his children be raised as Trappists.

Runyon was certain that by thinking only of himself and his success
he would always be a rope across a slippery deck for his family. He
slept until noon, because he said he worked morning newspaper hours,
which for him consisted of finishing his column by 7 P.M., at the absolute latest, sauntering up to dinner and a nightclub, followed by a visit
to Lindy's that lasted until 3 or 4 A.M.

He always lived no farther than three blocks from a subway, but his
interest was not in getting home. He never learned to drive, and used
busted-down heavyweight prizefighters as chauffeurs for his wife. He
never wanted one with him because then he would have no excuse for
being absent. He rode the subways only when trapped into it, and he
finally put an end to that. One night he was in front of Lindy's and
Eddie Walker, the fight manager, said he had to go downtown and post
bail for Eddie Borden, another manager, who had just been arrested
for running a dice game. As Walker and Borden hated each other,

Runyon thought that for Walker to post bail was the act of a truly gentle man. He said he would go downtown with him. Walker led the way to the subway, and when Runyon suggested that a cab would be quicker, Walker disagreed and kept going downstairs. Reluctantly, Runyon followed. When they got downtown, Walker posted the bail with a man sitting behind a barred window. Some minutes later, a guard appeared with Borden. The guard opened the cell door and told Borden he was free to go.

Borden pointed at Walker. "What's he doing here?"

"He's the guy who put up your bail," the guard said.

"Take me back to the cell," Borden said.

"You're lousier than I thought you were," Walker called.

"I'd rather die in jail than have you bail me out," Borden said. "Put me back in. I won't take bail off this man."

"You ain't got it to turn down. Give me my money back!" Walker shouted.

The guard put Borden back into the cell.

Runyon said, "Tough fella."

"You're taking his side!" Eddie Walker said, and walked off toward the subway.

Runyon stood alongside Walker on the platform. Walker read a newspaper and would not talk to him. When the train rushed into the station, Walker folded the newspaper, and was obviously finished with it. Runyon figured he would read the paper on the way uptown. Walker went over to a trash can and threw the paper in, then got on the train. Runyon went up to the street and hailed a cab. Nobody remembers seeing or hearing of him in a subway again. It took Eddie Walker years of being an open supplicant before Runyon accepted him again.

He usually went home by cab as the sun came up and washed the streets and started to awaken the city. At noon, Runyon woke with a cough and a groan, and spent a full hour wrestling with the morning until he finally opened the bedroom door and announced, "I'm up!" The children would be allowed to rush into the room and announce that one had hit the other or the canary was sick or their mother had been up early. Runyon would move to the bathroom and shave as they talked, saying nothing but looking at them in the mirror, which was pretty good, at least he looked. Ellen would pull the children out of the room while he slipped into the bathtub. The children now were allowed to make noise, until he walked into the dining room wearing a bathrobe and slippers. He sat alone at the large table and inspected the breakfast before him. The eggs had to be done exactly three and a half minutes, the toast a dark tan, no black, the bacon drained carefully. If anything on the plate was not what he wanted, he erupted. An amiable, even humble listener in the streets, he was a frigid, snappish king at home. When he lifted the first fork of the morning, he expected all mouths to be shut. Silence fell on the room. His children stood in the entrance to the dining room and watched him, hoping for a sign, a smile, an approving nod, to let them know he loved them. Usually there was nothing but the sound of the father grunting as he read something in the newspapers that interested him particularly. He drank four or five cups of coffee with his breakfast. After which he carried the papers into the bedroom. When Damon Junior reached age six, his father sometimes brought him in and told him his philosophies of life, those slogans Runyon himself never followed: "All horseplayers die broke."

Runyon spent the odd hour with the son, but only at rare moments did he ever grant the daughter an audience. Of course the son spent years never wanting to see the father, and the daughter spent her life boasting about her most magnificent dad. The first phone call Mary ever made was to her father. She stood on phone books and told the operator, "The *American* on William Street." Later she learned the number, Beekman 2000. His son remembers him in print this way: "His shy overtures of friendliness, his stumbling attempt to play the palsy Pop, was patently gawky. He seemed to be one of those parents who was at his best with a child too young to present an aggressive personality that might clash with his. He was not receptive to exchange in conversation."

Mostly, however, Runyon kept the bedroom door shut after breakfast while he dressed, keeping a most hostile eye for those outfits which he felt would not set him off properly from the throng. He was a man who regarded his suit as the first sentence of his day's story. After an hour of trying on different ensembles, and finally putting one on, he stood at the tie rack for another hour before pulling one out. During this time, he had not five minutes for wife or children.

Mary Runyon became louder at home and the nuns at Ascension reported that she was unruly in class and distracted others. At three each afternoon, the nun in third grade would station herself in the door and glare at the students who were filing out. As a mischievous one would appear, the nun's hand would go out. "Go back and sit down!" It was always a boy. The old uptown West Side Irish. On many days, however, as Mary Runyon reached the door, the nun's hand would drop and she would be sent back, the only girl in the school kept after class. But Mary would simply take a step back and wait for that moment when the nun would whirl to speak to someone else, at which point Mary would dash past the turned black back and head for the stairway and freedom. There were complaints from school and noise at home from a child wanting to be loved.

"I get the money," Runyon announced to his wife. "The kids are your job."

Through long Sunday mornings, his son remembered how he and his sister sat with their eyes at the door hoping for a sound, the first cough of the morning that would allow them to run inside and get the Sunday comics. Often they would have to sit there until midafternoon. Mary Runyon stopped waiting. She began to live in the morning and make noise with her feet and refuse to keep her voice at a whisper.

Damon Runyon, who promised hunting trips for his son, now had a grand idea for his daughter: a boarding school. Oh, not a warehouse, of course, just a place of magical halls where a young child can blossom and become even more loving. Why, send her just up the river a few yards. He had with him a brochure for the Convent of Mount St. Vincent on Riverdale Avenue, straight up the road along the river from where they were living.

This alarmed Agnes Fowler. She immediately had a plan. She caused Ellen to place her energy into forcing the husbands to cheat on their jobs, take a Saturday off and attend a bazaar for West Side schoolchildren. A photographer was there to take family pictures, and they all gathered together on chairs, and Agnes saw to it that Runyon had Mary in his lap, with Ellen holding the baby. Runyon pulled himself together and stared straight at the camera. His shy overture of friendliness consisted of looking down once, with a thin smile, at the girl wriggling in his arms. When the cameraman asked everybody to sit still, little Mary froze and posed for the camera. She did this so quickly and openly, and in such contrast to her usual behavior, that the two mothers laughed and Runyon looked down at her with genuine gladness. Impulsively, he put his head down and kissed the child on her blond hair. The cameraman instantly snapped the portrait.

"That picture will truly be worth ten thousand words to Alfred," Ellen Runyon said.

Later, they were walking on Riverside Drive when a heavy rainstorm began and they had to run home to Runyon's apartment, where Agnes Fowler went into his bedroom and tapped a finger on the wall.

"Oh Ellen, we will hang that picture in his bedroom and he will want to see that child every hour of the day," she said excitedly. "You can forget about some nasty boarding school."

"Well, mother, where's my picture?" Runyon said one night. He was unaccountably home for dinner.

Ellen called the local public school the next day and asked when the picture would be ready. She received a letter from the West Side school bazaar committee:

Dear Mr. Runyon;
    Unfortunately, the film taken by the bazaar committee photographer were ruined by the rain. The committee regrets this. If you will present your receipt for the photograph to the undersigned, a refund of your five dollars will be made. We regret this inconvenience. It was, however, out of the committee's hands.
                    Clifford Myers, chairman, bazaar committee.
267 West 89th Street.

Ellen Runyon took Mary to the Convent of Mount St. Vincent, which in those days was a twenty-minute ride by car. For a little girl, it was halfway to India. The place was on a hill overlooking the Hudson, but it had the gloominess in which Catholics seem to thrive, these the old wide hallways that were dim and smelled of incense. There was the heavy nun ready to take charge of this little girl who now began to scream to her mother and brother, "Please don't send me away, Mommy. I'll be good. Please don't send me away!"

Mary stayed and Damon Junior went home with his mother. He became a silent child.

At school, Mary would take her coat from the cloakroom and go to the room of a friend, Rose Bernabei, who was out of Greenwich Village. She was sent there because her father had business with Prohibition booze and didn't want her being shot on the stoop. Everybody would think Mary was out walking and they couldn't find her. Runyon never came to the school. Every weekend, Rose got the 10:58 train on Saturday morning in her school uniform: a blue jumper of shiny rayon like wool, black stockings and shoes. When she got off the train in Grand Central, she'd change clothes in the bathroom. All the students from girls' schools would be in there getting rid of their uniforms before they went out on 42nd Street. Mary always stayed in school for the weekends. She went off by herself on the grounds.

On his Broadway, the father could say quietly, in order to understate the meaning of such splendor, that "my daughter goes to a convent school. Costs like hell but it's a magnificent thing for a young girl. Young boy, too, for that matter. I wish my father could have done this for me." Which caused Owney Madden to grab his niece, Alice Marron, and say, "You're going to school with the swells." Which she did, and one day when a car backfired on the school grounds, someone said to Alice, "Maybe that's your uncle."

Mary Runyon came home rarely, and then only to stand in front of a mirror, dancing dreamily in the big foyer while "Blue Skies" played on the Victrola.

Into Lindy's at the end of a day came Jay Fagan, who looked like a large rare roast beef and was the first press agent in Broadway history. He had a staff of writers who wanted to get the first gags for radio shows out of their system, or perhaps even the first novel, but suffered from severe pain of the landlord. Jay Fagan had them work up the first-column "Notes": ". . . Fanny Brice betting on the horses at Belmont . . ." For providing such a note, Jay Fagan was given one free notice in a column for one of his clients: "Hottest act in town is the new chef at Reuben's."

"Do you know Walter Winchell?" Fagan asked Runyon.

"No."

"Do you know who he is?"

"The fella writes for the *Graphic*."

"He'd love to meet you," Fagan said.

"What for? He writes gossip. That's a girl's job."

The *Graphic* was a newspaper that made up the stories, and by use of scissors printed phony pictures with them. The publisher, a physical-culture fanatic named Macfadden, walked to work every day from New Rochelle, twenty-two miles away. Winchell was out of Harlem, where he had started in a song-and-dance team with George Jessel and Irving Berlin. On the road, he typed up a gossip sheet about the performers and hung it on the bulletin board backstage. The chorus girls loved it. He started doing a couple a week: "Janie Miles broke another farmer's heart back in Zanesville." When the gossip sheet clearly had more effect than his attempted dancing, he grabbed a job as ad salesman and theater reviewer for the *Vaudeville News*.

He caught on with the *Graphic*, where his energy carried him. He put three dots after every item, which was a good way of not having to write. He claimed to have invented the style, although sports pages had used it for a century or so. What Winchell did was become the first to find a way around the contempt most people had for illiterate gossip writers. As a megalomaniac, Winchell either damned people to hell or extolled them outlandlishly. But his lifelong policy was, "Never fire at a battleship." He ran an extraordinarily flattering note about writer Heywood Broun, who upon reading the notice announced, "Winchell is doing something new." Which he was. He was putting Broun's name in a show business column. Winchell tried flattery notices with Runyon, but there had been no reaction, so press agent Fagan sat at Lindy's, chewed on hard bread with big pieces of salt on the top and told Runyon, "I could do pretty good for myself if you'd just nod at the guy once."

"Then I'd have to listen to him talk. People tell me that's all he does. Talk."

"I'll be there to interrupt," Fagan said.

"Maybe someday. But give me a pass right now. You want to put on the feedbag?"

They were in Lindy's at two in the afternoon, eating breakfast of scrambled eggs, bacon, hashed brown potatoes, ten cups of coffee and a dozen cigarettes when the phone rang. Abe Scher, the cashier, nodded to him and said, "Cora." She was the operator at the *American* switchboard. Confidently, Runyon took the phone.

"I got a young one on the phone at the Greyhound terminal. She said you're expecting her."

"Not I, darling."

"Just another one of them."

"I guess so."

"Wait a minute," Cora said. Now she came back on. "She says her name is Patrice and she's up from Mexico and you told her to come here."

"That tyke?"

"She sure sounds young."

"She sure is," Runyon said.

"I lose her?"

"No, I can't do that. Tell her take a cab to Lindy's. I'll have a guy on the curb to pay the fare. Tell her where it is."

He grabbed little Pincus the waiter and gave him a few dollars and told him to stand outside and wait for a cab with a young girl in it. "A blonde."

"What else, Mister Runyon?"

Pincus went outside in a waiter's jacket and apron and stood in the freezing afternoon and waited.

"That is a nice guy," Scher the cashier said.

Presently, the cab pulled up. Pincus reached in and pulled out a big busted old suitcase. After it, a beautiful leg came out of the cab and into the freezing day.

"Look at that," Scher the cashier said.

Patrice came out of the cab in a leap. Her lips were parted in excitement and her eyes were afire. She waved as she saw Runyon in the window. Her eyes went everywhere as she saw the buildings and the lights flashing. She came almost running across the sidewalk and into Lindy's. He stood up and she ran right up to him and offered him a cold cheek.

"Mister Runyon?"

"Yes?"

"I'll put this in the checkroom."

"Thank you, Pincus."

"From Spain," Runyon said. He looked at Fagan, who was still standing with a napkin in his hand. "I got an item for our friend Winchell. Here is Miss Patrice Gridier, in town from Spain to conquer the Big Town with her gams. Great dancer."

He had given Fagan the Gridier name, which was new and not explainable or traceable, and therefore was a very great name. Fagan rushed to the phone. "He got an item for you!" Fagan said.

"Great. Type it out and I'll lead the column with it," Winchell said. "Now tell me what he said about me."

"He loves you," Fagan said.

"He does?"

"He thinks you're the greatest."

"Does he read me?"

"Every day."

"What does he think of my stuff?"

"I told you. He loves you."

"Where is he right now, Lindy's?"

"Uh . . ."

"I'm going right up there to see him. I better start hanging around there anyway."

"I think he left for the game. Walter, he's a little busy. I mean he probably has some trial he has to go back to. At any rate, I'll have him for you soon. Don't worry."

"All right, what do you need?"

Fagan had put a turkey on roller skates in a marathon on the dance floor of the International Club. The ASPCA, deluged by calls from Jay Fagan's staff, had sent people over to stop the turkey from being tortured by roller skates. But nobody had written about it. "I'm going to make the turkey famous," Winchell said. Jay Fagan hung up and told himself happily, I'll get there someday.

Runyon took Patrice over to the McAlpin Hotel, where the manager, a desperate horseplayer named McGlone, took him off to the side.

"I hate to pry, but this isn't the Acorn Stakes for you, is it?" he asked. The Acorn is the name of a very great race for fillies.

"Absolutely not," he said.

"Because I could save you a dollar if I could."

"The more the merrier. This is a young filly. They rarely stray far from the money," Runyon said.

"She's young. She doesn't mind moving around on short notice, does she? I can checkerboard her around empty rooms. Your wallet won't even take a deep breath," McGlone said.

Patrice checked in and Runyon went about his day's business.

"New York *Journal* and *American*."

"Cora?"

"Yes."

"Runyon."

"What's up with you?"

"The young woman that called the other day."

"Oh, you mean 'Up from Mexico.' "

"Cora, I don't want her driving me into an asylum. If she calls, take a message. But don't tell her where I am and don't look for me with the message. I'll get it when I get it. You know."

"You can't have her on the phone with you all day."

"You got it right."

The next day he came into Lindy's and spoke to Scher the cashier. "If a certain party starts calling me, just take the message. Don't ever say I'm in."

"The party is . . . ?"

"The one from the other day. Her name is Patrice."

"I tell you the truth, I don't remember her," Scher said.

"When I bring her around, you can put your orbs on her and you'll know what we're dealing with," he said. "A young blonde."

He picked up the phone and called the McAlpin. "I'll bet you're a hungry gal," he said. She was in Lindy's twenty minutes later. Runyon sighted along the top of his coffee cup as she walked in. His smile was not of the fatherly sort. Scher walked over so that Runyon could introduce him to the girl, and Runyon turned and glared at Scher and caused him to retreat.

Two days later, he sat along the ledge at the *American* and called the McAlpin.

"Miss Patrice Gridier."

"Gridier?" the operator said.

"She's in seven forty-two."

"I don't see her there."

"Then they put her in another room."

"I don't have it."

"You better look for it."

"I just did."

"Then look some more."

"Who are you, the boss?"

"I'm trying to be a gentleman."

"You're trying to be a boss. You want this Miss Gridier and I ain't got her."

His hand slapped the ledge. "Look for her!"

The operator clicked off.

He called back and asked for McGlone, only to learn the dismal news that it was the manager's day off. When he hung up, he told himself that this was all right, for of course she had to be looking for him at Lindy's. He went up to Lindy's and said to Scher, "Any messages?"

"Nope."

"There must be."

"None."

"You must have missed them," Runyon said, which was out of character, for he spent a lifetime enjoying service, and some say he nearly died of waiter's bow, but at the same time he never once so much as disagreed with anybody serving for a living.

He went home and called the McAlpin from the phone in the hallway outside his bedroom. The night operator had no record of Patrice and was snippy about it, too, but he could not raise his voice. He barely slept. In the morning he was up by ten. "Have to be in the office today to tabulate expenses," he said. He went directly to the McAlpin.

"She's in eleven twenty-three," McGlone said, picking up the phone.

"Miss Gridier? Here you are." He handed Runyon the phone. Her voice was beautiful in the morning. "Be right down," she said.

"You got her living like a gypsy," he told McGlone.

"Yes, but you said you wanted to save the grunt."

"Forget the grunt. I want her in the same room every time I call."

When Patrice came out of the elevator and into the lobby, McGlone said to her cheerily, "Well, you certainly had him worried."

He felt Runyon's murderous stare.

Patrice was, in the absence of a believable birth certificate, somewhere between eighteen and twenty. Looking at her now, it was obvious that she had more Mormon missionary in her blood than anything else, with the blond hair and white skin. Her years in these tough Catholic schools had stamped out nearly all of the Spanish in her voice, except for the now and then lapses with tenses, which often seem impossible for someone not born here. "I was tried to call you before I got on the bus," she said, in explaining how she came up from the Southwest. In Lindy's, Runyon began to write on a napkin the rules for tenses, but then he decided that was a waste. "Just learn how to say it the same way you learned your prayers," he told her. "Don't question what you say. Just learn it and say." In Runyon's honor she said she was twenty-one, but this was only because he admitted to forty, when he actually was forty-five, and a cigarette smoker's forty-five at that. He thought he was walking onto Broadway with her, but instead he went into the canyon that for ages has destroyed armies of men. On his arm was a young girl, her blond hair bouncing on her shoulders as if walking to school, turning to look at him admiringly, with breast brushing his arm, speaking to him as if his presence had caused her to lose all breath. And lining curb and building fronts were his people, who were delighted to see him with such a young woman.

Everybody approved. Damon Runyon was supposed to have a young broad. What did you want him to do, go home and watch his wife do the dishes? The touch of the young girl, the feel of her body grazing his, had him prancing down the Broadway sidewalk without even knowing he was there.

He had spent many hours on that sidewalk, talking with people like the great Caruso about the destructive power attendant to an older guy falling for a young girl. Now he forgot every word he had ever said or heard.

"He got no shot, surviving a young broad," Owney Madden said.

Madden's girlfriend at this time was named Bernadette Clancy, also known as Kimberly, and she had just despaired of ever finishing high school. She was seventeen.

Patrice is not in the town a week and she had a mention in Winchell's big column. Runyon took her shopping by the method of walking her up to John Wanamaker's store on Astor Place, handing her money and then leaving. She bought a new silk dress for $8.75 and, moving away from the sales racks, hit into $15 dresses. The middles were tight and the skirts flared, and she wore them a little below the knee. At Gimbel's, across the street from the McAlpin, silk stockings sold for three for $1; hundreds of silk dresses were on sale for two for $6 at Norton's, on 14th Street; she was not seen there. For hair, there was a Mister John at 12 East 42nd, who worked for $10 and gave waves that were many and tight to the head. Patrice looked at the sign in the window, sniffed and asked Leo Lindy's wife where she had her hair done. The name was Adolph, on Madison Avenue, and he was double what the guy on 42nd Street charged.

It was at this point that Runyon took her to Texas Guinan's, on that night when she sat there with Frank Costello and got a job as a dancer. Guinan's partner was a hoodlum named Larry Fay, who had a taxicab company that had a swastika emblem on the doors. He certainly was fairly dishonorable, but the symbol was not; this was years before anybody ever heard of Nazis. There was a chorus line of eight girls and no room to dance. Rehearsals consisted of learning to keep both feet on the dance floor and not have one of them put in under somebody's table. Guinan looked in at the start of the night and always said, "Anybody here want to be a nun?" She was a great big loud lesbian, which was fine, except look out for that word "loud," and this was her invitation to any of the girls. She never looked at Patrice because she knew Patrice's boyfriend.

Who was touting Patrice all over as the girl from a magic mountain. Every night after work, Runyon proposed to such crapshooters as Lou Clayton that she be brought along to the floating game to huff on the dice and make them wealthy. Clayton was against this almost to the point of violence. He sat in his room at the Alamac Hotel on 70th Street every day and argued on the phone with Jeannie Durante out in Flushing, who wanted to come into their West Side joint, called Club Durant, and sing with Jimmy. Clayton certainly wasn't bringing Runyon's broad to a crap game.

Runyon did bring Patrice to the private dinner parties that he and

Jimmy Walker had on the third floor of Leone's Restaurant on 48th
Street. Walker was always with Vonnie Shelton, the dancer for the
Ziegfeld Follies. He was desperately in love with her, and she with
him, until the night in the spring of 1925 when the Tammany Hall people decided that young Walker would be their candidate for mayor.
The governor, Al Smith, would not tolerate Walker's candidacy because he drank too much and, so much worse, had Vonnie Shelton as a
girlfriend out in public while his wife Allie remained home, putting on
weight, disregarding clothes, caring about neither as she realized that
her husband's great political quality, loyalty, was totally fraudulent.
Then, a couple of nights after the Fourth of July in 1925, a large crowd
was at Leone's. Walker departed abruptly and left Vonnie Shelton with
tears in her eyes. She got up and walked out angrily.

Runyon said to Patrice, "Go with her, will you?"

"A complete little weasel," Vonnie said outside.

"What happened to you?" Patrice asked.

"They send these cheap thief fuck politicians to tell me I can't be
seen with him anymore," Vonnie said. "He didn't come. Some old man
ready to die came and told me."

"Why didn't Jimmy tell you?"

"Because, like I told you, he is a cheap fucking weasel. Do you know
why he even was there tonight? Because I was going to put it in all the
papers that he was my boyfriend unless he showed up."

They walked up Broadway and then Vonnie impulsively said, "Let's
go in here and see real people." It was the Club Abbey, which was one
flight up. She led Patrice into the back, where, behind shower cur-
tains, the star of the show, Arleta Arlen, was getting ready. Arleta looked
at them in the mirror and talked. The moment she saw Vonnie's streaked
mascara she knew what it was about. She reminded Vonnie that she
had been the first to point out that Walker liked to stay out of crowds,
not because of claustrophobia, but simply because he didn't like the
idea of ordinary people touching him.

"You were right," Vonnie said.

"You new?" Arleta said to Patrice.

"Yep."

"From where?"

"Texas."

"Before we start," Arleta said, "I want you to know I did not work in
a whorehouse. I am a virgin. I am known as the Broadway Virgin. I am
fifteen. Aaggh! I couldn't kiss a guy's mouth. I hate his tongue in my

mouth. They took me to Philadelphia and I saw a woman have an affair with a dog. The only thing I ever did was shoot crap at night when the club was closed. I was not a loose woman, but I always gambled. Benny the piano player and Looey beat me. Lucky Luciano came in and told them to give me the money back.

"You know Runyon," she went on. "That's how you're starting. That's exactly how I started. With Earl Carroll. You can't work where I work unless you are from Ziegfeld or Earl Carroll. So I never would have been with Lucky Luciano if I hadn't been with Earl Carroll."

"Who is Lucky Luciano?"

"The man who comes to take me out."

Patrice proudly pulled out her notice from Winchell. "Oh, you have an item in Winchell. So do I." Arleta went into her pocketbook and produced a clipping:

"That scar on the thigh of the pretty little Indian Girl is from a stiletto."

"I am known as the Indian Girl," Arleta said. "That is my act. You must stay and see it."

"How did you get stabbed on your thigh?" Patrice asked her.

"It was an engagement party," she answered.

Arleta Arlen came out of Brooklyn as Arleta Altman, living on the top floor of a tenement on South 3rd Street in the Williamsburg section of Brooklyn. People on South 3rd felt they were living in the suburbs, for they were as much as a couple of blocks away from Havemeyer Street, which was packed with pushcarts and was as wide as a native quarter. They sat under low el tracks. The tenements were crowded and the rooms small and mostly windowless and filled with three and four in a bed. The roof directly over her head was a hotplate in summer and an icy tray in winter. Out of this crowded and gloomy neighborhood there rose an old gray span, the Williamsburg Bridge, which went over the East River, speckled with sun, and into Manhattan, where you had a chance. She went to P.S. 19 and Eastern District High School. Her mother brought her to Manhattan one day for dance lessons in a studio over the old Capitol movie house on Broadway.

"One other thing. They say I am a nude dancer. I am not. I am the Indian Girl. Oh. There is the music for my act."

Patrice stayed at the dressing room door as the band started playing "The Indian Love Call."

"That's my song," Arleta said. "See me? I am not naked." She had pulled her long ponytail apart, which now hung down in two braids that almost covered her breasts.

Swiveling on her high heels into smoke and tables with candles on them, Arleta Arlen, fifteen, her skin creamy and taut, feathers hanging from her hips and covering one area that, if exposed, would have caused even police on the club payroll to break in, swung her hips and danced in the middle of the Club Abbey, one flight over 54th Street and Broadway.

Two men listed as the Abbey's owners, the Schwartz brothers, sat at a table in the back and watched the room apprehensively. They figured, quite correctly, that on the best days they were trapped between the Irish mob of Owney Madden, who owned one half of the club, and the Italians, Frank Costello and Lucky Luciano, who owned the other half.

"If the Irish and dagos get mad at each other, who do you think they'll look around for?" one of the Schwartz brothers said.

As Arleta Arlen danced in the smoky club, the Schwartz brothers were more fearful than usual because sitting at one table was a large party with Dutch Schultz, the lumpy, light-haired bedbug who made the worst beer in New York. Schultz had Wanda, the fan dancer in the Club Abbey show, seated with him. But he really wanted to spend time with the Indian Girl, Arleta Arlen. Seated at another table was a party that included Chink Sherman, who also was a gorilla. Chink was in the club because he was truly in love with Arleta Arlen.

"One glance at Arleta is worth the cover charge!" the Schwartz brothers had put in their ads. Now two gangsters in the place agreed with the ad. Also, neither Madden nor Costello and Luciano were around to keep the place orderly. The only weapons the Schwartz brothers had were nervous smiles.

As Ardent Arleta Arlen danced, there was at one table the gangster Johnny Irish and Ruby Keeler. A girlfriend of Arleta Arlen's was off in the corner with a priest. The cigarette girl, who was supposed to be working, sat and held hands with Red Reese, who did not work for a living.

When Arleta Arlen, the Indian Girl, finished, the master of ceremonies asked for everyone to give a hand. Dutch Schultz and Chink Sherman stood up and clapped lustfully. They glared at each other. This was the part of show business Arleta loved the best. Two nights before, while she was taking her bows, one of the owners had rushed up to her and told her to sit with Lucky Luciano, and he had given her a hundred dollars before taking her up to Harlem, where some young boy played trumpet. Arleta was sure that the young boy stared at her all night long. She was thrilled because she knew it was against the rules, a death sentence, for a black to stare at a white woman in these places. Afterward, Lucky Luciano took her to somebody's apartment near the club, and two black men and two white women got down on the floor and performed in a sex circus. When Arleta went to the bathroom, in a dark hallway, somebody's hand grabbed her and then there was much commotion and here was Lucky Luciano and his bodyguards to save her.

"I almost got raped!" She threw her arms around Lucky. His men beat the rapist to a pulp like they should have.

"These men protected me. They were real gangsters!" Whenever she told the story, she insisted that Luciano took her home then, like the gentleman he was.

Now, at the Club Abbey, with Schultz and Chink openly growling at each other, the Schwartz brothers swallowed hard. Arleta Arlen clicked to the dressing room in her high heels and threw a black beaded dress over her slim body, inspected her makeup and ran excitedly out into the club. She went past Patrice and Vonnie, who were coming to get their coats. "See you," Arleta said.

She went past Dutch Schultz's table and Wanda, the club's fan dancer, said, "Arleta, come sit with us." Arleta Arlen, Indian Girl, stood at the table and posed in the light for Dutch Schultz. She smiled at him as he inspected her body inside beaded black. Instead, Arleta Arlen, Indian Girl, went straight over to Chink Sherman. When the orchestra played a dance tune, she and Chink got up and danced.

They were dancing close and she had her head on Chink's chest. Which must have caused some sort of growling from Schultz, which Arleta did not hear, but Chink Sherman sure did. He, too, growled. "Go back to the table," he said to Arleta.

"I want to dance."

"Go back to the table."

Arleta got as far as the table and saw Chink approach Dutch Schultz's table. Schultz got up and fired a gun. This was the first of three occasions on which Schultz and Chink resorted to weapons during these years. A year or so after this, Chink lost the third and most decisive gunfight by a wide margin. But this time at the Club Abbey he hit the floor breathing.

The priest stopped holding hands with his doll and jumped up. "Somebody'll find me here!" the priest said.

At this point, Vonnie and Patrice stepped out of the dressing room wearing their coats. In the noise and confusion, Arleta was crying, "Chink was so good to me!" She was bending over her fallen boyfriend. She was all right in a clutch, this Arleta Arlen. A very good girlfriend of hers, Marilyn, who was in the place, jumped up and grabbed her by the braids. "Are you crazy?" Marilyn yanked her toward the dressing room. Arleta pointed at the priest. "Go say a prayer and save his life."

This left the priest alone in the cordite. He went up to Chink Sherman and started saying a prayer in Latin. One of the Schwartz brothers wailed, "Are you crazy? What are you saying to him!" He yelled for the priest's girlfriend. "Get him out of here!"

In the rear of the club, Arleta and Marilyn grabbed their coats and led Patrice and Vonnie Shelton out through the kitchen and over to Dave's Blue Room, across the street on Seventh Avenue. There, Arleta made her entrance by announcing, "I never knew that when a gun went off it made so much flame."

With all attention on her, she said, "I feel so bad for Chink. The bullet went right into him. Is he dead, do you think?"

"I don't know. Let's just stay here," Marilyn said.

Within five minutes, all of Broadway had heard about the shooting. The famous Broadway detective Johnny Broderick rushed into Dave's Blue Room with a worried look. Which was caused by the two uniformed men behind him, who were sticking so close that it was obvious they smelled promotion. Broderick had a great fear of others getting ahead, particularly if they did so by honest means. He of course had his own view of how to do it. He joined the police force in January of 1923. By April of that year, he was a detective third grade, by May he was second grade and by the following March he was detective first grade — a rank more important in New York than that of President. At home he had a large portrait of politician Jimmy Hines hanging on the bedroom wall opposite his bed. Underneath it, in grotto style, was a candle in a holder taken from St. Patrick's Cathedral. Broderick wore hand-tailored suits and cream-colored silk underwear that was monogrammed, as were his shirts. When not at home in Yonkers, he had a permanent room and signing privileges at the Taft Hotel on Seventh Avenue under the name of Muldoon. He developed the reputation of being a great fistfighter, particularly during strikes, when he worked on the side of furriers and newspaper publishers and beat up pickets in side alleys. He also beat up a group of college students one night. During these fistfights, the other guys knew at all times that Broderick had a gun and would use it, and this became more than somewhat of an advantage for Broderick. But now, faced with the tremendous pressure of these two young and desperately honest uniformed cops standing behind him, Broderick started berating the girls.

"How could you duck out on us?" he said. "You're witnesses to a shooting." He took the four women to the police station on West 54th Street, where he left them standing at the desk while he went to talk to the lieutenant about the case. The two patrolmen did not go away, and Broderick and the lieutenant were nervous. Vonnie Shelton said she wanted to make a call. The detective let her use the phone at the front desk. Vonnie dialed Leone's and said very firmly, "Tell the little boy up in the third-floor private room that Miss Vonnie Shelton is at the West 54th Street police station. Tell him the item in question is a shooting."

Patrice got on the phone. "Tell Damon Runyon his girl is in the police station."

Only minutes later, a lawyer, rubbing his eyes, rushed into the station house and declared that he was Miss Shelton's attorney. Then in walked Dan McKettrick, an old fight manager who was a Tammany Hall burglar. He and the lawyer went into the back to speak to an inspector. Runyon now entered, carefully playing the wall. A detective, still thinking he had a legitimate investigation, came out of an office and said to Marilyn, "Come in here for a minute. We want to ask you something."

Marilyn became very nervous and patted Arleta's hand, slipping something into it. She said under her breath, "Hold this for me. I can't have them find it."

Marilyn went into the office with the detective. Patrice and Vonnie stood in the middle of the precinct floor. Arleta Arlen, age fifteen, ran one hand through her hair nervously while the other was clenched tightly on something. When Runyon saw the big ceiling light glint on the tinfoil peeking out from Arleta's hand, he walked over to Arleta. "What are you holding?"

"What Marilyn just gave me."

"But what is it?"

"I told you. It's Marilyn's."

"Are you crazy? Go into the bathroom right now and get rid of that."

Runyon walked up to the desk sergeant. "The lady has to go to the bathroom."

The policeman looked up. "Right in there, Miss." He indicated a door. When Runyon heard the toilet sound he relaxed and walked over and began talking to cops. Later, McKettrick and the lawyer came out of the back, and without any talk everybody left for home. Arleta said to Runyon, "It's lucky you could notice the way I was trying to hide it in my hand. You're the first man who ever looked at one of my hands."

Outside, McKettrick and the lawyer hustled Vonnie into a car. "They're so worried about me," Vonnie said sarcastically.

Runyon walked Patrice away from the precinct. When she said that he seemed extremely nervous, he became irritated. "You saw me in a worse place than this," she said. Runyon shook his head. "You're from Spain." She looked at him carefully and was surprised to see that he meant it.

Later that week, Walker showed up at a Democratic dinner with his wife, Allie. At the end of the dinner, he took her to their house on St. Luke's Place in Greenwich Village, turned around and went to an apartment on East 58th Street that had been rented by a man named Grasshoff, who had a soda water company in which Walker somehow had an interest. The apartment had a bar and bartender, but a locked-door policy for any and all women, including Vonnie Shelton. Nobody was able to see Walker drunk or out with any woman but his wife. Instead, there were many newspaper pictures of Walker and his wife Allie out at charitable affairs. The pictures were to get Walker the nomination of Tammany Hall for mayor. Allie Walker kept a warm smile and made it appear that they were a loving couple. Allie Walker did this for the simple reason that she was living in the year 1925 and didn't know how to do anything except what she was doing, and loathing it.

FIFTEEN

ON THE afternoon of June 1, 1925, a Monday, Babe Ruth was back from what was supposed to be a stomachache, but some said it was a mysterious disease, although not so mysterious to people at the Forrest Hotel, where syphilis was a word that was worn. It was Ruth's first game of the season, and it was against the Washington Senators, who had Walter Johnson pitching. Johnson walked Ruth in the fourth inning, and when Bob Meusel hit a double behind him, Ruth tried to run from first to home. By now, he had this beer belly heaving and he actually wobbled as he started for home. The throw to the catcher, Muddy Ruel, was ahead of Ruth, who flopped on his stomach like a fat fluke and was tagged out. In the eighth inning, the Yankees sent a reserve first baseman, Lou Gehrig, up to bat for shortstop Pee Wee Wanninger. Gehrig grounded out.

In the dressing room after this game, which the Yankees lost, Miller Huggins, the Yankee manager, had to get angry at someone, so he started picking on Wally Pipp, the veteran first baseman.

"I hit two ninety-five for you last year, don't forget that," Pipp said.

"You're not doing it now," Huggins said. He turned on Pipp and walked off.

Pipp, Runyon, Patrice and Edward Frayne, sports editor of the *American*, left the stadium and went downtown by cab. When Pipp got out at the Hotel Ansonia at Broadway and 72nd Street, he asked Runyon and Frayne, "Why does he start on me? I delivered last year. He got a whole team to pick on. The hell with him. When I see him tomorrow, I'm going to tell him."

"Why argue?" Runyon said.

Frayne joined his hands in prayer. "Oh, it doesn't pay to argue with those in charge," he said.

"I don't think I feel good," Pipp said. "I'm taking a day off from this."

"My friend, you never leave white space. You always fill it," Runyon said.

As Pipp did not quite catch the full meaning, Runyon said, "I am owed many days off by the newspaper. I could just as well get out right here and walk home. But I would be leaving white space. This man here" — he indicated Frayne — "has white space blocked out for me in tomorrow's paper. If I do not fill it, he will get somebody to do it. Fella, the thought of that makes me uneasy. So I am now going all the way downtown to sit and write and most likely finish late. But I will finish. Don't ever leave white space."

Pipp sulked on the sidewalk. "You'll feel better in the morning," Runyon assured him.

Patrice touched his arm. "Can I say something?"

"Sure you can."

"Mr. Pipp, I don't know you. But I know that Mr. Runyon is one of the smartest men in all of New York. I know personally that big generals in a war had respect for him. I wish you would listen to this man." She touched the arm of her boyfriend, who was so busy glowing that he didn't see Pipp walk off.

The next day, Pipp, a genius, arrived at the stadium. During batting practice, a kid trying out, Charles Caldwell Jr., son of an Ivy League football coach at Princeton, couldn't throw straight and grazed Pipp's head. Immediately, Pipp decided he was mortally wounded. That would fix this freaking Huggins. He told manager Huggins, "I got a bad headache."

"You're sure?" Huggins said.

"I got too bad a headache to play baseball," Pipp said.

Huggins sighed. "I guess I'll just have to go with this kid Gehrig."

Two thousand one hundred and thirty games later, and only when he was at death's door, did Gehrig come out. Pipp died pounding his fist into his glove hand and muttering, through half a coma, "I'm ready to go back in, Miller."

Across the street from the Forrest on 49th Street, a street ten yards wide, the amount of a first down in football, in front of Mike Jacobs's ticket agency offices, were a few yards of cement known as Jacobs Beach, so named because fight managers used to lean against the wall of the ticket agency and lift their faces to the sun. It was at times interchangeable with the sidewalk in front of Lindy's, particularly before any fights at Madison Square Garden. The guys on Broadway began to come around Jacobs Beach in dark suits, black shirts and white ties, which made them look ridiculous and Runyon even more classy as he emerged from the Forrest in his subdued outfits. He had Patrice shuttling between her own room in the McAlpin and his part-time life at the Forrest. At this time, however, he was so filled with dreams of finding a heavyweight fighter who would make him rich that he paid no attention to what clearly was his fortune.

He is at Aqueduct and an usher who lived in the area tells Runyon about an Indian burial ground a few blocks from the racetrack. The dead Indians were the Jameco tribe, around before Columbus. Their burial ground had been sold to a Jewish cemetery, which immediately started slapping old man Roth right on top of Chief Slow Horse. Runyon wondered whether he could excite all New York on this issue, as he once made Denver enraged over an Indian statue. Why should a decent New York person of Jewish ancestry be made to sleep forever with filthy murderous Indians?

After the last race, he and the usher drove to the cemetery, off Liberty Avenue in Ozone Park. They were in high weeds in a corner of the cemetery that was unused. The guy told Runyon this was where the Indians had been planted. They were interrupted by an imposing man who came out of a house directly across the narrow street. He was imposing because he carried a sawed-off shotgun. He said his name was Angelo the Ox, as if this had some meaning, which it did if you lived in Queens at this time. But as Runyon did not, he could only go on instinct, which was to identify himself to Angelo right away. This seemed to relax Angelo. Sportswriter. But when Runyon said he wanted to dig up Indians, Angelo said, "If you do, I shoot you."

Runyon left. But after many discussions on Broadway and the racetrack as to why Angie the Ox took the burial ground so personally, he was advised to return to the cemetery, and this time Angelo would be more mannerly. He was. He explained that there had been a major war between Sicilian and Calabrese immigrants, with shotguns being fired in the marshlands and fields running along Jamaica Bay. It was their way of making it in the New World. During this war, the boss of the Sicilians, Big Mike from Catania, passed. So did Buster from Reggio, who represented the Calabrese, but not for all that long. He was stabbed in his bed during the second week of the great war. About a dozen others, representing each side, became deceased. Angie the Ox survived, for a good reason, in that he shot people before they could shoot him. "They turn-a their backs and, poof!" he said. All bodies were put into the earth alongside Chief Raincloud and his outfit. Then the burial ground, billed as an empty lot, was sold for a Jewish cemetery. As funerals began to fill up the ground, the bodies were getting closer by the foot to the area where beloved Herman Goldstein would be dropped into the ground right atop some murdered Italian, who in turn was atop the bones of a despicable redskin. But until such time, Angie the Ox was the patrol officer for the burial site of all murdered Italians, and he said he would appreciate it very much if nobody gave the cemetery a write-up.

Runyon decided he could use all this in a short story later, and wrote nothing in the newspaper and also invited Angie over to Broadway. Angie arrived in the big city with his sawed-off and a burlap bag. He walked up to Bob Warren, the crap game operator, and threw the burlap over his head. Warren collapsed on the sidewalk. Angie roared, "I bet you think I was going ta kill you."

Runyon took this in, but did nothing with it because he was very busy at this time with Harry Levene, a huge heavyweight from Poland who was costing a fortune in restaurants. Levene had a shaved head, and trainer Harry Lenny kept muttering, "I wish this guy had hair." Then in the gym one day a sparring partner hit Levene on the chin and knocked him flat. In the dressing room, Harry Lenny worked over the fallen Pole. The big lamp from the ceiling glared on Levene's head. Lenny walked out and called to Runyon, "His hair is starting to grow in. It's all gray. The guy must be a hundred years old."

All Runyon was doing now was wasting time and money. It was years before he remembered to do something with Angie the Ox, whose name and burlap bag were important in a short story called "The Old Doll's House."

In the twenties, during the summer in New York, people kept the shades drawn and put slipcovers over their furniture. Women went around the house in slips and drank iced tea. The men wore undershirts and bare feet. They kept movement down and even the conversation was slow, as if sitting at the courthouse square in some Alabama town.

In nightclubs, which were nearly all in basements and didn't have enough fresh air in winter, much less for the evening of a 95-degree summer day, they put fans blowing on large cakes of ice and hoped it could save the customers. As the fans-over-ice were there for the customers and not the workers, Patrice danced at Texas Guinan's club each night with her body dripping with sweat. The ice was delivered early in the evening and once more later at night. Guinan noticed that the ice man from Mondello Ice and Coal was hanging around in an alcove with his burlap wrapping for the ice and tongs. The ice man was young and had arms and an upper torso that almost, but not quite, excited even Texas. Soon, she could tell by the number of young women going to the ladies' room, and grazing the ice man as they did, that he would deliver the ice for nothing.

She decided that he would make the perfect signature piece for her summer revue. The chorus girls came out wrapped in fake fur stoles and sang, "Put your wife on ice . . ." Then the production singer sang some sort of winter song while they wheeled out a girl frozen in a block of ice. Whatever the stage trick involved, the girl still was good and cold, and that is where the ice man came in. Texas had him go right out on the stage, smack the ice apart with those big bare arms, pull the freezing girl out and start warming her up right on stage. It was apparent right away that he was the only one in show business who didn't care if he was in or out of the spotlight. He wanted to put on the first live sex act. Guinan, as host, came out each show and stopped it: "They're not married!"

The new show, featuring "the World's Hottest Ice Man," was blazing away on the night Runyon came back from a trip with the baseball Giants. He got right to Guinan's and was shocked to see the brazen floor show his girlfriend was in. "I can't have you in a cathouse like that," he told her. The argument went on for some days.

One night, on the elevator at the McAlpin, where she still more or less resided, a distinguished-looking older clergyman, erect, gray hair neat, red piping on his black front to indicate high religious rank, said hello. "I am Bishop James Cannon," he said.

"My name's Patrice," she said easily.

The following afternoon, a lashing rain sounded on the glass doors of the McAlpin lobby. Two women remained a few paces away from the entrance, while people in raincoats rushed in from 34th Street and stood shaking themselves like dogs. Patrice sat in a chair and read the paper; Runyon was sending a prizefighter with a car to pick her up. The other women discussed how to get home in the rain and also how to pay the rent when they got there.

Across the room came the distinguished-looking older man, the bishop from the night before. But he wasn't in clerical outfit now. "Is it raining out?" he asked the women.

One woman gave a dazzling smile. "Yes," she said.

The woman said she was Helen McCallum, and the other was Vera Watson.

"I'm Stephen Trent and I am a writer. I am here from the South." Bishop James Cannon lied easily and immediately.

Mrs. Helen McCallum was forty-three and a widow, but this did not make the bishop, sixty-five, uncomfortable, even if she was far older than his volunteer secretaries at the Female Institute at Blackstone.

The bishop offered them a ride to their door, and Mrs. McCallum said she and her friend were happy to accept. The bishop put on a coat in order to go outside and hail a cab. Patrice heard Mrs. McCallum say she and her girlfriend were going to her apartment at 85th Street, a few doors off Amsterdam Avenue on the West Side. Which was fine with Bishop Cannon, for this meant he still would be on the same side of town as the Pennsylvania Railroad Station, and therefore would not miss the four-thirty train home to Richmond; his wife, ill, was depending on him to relieve a daughter who was spending the day attending her mother. None of this was said to Mrs. McCallum. How could he, writer Stephen Trent, have such problems when he already had assured the woman that he was single?

When he got Mrs. McCallum and her companion to the door, Cannon leaped out, held the cab door and was about to take his leave when Mrs. McCallum asked him if he felt like a cup of tea. He paid the cab driver and followed her breathlessly. Inside, they sat and chatted awhile, this kind stranger and the two women, until Mrs. McCallum's friend found an excuse to step out of the room. Left alone, the couple fell insanely in love. The bishop said later that the two found they had a strong common bond, a mutual antipathy for Alfred E. Smith, the wet governor of New York.

When she walked into Lindy's in the afternoon to have breakfast with Runyon, Patrice said, "Oh, dear Damon, you're so mad at me about a little nightclub show. I think you should look into these bishops going around after girls."

"What bishops?"

"I'll show him to you. His name is Cannon."

One afternoon when he came to pick her up at the McAlpin, she had the manager, McGlone, look into his register. "Bishop James Cannon,

Richmond, Virginia. Not here now. But we've had him with us." Runyon told McGlone to call the next time the bishop arrived. McGlone said he would. McGlone was an efficient man. It took him time because he was a busy man trying to stay even with bookmakers. But as you shall see, McGlone could complete a task.

Through the summer and into the fall of 1925, Walker was running in the primary for mayor against the incumbent, John F. Hylan, who was known as Cementhead even among relatives. Hylan was supported by Hearst, and strongly so. Over a lifetime one of Hearst's major characteristics was an aggressive, fanatical love of stupidity. Hearst was out in California, but he sent wires and made many phone calls to his people in New York, including a man named Moore, who was the editor of the evening *Journal*, and Gene Fowler, who was in command of editorial opinion, which meant he was an exciting stenographer. The *Journal* ran a cartoon showing Walker smiling while watching a dope dealer sell to children.

Al Smith, as governor, campaigned for Walker. In the early years he had opposed Walker because he said the little guy didn't know how to behave. Most of Walker's friends, Fowler foremost, had trouble believing Smith ever could take such a position. Fowler once ran a New York Press Club Christmas party in the *Times* building on Times Square and had an elephant brought up to the third floor for kids, and then found his job was only beginning: Al Smith had a bad stomachache from some rotgut. A prescription blank for opium was filled out by somebody at the party, but the pharmacist downstairs said it was a forgery and wouldn't touch it. Fowler, as head of the Press Club, requested that a mounted cop ride down 42nd Street to a pharmacist who said he could wait until the next day for a prescription. The medicine was brought back to Smith, who swallowed it and soon said he wanted to ride the elephant. When the pharmacist asked for the prescription the next day, he was promptly arrested for selling drugs without a prescription.

Campaigning for Walker now, Smith said that Hylan had close ties to the Ku Klux Klan and "gave blind, obedient subservience to a superboss." Hearst wrote a reply. "The distinguished Governor of the great State of New York has taken three days laboriously to prepare a vulgar tirade that any resident of Billingsgate or any occupant of the alcoholic ward at Bellevue could have written in 15 minutes in quite the same style, but with more evidence of education and intelligence."

One evening, barside, Perry's Drug Store, also known as the Pot of Glue, Fowler grabbed copy paper and scrawled out an editorial for the next day's paper. "Boy!" he roared. A copyboy, stationed at the bar, snatched the copy and rushed it down to the *American*.

"Does anybody regard himself as an expert in Homer?" Fowler announced.

"Why him?"

"Because an intelligent discourse on the man and his works shall carry us through until morning. Bartender!"

"Do you think," he was asked, "that you might want to go back up and look at the editorial?"

"That classic I just sent in guarantees my employment with Mr. Hearst until the moment after I take my last breath," Fowler said.

The editorial, which started on the first page in huge type, stated that Hylan was the Abraham Lincoln of New York.

One night after Patrice finished the last show at Guinan's, she came out to meet Runyon and found him at a table in the corner, with the view blocked by men standing guard. He was sitting with Fowler, Walker and two chorus girls from another club.

"I thought you guys hated each other," she said to Fowler and Walker.

"Oh, my darling, you don't understand. This is the way men do things," Walker said.

"No, it isn't," Patrice said. "It's how bad girls do things."

The moment she said it, she saw that Runyon was upset. Afterward, when they were alone on the street, he began to berate her and she said to him, "Where is your wife tonight?" He did not answer. "Are you going to stay married to her?"

"What does that have to do with your embarrassing everybody tonight?" Runyon said.

"It has to do with you yelling at me like you own me. If you aren't going to leave your wife, then I don't know why I let you yell at me."

When she saw the white anger in Runyon's eyes, she stamped her foot on the sidewalk and shouted at him, "Maybe I should go home and call your wife up on the telephone and ask her what she thinks of you staying out all night with some girl you think you own."

Runyon walked away. He felt at that moment that she was a blond hemp about his thin neck. At noon the next day, over lunch with Phoce Howard, Runyon mentioned the fight. "I can't have her closing in on me like this," he said.

"Yes, but you must go and call her right away," Phoce said. "Always call the next morning, whether the night before was good or bad. The absence of a soothing word the next day has caused civilizations to totter." The only reason florists open before noon is for guys to make up for the night before.

Runyon called but was distant and made no date to see her that night. Then, at 7 P.M., he was on the sidewalk in front of Lindy's and the gray cement turned yellow as the first Times Square signs flashed on. Suddenly, the loneliness ran through and flared into a fever. He looked into Lindy's and saw Scher, now the night manager, on the phone. Why is Scher talking on the phone when I need it to call Patrice? He went inside, stared Scher off the phone, called Patrice and met her in front of the club when she arrived for work. He spent the night sitting with her at a table and watching her perform. He was never happier.

One night, in Billy LaHiff's on 48th Street, Frank Costello came in to meet a bookmaker named Clancy. While Clancy was the name, his background was slightly different. "What-a you want?" Clancy asked. He had been handling Costello's bets for some time. Handled them with great confidence because Costello was being touted by Harry (Champ) Segal, and Clancy had about no respect for Segal's ability as a handicapper. That Costello lost quite a bit bothered Costello more than somewhat, but not nearly as much as Clancy's attitude. Each time Costello came in to pay, Clancy's chin rose and his mouth went into a mild sneer. Worse, Costello understood that each time he made a bet, Clancy called a private handicapper named Minch and asked his opinion on whether to keep the bet or lay it off with the racetrack. As Costello was betting Clancy man to man, or so he thought, he felt violated. On this night he came in and took out a sealed envelope and said to Clancy, "This here is a nice bet. It is on the fifth race at Hollywood Park tomorrow. I want to keep the envelope sealed, and after the race we'll both open it. We'll leave the envelope here with LaHiff personal and we'll meet tomorrow."

"So leave it. Why-a you don't trust?" Clancy said.

"You could sneak a look, which I don't want you doing," Costello said. As he handed the envelope to LaHiff, he said, "I got a word with you. This don't get opened until we're both here tomorrow night."

"You got a word," LaHiff said.

"This little girl is lucky?" Costello said to Runyon.

"Magic," Runyon said.

"Run your hand on the envelope for luck," Costello said.

Patrice ran her hand on it. Costello gave it to LaHiff.

"Are you really lucky?" he asked her.

She held her hand over her head and pointed at the ceiling. Why not?

The next night, Runyon and Patrice are at the table and Costello walks in. LaHiff drops the envelope on the table. Clancy arrived at eight o'clock sharp. He had a scratch sheet marked with the results of the fifth at Hollywood Park. The winner was Saltine Sea, paying $22.40 for every $2 bet.

"Go ahead open it," Costello said.

Clancy ripped it open and looked at the bet: "5 Hollywood. Saltine Sea. $100,000 Win."

Clancy's head came forward and smacked onto the table. Costello looked at him. "His eyes are open. Damon, this guy's gone." Dead he was. Without even thinking, he said, "Gee, this broad can kill you with her luck."

Patrice screamed.

Runyon took Patrice to all the fights, including the first Dempsey–Tunney fight, in September of 1926 in Philadelphia, which drew over one hundred thousand people and was supposed to be a display of Dempsey's deep jungle strength. A week before the fight, Runyon leaned against the ring at Tunney's training camp and listened hard. He had a theory that when a fighter was in the best condition, he groaned like an old cow when he threw a punch. As Tunney boxed, Runyon heard only the squeak of his shoes on the ring canvas. No other sound. When Tunney threw a punch, it made a great deal of sound as it landed on the sparring partner's nose. Runyon heard no grunt. Before the fight, he told this to Jimmy Walker at a party in Walker's private railroad car on the tracks alongside the Philadelphia Municipal Stadium. "I was going to make a good bet on Gene," Walker said. "He's one of the neighbor's children." Runyon insisted he remain clear of betting. There was no way to bet on Dempsey; he was a prohibitive favorite.

In the opening moments of the fight, Tunney walked out and hit Dempsey with a right hand. There was no grunt, but Dempsey's knees bent in half. His chances in the fight went out into the night air.

Walker looked frantically for Runyon. When he saw him, he tapped Runyon's ear and said, "Next time, get yourself a hearing aid."

Which was great sport, but there never was anything like the second Dempsey–Tunney fight in Chicago in 1927. Upon arrival, Runyon had a chauffeur, Charley Guzik, son of Jacob (Greasy Thumb) Guzik. When Runyon said he would drop Patrice off at the hotel, Guzik said that there had been an official request for her to accompany Runyon to fight headquarters, which were in the offices of Dr. A. Brown at 2146 Michigan Avenue. Here was big Dr. Brown, real name Al Capone, seated in a swivel chair that had armor plating on the back.

"Al."

"Shhhhh!"

Capone held up his hand. He smiled at Patrice and Runyon and waved them to seats. He made a whistling-wailing sound to imitate a clarinet: "Wa-wa-wa-waaaa da-da-da-da . . ."

"What is it?" Runyon said.

"Wa-wa . . . *Rhapsody in Blue*, what do you think it is? . . . Da-da-da . . ."

Capone kept his hand up for silence. For the next twenty minutes, he sounded every note of *Rhapsody in Blue*. When he was finished, he beamed. "How do you like it? Do I know the whole thing? Every note, yeah? I'm going to do it in the ring before 'The Star-Spangled Banner.' "

Runyon laughed.

"Hey, I mean it," Capone said.

"Would you tell him?" Guzik said.

"The crowd won't sit still for it," Runyon said.

"You see?" Guzik said.

"I know the piece," Capone said.

"I'll bet you do," Runyon said.

"I know every note."

"But they won't sit still for it."

"What do you think?" he said to Patrice.

"Oh, Alphonse, you know that I think you have exquisite taste."

"Yeah, but I want to know."

"Not in a prizefight ring —"

"You see what I tell you," Guzik said.

"Will you let her finish!"

"I'm thinking of a big band somewhere," Patrice said.

"Yeah, but that means they play. What do I do?" Capone said.

"You conduct," Patrice said.

Runyon repeated the opinion over the next couple of days. Finally, Capone called for a bandleader named Jule Styne. "Do you know Gershwin?" Capone said haughtily.

"I think so," Jule said.

"I want you to listen," Capone said. He opened his mouth and out came the first notes of *Rhapsody in Blue*.

Jule Styne sat like a mummy.

"What do you think?" Capone said.

"Al, I never heard anything like it before in my life."

Capone nodded. "You're hired." Capone had taken the Hotel Metropole for the entire week of the fight and booked entertainers Sophie Tucker and Harry Richman, who refused to appear in any club that did not feature gangsters. Now little Jule Styne listened respectfully and said that while he appreciated the offer, he couldn't fill the date because he was booked at the Granada, which was owned by Meyer Marks. "Meyer Marks won't let me go," Styne said.

"Meyer Marks is dead," Capone said.

"What time do you want my band at the Metropole?" Jule Styne said.

"Meyer Marks is alive!"

On fight night, Capone, who had been taking lessons on how to enter a room from a young guy brought in from New York, George Balanchine, made a subtle arrival. Gorillas rushed down the aisle and threw everybody in it into the rows, whether they belonged there or not. Then, with the aisle clean, here came Al Capone in a fine understated stride. "He looks like he's goin' down to get married," one of his men said with great admiration. He took a seat where, on one side of him, sat Jule Styne. On the other, Patrice Gridier.

When the fight began, Capone leancd toward Styne and began to sound out *Rhapsody in Blue*. Styne nodded. Then Capone swung over to Patrice and began to hum it for her. She, too, nodded. Capone had no interest in the fight.

Dempsey had Tunney on the floor once for what appeared to be more than ten seconds. Dempsey failed to go to a neutral corner and the referee refused to count until he did. Tunney remained on one knee and waited until the referee eventually got around to nine. Tunney probably could have risen whenever he had to, and when he did get up, he went backward until ready. The story is not in the long count. Rather, if Dempsey was such a champion, he would have left Tunney on the floor for thirty minutes. After the knockdown, Tunney issued a major beating to Dempsey. Tunney on his best night was a nice average heavyweight boxer with more fortitude than talent. His major ability seemed to be in reading good books, or at least saying he did.

This takes care of the cheap prizefight. Now the main event of the twenties took place. After the fight, with the ballroom at the Metropole packed with some forty senators and congressmen, with the mayor of Chicago and every other politician in the city, with all of Midwest society clawing to get in the door, here was Al Capone out in the hallway, wearing a tuxedo and white gloves, humming his concert. The gorillas with him nodded as if symphony hall regulars. He greeted the newspapermen as they arrived from writing their stories. "Wait'll you see this," he assured Runyon.

Capone went inside and stepped up to the bandstand. Jule Styne handed him a baton and went into his pocket and pulled out a sheet and read from it so he wouldn't make a mistake. "Ladies and gentlemen. Al Capone now will conduct George Gershwin's *Rhapsody in Blue.*" The room fell silent. Capone's white gloves and baton went up. The fingers wiggled. The first sounds of a clarinet ran through the room.

For twenty minutes Capone conducted the orchestra. Jule Styne, crouching alongside the piano, kept signaling Al to calm down. He was getting so excited that he looked like he was breaking somebody's head. At the finish, Capone turned to the audience and stood erect, chin up, hands at sides, eyes closed in positive rapture as the applause ran over him. Then, with the spotlight on him, he took a great bow.

The next day, everybody talked throughout breakfast about big Al's performance, and not the fight. Runyon was impatient for the late afternoon to arrive, so he could speak to Jule Styne about somebody to give Patrice vocal lessons in New York. He had to get her out of the chorus line at Guinan's.

The task of keeping a marriage and a girlfriend at the same time fell apart in the summer of 1928 when he came down with appendicitis. The operation was performed by Dr. Edward L. Brennan, who had the surest pair of hands in the city of New York. "Has to," Jimmy Walker assured Runyon. "Any fella who takes what this fellow gets from workmen's compensation claims would shake like a leaf. This guy is unconscious. He orders an x-ray for a sprained ankle."

"You're sure?" Runyon said.

"Ask my brother," Walker said. His brother, Dr. William Walker, had put $431,258 in the bank in Walker's first three years as mayor. William Walker had confessed that he was afraid to attempt any of the cash moves that Dr. Brennan did casually.

The appendix was removed at Polyclinic Hospital on 50th Street. Before the operation, Runyon tortured himself for memories of enough good works committed during his life to outweigh the evil he felt he had perpetrated. When, finally, he decided that the enthusiastic cash support of a family was the number-one corporal work of mercy, there was no workout on earth that would better prepare a man to win handily when entered in the biggest race of them all, the rush to the gates of heaven. "I've heard of a hundred cases of guys visiting people in prison and then handing out money to the poor on street corners, and all the time their own families don't see a dollar from them," Runyon said. He sat back in bed and began to consider himself a saint. After the operation he was sent home to the same wife and children who were responsible for his self-canonization. He had a son who stood in the doorway and could not wait to run an errand. The daughter smothered him with kisses. And the wife brought food and newspapers and fresh water. He hated it. He missed his girlfriend. The phone was in the hallway and Runyon was in too much pain to get up and use it. Frequently, Cora, the operator at the *American,* would call and leave a message. "She sends her love," Ellen Runyon said. In bed, Damon grunted. Cora was sending him a message for Patrice.

Finally, at noon one day while his wife was preparing lunch, Runyon got up creakily and made his way to the phone. He called the Forrest, where Patrice was house sitting. He knew he was supposed to speak in a low voice and pretend to be muttering to somebody on the sports desk, but instead he grew snappish. What was she doing in bed so late? Does that mean she had been up all night? What was she doing? "I didn't go anywhere," Patrice said. Of course this statement drove him insane. Suspicion breeds more illness than a jungle. Within twenty-four hours, almost recovered from an appendix operation, he came down with pneumonia. The doctor said, well, you never can tell about infections.

In bed, the fever making him even angrier, Runyon said to himself, A doll can kill you.

In despair he ordered a radio. His son remembered it as an "infernal machine." A corner of the room was cleared away and the pile of batteries, wet and dry, was placed there. The box was two feet long, one foot wide and eight inches high. There were three big dials and two smaller knobs that had to be adjusted. On top was a tall loudspeaker. Aerial and ground wires were required. When the radio deliveryman had the set fixed just right, Runyon, impatient, told him to go, that he would handle it. The moment the guy was gone, Runyon touched the dials. A blast of static came out of the loudspeaker.

He wanted to hear the Democratic National Convention, as Al Smith was being nominated. On the first day he heard the crowd roaring at the keynote address and got static for the rest of the day. He had Damon Junior run to the radio store on Broadway for instructions. He returned with a new battery. It was the first of many trips. The only familiar sound to break through the static was the voice of the announcer for station WEAF, Graham McNamee. He once had called trains for the Rock Island Railroad and came to New York as a baritone, but the only opening he could fill was in a church choir. He had been doing jury duty for a living, earning two dollars a day, which was only three dollars below what people were getting for a full day on a regular job, when he walked past WEAF, 165 Broadway, decided to go in and asked for a job. Which he got. Runyon switched to WJZ, with Major J. Andrew White, editor of *Wireless Age*, and Norman Brokenshire, who talked more than a politician.

When Runyon's radio finally became clear enough for Al Smith's acceptance speech to be heard, Brokenshire began talking during it. Runyon was infuriated, switched stations and ran into forty minutes of static. Just when he thought he had everything back, the speech turned out to be over and all he heard was Graham McNamee extolling himself. "I am the forerunner of the new speech form, radio announcing," he proclaimed. Now, for the first time in electronic reporting, somebody on the broadcast said thank you to Graham McNamee, and this practice never stopped. It became as much a part of broadcasting as the station signals. Runyon, who came out of a business where you went home penniless if you didn't get the story, listened to another lobbygow gush, "Thank you, Graham," and McNamee, preening so much that you practically could see him on the radio, said, "I appreciate that very much."

"I thought you got paid for this," Runyon said to McNamee on the radio.

During those days in bed, he began to notice that Ellen was a little bedraggled in the morning, but crisp and efficient throughout most of the day, until late afternoon when she began to grow loose and giggle, and here and there forget things. By nighttime, she was frequently out of hearing of his voice. When he needed something like water, it was daughter Mary who came in with it.

Also while he was home, the children were not allowed to make noise, except when, recovering, Runyon began to take baths. During that time, the children could speak.

*   *   *

The night is Sunday, November 4, 1928, and there is going to be a murder, a great New York murder, one which will bring joy to all those who consider the victim a great louse, and the line forms to the left for that. It also is the murder that starts the phase of Runyon's career where he gets paid big money. In other words, it is the start of his whole career.

He is sitting at the table in Lindy's with Arnold Rothstein. While both men are immaculately dressed, Runyon's Sunday blue is the winner by a couple of lengths. This is not easy. Rothstein is such a splendid dresser that he even advises Lucky Luciano on how to dress.

"You're a hoodlum, get a genteel tailor," Rothstein told Lucky.

"What are you telling me, I got a Roman Catholic tailor now!" Luciano said.

While Runyon sat resplendent in understated garments, Patrice, directly around the corner at this moment in the chorus line at Owney Madden's Parody Club, Jimmy Durante headlining, went to work wearing big rings, and her new dress, like all her new dresses, was cut so that her chest would be the first thing noticed by those entering the room. Runyon sat with Rothstein in Lindy's because Sunday night was "wash" night, when he and his bookmakers met and straightened out the previous week's sins, of which the only one recognized on Broadway was losing. As a gambler, Runyon was always in need of money for these "wash" occasions, and Rothstein loaned money to him for twenty-four hours at no interest, which was Rothstein's way of acknowledging greatness. Rothstein had the money and ego to rule everyone around him except Runyon. Once, Arnold had watched newspaper presses run in the *American* building. "They do not stop," he concluded. "You are not fighting a man with a pen. You can kill the man with the pen, but the press will keep rolling. So you really are fighting a printing press. That fight cannot be won."

Rothstein, however, does not back off when the matter consists of nonpayment by a newsman. Which was one of the problems on this night. Runyon and Rothstein discussed the problem of Arthur (Bugs) Baer, who wrote a column for the Hearst papers. Somehow, over the years, Baer took on this impossible nickname, which smothered the recognition of his ability to think, which he could do rapidly and delightfully. He was far from the cheap buffoonery the nickname implies. He argued that Niagara Falls shouldn't be listed as one of the even wonders of the world because people living on the very edge of the falls had to pay more for electric power than people in the Sahara.

Bugs had a secretary named Jerry Finnegan, who borrowed $2,000 from Rothstein, saying it was for Baer. Rothstein loaned him the money. Jerry Finnegan borrowed because he was such an insufferably dull man that he had to buy women everything in sight just to get them to have lunch with him. Baer had never borrowed a dollar in his life. He was a lender, not a borrower. He earned $25,000 from Hearst, lived on 89th and Park for $285 a month, paid the maid $15 a week and kept the car in a garage on 88th Street for $25 a month. He used to get $1,000 for after-dinner talks and $1,000 for articles in *Collier's*. So Bugs was all right. But Finnegan was not. Not only did he take the money from Rothstein, but he never returned it. Rothstein, who once walked through a snowstorm to collect $100, demanded his $2,000 from Baer, who thought it was a practical joke and laughed. Rothstein became surly. Bugs, nervous, asked Runyon to find out what was going on.

Now, at the table in Lindy's, Rothstein complained to Runyon, "Baer treated me like a clown."

"He sees the world funny," Runyon said.

"I don't laugh at money," Rothstein said.

"You'll laugh when you find out where the money is," Runyon said. "Bugs never got it. The guy used Bugs's name and blew it on a doll. Neither you nor Baer will ever see it again."

At this moment, outside, is Manny Manishor in a snap-brim pearl-gray hat and a tight-fitting black topcoat. Manny's clean-shaven, tough chin is out, and when Manny adjusts his hat you see his hair is black and wavy. Manny Manishor, thirty-three, lithe, his hands fast and heavy, stands on Broadway very alert for any presence of Champ Segal, who is not there, which is important because Manny doesn't get along with Champ Segal. In front of Lindy's, however, he does bunk into Nigger Nate Raymond, whose occupation is dishonesty.

"I need twenty-five hundred," Nigger Nate says.

"I don't have it with me. Have you asked Rothstein?" Manny says, indicating the restaurant inside, where Rothstein sat in the window with Runyon.

"Him? That's why I need the twenty-five hundred. The rat bastard Arnold robs us in the game."

"So I'll take from Arnold and you'll pay me back."

"Thanks, Manny."

"You won't mention it."

Manny goes into Lindy's and says excuse me to Runyon and says to Rothstein, "Arnold, I got to borrow twenty-five hundred."

"For you?" Arnold says to Manny.

"If I take the money from you, it's my worry to give you the money back."

"But is it for you personal?"

"No, you know I don't need your money. But I'm taking it for a guy."

"All right," Arnold said.

He turned his back and went inside his silk shirt and came out with a packet of money and began counting it. He grunted and handed it to Manny. "That's twenty-five hundred."

Manny nodded and stood there and openly counted the money. "I only got twenty-two five," Manny said.

Rothstein didn't say anything.

"I'm shy two-fifty here," Manny said.

"No you're not. That's off the top."

"You mean you're charging ten percent interest?"

"No, I charge the same two percent a week. The ten percent is expenses off the top. I got to pay to get money too."

Manny folds the money in half and hands it back to Rothstein. "No, I prefer not to do business like that,"he said.

"Suit yourself," Rothstein said.

"I do," Manny said.

As it was not his business, during all this Runyon remained mute. Manny Manishor walks out on the sidewalk and tells Nigger Nate Raymond to forget the loan. Raymond is furious. At the same moment, a man named George McManus walks up. He is called Humpy, but he is six foot two and with much weight on the frame. George McManus wears a plaid coat that must have cost like hell and could be seen for a block. He is accompanied by Red Martin Bowe, who will be immortalized before all this is over. Raymond tells McManus and Bowe about the loan and the three explode at once: one smacks his fist into his palm, one spins around and spits, one growls. They are all so mad at Arnold Rothstein that they cannot control themselves.

This moment has a history:

One week before, on October 28, McManus had been in a card game with Rothstein in the Park Circle Hotel, a full five blocks up Seventh Avenue. Playing in the game were such as Nigger Nate Raymond and Titanic Slim Thompson, who got the nickname, he explained proudly, "because I sink everybody." Also attending were Meyer and Samuel Boston, who came from Brownsville, in Brooklyn, and were early members of a group known in newspapers as Murder, Inc.

Rothstein sat down at the game at midnight. Nobody talked much and there was only the sound of the silky shuffling of cards. They played stud poker and Rothstein drank only water and smoked cigarettes. He also went to the men's room more than normal and came out hyper. Whenever Rothstein won he took the cash out of the game, and upon losing a hand, put up an IOU. He won $40,000 in cash and pocketed it. When he stood up some thirty hours later, his markers ran up to, everybody maintained, $284,000. At the end of the game, with daylight flooding through the windows and onto the dining room table where they had played cards, Rothstein said, "All right, I made a note on how much I owe. Now just give me the IOUs back so I don't have them around for somebody to look at."

"How do I get paid?" George McManus said.

"You'll get paid."

"What do you mean?" Nigger Nate Raymond, who also was owed money, said.

"I'm betting a parlay that takes care of everything," Rothstein said. "I'm betting Hoover to beat Smith, and Roosevelt to become governor in New York. Your money is good that night."

The national election was a full week off. Smith was going to be buried, but the second half of the parlay, Franklin D. Roosevelt, looked tough. He was not known and not such a hero around the entire state of New York. George McManus didn't even know Roosevelt's name. All he cared was that he had won money in the game, yet he had no money. Rothstein had lost money in the game and yet he had money from the game in his pocket.

"Would somebody please explain this to me?" McManus said.

That is the history of the game. Now, some nights later, here on this Sunday night in front of Lindy's, the harbor for ill feelings was bigger than Liverpool. There was such anger that Manny Manishor observed, "Talk like this could get somebody hurt."

"That would be awful," McManus said.

Now Manny Manishor walks off to his nightclub on West 52nd. He doesn't acknowledge Champ Segal as he passes him. The Champ stations himself in front of Lindy's, and he too sees how mad McManus and Raymond are, as is Red Martin Bowe. The three leave for the Park Circle Hotel and the Champ remains outside Lindy's.

Miss Temple Texas now walks up. She is young and blond and shivering in a thin cloth coat. She has the coat pulled around her and her arms folded in front in an attempt to keep warm. The one wrist show-ing had a bracelet with diamonds in it.

"I'm freezing," Miss Temple Texas announces.

"Isn't the coat warm enough?" the Champ asks.

"Not close. This is something you wear in the spring in San Anto-nio." She held out a wrist. "Every time my boyfriend goes out to buy me something, he brings me a bracelet. Or this." She opened the coat to show a necklace with a large diamond on it. "I never realized that a diamond don't keep you warm. I'm freezing to death and all they buy are these things. Diamonds. Nobody buys me a coat."

"So you take a couple of the diamonds to Simpson's and buy your own coat," the Champ said, Simpson's being the best hockshop in town.

"I can't," Miss Temple Texas said. "I'd lose my boyfriend. He wants to see me wearing these things."

"Tell him you want him to buy you a fur coat," the Champ said.

"I told him. He promised he'd get me one. But he's afraid to go to the furrier because his wife is always going into the place. So he came and said he was sorry and he gave me this." She showed her second wrist, with its second bracelet.

"Why does it have to be a fur coat? The guy could go into a store and buy you a nice big warm cloth coat," the Champ said.

"Oh, he did that," Miss Temple Texas said.

"Where is it, then?"

"I threw it at him. A cloth coat. Is that the best he can do for Temple Texas?"

Meanwhile, Runyon was in Lindy's, performing the act most crucial to his profession, sitting. The job of newsman requires an ability to sit for such long periods that a top-flight park bench sitter, a retiree from the transit system who cannot stand being home with his wife of thirty-seven years and thus has been known to sit even on the longest rainy day, would retire at the end of the eleventh hour with numb legs. Run-yon would still be there. Gangsters, who are in that trade because they don't want to work, spent nearly all their hours seated. A gangster needed wind and limb for only the shortest of dashes, the few odd yards from his car to that of the man he is going to shoot, and thence to re-turn. A big gangster like Rothstein didn't have to put out even that much effort. He could sit for long hours on almost anything that didn't have a nail sticking out of it. But when you get into championship sit-ting, and you have a guy like Runyon, who starts his thirteenth hour with a thin smile, the realization strikes that something more than a hard bottom is needed, that imagination must control mind and body. For by now, sitting is so strenuous that each thought about it causes the body to squeal in pain. Runyon, the son of a daydreamer, and who grew up alone in back alleys and railroad stations while imagining that he was living in China in the morning, in a gold-mining camp in the afternoon, had no limit on his sitting. Here in Lindy's, he only needed a cup of coffee in his hand, a haze of smoke to stare through, and he was good for an entire day. "I am the sedentary champion of the city," Runyon said. "Any young dope who can't sit still long enough to read a page can go out and jump low hurdles. In order to learn anything of importance, I must remain seated. Why I am the best is that I can last an entire day without causing the chair to squeak."

He once sat for seven hours on a court hallway radiator while awaiting a jury verdict. He recalled that he actually was on a tour of the Sistine Chapel, a private tour because the Vatican recognized him as a great worldwide talent whose children were being raised Catholic. The pope himself was in the chapel and was reciting some of Runyon's better lines when the jury ruined the scene by returning with a guilty verdict in a Staten Island love-triangle murder. Another time, he sat on one bench through a whole day in the Colorado statehouse waiting for the appearance of some papers dealing with a land scandal. That was the day he sang in the Denver opera. He established all sorts of records at his favorite event, as we will see it is, the Six-Day Bike Race. Here in Lindy's, he saw songs and stories and movies and love affairs and crime, all sorts of crime, from championship purse snatching to the main event, homicide. And as he dreamed, he also could keep up with the two to three different conversations going on around him, and that is another prerequisite for a decent newsman. The guy across from him, Rothstein, had been raised in a house where the older men sat and read religious books for tremendous amounts of hours, but Rothstein's attention span always betrayed him. After nine or ten hours, he would commence fidgeting and would actually get up from his chair and go out and stand in a doorway on Broadway, or jump into a cab while it was still moving and fly off to see some woman.

Therefore, when the phone in Lindy's rings, Rothstein is ready to jump out of his chair even before hearing that the call concerns him. Abe Scher, the young cashier, answers. The caller, McManus, shouts, "Tell Rothstein to get up here to Three Forty-nine of the Park Central right away." McManus hangs up before Scher can hand the phone to Arnold. Scher told the contents of the call to Rothstein, who listened and went briskly to the corner table of Jimmy Meehan, who was a tremendously honest person, according to his criminal attorney. Rothstein and Meehan went downstairs to the men's room, where Meehan apparently gave Rothstein the smallest gun he had on him, and he always carried a couple, for when Rothstein came up from the men's room he had in his jacket pocket a short-nosed Smith & Wesson .38.

Arnold told Runyon that he had to leave. Runyon decided to go around to the Parody Club to see Patrice dance, and afterward go to the Six-Day Bike Race. When he noticed it was too early, he decided he would hazard the walk of four short blocks with Rothstein up to the hotel. When the two got outside, here was Champ Segal studying Rothstein's face. Champ Segal asked Arnold, "What's the matter?"

"Somebody told George McManus I cheated him in a poker game and I have to meet him at the hotel to straighten it out."

"You have a gun on you, Arnold?"

"What do you want to know for?"

"Because McManus is a big guy, and if you get into a real hot argument with him you might be tempted to do something you'd be sorry for. Why don't you let me hold the gun?"

"Not a bad idea," Rothstein said. He gave Segal the gun. Frankly, many people thought the Champ wanted the gun so he could shoot somebody himself that night. Then Runyon and Rothstein passed through the gamblers and touts. Automatically, Horse Thief Burke fell in with them and they walked up to the Park Central.

"I'll be down in a couple of minutes if you want to wait," Rothstein said. "I just got to calm this guy down a little."

It was a minute or so after 10:30 P.M. Runyon said he would wait for a half hour. He bought a pack of cigarettes and a magazine for himself and the racing newspaper for Horse Thief Burke and the two sat in the lobby.

They did not have to wait any half hour. Barreling out of a door under a red exit sign, which showed he had just pounded down the stairs, came George McManus. Now the elevator doors opened and here came Titanic Thompson on all ahead. "I am not here!" he yelled at Runyon. The next elevator popped open and several men jumped out with their hands over their faces so nobody could see who they were. But one of them, Nigger Nate Raymond, cried out, "It wasn't suppose to come to this!" He fled.

Now Bridget Farry, a chambermaid, came into the lobby with a loud plaid coat over her arm. "Don't he want this?"

"What happened?" Runyon said.

"You couldn't hear it?"

"Hear what?"

"The shot. The whole hotel heard the gun go off. The guy got shot is in the hallway."

"Who is he?"

"Rothstein. I know that. I don't know whose coat this is. They told me to get rid of it. Why don't I leave it with you?"

Runyon kept both his hands on the lowered magazine. Horse Thief Burke took the coat out of habit. He saw the name inside printed in indelible ink: George McManus. The label said the coat was made by Harold L. Wallach, a tailor on West 57th Street. Runyon neither looked nor asked. He was right on that line where he had no objections to whatever happened. What was most important was that Rothstein was going to be a better character in stories now that he was wounded or dead than he ever would be if he remained alive and kicking. At this moment one of the hotel managers came rushing over. In his hand was fresh unfolded money from the hotel cashier's counter. "Mr. Runyon, the shooting happened right outside the hotel. It did not happen inside."

Runyon did not touch the money. Horse Thief's hand came out to snatch it, but Runyon knocked it back. "Not in time of murder," Runyon later remembered he had told himself.

Now the chambermaid said, "What am I going to do? I'm checking rooms to see which beds I got to turn down. I find this man sitting on the floor in front of room three forty-nine. He says to me, 'Get me an ambulance. I've been shot.' I called the police right away from the room."

"That is irresponsible of you!" the hotel manager said. "The man was shot outside the hotel. He is being put in an ambulance right now." He ripped money off the desk, gave her some and looked helplessly as Runyon and Horse Thief went on their way. The dizzy manager almost had them an unwilling part of a conversation that for sure could wind up on a witness stand. And Horse Thief now had both feet in a homicide case because he had the shooter's coat over his arm and he was not going to get rid of it, for he had ambitions of wearing it himself.

Police took Rothstein to Polyclinic Hospital, on 50th Street between Eighth and Ninth avenues, and rather than the usual platoon of superior officers watching the place, he was practically left alone. Nobody thought he would die, and anyway, there would be no crowd control at any hospital vigil for him. Patrolman William Davis was left to call Police Commissioner Joseph Warren's confidential squad. Mayor Walker's orders were that the confidential squad must be called for any major crime dealing with the guys out on the Big Street. When the mayor's cops arrived, Patrolman Davis said, "Some guy McManus supposed to have left his coat here, but I can't find it." The confidential squad man, Detective John Cordes, pushed the officer down the hall. "Whatever you heard or saw means nothing. We'll take care of this."

Runyon and Horse Thief, carrying the coat, had walked the four blocks to the Parody, where Patrice was in the midst of a spontaneous party being thrown by Lou Clayton. "I don't deserve this," Clayton said. "I don't deserve that Arnold Rothstein should get shot." Runyon, Patrice and Horse Thief left by cab for the Six-Day Bike Race. As Broadway was still a small village, the guy present at the start of it all, Manny Manishor, was only yards away, running his club in a brownstone at 137 West 52nd. It was called the Furnace Club, "the Hottest Spot in Town." As you came up the steps to Manny's club, the staircase was made out of blocked glass, and inside the glass there were red flames leaping. You were walking up to the home of devils.

Manny is at the bar, with Canadian Club, owned by the Rosensteils of Montreal, and Black Label, owned by the Bronfmans of Montreal and delivered to New York by Frank Costello and Lucky Luciano. The five-piece band is playing and the girls are singing and the guys are looking them over. Into the bar comes Nigger Nate Raymond and George McManus, coatless.

"There's been a comeoff," Raymond whispered to Manny. What was he, Raymond, supposed to do, keep quiet? He had just been at a thrilling shooting.

"What was it?" Manny whispered back.

"George shot Rothstein under the table."

"You all right?" Manny said to McManus.

"I am. Rothstein isn't. I shot him right through the prick." McManus fell silent. "The coat," he muttered. "I wish I would of thought to get it before I started running."

"They get a coat don't prove you shot him," Raymond said.

"The inside pocket is full of bullets," McManus said.

There was so much talk in the precinct about this missing coat of McManus that one detective, who wasn't part of the show, said, "I don't know what happened, but if a coat doesn't show up there soon I'm going to say something. I'm not losing my job over something I don't have nothing to do with."

All of a sudden, a chesterfield coat, with the name George McManus inside and a room key from the hotel in the pocket, appeared. The assistant district attorney thought it was great evidence. It was not quite as good as the real coat, a bit singed with gunpowder and the like. Still, detectives said that now somebody would have to lose a job for sure if this chesterfield coat ever got important in court. Some detective would have to say that he grabbed the coat from McManus's house and therefore was guilty of overeager prosecution. He then would have to place trust in the mayor for his living. "If it comes to that," Detective Cordes said.

At this time, the coat with the bullets in the inside pocket, which made it the real coat, was draped over the rail in front of Horse Thief and Runyon at the Six-Day Bike Race at Madison Square Garden. Runyon sat back, lit a cigarette, smiled and held Patrice's hand. The Rothstein shooting had the town upside down, he expected, and of all the places in New York, he knew of no fortress that could give a man better protection than the bike race. He figured that later on he would make one call and McManus or one of his people would pick up the coat. Meanwhile, there were at this hour virtually no decent people at the bike race, which was why he found the place so comfortable.

The Six-Day Bike Race meant exactly what it says, six days of riding, on a banked indoor track, twenty-four hours a day. Teams covered about two thousand miles in the six days. There were nineteen two-man teams from all over the world, with Poland, Belgium, Italy and the Netherlands usually sending in the strongest teams. The race was known as the ride to nowhere, because nobody understood what it was all about, and the scorekeepers were so dizzy by the third day that the elaborate standings they handed out were as accurate as wrestling results. A $1.50 ticket allowed you to sit through the entire first five days of the race. Everybody then had to clear out to make way for the enthusiasm of the last day's crowd, paying new admissions. But for those five days on one admission, of which this night was one, it was a poor man's hotel room. You might get a bit gamey, but for $1.50 you could be dry and warm for the whole week. Try standing outside in a blizzard for six nights.

Through most of the hours of each day, the riders went just fast enough to keep the bikes from wobbling. There were sprints at midnight, 2 A.M. and 5:30 A.M., and they drew every degenerate, show-off, busted valise, gangster, pickpocket and cheater in the city. Cash money on the spot was awarded to the teams that raced insanely around the oval and finished first. But the great sprints were started when somebody, usually a mobster or a show business name, got up and promised hundreds to the winner of a special sprint. This sent the riders and the crowd crazy.

Sophie Tucker sat in front of Runyon and Patrice. She had her legs propped up on the seat in front of her. The shoes had the highest and slimmest heels that could support her. She turned around and introduced the man with her. "Damon, I want you to meet my new pimp." The man was hunched forward, clutching Sophie's fur coat. Throughout the arena, men sat leaning forward with arms wrapped around their overcoats, much as a good fullback hugs the football when charging into the center of the line. Horse Thief Burke stood up and announced he was going to the men's room. The three coats, Runyon's, Horse Thief's and George McManus's loud plaid, were on the rail. Runyon sat back and smoked his cigarette. Nobody ever touched a coat of Damon Runyon's.

Bike riders moved slowly, in single file, around the banked wood track. The straightaway was canted to an angle of 25 degrees and the turns to 48 degrees. The most memorable Six-Day was when the promoter used plans from the original Madison Square Garden to lay out the track which were no good for the new Garden. This had been discovered by carpenters putting down the track at 7 o'clock on the night the race was supposed to start at 8. They had the whole track down except for some gaps; the wood wouldn't fit because it had been sawed to specifications of fifty years before. There were forty carpenters out there hammering away, and a band played "Yes, Sir, That's My Baby." The crowd sat and watched the carpenters work until 1 A.M., when the race had finally begun.

In the infield, in small wood cubicles of the sort used by chow chows in the Westminster Kennel Club show, other bike riders slept on cots until it was their turn to get out on the track for three or four hours. There was a man with a chef's hat on, standing at a steam table that carried a big sign, "Catered by Leone's." In the infield, too, Jimmy Basile and his eight-piece band played music. Shirt collars were open and, upon close inspection, the band seemed in terrible condition. Their eyes were puffy and red; their faces seemed to have had cigarette ashes rubbed into them. Their clothes smelled.

It is 2 A.M., and the scoreboard showed that George DeBaets and Alphonse Goosens from Belgium were leading Reggie McNamara and the fabulous Aldo Georgetti, who said he lived "near Rome," for the lead at the 101st hour. The Belgians had covered 1,646 miles and claimed they were challenging the all-time record of 2,003 miles, set in 1914. At this moment, however, one member of each team circled the track lazily and the other slept in his kennel.

Into the arena they came, the one gunman walking first, then the broads, and now here was Joe Adonis, the big new guy from Brooklyn, in a dark blue suit with a dark shirt and a tie so sparkling white in the light that it could have been made of pure silver. His correct name was Joseph Doto, but he took the name Adonis because that was exactly what he thought he saw when he looked in the mirror, and all the guys around him always said, "That Joe got the right name. He is a real Adonis."

There was the night that Heshie from East New York was honest enough to ask, "What is an Adonis?" Not one of the guys had an answer, and the only way out of this embarrassment was to give Heshie a good slap in the mouth.

In the stands, Joe Adonis raised a hand and snapped a finger. An usher came running over. Adonis stood up, took out a bankroll and removed $500 from it. The usher ran down to the track announcer, Joe Humphreys, who took the microphone and called out, "Mr. Joe A. from Brooklyn puts up five hundred for the winner of the next sprint!"

This was the custom that began in the early teens when Enrico Caruso would stand up at three in the morning and offer $1,000 for the winner of a sprint in his honor.

With a shout, the arena came to life. Officials ran around the infield, rapping hard on the tops of the cubicles. Riders came out on hands and knees, shook the sleep out of their heads and arose for the sprint. Two guys, Benny Davis and Harry Akst, rushed across the track to the piano used by Joe Basile's band. Joe Humphreys now announced, "Writers Benny Davis and Harry Akst would like to introduce their latest song, which will soon be sung all over the world. Here they are with 'Baby Face.' "

Harry Akst sat at the piano. Benny Davis stood at the microphone and in the worst possible voice, but one alive with spirit, began singing: "Baby Face, you got the cutest little baby face." The joint began to clap hands in rhythm to the song, which was one of these dynamite keg songs that blew the roof off at first hearing.

The first song introduced at a bike race was in 1913 when Fred Fisher and Al Bryan looked up at an arena loaded with whores and gangsters

and at two-thirty in the morning they began singing "Peg o' my heart
. . ." It was such a hit inside the arena that the word was all over town
within days, and soon every songwriter in New York knew that the
moment the Six-Day Bike Race began, they would get up there with
their new great tune, of which everybody had one or more.

The instant they finished singing "Baby Face," an usher was alongside Joe Humphreys, who read aloud, "Mr. Buster from East 107th
Street puts up six hundred for the next sprint!"

One section away from Adonis, a redhead with practically nothing
over her front explodes in glee. Next to her is her boyfriend Buster,
who smiles and waves a hand over his head as if he has just won a big
fight.

Now an offended Joe Adonis signals to the usher, who disappears
through an exit on the dead run and appears on the track.

"Mr. Joe A. of Brooklyn puts up seven hundred for the next sprint."

And, momentarily, "Mr. Buster from East 107th Street puts up seven
hundred and fifty dollars for the next sprint."

"Mister Joe A. of Brooklyn puts up eight hundred dollars for the
next sprint."

"Mr. Buster offers nine hundred dollars to the winner of the next
sprint!"

"Mister Joe A. of Brooklyn offers nine hundred and fifty!"

Buster figures Runyon has the weight to be the arbiter of the underworld at this moment. He runs over and says, "You don't know me.
I'm Buster from 107th Street. I'm in with good people. What do you
think, I keep this up? My girl loves me for it."

"Adonis doesn't," Runyon said quietly.

"Yeah, but I got a girl loves me to show people up."

"Yes, and your Mr. A. does not want to go to a grand because he
knows it is too much and he doesn't want to look like a sucker. He hates
that."

Joe Adonis stands in the Garden with two adoring broads in the seats
staring up at him and all the wise guys eyeing him and slowly Joe A.
takes out a cigarette case, taps out a cigarette, lights it and, smoke
streaming out of his large nose, holds his head high. All that is needed
to make a statue out of him is a fountain. Buster from 107th Street
quits. His red-headed girlfriend starts berating him for having no guts.

On the track, the riders move together slowly, ominously, and suddenly a gun goes off and the forty-lap sprint, five miles, is on. The riders tear around the track as the crowd screams, and after many laps,

Georgetti slows his bike while in the infield Reggie McNamara starts running alongside. The two do a quick leap, one off, one on, and the bike is back into fastest speed as the crowd is standing and screaming.

Standing being indisputably the most important act. For here were filthy ruffians scurrying out of staircase entrances and from empty sections, where they had been pretending to sleep. They rushed along the last rows of seats — where people had left coats as they stood and cheered the bikers — whisked away overcoats and continued running. The brazen tripped down the aisles and sought anything that looked good over a seat and simply reached in, filched it and fled in the same motion.

One of these ruffians worked on his hands and knees like a dog, crawling along behind the last row of the good seats. The suckers had been at the races for a couple of days and, with feet swelling, were in stocking feet. A hand reached for the spike-heeled women's shoes under the seat of Sophie Tucker, who had her bare feet up on the rail. One heavily made-up eyelid raised. She shouted, "Hey, fuck!"

With loud huzzahs, the sprint was over and the Georgetti team won another bundle. The crowd applauded and sat down.

Now here a fist slammed backward into the seat. "They beat me for my fucking coat!"

And over here a woman shrieks, "Genie! My shoes!"

The guy was on his feet, looking around. "The fuck!"

"Genie, how could they do this to you! You told me you were a big gangster. Who steals shoes off a big gangster's girlfriend?"

This gangster was suddenly part of an old joke: "Isn't that romantic the way Eddie carried his girlfriend in his arms all the way to the subway?"

"He's not gallant. She got her shoes stolen at the bike races."

It was common. Always there were people walking barefoot out of the six-day races and leaping into the air as they stepped on a piece of glass.

Runyon was laughing out loud and clapping for the bike riders. He reminded himself that this was the greatest sport in the land. Then he looked at the rail in front of him. His coat was there, all right. Horse Thief's coat was also there. But George McManus's coat, with a pocket full of bullets, was gone.

This was his first experience of being a robbery victim and he found the pain excruciating. "I want him killed!" he shouted. He glanced over at Adonis's party, but he knew that in telling anything to Adonis, even after two or three separate oaths on graves of mothers, Adonis would tell an Italian detective that George McManus shot Rothstein and tell him go ahead, this is a good pinch for you, an Irish bastard. Runyon even could hear Adonis leaning forward and whispering to some eager district attorney, "You know how I know? Let me see if you got the guts to axt somebody important about the case. Why don't you go and axt Damon Runyon if he knows who shot Rothstein."

Looking around, Runyon saw a big guy named Nolan, who once worked as a waiter at the Club Durant and now was doing things on his own. He went over and asked for help in getting a certain coat back before it caused a national incident.

He and Runyon left Patrice and Horse Thief and were walking along under the el on Third Avenue, with the cold morning sunlight coming through the tracks and falling in oblongs on the sidewalk. It is close to 9 A.M., when all the hockshops lining the streets in the 40s and 50s will open up. Already there are people lined up on the sidewalk to hock suits, watches, radios, anything that can bring expenses for the day, mostly and including food. Nolan leads Runyon past these legitimate people. He is looking for guys with their arms full of coats that have been accumulated during the night's foraging at the bike race. The problem was, there had been an early cold snap, and some of the thieves in the Garden were in such a wretched state that they needed the coats for themselves. With the onset of winter in New York, the heritage of the city was for a man without a coat to choose someone of about the same size and follow this well-clad person around until he stopped someplace, usually for lunch, and took off his coat. In snatching the coat, the thief never risked a stupid blind stab for a garment that would be of no benefit to him. There was nothing more forlorn than a man hitting the sidewalk outside a cafeteria on the rull run, darting around several corners, leaning against a building, chest heaving, only to find the coat he just filched was too small for him. So if the coat had been grabbed by a man in need of warmth, they were in trouble, Runyon thought. The coat was large enough to cover anybody. That would leave a stranger walking around the streets as the key to a shooting.

The people who had been in the Garden solely to steal were now skipping out from behind el pillars on Third Avenue and suddenly disappearing into the shadows, crying out to each other that an angry sucker was on the way. One man with coats over his arms moved with such speed that when Nolan began to run he quickly stopped, for he saw there was no chance of ever catching up with the guy.

Runyon shivered in the cold and his apprehension rose. He thanked Nolan but said it was hopeless. He went to the Maurice apartments, nodded to Madden's man, who always sat in the Duesenberg car at the curb in case of dynamite, and went upstairs. A pair of bloody eyes answered the door. "You go back to your Forrest and hang out. I can't promise anything. We'll have a look."

Runyon went to the Forrest Hotel and wrote a story in which he said:

Life for the average man who minds his own affairs is even money. When he walks out of his door in the morning, it is 50-50 that he will return safe and sound.

Arnold Rothstein was the only man I ever encountered who was "NO PRICE." When he stepped beyond his threshold he was "out" in the betting.

When he finished, Runyon put a Baltimore dateline on the story, to indicate to all gunmen that, as the gunfire was so close to him, he would remain at a distance. His typewriter was not the tool of a stool pigeon. He went to bed.

Both the phone and the bellhop woke him at 1 P.M. "There's some guys to see you out at the curb," the bellhop said. "Fella name of Bieler."

Runyon put on clothes and went downstairs, patting his hair into place as he stepped out onto the street. Bieler was lounging at the wheel of a car. In the back seat were two people whose occupation seemed to be hoodlum, and between them was a guy, scrawny and scruffy, and afraid, which he should have been. He couldn't voice his fear because of the hand clapped over his mouth.

"Here you are," Bieler said. He held out George McManus's plaid coat.

"Why don't you give it back to him?" Runyon said.

"All right," Bieler said.

"Thank you. And who's that in the back?"

"He is no more," Bieler said.

The guy in the back moaned so loudly that the sound went through the hand over his mouth.

"Fellas," Runyon started.

"Forget about him, he's gone," Bieler said.

"No, no," Runyon said excitedly. He explained with great care and logic the idea that even if the homicide of this unfortunate went unrecorded, it would weigh so heavily on Runyon that he would never be able to work again. He asked to talk to the guy. The hand was removed from the mouth.

The guy said with great desperation, "I want to live."

"Where?" Runyon said.

"Anywhere you say."

"Asheville, North Carolina," Runyon said.

"I'll go there right now if you let me live," the poor guy in the back said.

Once Bieler was satisfied that it was all right with Runyon, he warned the guy that if he appeared in the city again he would cut his head off and feed it to his cat. He then took the guy to the Capitol Bus Terminal on West 50th Street and put him on the bus for Raleigh, with a transfer to Asheville.

At the same time, Detective Johnny Broderick, the highly promising member of the police commissioner's confidential squad, came into the Furnace Club and asked Manny Manishor if he had heard about what happened the night before.

"I get on the train to go home to Brooklyn last night," Manny said, "and I pick up the paper and what do I see? This person Rothstein got shot. You wonder what kind of a world it's coming to."

"Was George McManus in your place?"

"Certainly. He was with Nigger Nate. I talked to the two of them."

"What did he say?"

"Hey, I'm in a nightclub. I say, 'How do you like the music? I hired a new trumpet player.' He says he likes the new trumpet player. I know they were right here in this bar and for a long time."

"What time did they get here?"

"What time did they say they got here?" Manny said.

Later, in the basement of police headquarters on Centre Street, a harsh voice calls up to the hot white lighted stage, "All right, bring them in."

Eight men are brought onto the stage and placed against the wall, which has ruler lines to show the height. Their eyes narrowed in the blinding light. This was a lineup in which perpetrators were identified by witnesses who remained hidden in the dark. Like all good methods of frightening the accused, it was a Catholic invention.

In the dark, chambermaid Bridget Farry, of the Park Circle Hotel, as eyewitness, sits with Detective John Cordes, a partner of Broderick's on the confidential squad.

"Take your hats off," Detective Cordes calls out.

One of the eight, George McManus, pulls off his hat and stands nervously.

Bridget Farry gets up, points at George McManus and cries, "That's not the man!"

Elsewhere, criminal justice did not function so well. Some uniformed cops had kept Red Martin Bowe in the back of a precinct for many hours and when Red Martin Bowe passed remarks about one cop's wife, the cop pummeled him. The moment he was set free, Red Martin Bowe, genius, wanted Runyon, or Winchell, to put a note in the paper about the way the same cops who took money from him for years had the nerve to question him about the Rothstein murder.

"How long was Arnold in the game?" Runyon asked.

"Not so long. We are there way before him."

"How long had you been playing?"

"It goes on for twenty-six hours and does not stop, yeah?"

"How did you do?"

"I lose."

"What about Meyer Boston?" Runyon said.

"He wins."

Damon Runyon suddenly stopped talking and stared off. Martin Bowe, speaking present tense, and then not using a contraction — "It does not stop" — caused Runyon to hear, in excitement, the sound of his Broadway characters. Here in Manny Manishor's saloon, when Runyon heard Red Martin Bowe's past-present tense, or the historic present as somebody said, the "I lose" and "He wins," he believed he was hearing someone speak this way for the first time ever. He particularly liked it when guys spoke in a stilted way, with no contractions, and used the language earnestly, the more to highlight their underworld positions. And now he, Runyon, and not Brisbane or Coleridge, was entitled to claim the whole of first person present as his own.

Damon Runyon heard it with those ears that had listened to people speak in army barracks, in saloons in the West where they still carried guns, on trains and in police stations, in baseball dugouts and fight gymnasiums, at ballparks and racetracks. Heard them speak with twang, brogue, nasal, guttural, heard of Italians called Meyer because they always said "My-a," heard ten thousand Jews lead with the verb, and heard the Germans in New York do the same — "Make the door shut," "Take a haircut" — heard all this speech, and heard well, because Runyon was the great listener, but nothing ever stayed with him the way Red Martin Bowe's line did. He had always liked the first person in the present tense and had used it in a couple of stories. But this was all in a warm-up of his later style. It never had the same effect as it would, from Red Martin Bowe on, coming out of the mouths of gangsters. In the ear of the reader, the gangsters seemed to speak in a British accent. So did the narrator, who revealed nothing of himself. The wall remained up, so that neither friend nor reader ever would be allowed to peer at his insides, which were frozen by loneliness. Had he realized that this reluctance to give of himself would prevent him from going past a short story and trying a novel, which requires you to sell your mother and then pull the covering off your soul, he would have said, well, there'll be no novels from this guy. His insides were to live in secrecy. A narrator hiding behind a false voice was the closest he ever would come to allowing his life to be seen and felt by others.

If everybody wasn't cursed with the electoral system, there never would have been a trial for the Rothstein murder. "Let sleeping documents snore," was the motto in the district attorney's office. Then in the fall of 1929, Walker had an opponent, Fiorello La Guardia, in the mayoralty election. Walker, hair slicked, suit without a crease, voice charming, appeared in the first filmed commercial in political history. It was done by Movietone News, the newsreel outfit, and showed Walker standing in front of subway construction and reciting a Runyon script. "I think the working man's time is sacred. These new subways will speed him home to family and hearth." Many, many movie houses showed the commercial between films rather than have city firemen arrive and look for violations.

This caused La Guardia to cheat and start using the truth. He said that Walker knew who killed Rothstein and was covering it up. Near the end of September, La Guardia said that city magistrate Albert Vitale of the Bronx, appointed by Walker, had received a loan of $19,940 from Rothstein. When reporters looked for Vitale, he was not in court. He was discovered making a campaign speech for Walker. "Remember this," Vitale told the audience, "La Guardia isn't a Catholic. He's a Mason."

A couple of nights before the election, La Guardia stood on street corners and called out into the chill fall air, "Walker knows who killed him and the police know but they do not dare bring the murderers to trial because they fear the murderers will tell what they know and bring to light a most revolting scandal."

Walker won the election by 500,000 votes, but on election night, amidst the cheers and toasts, Joab Banton, the district attorney, whispered, "I wish I didn't have the job. Everybody voted for you, but they are still complaining about the Rothstein case. We have to take McManus to trial."

The case was scheduled for November. An assistant district attorney named Ferdinand Pecora was given the files to prepare the case. He asked Detective Cordes to get him a set of Rothstein's fingerprints. Prosecutor Pecora had what he knew were Rothstein's prints on a glass of whisky left in the hotel room, but he had to match them against prints of Rothstein on file or he wouldn't be able to prove that Rothstein was even in the hotel room. Detective Cordes went downstairs to get the prints. He took quite a bit of time. When he returned, Cordes said, "I don't know what to tell you, but they got no fingerprints on Rothstein. Somebody took them out, I guess."

Then all of Rothstein's clothes from the murder night were missing. The dead man's vest, shoes, socks and underwear were nowhere to be found. After this, papers were filled out to obtain travel vouchers for a witness, Ruth Keyes. The city comptroller turned down the expense request with the complaint that the cost of bringing the witness was prohibitive.

The trial began in late November, and at the end of the second day of testimony, McManus's lawyer, James D. C. Murray, appeared to be in pain. Everybody assumed that Murray had just learned the day's race results. He was a helpless gambler who spent his life riding buses to Belmont Park so he could have a few more dollars to bet. But this time, Murray was muttering that he had no faith in juror number two, Eugene Riker. "He acts like something important happened," Murray said.

"Where does he live?" somebody asked.

"In the Village, I think. The clerk got the home address," Murray said.

The next morning, November 23, Riker was standing in the hallway waiting to present the judge with a doctor's note saying he was too nervous to continue as a juror. "We need lads with good steady nerves for this one," James D. C. Murray said. Usually, this would call for a mistrial, but the judge suddenly came up with something from *Abbott's Trial Brief.* An obscure section said that the judge could select a new juror, have all previous testimony read to him and then allow the trial to go on with the new juror in the box Rather than ask for a mistrial, defense attorney Murray glanced at the rule and termed it brilliant. A new juror, given a cram course, would be perfect for him.

The door opened and in came the new juror. He was at least heavyset. His face was jowly and pleasant. He had one hand in his jacket pocket, jingling change. He acted as if he knew everybody in the room. The defendant, McManus, had to look away, to ensure that no smile appeared involuntarily. The juror gave his name as Edward Shotwell. Defense attorney Murray bowed. He had no objections.

Shotwell sat down. "Let's go," he said. He was a working man, was Edward Shotwell, and as long as he was here to do a job, he wanted to get on with it. He was directed to a chair that was off to the side of the jury box. "I always run good from an outside post," he said, looking at Murray, who he knew was a gambling degenerate.

An assistant district attorney named McDonald brandished the three hundred pages of transcript that he would be reading to Shotwell.

"Can you pay attention to all this reading?" Judge Nott asked.

"I'm a great listener," Shotwell testified.

The chair creaked as Shotwell made himself comfortable. The assistant district attorney, McDonald, began to read. Shotwell fell asleep with his eyes wide open.

In the next morning's paper, Runyon wrote approvingly, "Mr. Shotwell settled down to steady, dogged listening that aroused the admiration."

All through the second day, the assistant district attorney read more and more pages of testimony to Shotwell. The large man did not waver or blink.

At 4:30 P.M., the assistant finished the reading with a flourish. "Well, Mr. Shotwell, are you satisfied that you have heard it all?"

Shotwell did not move.

"Mr. Shotwell?" the judge said.

"Payson Avenue," Shotwell said.

"What's that?"

"That's where I live. Payson Avenue, up in Inwood."

The judge was silent. Then, realizing that he, too, had his part to play, he ordered Shotwell to take the number two seat in the jury box.

Runyon's incisive trial coverage consisted of printing a complaint about the court hours. "Commodore Dutch, skipper of the Broadway Navy, is said to be in charge of pulling all defense witnesses out of bed in time for the 10:30 A.M. post time in court. These hours are really tough on a lot of folks who will figure more or less prominently in the trial. Some of the boys are wondering if Judge Nott would entertain a motion to switch his hours around and start in at 4 P.M., the usual hour of adjournment, and run to 10:30 A.M., which is the bedtime for gentlemen."

On Saturday, November 30, 1929, Mayor Walker, Runyon and Phoce Howard went to the Notre Dame–Army game at Yankee Stadium. Runyon and Phoce went to the press box. They could see that during the game several people dropped by Walker's box and whispered to him, and that these visits appeared to leave Walker elated. During the game, Walker drank from several silver flasks. Phoce looked at him in disdain. On Monday, Walker couldn't make City Hall. He was in bed with a "flu." Phoce saw Runyon after court that day and said, "He is a fool and he will soon be gone."

On Wednesday night, the *American* was informed by the judge's secretary that the case was going out in the morning. At 9:50 A.M. on Thursday, Judge Nott declared that the prosecution couldn't even establish the fact that Rothstein was in the room where McManus supposedly shot him. "I am dismissing this case," he announced.

George McManus and his wife hugged each other. Attorney James D. C. Murray, in a wing collar and bow tie, thanked the judge and then rushed for the door. He was going downstairs to reclaim the $50,000 McManus had put up as bail. It now became Murray's fee.

McManus grabbed the chesterfield coat that was supposed to be evidence against him and tried to run after Murray so he could at least split the $50,000 with him. But McManus's wife took his arm and photographers held the couple up for pictures. McManus smiled for the cameras and blew the bankroll. All now went to Dinty Moore's, then the Parody Club, and after that Lindy's. It was to be one of Broadway's biggest nights. Juror number two, Mr. Shotwell, said he enjoyed the party immensely and posed for several newspaper photos during the long night. "I was ready to do my duty, but they didn't give me the chance," he said.

At dawn at Lindy's, Runyon went through the paper and stopped to show the crowd a short dispatch from Washington that was at the bottom of the trial coverage. It said that the U.S. Board of Tax Appeals had ruled that Natalie H. Duke, widow of James B. Duke, the tobacco magnate, was absolutely correct in claiming that stock she purchased for $100 and sold for $127 had resulted in a $57 loss on each share.

SIXTEEN

He WENT home to the Forrest Hotel that night and took out a pad and went to bed with his girlfriend Patrice. He put the yellow legal pad against his knees and began writing in longhand. He spent several days on a fiction story about Rothstein's murder, but he was too close to it and found the story all chopped up inside him. One night he simply decided to choose a subject so simple that he was almost ashamed to let the pen touch the paper. Walter Winchell. An imbecile, but a useful imbecile. Runyon started out by writing down the name Waldo Winchester.

Phoce Howard called and asked, "How is the Rothstein story?"

"I'm not doing it."

"You must. You can't let it go by."

"Don't worry," Runyon said. "I got the night in cold storage."

He went back to writing:

> Only a rank sucker will think of taking two peeks at Dave the Dude's doll, because while Dave may stand for the first peek, figuring it is a mistake, it is a sure thing he will get sored up at the second peek, and Dave the Dude is certainly not a man to have sored up at you.
>
> But this Waldo Winchester is one hundred per cent sucker, which is why he takes quite a number of peeks at Dave's doll.

He wrote and rewrote the story by hand for several weeks before typing it. Longhand is still the best way to write, because the closer the hand gets to the words, the richer the words. Yet it was when he typed the pages that the best passages came. In starting to type, all he told himself was that he was merely copying this down, just typing it for neatness, and immediately the pressure and anxiety of actual writing was gone, and out of this freedom, without even thinking, things came out naturally, the phrase that made the story, the scene that suddenly came to mind, and the finished typewritten story was so much better than the handwritten version.

He spent a couple of days thinking of a title. He walked up Eighth Avenue and dropped the manuscript off at *Cosmopolitan*. At the magazine, stories are recorded on small numbered index cards when they come in. At the bottom of most is the date on which they were returned to the author. When Runyon's manuscript arrived, the secretary, before sending it around to the editor's, typed out on card number 1640:

> "Romance in the Roaring Forties."
> Author: Damon Runyon, Forrest Hotel, 224 West 49th Street, New
> York.

When the editors were finished, the secretary typed out on the bottom: "$500." There is a scratch mark through her typing. Over it is scrawled "$800." Under this was typed: "All English language rights."
Card number 1689 said:

> "A Very Honorable Guy."
> Author: Damon Runyon.
> Address: Forrest Hotel, 224 West 49th Street, New York.
> $800.
> All English language rights.

Card 1745:

> "Madame La Gimp."
> Address: Forrest Hotel, 224 West 49th Street, New York, New York.
> $900.
> All English rights. No film rights.

He said he wrote only for money, and his second and third stories to some of these magazines would send his fee up to $5,000 — and this in the middle of the Depression — for one three-thousand-word story. Yet even if a writer owes so much rent that the landlord is helping move the typewriter carriage, he needs all of his other emotions more, the unyielding conscience and pride to tear all of his insides raw while hunting at full speed a phrase that will bring sighs of delight from a reader. Without this, someone trying to scale the face of a short story will come down with hands empty and bloody. The length, a story told in at most six thousand words, at this time was the literary form of the superior writers in America. If you sent a short story to such magazines as *The Saturday Evening Post, Collier's* or *Cosmopolitan,* you were attempting to put your work amidst new short stories by Hemingway, Faulkner, Saroyan. In trying to write one of these stories, then, money could be a partial motive at the start and a measure of success at the finish, but it had to be the last thought during the writing.

The short story was the best for a writer in America, where life is lived so swiftly. Years in a room overlooking an English brook produce all these interminable novels of which nobody ever reaches the end. Life lived in a rush hour produces these rapid thoughts, compressed narrative, stories that get to the end when they should. At the same time, it is excruciating to write them, for while anybody can throw off tens of thousands of words without thought, it is another matter to be brief and still subtle and delicate, qualities without which the story is just another effort by some pretender given the use of a typewriter. The short story always has been thought of as a kite in the sky, riding on cord, pleasant and calming. Then a breeze catches the kite and the kite shimmers and dances in the sky, catching the eye and breath, and then the breeze is gone, the dance is over, the delightful moment has ended, as has the story. The writer who does not realize this, and attempts to prolong the moment, ruins it and has no story left.

Runyon's made the most money and lasted the longest because he was writing about people with at least one foot in the underworld, and he kept both eyes on one part of his audience, movie producers. Because of them, he had no need to find the right literary saloon, dine with the critic of the moment and attend the better parties. The other writers had to suffer through nights with people eager to exploit or plagiarize. Of all their works, only the odd one or two that wound up on the movie screen lasted. Runyon knew he would please none of the literary judges because he was mostly writing about small thieves and other minor criminals, and he made them humorous and even romanticized them. This horrified people who at the same time saw nothing wrong with a long book calling the Harrimans terrific people even if they did fleece working stiffs who came to their bank.

In the fall of 1928, while leaving Jamaica Race Track in despair, Runyon met a short, energetic man dressed so splendidly that Runyon immediately was attracted to him. Even more so when the man excused himself for a moment, went to the cashier's window and collected a slight stack of hundred dollar notes. His name was Ben Reuben and he was out of the Hebrew Orphanage in Cleveland. While grateful to the orphanage, he did not wish to return. He believed fervently in serving suckers. With a straight face, Ben told Runyon that he sold stock in his companies, such as "Internal Combustion of Canada." He had a small company that made snow shovels that were not selling. What did that matter to Ben Reuben? He put out stock called "Minnesota Snow Removal." When Runyon started to introduce him to Phoce Howard, who was also at the track, he found they already knew each other. Reuben told Runyon that he spent winters at Hibiscus Island, just off the Venetian Causeway in Miami. He described a room in his house that would be perfect for writing.

Runyon practically made one of his short stories happen first in real life, and then wrote it and profited marvelously. It started in February of 1929, when there was a wonderful mass murder in Chicago, the St. Valentine's Day Massacre, which people would live off for years, but as Runyon couldn't use a thing this obvious for a short story, he spent time looking. Everybody had said right away that Capone had perpetrated this crime. Capone screamed, "How could you say a thing like that there!" At the time, he was in the sun at his house on Palm Island in Miami.

A couple of days later, Runyon and Patrice arrived at Ben Reuben's house on Hibiscus Island, which was alongside Palm Island. Runyon intended to give giant write-ups for a few weeks to an outdoor fight in Miami between Jack Sharkey and Young Stribling. He happened to have a piece of the show. Ben Reuben's house was at 297 Hibiscus and the house next door, 305, was a twin building, almost attached except for a small passageway between them. Both houses were behind a common wall to keep purely honest people away. Number 305 was owned by Ed Strong, a disbarred Cleveland lawyer. In Reuben's house, Runyon and Patrice had their own bedroom in a private wing on the second floor, which had its own staircase. Patrice was up early each day to talk to workmen about building a white house a few doors down. It was going to be her taste and his money and, at the end, her house. When Runyon got up, they went for the day's sport at Hialeah. On many evenings, the adults had dinner parties at Reuben's house. Then Ben's young son Bill and other kids from nearby houses would cross the bridge over a small canal to Palm Island, where the happy Capone brothers, Ralph, Bottles and Mario, could be found with a waist-high pile of golf balls, which they hit into Biscayne Bay until the pile was gone. The older Capone, Big Al, always remained inside. "I stay in the house at night because I don't like to come out of the house at night," he explained. Every Sunday night, Capone had an open house and the Reubens, Strongs, Runyons and all persons unencumbered by legitimacy gathered. "When you got citizens around, you can't even talk about nothin', account of every one of them is a potential rat stool pigeon," Capone explained.

Runyon told Capone one Sunday night that the publicity from the St. Valentine's Day Massacre was harmful. In Chicago the previous Wednesday, two of the gunmen from the shooting had been blown up at a banquet while standing proudly, as if being honored for civic virtue. It was such a unique and brazen killing, coming right on top of the St. Valentine's Day mass murder, that a young assistant U.S. attorney for Illinois, Edwin L. Weisl, sent marshals attached to his office to Miami to see Capone. The marshals were not susceptible to outside pressure, such as J. Edgar Hoover telling them to go home and leave this nice sportsman Capone alone. They accomplished nothing outwardly, but they made Capone uncomfortable and unsure.

"You'd think they'd show some appreciation," Capone muttered to Runyon and Ben Reuben. "Guys get punished for the terrible thing they done, and instead of saying thank you, they send bulls to see me."

Runyon told Capone that anybody who gets in the newspapers so often gets blamed for the nearest traffic accident. He said that the gangsters might try to imitate truly rich women, whose names appear in the paper only at birth, marriage and death. "What do they do if they want to see their picture in a paper?" Capone wondered. Later, Patrice told Runyon and Reuben that she had occasion to speak to a young woman present at dinner who said Capone had syphilis and went insane and put his fist into the wall when she brought the matter up.

The heavyweight fight in which he was slightly interested was between Jack Sharkey and Young Stribling, who was from Georgia and best known for having terrific parents. His father and mother worked as seconds, so they could swab him down between rounds and then push their son out to get his face punched in. In real tough fights, the mother even gave him a kiss on the cheek before sending him out to get destroyed.

Runyon inspected the box office one day and found a ticket seller dozing. Runyon returned the next day with Capone, who stood proudly while photographers took pictures of him with Sharkey, who loved it. In New York, the *American* ran a two-column photo of Capone, straw hat in hands, wearing a string tie and double-breasted suit, standing alongside the fighter. The caption, written by Runyon, read: "The somewhat portly person on the left is none other than 'Scarface' Al Capone, once a well-known Chicago gangster, now residing quietly in Florida, who has never been photographed. Although the police have lately mentioned his name in connection with the Chicago rum massacre — which Capone says he knows nothing about — the hitherto shy Al consented to this pose with — guess whom? — Jack Sharkey, the sunshine of Miami Beach."

Runyon suggested that Capone ought to bring all the sportswriters in town to a pre-fight party at his house. Capone said, "What time?" He had more than sixty people at an affair that featured a young woman who passed out from champagne. When she awoke on the living room couch, she complained of her back aching. She felt underneath her and pulled a shotgun out from under the pillows. At dinner's end, right after peaches with espresso, Mrs. Al Capone went up to her bedroom to try on a new outfit — why have a gangster for a husband if you have to wear the same clothes all night? — and let out a scream when she found that her best diamond ring was missing. Big angry gangsters ran all through the house. Suddenly, Capone said the ring had been found. That was for his ego. The ring never was found, and in private Capone screamed, "I know these poor bastards on newspapers can't help themselves, that they got to steal every fucking thing in sight, all of them, because that's what they are, thieves, but they better get some rules for stealing. I thought they knew enough never to take something off a friend in his house. Because I tell you what that brings on. That's what makes six or seven guys get killed all at fucking once, do you hear me? Six or seven at fucking once!"

Because of Runyon's press party, Capone was written about by dinner guests such as Paul Gallico and Ring Lardner, and nobody mentioned the fact that some rat sportswriter stole Al's wife's ring. Capone now got a phone call from Johnny Torrio in Chicago, who asked Capone if he had gone crazy. Torrio, a murderer from the Sheepshead Bay area in Brooklyn, moved to Chicago and found the town so backward that his 78 IQ made him Boss of all Bosses. Capone blamed Runyon. Torrio told Capone that Runyon was nothing but a user and Capone ought to kill him. At the racetrack he went up and complained to Runyon, who was amazed and irritated. He said he could not imagine why Capone was upset, particularly with the way the New York papers played the story. Later, Runyon called the newspaper in New York and got Hype Igoe in the sports department on the phone and handed the receiver to Capone.

"I'll tell you one thing," Igoe said. "Boy, you sure sell newspapers in this town. Anybody who sees this paper today would never convict you if they had to sit on a jury."

"Well, I come from there, you know that, don't you?" Capone said.

"Sure we do. We got extra trucks going to Brooklyn," Igoe said.

"Do they want my old street address? Ninety-five Navy Street. Off of Myrtle Avenue. I'm baptized right around the corner. You want the church? Saint Michael's."

"That's great," Igoe said.

"Don't you want to know who my godfather was?" Capone said.

"Who?"

"No one," Capone said. "Since the church was put up, I'm the only guy never had a godfather. Do you know why?"

Igoe was silent on the other end of the phone.

"I just axt you to axt me a fucking question!" Capone said.

"Why?" Igoe said.

"Because I'm the godfather of everything." Now Capone paused. Then he said, "I got married Mary Star of the Sea on Court Street."

On the night of the Sharkey–Stribling fight, on February 27, 1929, held outdoors in Miami Stadium, a great smile covered Capone's face as he sat in the lights of photographers' flash bulbs.

Back in New York, Runyon told Owney Madden that Capone had something wrong with his prick, although he would let nobody get near it, particularly a doctor, and it was making him even crazier. Instead of a legitimate mob killer he was becoming a homicidal maniac. Madden, the librarian of the underworld, had read too much about Capone. "What do I do about the guy?" Madden said.

"Call a convention," Runyon said. "Do it like the Democrats." The vision now took over his mind and his cigarette waved at Madden. "Go to Atlantic City. You got the place. Cut down the murders and cut Alphonse down before he takes you all with him. Safest place in the world for him is jail."

Again, there was the most ecstatic feeling of the poet as dictator. He would direct a writer to turn his chair away from a window and stare instead at a blank wall. Now he would tell gangsters how to conduct all of crime. What was the difference? He loved to put his opinions into law. He had nothing against Capone. He rather liked Capone. But his urge to direct everything was more important to him. After me, you come first, Al.

Madden left his office on Broadway to find Frank Costello, who was at the Waldorf-Astoria barbershop. Costello didn't like Madden because he was Irish, but like Madden he knew enough to refrain from all bigotry that cost money; Owney never cheated him by an unconscionable amount. Costello also knew that while Capone often was just playful, he was using real guns. He agreed with Madden that a meeting was necessary. It was held in Atlantic City in May of 1929. By this time, Capone was a national issue. In brazen nepotism, he arrived with a staff of six, three of whom were his brothers.

A half block from the boardwalk, in a two-story stucco house on Iowa Avenue, Louie Kessel, a 260-pound man with a waxed mustache, walked into the bedroom of Mayor Nucky Johnson at 3 P.M., a full hour earlier than the mayor's usual rising time. Kessel chopped his strong hands on the back of the mayor, who as usual did not feel well from whisky the night before. Kessel threw him into the shower, then had the maid bring in breakfast. He helped Nucky dress in a blazer and slacks. Leaving the house, Nucky put on a straw hat. The moment the sun hit his eyes he winced. But when Nucky got a toe on the boardwalk, his face broke into a smile and he had a hand in front of him, reaching for the first citizen he could see. As photographers were present, he had his staff out on the boardwalk, and immediately they rushed a panhandler up to him. Nucky went into his pocket and brought out bills. Watching this, adjusting a double-breasted dark blue suit, white tie and big gray gangster hat, was Al Capone, who was so shaken by the mayor's entrance that he had his two Great Danes brought. Nucky Johnson walked over and kissed Capone on both cheeks. They started walking the boardwalk, Capone's dogs trying to pull Capone and thus providing excellent action for the cameras.

"This goes on the front page, right?" he said to the photographers, who walked backward in front of him.

"Sure, Al."

"You sure?"

"Sure, Al."

"If it don't, yez'll all get killed," Capone said.

The cameramen and onlookers convulsed in laughter.

In the hotel entranceway, conventioneers Owney Madden, Lucky Luciano, Meyer Lansky and Costello watched. The others turned to

Madden and said it was a good thing he had called this meeting because obviously they had a lot of trouble.

In a private dining room of the Shelbourne Hotel, 125 people assembled, the most murderers ever to gather in one place, including peni-
tentiaries. When the convention began, all present took an oath of silence, called *omertà* by the Italian faction. Then everybody ran to the
phone and called everybody they knew. The gangsters despised the
meeting because it reminded them of grammar school, which they all
hated, or a courtroom, which was nothing more than a grammar school
that hurt. Therefore, nobody sat up straight. Albert Anastasia gave Bugsy
Siegel a hotfoot. They all told Frank Costello that Walter Winchell was
fucking his girl in New York and Costello couldn't have Winchell killed
anymore, as Owney's meeting was against murder. "I won't vote for
you to hit Winchell," one gangster said. Costello continually ran out to
the phone to call his girl. Champ Segal appeared in the lobby. The
Champ had heard about the big meeting and came down to put the
bite on everybody. He banged on the meeting room door while they
sat in silence, pretending not to be there. Finally, Joe Adonis went to
the door and told Segal, "Here's a little traveling money." He slammed
the door. Segal cried out, "This won't take me to Toledo!"

The minutes of the conference show that Madden was a seasoned
politician. He had the major issue settled before he walked into the
public meeting.

"We have to get to the rut of the matter," he said in his harsh northern England voice. Everybody was looking at Capone. "We just voted
you go on a trip."

"To where?" Capone said.

"To college," Madden said.

"Let me axt you a question," Capone said.

"Certainly."

"When do I laugh?"

"When the wee little man opens the door to let you out."

The idea was so direct, that Capone, in the vortex of all controversy,
would simply walk across the street and into a jail cell and end the heat
for everybody else, that the gorillas growled in agreement. Capone,
dazed, sat down and started swallowing red wine. The next day, pout-
ing, he walked out of the place and took a train to Philadelphia, where,
changing for the train to Chicago, he was met by two detectives. Capone held up his arms and said, "Yez nailed me carrying a gun." He
was en route to a year in the can.

Back in Atlantic City, Madden spread out street maps of New York on the floor of a hotel suite. He had seen West Side politicians doing the same thing. He walked around the room, bending down with crayons to draw lines on streets, indicating which bootlegging territory was owned by which gang. The Chicago, Detroit and Philadelphia people remembered what he did so that when they got home, they could do the same on their own street maps. Madden also established rules for murder. Nobody could be hit unless a local commission passed on it. The first commissioners were named at the meeting, including Lansky, Luciano, Madden and Costello for New York. When Owney finished, Costello reviewed the work. "Owney will save us a thousand murders," he said. In the end, probably more than that. Costello was confident that by numbers and incentive, this crime organization would turn into a syndicate mainly with Italian names and become known as the Mafia, if they didn't all murder each other first.

After the redistricting, the mobsters threw a banquet to honor Madden. Big Frenchy DeMange was told to present Madden with a watch for service to the American underworld. "You got a watch, Owney?" he asked. Madden held his wrist out. Frenchy took the watch off and threw it on the floor. He stomped on it. Then he handed Madden a box. "Here's a new one."

Madden is not in New York twenty minutes and he tells Runyon that the conference was hindered by Costello's many dashes to the phone at key moments. Costello was afraid that Walter Winchell was stealing his girl in New York. The girl had dark hair. "Dark Dolores" now appeared as card 1745 at *Cosmopolitan:* "I am in Atlantic City with Dave the Dude at the time of the big conference."

On the day the magazine was delivered to the Waldorf-Astoria newsstand, Frank Costello was upstairs having his fingernails manicured. Costello read while Jeannie, the manicurist, waited. Then Costello muttered, "He put the whole thing on me."

A week later, Costello is sitting in Dave's Blue room with Dark Dolores.

"You bring me anything?" Dolores said.

"Myself," Costello said. "What else was I supposed to bring?"

"Something good."

"Like what?"

"Like a car. Every place I go people tell me about the story Runyon wrote about me. I'll bet you I'm going to have somebody play me in the movies. I'm going to be a famous person."

At the Kentucky Derby that year, 1929, Runyon and Phoce Howard took a suite at the Hotel Kentucky, on 3rd Street in Louisville. The day before the race, they stood on the sidewalk outside the hotel and searched the crowds surging back and forth between the Kentucky and the Seelbach Hotel up the street. Diamond Jimmy Moran of New Orleans, who was staying in a private Pullman car out at the train yards, came down the street with the diamonds in his teeth flashing and his hands waving as he led his personal marching jazz band. He stopped the parade and introduced Runyon to Clyde Van Deusen, the trainer. Van Deusen had a horse in the Derby under the same name, Clyde Van Deusen.

"I am going to win the race," trainer Van Deusen said.

After he left, E. Phocian Howard announced, "I cannot stand such a man. I said in my report to my own paper that the horse will win. Now I hope something will come up to beat him. I am willing to sacrifice my flawless opinion just to see the look on his face when he loses."

It came up rain late that night. It rained harder through the early morning. "The mud will ruin the horse," Phoce told Runyon in the hotel lobby. "The horse can run in your usual mud, but this is an entirely different matter down here. We deal with earth that has a great deal of limestone in it. The mud is deeper. Once this horse sinks that extra inch or so into mud, believe me, he is a goner."

At Churchill Downs, Runyon went to the jockeys' room and looked for Linus McAtee, who was to ride Clyde Van Deusen. He was told that McAtee would not be around until it was time to get dressed for the Derby. "Doesn't he want to get a feel of the track?" Runyon said. The jockey's valet shrugged. Runyon walked under the stands to the track. He ducked into an office used by workmen and borrowed one large rubber boot from a pile on the floor. He went out to the track and put his foot down. The foot disappeared into the mud. He stood there in a white panama hat, a cigarette holder clenched between his teeth and a victorious smile on his face. In all this great crowd, only he and Phoce knew that Clyde Van Deusen could not survive mud this deep.

Watching this from the rail was Hirsch Jacobs, the young trainer from New York. "What is your object?" he said, speaking softly.

"This limestone soil certainly makes deep mud," Runyon said.

"I think it is the rain that makes the mud," Jacobs said.

"I just wanted to see the condition of the track. The jockey doesn't want to get a feel of it. That means I have to do it myself. I get penalized for losing. He gets paid for it."

"If the jockey gets a feel of the racetrack, I would say he is in trouble," Hirsch said, "because that means he just fell off the horse."

"I know I'm going to make one of the biggest bets of my life against him," Runyon said. "I fancy the Bradley entry."

"I do not want to influence you," Jacobs said. "But did your foot in the mud have anything to do with it?"

"Absolutely. Clyde Van Deusen can't run in deep mud. He can only run in light mud. He sinks down too much in deep mud like this. I am going for the lump on Blue Larkspur."

"Isn't the mud just as deep for Blue Larkspur as it is for Clyde Van Deusen?" Jacobs asked.

Runyon had no answer, which was the usual, for a true gambler has so much ego that he cannot see or hear of any other animal or human being.

Jacobs smiled warmly and left. He would go on to train the winners of three thousand races, but he did not think it was good business to alienate a sports columnist. Upstairs in the stands, Phoce Howard was irate when Runyon mentioned Hirsch Jacobs's opinion. "He is trying to sway us with racetrack terminology. A front runner like Van Deusen cannot make it in the mud. Besides, the trainer is a lunatic. Having the horse named after him. Go with quality. Go with old-fashioned understatement. Colonel E. R. Bradley."

Runyon and Phoce Howard went to see Bradley in the clubhouse boxes. Bradley said Blue Larkspur was a wonderful prospect. "It's still only May," he said. "We hope we have a long way to go with him. He might even have a chance today. That is all I can tell you."

"He means he will win by a thousand yards," Phoce said.

Runyon went to the window and bet $2,500 on Blue Larkspur and went to the old press box high on the roof. Out of the starting gate and into the wet, gloomy afternoon came Clyde Van Deusen. His lead foot took this enormous stride and the full weight of the horse came down on an ankle so thin you could fit a bracelet around it. The foot plunged into the deep mud. Then the other foot came plunging right straight into the mud. Simultaneously the two rear legs went into the same mud and the two front hooves came out of the mud as the rear legs sent Clyde Van Deusen's body practically whistling through the wet air. He was on the lead with the first jump.

The slop will eat him up, Runyon said to himself.

Clyde Van Deusen was first going past the stands and he entered the backstretch first. Now Blue Larkspur showed wonderful running form and came up to third, except that running was difficult because Clyde Van Deusen, out there in the lead, was throwing a great amount of mud high into the air and the other horses had to run through it. This is where the phrase "mud in your eye" stems from. The phrase often carries quite a bit of meaning. In this case, Clyde Van Deusen was two lengths ahead at the finish, and Runyon, writing the account, was sick to his stomach.

Runyon and Phoce then entrained for New York. At Penn Station, Ben Jones, Phoce's chauffeur, met them. He had chicken on the back seat, a sign that he knew the riders were broke. He dropped Runyon off at the Forrest. "Just go up and write," Phoce said. "Your only way out is with a typewriter." Then he went home to the Plaza. His mother asked him how he had done in Louisville. "Wonderful. I always cash a big bet when I see you."

Any good record of the times, such as the blotter of the 16th Precinct, West 47th Street, shows that Phoce Howard had clear eyes.

June 22, 1929
Complaint
4:40 A.M. Ptl. Quilty J. reports that some unknown citizen informed him of a crap game at 231 West 50th Street. Sgt. McGuire sent to investigate.
5:10 A.M. Sgt. McGuire reports that report of crap game at 231 West 50th St. is unfounded.

Oct. 15, 1929
Complaint
3:05 A.M. Ptl. Ryan C. reports that some unknown citizen informed him of a crap game in premises 321 E. 48th Street. Sgt. McGuire sent to investigate.
4:05 A.M. Sgt. McGuire reports that report of crap game at 321 E. 48th Street is unfounded.

"I used to feel sorry for Sergeant McGuire's family, what with him being on permanent night duty," Feet Edson, the nightclub head waiter, also known as Feet Samuels in stories, said one night. "Then I was at the dice game at the Hotel West Virginia. Doesn't the guy bang down the door and say he is going to bust the game unless we find a way to change his mind. I see what everybody has to give him. You can bet me the guy makes more around here than a singer does."

16th Precinct, November 20, 1929
1:25 A.M. Miss Lora Lee present with key marked Breslin Hotel room
706 which was thrown from some unknown taxi at 49th and Broadway. Hotel Breslin notified.

It can be stated with some historical knowledge that not only was the
Hotel Breslin, located at 29th and Broadway, notified by phone, but so
was the occupant of Room 706. The guest was Mr. Samuel Gluckstern.
He was home with his wife. He got a call from the West 47th Street
desk lieutenant, who said that a Miss Lora Lee had the room key and
wanted to know if he thought he forgot anything else. Sam said that if
there was, he would be at Lindy's the next day to attend to it. He was
a ticket speculator, and he arrived on Broadway with tickets to the Yale–
Harvard game, which he handed out to gamblers in hopes they would
refrain from spreading the room-key story. The better seats at the game
were filled with people like Irving Caesar, who bet Yale and then sat
through the game reading and discussing *Variety*. In a short story, "Hold
'Em Yale," Sam Gluckstern became Sam the Gonoph. He also came
down from the game at New Haven and once again checked into the
Hotel Breslin for the night.

Outside of Phoce Howard, Runyon's literary circle now consisted of
people in gray shirts in filthy city rooms. At the Hearst papers, the
chief copyboy, Al Marder, was in partnership with Bugs Baer and a
new reporter, Robert Considine, in marketing a hearing aid that consisted of a metal bug to be fitted into the ear. The bug was attached to
nothing, and did nothing. The hearing aid sold for a quarter. "When
you wear it in your ear, people see it and start shouting at you," Marder explained. "That's a hearing aid, isn't it?"

Runyon's other circle, on Broadway, consisted of people like Billy
Lustig, who came up from the East Side and dared people to play Russian roulette with him for $1,000 a try. "Go ahead, you're faded,"
somebody said to him one night. Billy stood in front of Lindy's and put
the gun to his head and pulled the trigger. The click sounded like an
earthquake. "Give me my money," Lustig said. The bettor, Max the
Chef, said, "The gun ain't loaded." Billy put the gun to the palm of his
hand and pulled the trigger. The explosion caused everybody to drop
to the pavement like experienced infantrymen. Billy stood with the
blood running out of his hand. "Pay me my thousand. And go inside
and bring me a napkin."

All his waking hours now were spent in silence, with the enthusiasm and emotions that went into writing pouring through Runyon's mind. As he wrote "Madame La Gimp," he more and more believed that Patrice was a Spanish countess, and on a couple of occasions he asked her about the Amati diamond. This was the diamond of over 30 carats that was owned by the family in Spain that Madame La Gimp's daughter had entered. By now, he did not mind in the least that he found himself believing that the gem existed. And Patrice had no quarrel with living in illusion: she said that the diamond was in a bank vault. She had an appraisal from some expert who didn't spoil the night by asking to see anything except a showgirl. She then insured the Amati diamond for $200,000. One day she called the offices of the International Diamond Exchange Investors Service, which kept track of all the world's major diamonds, and announced that she was Damon Runyon's personal girlfriend and she owned the Amati diamond. The service thanked her for calling, and the official world diamond records showed thereafter that the tenth largest diamond in the world belonged to her. Nobody questioned the matter further, because she was regarded as being rich and prominent.

Soon, at the offices of *Cosmopolitan*, a secretary typed out card number 2204 for a story called "Butch Minds the Baby." The fee on the bottom was listed as $1,000.

And then card number 2650:

LITTLE MISS MARKER
Author: Damon Runyon
Address: c/o Reuben, 297 Hibiscus Island, Miami, Fla.
Rep: Paul Small, the William Morris Agency, 1640 Broadway, New York City.
$1,500.
First North American serial rights only. NO FILM RIGHTS.

E. Phocian Howard's opinions began to talk through the mouth of a man named Frank Capra, who sat in Hollywood and read, once again, "Madame La Gimp." He had directed a movie for Columbia Pictures, entitled *The Bitter Tea of General Yen*, a romance with a yellow man and a white woman. It had blown money because all of the British Empire banned it. He also had not won an Oscar. So, in Hollywood, he decided to go to the other side of the street. He liked a story about "these ragtag mugs scrounging for crumbs in the twilight zone between the underworld and the supposedly decent." Capra loved the

first person present and the outlandish metaphors. He also was in-
trigued by the notion that "some eggheads dismissed the style and
his beggary Guys and Dolls — petty mobsters, pickpockets, molls,
grifters, touts, pool hustlers, and panhandlers — as another passing
Broadway fad. But knuckleheads loved the fey antics of Louie the Lug,
Harry the Horse, the Lemon Drop Kid, Dave the Dude, the Weasel,
Butch, Madame La Gimp — all of whom considered honest work a
human catastrophe."

Capra decided to go for the paradox. His *Bitter Tea* had a cool, blue
tinge. Harry Cohn, the head of Columbia, had called it "arty dreck"
and kept saying that the picture had lost money. This was virtually an
impossibility in these days when movies still were called photoplays
and they were the only form of mass public entertainment. Anyway,
Capra was going with the other end of the story spectrum, as he called
it, the warmer, red end. At least the British Commonwealth couldn't
ban a Runyon fairy tale. He had a letter sent to Runyon at the *American*, offering him $1,500 for the story. When Capra, who pretended to
be a romanticist, sent the letter, he said, "Wait until a sportswriter
gets the letter. This will make his life."

In New York, Runyon sat at his typewriter at the *American*, reading
Capra's letter. His life now was such a total illusion that he forgot the
figure as rapidly as he read it. Oh, somewhere in the back of his mind
was the fact that $1,500, while pretty good money in a depression, wasn't
this great Hollywood gold he always dreamed of. He also thought of
Hollywood as being the slowest and unsafest of roads, that to get from
story to movie on the screen was a couple of years at best, but he brushed
this even further back into his mind. He could not wait until he got to
Lindy's, where he told Pincus the waiter, "I guess you're serving a big
shot this time." He sat and looked out at Broadway in the night like a
man staring at his front lawn.

At this point, Frank McGlone, manager, McAlpin Hotel, 34th Street,
completed the task he promised to do in 1925. On the phone to Runyon one evening he said, "You told me to tell you when that bishop hit
my place."

"Did I ever."

"I tell you what. I am standing in the lobby and he shows up here.
But only to pick up this woman. She was shopping across the street,
you know how they all do that. This was the meet. He comes up from
the railroad station and he meets her here."

"And they went?"

"I had the doorman go on the earie. He told the guy to take him to the West Side. Amsterdam and 85th. I hope it's some use to you."

Of all sports of the twenties and thirties, as it has been since the start of man and woman, the greatest of all sports, revenge, was played with abandon. And for those who trafficked in Prohibition, it was going to be swift and certain. You will remember that at the start, William Anderson of the Anti-Saloon League had told five hundred Methodist ministers that he believed that "Catholics are indignant over what they feel is a Protestant victory for Prohibition, and are in sympathy with Tammany efforts to destroy that victory and bring back the saloons."

If it were not for the handcuffs biting into his fat wrists, Anderson would not have believed it when detectives came for him one afternoon and said he was being arrested for bribery and forgery. At the district attorney's office, Anderson saw C. Bertall Phillips, that dirty little fund raiser. "Why are you here?" Anderson asked him. "For your health," Phillips said.

Everywhere Anderson looked, from detective to district attorney, he saw Irish Catholics. His friends tried to assure Anderson that somebody as high as Governor Smith simply would not practice revenge right out in the open. "They'll drop the case after a while," Anderson's lawyer, Charles Whitman, said.

When the trial started, the judge was Arthur S. Tompkins, who was the New York grand master of the Masons. He had his job because of an agreement between Tammany Hall and the cardinal of New York to give the Masons one judgeship every five years. The day Tompkins was told that he would be a judge, his wife stood on the steps of the cardinal's residence on Madison Avenue. She begged the Irish parlor maid to go inside and get her the cardinal's autograph.

At the trial, the first juror picked was David Alexander, who had red blotches on his face that were from "mosquito bites." The judge said he would be a tremendous juror. On the second day, C. Bertall Phillips came walking up to the front of the room.

"Why is he here today?" Anderson said. "I thought the defense case goes on last and the prosecution first."

"You have that right," his lawyer said.

Witness Phillips was asked if he split Prohibition funds with Anderson out of the goodness of his heart.

"It was done under threat!" Phillips answered.

The jury took fifty-six minutes, and foreman David Alexander seemed proud and happy to announce: "The man is guilty."

On his way into a prison cell in Sing Sing, Anderson read the only wire any Protestant in the country sent. It was from Bishop James Cannon: "Verdict not surprising that a pure-blooded American, who has fearlessly, successfully fought beasts at Ephesus, be convicted in a court with wet, foreign-born Tammany people and with a jury in a city where confessedly Satan's seat is."

Following which, the bishop attacked Al Smith by announcing to the Southern Methodist press: "Governor Smith wants the Italians, the Sicilians, the Poles and the Russian Jews. That kind has given us a stomach ache. We have been unable to assimilate such people in our national life, so we shut the door to them. But Smith says, 'Give me that kind of people.' He wants the kind of dirty people that you find today on the sidewalks of New York."

During this, romance flourished between the bishop, who ducked into Mrs. Helen McCallum's apartment to experience the fullness of life, and the woman who got the rent paid and now could browse for some fashionable clothes. When he was not with her, he wrote.

My Dear Madam,
   I am so distressed about your financial difficulties and that I was unable to assist you with more than twenty dollars yesterday. I am doubly distressed that you do not seem to think I am unselfish enough to really be able to help you. I could do no more yesterday as I needed to have cab fare for the rush to the railway station to board the eight thirty to Washington. It was the very last train of the day.
   I believe that the enclosed hundred dollars is a measure of my willingness to assist you at this time.
   Dear Madam, I do want you to feel a greater sense of security now that I have stepped into your life. It was such a joy to be with you yesterday. It was such a joy to hear your voice, to look into your eyes. Dear Madam, I must come to New York again immediately. I must tell you of myself and work you must help me in. Let us win the victory, dear heart, for the future years.

                                             Hastily,
                                             James Cannon Jr.
                                             Doctor.

(I shall explain this title to you upon my next arrival at your wonderful domicile.)

Mrs. McCallum liked the letters so much that she took them down to her bank on Broadway and placed them in her safe-deposit box, which she had purchased with the start of the bishop's cash money flow. She and the bishop shared many blissful months together in the apartment on West 85th Street.

The bishop had been helping her move furniture early one evening, and when she went out to a store on Broadway, he called the Sibley Hospital in Washington to see how his wife was doing. What he heard so alarmed him that he was waiting on the sidewalk when Helen McCallum returned. He kissed her goodbye and said he had a terrible emergency to attend to. He rushed to Penn Station and caught the last train to Washington, and just did get to Sibley Hospital in time to see his wife kick. At graveside, the bishop wheeled in grief, walked off amidst the tombstones and disappeared over a knoll. Fearing he was on his way to committing suicide, friends rushed after him. The bishop waved them away. These fools would make him miss his train to New York, where an understanding Helen Hawley McCallum waited for him. He stayed with her for some time, and then once more had to travel abroad. He left her in the apartment.

Around the corner, upstairs in the local firehouse, Johnny Weissberger sat on a bunk and made bells ring in his head.

Bing . . . bing . . . bing-bing, bing-bing.

One one two two. Box 1122. The corner of Broadway and 80th Street.

Bing . . . bing . . . bing-bing, bing-bing-bing.

One one two three. Box 1123. Riverside Drive and 81st Street.

Box 1124. The corner of Amsterdam Avenue and 81st Street.

Johnny Weissberger learned the fire calls when he moved into a different firehouse — particularly this time, when he was on business. Weissberger, a reporter for Hearst's *New York Journal* newspaper, had just taken up temporary residence, along with two other reporters, on the second floor of the firehouse occupied by Engine 74, at 120 West 83rd Street, a couple of doors off Amsterdam Avenue and two short blocks down from Helen McCallum's house, which he did not know yet but soon would. He was stationed here at the request of all his editors, who got the idea from Damon Runyon and, Weissberger knew, from Mayor Walker. They wanted to find the bishop with his broad, and he, Weissberger, would produce him.

Bing . . . bing . . . bing-bing, bing-bing-bing-bing.

"What's that, Johnny?" Austin O'Malley, a reporter on the *New York American,* said to his fellow worker Johnny Weissberger. O'Malley was a Roman Catholic. With them was the third reporter, Sid Livingston.

"Amsterdam and 85th," Weissberger said.

They ran up the street again. This was the fifth false alarm in the last three days, during which firemen emptied the houses. The three reporters, clutching descriptions of the bishop's girlfriend, as given by the Hotel McAlpin manager, checked all the women on the sidewalk in front of the building that was suspected of being afire, 230 West 85th. Here she was. Weissberger grabbed a fireman, who went up to the woman and asked her her name. "We're keeping lists." Helen McCallum gladly gave the fireman her name and apartment number.

The same apartment at which the three Hearst reporters soon banged on the door. When Mrs. McCallum opened it, O'Malley whipped out a copy of a story that the United Press had sent out on its wire with a Huntsville, Alabama, and, on the second run, a St. Louis dateline. The dispatch said that Bishop Cannon had wed Mrs. Mary Moore McCoy, of Athens, Alabama, the widow of Bishop McCoy. At this time, Bishop Cannon was in Europe on more missionary duties and had written only two letters to Mrs. McCallum, both prosaic. Mrs. McCallum was in an emotional state on reading the dispatch and did not take the time to discount it, pending arrival of verification. Of which none would ever be forthcoming. The United Press story from Huntsville quoted Mrs. William H. Moore of St. Augustine, Florida, who said she had received "indirect" word of the wedding of Mrs. McCoy, her sister-in-law.

The indirect word happened to come up when a reporter from somewhere asked her if she had heard the news about the bishop and Mrs. McCoy being married in North Africa.

As she read the dispatch in her apartment, Helen McCallum shook with anger. She asked the three reporters to wait until she was dressed. Afterward, she took them to a bank on Broadway, where she went into the safe-deposit box and pulled out a packet of letters, which she handed to Johnny Weissberger.

THE BISHOP'S LOVE LETTERS TO A WIDOW

The Methodist Church throughout the entire civilized world was rocked today by the announcement that James M. Cannon, Jr., militant leader of the Southern branch in the United States, has had an ardent courtship with a New York City widow, Mrs. Helen McCallum.

The venerable Bishop Cannon is 65 and Mrs. McCallum is thought to be 42.

Today they are revealed to the public for the first time.

It was Romance with a capital R — this tender association of the

M. E. Bishop with the comely widow. It was Romance from the instant of their meeting in a hotel lobby in New York.

Perhaps the greatest height of Romance scaled by Bishop Cannon in his correspondcence with Mrs. McCallum was the sentiments expressed on a card he mailed to her the day after his arrival on the Bremen last April from Europe. It was a ship's menu card, and the message was dated April 9th. At that time, Mrs. McCallum was ill.

"My doubly Dearest Madam," the message read. "I am so distressed about your sickness. But the time for you to be in travail alone has passed. My doubly dear Madame, we must find a way to join hands in life, at the first suitable date. I do not care to continue my vital and exhausting undertakings without you at my side."

On the night before his wife died, Bishop Cannon visited Mrs. McCallum at her apartment on West 85th Street.

This Godly man, one of the pillars of the Methodist Episcopal Church in the United States, found this comely widow a fascinating companion. She had the gift of listening intelligently to a man when he talked. Bishop Cannon was with her on the night he learned his wife was fatally ill in Washington. He left on the first train for his wife's bedside. After the funeral he returned again to the apartment of Mrs. McCallum and she comforted him.

"Adultery!" Bishop Costen J. Harrell, one of the pastors of the Virginia Conference of Methodist Episcopal Churches, addressed a roomful of highly regarded and completely shocked ministers in Richmond.

"Bishop Adultery!" Jimmy Walker, mayor of New York, introduced by Gene Fowler, stood in the crowded basement dining room of Leone's Restaurant and spoke to all the guys, who turned out to celebrate the three Hearst reporters who had performed what most agreed was the best journalism the city had ever seen.

"I say to you that the last thing this fair city of ours can tolerate is adultery by bishops," Jimmy Walker said. "We have enough of laymen committing adultery around this town without the Southern Methodists getting into the game. I would ask two things at this time. One, would the Southern Methodists be so kind as to inform us if we have any more of their bishops living in mortal sin in our town? And two, would the waiters please do a little work around here? I see empty glasses!"

It was only days after this that Patrice and Runyon walked down Broadway, her hand holding his arm. She was smiling sweetly for all to see, and at the same time she was informing Runyon that she wanted him to leave his wife. When he said, mildly, that he already had, if she would look on the other side of the bed, she said, "I want to live on the red board." This was a reference to the red light spelling out the word "Official" when race results were put up on the pari-mutuel board. Initially, Runyon was hesitant and uncomfortable, because while he only felt alive when he was with her, and was in constant pain when he was forced to be at home, he had never so much as emptied the furnace in a house, not to speak of the far more painful job of placing the ashes of his life out on the street for all to inspect.

He mentioned his circumstances to E. Phocian Howard, who had not been married for many years and had, in Runyon's opinion, the long view necessary to give advice. Phoce asked Runyon the age of his intended, and Runyon said that she was twenty-three. He was so proud of having a young girl that he cut the age down when he gave it. Phoce then committed the unpardonable sin of asking Runyon his age. Damon compressed his lips a moment but finally said he was forty-seven. Phoce thought this over. He knew that Runyon's forty-seven could mean that he was fifty or fifty-two. Actually, Damon was a flat fifty on this day in 1930, and his beloved Patrice was twenty-four. Phoce began to talk to Runyon about the effects of age on a marriage.

"After a game, who do you go to talk to, the manager or some twenty-three-year-old hillbilly from Arkansas who got the most hits?" he asked Runyon.

"The manager. He's the only one has anything to say."

"Who do you think a young person would want to see, the old manager or the young player?"

"What's that got to do with it?" Runyon said.

"Everything," Phoce said. "Calendar determines interest. What is a daily surprise to you, the score of the Giants game, the whereabouts of your dear mayor, could not be of less interest to a twenty-three-year-old woman. She wants to hear song and dance. Tell me, Damon, when was the last time you danced with this young girl?"

"She dances for a living," Runyon said.

"I said with you."

"Are you just talking only about dancing?" he said, a bit defensively.

"Oh, I dare not even go into personal matters," Phoce said. "I am afraid that is something you must face by yourself. That is the final struggle of that definitive battle, man's desires against the age of his own body."

Runyon was silent. "I can tell you something," Phoce said. "I have my annual Winter Book handicapping on these events. I will tell you that the prices have never changed."

He then listed the same odds that he had been placing in his newspaper's January 1 issue for the last ten years:

28-year-old girl versus 55-year-old man. Girl 3–5.

25-year-old girl versus 60-year-old man. Girl 2–5.

20-year-old girl versus 63-year-old man. Girl 1–5.

18-year-old girl versus 70-year-old man. Girl 1–10.

17-year-old girl versus 70-year-old man. WA. (Walkover; no contest. Man does not show. He dies.)

Runyon attempted to smile as he looked at Phoce's form chart, and he surely would have smiled, except for the pain spreading from the pit of his stomach. He turned away and said that he had a problem in that under Ellen's Catholic religion there was no way she would agree to any divorce, and under New York State laws the only sure way of gaining one would be through adultery. As he could not believe that Ellen would ever do such a thing, and he knew that he was living in sin, it would be his life thrown on a billboard, and this he could not have. He decided that he was going to have to split the difference. He would simply move out for good. When Phoce asked him how he was going to tell his wife, Runyon said that he intended to go home and have a totally reasonable discourse with the woman.

Ellen Runyon, her daughter in boarding school, now alone with her son, followed the life of most women who had lived in at least some of the excitement of the news business and then had an unreliable bum walk out. She had gone around with her son and shown him all the places where his father had worked. She took the boy to the Park Central where she pointed out excitedly the place where Arnold Rothstein was shot, and to the piers for the docking of the liner *Leviathan*. Through long nights, she drank while he slept somewhere.

In time of trouble, alcohol always betrays. At night, the whisky couldn't even get her boasting to herself, and she woke up with whisky sickness accompanying her loneliness. Her husband came home one night and all of his passion for his life on the street turned defensive when she demanded that this life be explained. He walked about in impassive silence while her shouting caused him to wince. Then he called her a drunk. Ellen said that she had stopped, and besides, he had a girlfriend. Runyon detonated. How could she say such a thing about him! "Her name is Patrice," she said. Searching for a tactic, he

pulled open a closet door and studied it, as if actually looking, and here
up on a shelf was a bottle hidden, which he now brandished as he
screamed back at her, packed and left. He calmed down the moment
he got to Lindy's and called his Spanish countess to tell her to arise,
that he was out of the house.

Ellen moved with her son and an Irish housegirl to Pondfield Road
in Bronxville, in a garden apartment in a series of pleasant, attached
buildings that were favored by artists and writers. The grammar school,
set back on wide lawns, was directly across the street. The boy went to
school and his mother drank herself to death. Runyon put up enough
money to keep the family from intruding upon the creative atmosphere provided by a young doll. Summers for his wife and children
were spent at Lake Placid, where Ellen Egan stumbled through a cottage; on a cruise to Bermuda, during which sometimes she couldn't get
up because she was "seasick"; and at Rehoboth Beach, Delaware, where
the children took a walk on the beach and decided the drinking was an
illness. Mary blamed the mother for not getting a divorce; the son hated
the father because he had walked out. And the father never would return unless the mother suddenly dropped twenty-five years in age. So
Ellen stayed home and drank until she turned undertaker's yellow. In
Bronxville on the morning of November 4, 1931, she called to her son,
"Let me see you. I might not be here when you come back. All the
Egans die on November the fourth." When he came back after school,
the mother was still in bed. On November 9, however, she called for a
priest and the family doctor, who said he couldn't help her anymore.
Ellen looked up at her son and said, "Don't worry." She turned to face
the window and closed her eyes.

Her son was across the street on the school grounds when somebody
called to him that his father was home. He shrugged and played on.
His father never had shown up in this house. When the boy did come
home, he found neighbors in the house, his mother's body being brought
down the stairs and his father upstairs crying.

The daughter wrote an account in a notebook:

> I talked to my mother on Sunday. She told me she had a blazer that
> she hated and that I could have it. On Monday morning, my mother
> wasn't well. The maid, Bridey, called the Catholic church. My mother
> looked up and saw the priest and she was frightened by the priest and
> died. My mother died before nine o'clock on Monday morning. She
> wasn't quite 45. I never was told until Wednesday. The superior told
> me and they took me to the railroad and I went home. Poor daddy

had just had pneumonia. My mother left a letter and my father and I
read it. She wanted Colorado marble on a hill in Woodlawn Cemetery. She wanted the casket in a vault so it wouldn't touch the ground.
My father said, "She'll come back and haunt us." When we were at
the funeral, at the cemetery, I looked around and I saw this crowd of
200 people walking up to us. They had suitcases and paper bags. I
said "Who are these people?" I was told that they were railroaders.
They had known her all their lives. They had come by train from Colorado. They didn't say a thing. They just walked across the grass. They
had suitcases and paper bags. Then they just stood there while mommy
was buried. They turned around and walked away.

Runyon had no room for children in the one-bedroom penthouse
suite at the Forrest, or in his life, which by now consisted of sitting on
Broadway until the last of the night dissolved into a morning sky. He
slept until midafternoon. With him at almost every moment was Patrice. He brought the children down to Washington, where Ellen's sister took them, smiling at the children and casting the coldest eye on
the father. Shortly afterward, Mary was sent up to New York one
weekend and arrived at the Forrest to find this trim woman with an
armful of yellow flowers in the living room. "Oh, you must be Mister
Runyon's daughter," Patrice said. She placed the flowers in a vase and
out of the bedroom came Runyon, who was embarrassed.

"Oh, dear, have you met my daughter?" he said to the woman, who
nodded and left. She felt no uncertainty; she and Runyon already had
a marriage date.

Mary Runyon McCann's memories state: "My mother had just died,
and yet he was getting married and Patrice wanted me as the maid of
honor. She knew Stanwyck and Crawford and those girls, yet she wanted
me. She took me to Wilma on 57th Street, where gowns for $1,000
were nothing. She bought me a pale peach satin slip with black lace
over it."

Sam Becker, Runyon's lawyer, recalled that for the wedding they
had a suite at the Sherry Netherland on Fifth Avenue and 59th Street.
Mary, the maid of honor, and Patrice, the bride-to-be, went out one
day before the wedding and when they returned home by cab, the maid
of honor was about half stiff and the bride had a red right eye that turned
into a shiner even when a great amount of ice was applied. "She socked
Patrice," Becker said. "Damon acted as if he never saw it."

Jimmy Walker, nervous and emaciated, married them in the apartment of Edward Frayne, the *American*'s sports editor. Walker, who

had won by half a million votes over Fiorello La Guardia in 1931, now
in August of 1932 had one foot in Sing Sing because of the blanket he
had thrown over the Rothstein murder case. Just before Runyon married Patrice, he asked Walker to get his first marriage records so he
could destroy any record of his age. This was just before Walker had to
leave town, and even dogs gave chase when he appeared on the street.
He told Runyon, "Damon, if I'm going to jail, let it be for scuttling a
ship. If they get me for stealing a marriage license I'll have to kill myself." The fearless Broadway detective, Johnny Broderick, had called
the host, Frayne, and asked to be excused from attending the ceremony. "I got a lot to do, such as remaining alive," he said. Walker
spent much time on the phone trying to reach Big Bill Dwyer, the old
bootlegger, for a loan. He knew enough not to ask Runyon. Before the
reception was over, Walker was relieved. A check for $2,500 had ar-
rived by messenger from Dwyer. Walker went home, resigned as mayor
and left town aboard the liner *Conte Grande*. He was broke, whisky-
ridden and defeated.

Damon Runyon, only a couple days short of his fifty-second birth-
day, was married to a twenty-six-year-old blonde. Along with his new
wife, he took his son and daughter and his friend Ben Reuben's son,
Bill, on the Chief for the train ride to the West Coast and the 1932
Olympics. They stayed at the Biltmore Hotel in downtown Los Angeles.

Damon was swept up by amateur sports, mostly a scene at the
Olympic Village. There was a doorknob to one building that was stuck,
and the great American athletes twisted, yanked and slammed it but
couldn't open the door. They left for another entrance. Then a woman
athlete approached the door, slapped a large hand on the knob and
twisted. The door opened and in she walked.

"Babe Didrikson," Runyon said. When he got back to the hotel that
night, he couldn't wait to tell Patrice and the kids about it. The anecdote made a stunning impact on Patrice. How could Runyon be telling
her about a doorknob? She wanted to know where they were going for
dinner on her honeymoon. The kids sat glumly in the living room.

Runyon's newspaper stories of the Olympic events reflected the
keenest observations and also were uncommonly warm. They were
written by someone who sat alone in a row behind the press box. There
were empty seats next to him, which he had reserved for his family,
but nobody was interested. He'd bring young Bill Reuben with him,
and his chauffeur, Charley Guzik, Greasy Thumb's son. Bill Reuben

took Mary out on a date one night. When they returned to New York, Runyon sent his son and daughter back to live in Washington, and he and Patrice moved out of the Forrest, to the elegance of the Parc Vendome building on 57th Street. He sat there with a fireplace, and the Hearst newspaper national headquarters just down the street, and Stillman's Gymnasium only two blocks farther. His new wife sat with him for about as long as the form chart for these things indicated that she would.

SEVENTEEN

THE MOTHER stood on the sidewalk and screamed at the window on the third floor.

"Vigiliacco!"

Hearing himself called a coward, Primo Carnera's great head shot out the third-floor window and glared down at West 48th Street, where the mother stood with her daughter. The mother wore her gray hair pulled back in a bun and a black dress and stockings. This was to let you know she was a widow. Her daughter at this time appeared en route to motherhood.

Now the mother screamed at Carnera, "Animale!"

Carnera, leaning far out, roared unintelligibly. A German shepherd pushed his snout past Carnera and began barking. Another man appeared at the window, a dark-haired man with a square face. He slapped the dog on the nose, and the dog disappeared. The man tried to push Carnera back into the room.

"Go wan," he yelled down at the mother and daughter.

Now the daughter, a lovely little woman with, as noted, an expression of pure life showing in front, suddenly opened a mouth the size of a small clam and shrieked, "La vostra madre puttana!"

Carnera now became furious. He wanted to jump out the window at the girl. Watching this, Patrice and the girls with her understood very well that Primo's mother was being called at the least a whore. The girls, all alumnae of Texas Guinan's chorus line, were going into La-Hiff's Tavern, which was on the ground floor of the building. They were Ruby Keeler Jolson, by now married to Al Jolson, Hannah Williams, who also married a rich guy, and Patrice. The dark-haired, square-faced man next to Carnera in the window, Bill Duffy, called down to

Patrice, "Don't ever tell Runyon I don't do no work. I'm trying to train this guy up here. Look what I got to put up with."

The widow on the sidewalk was certain he was making fun of her. She pointed her finger up at Duffy and screamed, "Su madre!"

Duffy was about to spit on her when he reminded himself of the presence of the women. He waved a hand in disdain.

"You don't train him in a gymnasium?" Patrice called.

"I want him here personal, with no prying eyes," Duffy said.

"Nobody can see?"

"You can. Come on up and take a look. You can do the reportin' for Damon."

"We can't. We're going in to lunch."

"Who says I want you here for the day? Come on, walk up. It'll take you a minute."

Ruby Keeler Jolson and Hannah Williams, upon seeing the long flight of stairs rising at the angle of a housepainter's ladder, said they would prefer to sit over cocktails. They went into LaHiff's and Patrice climbed the stairs, those firm dancer's legs propelling her up. At the top floor, Duffy, in a dark blue polo shirt, held the door open. "Yahhh!" He shouted at the two huge German shepherds, who scurried off, claws sounding on the bare floor. Inside the front room, which was the size of a small factory loft and had a fourteen-foot ceiling, was Primo Carnera. He was bare from the belt buckle up and wore huge boxing gloves. He was six foot six and weighed 275 pounds, which on his upper torso were taut and glistened with perspiration. When he smiled, he showed teeth as big as your fingers. For an instant, standing with his huge grin, and a face twice the size of anything people were used to seeing, he looked like some sort of carnival act from a circus, which was his background. But as the smile took hold and revealed the gentleness in his eyes, Carnera became absolutely adorable. Which, as Duffy explained, was his problem on the street.

"He got nine paternity suits," Duffy told Patrice.

Who heard nothing. Suddenly, she had a secret that she wanted no one in the world to know, but she could not keep it hidden and it was all over her face, with lips parted and eyes locked on him, this warm giant, his eyes sparkling with friendliness. Friendly? How can you think of this man as friendly? Patrice cautioned herself. The dreamy moment was interrupted by a vision of Damon, dressed impeccably, with the round wire glasses and the hair slicked back. So neat. He also looked old. Oh, I love him, she said. She meant Carnera's torso.

Duffy, who lived mostly at night and had watched this scene a thousand times in his own club, attempted to keep it business. He turned to Leon See, the slim man who sat in the corner. "Here, Leon, tell him that this is Patrice Runyon, the wife of the big sportswriter Damon Runyon. If he's nice to her, she'll make Runyon give us a real good write-up."

Duffy said this pointedly, for Runyon had not written more than a few lines about Carnera. Runyon hated the name and sight of Carnera because he wasn't in on the deal. A guy named Good Time Charley Friedman had found Carnera in a circus in France and brought him to New York, where he acquired as managers Owney Madden, Duffy, Big Frenchy LaMange and practically anybody else who came around with a loaded gun. Runyon was in Florida when they brought Carnera back, and was unforgiving when they didn't remember to cut him in.

Leon See relayed the conversation to Carnera in French. Duffy said, "That's all he knows. French and Italian and Spanish. It's a shame he's not smart enough to speak English. I can't tell him nothin' straight."

Patrice spoke in Spanish to Carnera. He laughed delightedly as she told him that she was glad to meet him and hoped he liked New York. Carnera said he could not go to as many places as he wanted, because he was always in training or traveling. He said he had been in Los Angeles mostly. When Patrice asked him how he liked Los Angeles, he laughed and spoke the only English he knew. "I knock him out in two rounds." It was the line Duffy had given to him to use in every town they hit. Patrice said to him in Spanish, "The girl down in the street who came with her mother seemed to have met you." He laughed and held out one of the old, creased, soggy, brown-wine gloves. It was as heavy as a cement block. He told her this was how he spent his time.

"We got the glove weighted," Duffy explained. Carnera had to learn to hold his hands up higher, and when he was finished training with these particular gloves, he would find the gloves used in a fight so light that the hands would remain high. "When he gets up in the morning, I make him put on the gloves," Duffy said. "He don't get them off till he goes to bed. I made these gloves myself for him. I sewed lead into them. Here, you see?" On the wrist, in tape over the manufacturer's name, Everlast, was printed in ink, "Bill Duffy Model."

Always, there was a small problem in that Carnera not only didn't happen to be a professional prizefighter, but he also wasn't even close to being an amateur prizefighter. Duffy had him three floors over a restaurant, and directly across the street from one of the clubs he and

Owney Madden ran, the Parody, and through long days, as he did now
for Patrice's benefit, he showed Carnera how to hold his hands and
plant his feet properly. The feet were size 16. She asked Primo where
he bought his shoes, and he said he was having trouble getting any to
fit. He told Patrice that he had grown up without shoes, for shoes of his
size had to be specially made in Italy and his family didn't have money
to buy them. He went around with bags and newspapers on his feet,
he said.

"You can't get shoes in this whole big city?" Patrice said in Spanish.

"I look. Once in a while I find a pair."

"The least I can do is help you get a nice pair of shoes that fit," Patrice said.

Patrice said goodbye and felt Carnera's eyes on her as she left the
room. In the restaurant, she ordered a Coke. "With gin."

"When did this start?" Ruby Keeler said.

"Lately."

She had been married to Runyon for only a year, and he was twenty-
six years older than she. He also was writing fiction, which caused him
to became vacant in the middle of a conversation with her and begin to
stare into the smoke of some night joint. She knew he was composing,
but after the first thrill or so of watching a short story turn into a movie,
she became irritated with the idea of being much less interesting to
him than the tablecloth, which he often brushed a hand over as he
thought. If he was deep into a short story, he would finish his newspaper column and then sit up through the night writing fiction, smoking
so many cigarettes that he flopped into bed at sunrise barely able to
breathe, much less summon the necessary energy to be a husband.

Then there was the gambling, from which he could not stay away.
"This is it," Regret announced one night in a room in the Paris Hotel,
across the street from the Fulton Fish Market. Tough Willie McCabe
was shooting and the point was four. Regret's money was gone. One of
the players, the famous Nick the Greek, smirked. "When you're broke,
you're a joke." Regret was furious. "They don't have a gambler in my
league in this town," he said. The Greek pointed out the window at the
dawn sky. "There so happens to be millions of broken-down bums out
there." Tough Willie McCabe growled, "Number!"

His point was four. Regret took out four quarters, threw them on
the table and said, "He does with the gag." He meant that McCabe
would make his point with a pair of twos. "You're covered," the Greek
smirked. Regret was getting 8-to-1 odds. McCabe threw once. Five

and three. Tough Willie threw the dice again. They skipped the table, clicked up against the wall, fell back and stopped. Two and two. "Yahhhh!" Regret said. Runyon, about to go home, took off his coat. By noon that day, Regret had $110,000 stuffed in his pockets and waistband. By 10 A.M. the next day, Regret had $300 left, and Runyon stood at the window and looked at the East River, silver and cold in the winter morning. A freighter moved slowly toward Pier 44, which was directly across from the Hearst plant. Men around the table were shaking glasses that had ice cubes in them and the noise was irritating Runyon. This had never happened to him before and he wondered why, and for an instant there was a sound in his mind that reminded him of his age: born in 1880! He threw it out of his mind. Now, from somewhere else, a kinder thought attempted to express itself: you're not as young as you were. Just as suddenly, he banished the thought. It did not stop the ice shaking against glasses from causing him to become increasingly nervous. Finally, at noontime, when Regret pulled out his pockets to show all that he was officially through, Runyon left for the Parc Vendome. He got home and flopped on the bed and was disappointed that Patrice wasn't there so she could pull off his shoes. He was too tired to do so. He closed his eyes against such a thought. He was terrified of age.

By the winter of 1933, construction and furnishing of Patrice's white house on Hibiscus Island, which she called Las Melaleuccas, was finished. On February 15, Damon Junior, fourteen, was visiting the Riverside Military Academy, which was at Gainesville, Georgia, but had its winter headquarters in Hollywood, Florida, land still being that cheap down there. Damon came up to Hollywood from Hibiscus to visit the school. He had taken his son to see the famous New England prep schools, such as Andover, where he claimed he had a hook, but now decided that the military school, with its closeness to Hibiscus, was best.

While Runyon visited a child's military school, down in Miami, eighteen miles away, Joseph Zangara, a New Jersey bricklayer, stood in a crowd watching President Franklin D. Roosevelt and Mayor Anton Cermak of Chicago arrive at a rally. Zangara had stomach pains which he believed were being caused by Roosevelt. Zangara got up on a bench and held a pistol straight out and fired five shots at the President. He missed Roosevelt but hit Anton Cermak, the mayor of Chicago, and four others. A New York man, William Sinotte, a detective in Miami on vacation, was hit in the head and went down as if dead. The crowd of fifty thousand panicked as Roosevelt threw his arms around Cermak and the car rushed off to Jackson Memorial Hospital.

In the Miami city jail, Zangara said he was sorry that he had missed Roosevelt because he still suffered from a stomach operation and this made him hate "all the rich and powerful." He was furious with the crowd, which was so large that it spoiled his aim. He said the same crush of people had kept him from killing the king of Italy ten years before this.

Walter Winchell rushed into the jail office and shouted at the sheriff, "I'll put your name in every paper in the world. Get me in to see Zangara." The sheriff took Winchell upstairs for a moment. Winchell spoke to Zangara, who was still mad that he had missed the king of Italy. Winchell was running out of the jailhouse to write his great interview as federal agents were coming in to close the place down. This guaranteed that Winchell's interview was exclusive! Winchell went to the Associated Press office in Miami and typed with his hat on. He had a joyous sensation as he sat in a newsroom and wrote a story that would cause the eyes of a nation — no, those of the entire world — to stop cold and read every word of what he was writing.

When he finished, Winchell gave his copy to a clerk to telegraph to the *Mirror* in New York. The Associated Press clerk put the copy on a pile. Winchell was so inexperienced in reporting news that he did not remain until his copy had been sent to New York and a receipt acknowledged by his desk at the *Mirror*. Instead, he was so impatient to get to the Roney Plaza Hotel and start bragging to the crowd at the end of the night that he bolted out of the Associated Press newsroom. Through the rest of the night, he did not call his office in New York to check on the story.

At the Associated Press office, Steve Hannagan, a press agent, had wandered in to help out on the phones. When the rewrite men couldn't turn out all the work piled on their desks, Hannagan went to the stack of copy and looked it over. Noticing Winchell's story, he snatched it, rewrote it and turned in his version to the desk. The Associated Press now had the Zangara interview, without a byline, on the wires to 3,500 papers, including the *Mirror* in New York, long before Winchell's exclusive was telegraphed to the *Mirror*. When it finally did reach the paper, on East 45th Street in Manhattan, the *Mirror* deskmen assumed that Winchell had stolen his "exclusive" from the wires. They ran Winchell's great story as a short piece. The accountant had the

telegraph tolls of $11 taken out of Winchell's check because his con-
tract called for him to use the mails — his column was as timely one
day as the other — in order to prevent Winchell from sending a wire
every ten minutes announcing where he was and what he was doing,
which he thought was important. When Winchell said he would quit if
the accountant wasn't fired, Hearst personally gave him the $11 back.
Hearst also admonished the accountant by note: "A grateful publisher
thanks you for your efforts in keeping the newspaper solvent. Please
don't stop."

The Zangara statements about his stomach, rich people and the king
of Italy sound true to anyone unfortunate enough to have had any contact with one of these loners with hot eyes dancing in a vacant face who
have demoralized our history.

When Runyon got back to Miami, he wrote that Mayor Cermak was
"game as a pebble. They don't come any gamer than this chunky chief
of the big town on the shores of Lake Michigan."

Then, at a small press conference, Roosevelt said to Runyon, "I should
like to amend that line of yours. Mayor Cermak is a boulder in this
nation. I will tell you what he said to me, but I have to leave it to you
whether you want to print such a personal line or not. But the first
thing Mayor Cermak said to me after being shot was, 'I'm glad it was
me, not you.' "

Standing next to Roosevelt, his wife, Eleanor, gave a small startled
cry of shock and surprise.

"She done that when he said it last night, too," a photographer next
to Runyon said.

For the rest of the interview, Runyon gazed into the distance and
saw a vision of Anton Cermak, right out of Chicago, diving at a gun to
protect this rich man from New York. Did Anton throw his chest out
as a target? Or did he just dive atop Roosevelt with his arms flailing?

"I think I have just heard another great saying that never was said,"
Runyon told the photographer.

On the twentieth of February, Zangara was in court and pleaded
guilty to shooting five people. By now Cermak was quite dead. The
Cermak murder was not involved in Zangara's sentencing because the
case would have taken too much time, and the state wanted to get Zangara out of sight and mind as soon as possible. Zangara stood in court,
his voice high and shrill, and said, "How much you gimme, judge?
How much? Eighty years? You too stingy. Why you no give me a hundred years?"

One of those shot was Sinotte, the New York City detective, who, when carried off to the hospital, looked a cinch to be dead. Nobody knows how, but in a couple of weeks he was awake. Sinotte's first visitors were Runyon and his guest for the middle furlongs of winter, Regret. When Sinotte told them that his address was 612 West 178th Street in Manhattan, Regret said, "We are playing that number right now. I think I can feel it got a chance to win. Give me a couple of dollars. It's a better thrill, you play your own money."

Sinotte tried to pick his head up from the pillow, but couldn't. "I feel like I got shot in the head," he said. The realization promptly caused him to pass out.

When he awoke, the nurse had a note from Regret that said, "I put it up for you. We blew today. Number was 572. I'll return. Wether fair track fast."

That Saturday, Runyon and Regret arrived in Sinotte's hospital room carrying a pile of racing papers. Runyon and Regret spread out so much in the room that Sinotte's wife was pushed into a corner. Regret held out a hand to Sinotte. "Give me twenty dollars your end, first race." Sinotte's hand came out from under the sheet and held up the gold badge of a New York City detective.

"Here's your money," he told Regret.

"Why you're nothin' but a bull," Regret told him.

At this, Mrs. Sinotte spoke up. "Why are you talking to him like that? You're nothing but a common bookmaker. My husband is a hero. He took a bullet that was meant for President Roosevelt."

"You could be right," Runyon said.

"Not could be. I am right. Do you know how I know? Because President Roosevelt himself called here and he told me this with his own lips. He says to me, 'Your husband took the bullet for me.' "

In keeping with his role as a great father, Runyon now had a son stored in the military school and a daughter, age eighteen, who now was out of the Catholic school in New York and with an aunt in Washington. The aunt lived at 14th and Delafield streets, and around the block, at 15th and Decatur, were the McCanns, the father a champion hand typesetter with the federal printing office. There were seven children in the four-bedroom house. One was Richard, age twenty-two, a sportswriter on the *Washington Daily News*, a Scripps-Howard tabloid. When Richard saw this young woman around the corner, he was somewhat impressed with her last name, but much more so with her beauty. Soon, they were bouncing around 9th Street to one of the acceptably Irish nightclubs, one flight up and owned by a man named Jimmy Lake. Also living in the 14th Street neighborhood were two distinguished people, Shirley Povich, the sports columnist for the *Washington Post*, and his wife Ethel.

Mary Runyon McCann states that she was starting out in the newspaper business at this time. "The city editor of the *Washington Herald* knew about me, and he would call me up if he had some assignment he wanted handled. I also was working for a small paper in the area."

Dick McCann's sister, Helen Grau, remembered that "we all loved Mary. She was a doll. Did Mary Elaine work? Oh, heavens, no."

In March of 1933, right after an earthquake in Los Angeles, Harry Cohn, the head of Columbia Pictures, told Frank Capra, "Listen, Dago, you wanted to buy that old-lady story. I didn't. You wanna make all the decisions, then don't give me maybes. For three thousand a week, I want pictures out of you, not excuses."

Bob Riskin, the screenwriter, told Capra he had a better title, *Lady for a Day*, and they went to Palm Springs and put together a script in six weeks. Capra said they worked well together because they were both going bald and were bothered to death by it. When they finished, they tried for Marie Dressler as star, the only older woman working with any success, but she was under contact somewhere else. They asked May Robson to come in from the Broadway stage. She was seventy. At the first reading, her great stage voice boomed through the bare Hollywood studio. Capra was disheartened. He told her, "Miss Robson, I forgot to tell you. There are two detectives who suspect you're not on the up-and-up. They follow you and eavesdrop. And you know it. So try the same lines in a hoarse whisper so they won't hear you, understand?"

May Robson said, why, of course, she would read the lines so they would not be overheard by these two rat detectives. She spoke in an anxious, urgent, low voice, filled with fear of the lawmen shadowing her and despair at the thought of failing her daughter. Capra realized what he was dealing with. If he had asked this woman to sing, she would have burst into song. He had become so accustomed to limited Hollywood talent that he had forgotten that a veteran Broadway actress such as this was capable of anything and needed notice of about a moment or two.

"What else would you like?" she asked.

"For you to sign a contract for the part," he said.

He wanted James Cagney to play the Costello part, Dave the Dude, but he also was unavailable. An actor from the Columbia pool, Warren William, was cast. The character actors were Walter Connolly, Guy Kibbee, Ned Sparks, Nat Pendleton and Ward Bond. Harry Cohn saw the finished movie one morning in the Columbia screening room on Gower Street in West Los Angeles. The film ran eighty-eight minutes. After which, Cohn walked into his office, where he sat with a riding crop, slapping it against the desk as his secretary called Columbia executives in New York, waking them up. "Get up, you lazy stupid sonofabitch," Cohn yelled. "I got a hit and you got nothin' but trouble comin' from me."

In Miami that winter, Patrice let out a moan as she read that in New York the night before, Carnera had knocked out Ernie Schaaf of Boston with a weak left jab. The crowd had shouted "Fake!" Which was normal, because most of Carnera's fights were what Good Time Charley Friedman called "mischievous." But after the crowd stopped screaming "Fake!" Schaaf did not recover consciousness. He was taken to the hospital. For three days, she had Runyon keep calling New York, and finally on the third day he told her, "He died." She said, "Poor Primo." Runyon told her that it certainly wasn't Primo's worry. "That fella took a desperate beating from Max Baer and shouldn't have been in the ring." She still was saddened, and she and Runyon never discussed the reason for such prolonged sadness.

When they came back to New York in the spring of 1933, she insisted on going to Pompton Lakes, New Jersey, where Carnera trained for his heavyweight championship with Jack Sharkey. The fight was to be held in June at the Long Island City Bowl, an outdoor wooden arena built over the railroad tracks just across the Queensborough Bridge from midtown Manhattan. Runyon knew John Buckley, Sharkey's manager, was a man who would scuttle a fleet. And of course there was Duffy and company. All day before the fight, he looked for Duffy and Madden, and both of them, hearing he was after them, ducked over to the West Side. They thought he wanted to talk about Carnera and Patrice, and they had no way to answer him. He was only looking to cash a bet. When he couldn't locate them, he wrote in his column that he had no opinion as to the winner of the fight, that it was at best a high-risk bet either way.

Which it wasn't, really. Carnera came into the ring all by himself, as his cornermen did not like the full glare of publicity. They remained down in the corner with the water buckets and only between rounds did they come up, wearing big caps pulled over their eyes. Carnera fought standing straight up, with his head motionless and his huge jaw framed beautifully. Despite all those hours of wearing the weighted gloves, he carried his hands far too low. Each time he jabbed, he dropped his hand to his side as he brought it back. This is a terrific way to get killed. It made no difference. In the sixth round he hit Sharkey with half of a right hand uppercut, if the punch really did land. The thing about boxing is that usually only two people know about a punch, and they are too busy fighting to judge it. Sharkey went down on his face and never moved. Duffy leaped into the ring and Carnera held him high. They owned the biggest title in sports. Duffy stood in the ring and would not let Carnera remove the gloves.

"I want a commissioner," Duffy said. He kept pointing at the gloves. He wanted them inspected so that nobody would be able to claim he had put weights in these gloves, too. Finally, Bill Brown, a commissioner, came up the steps and into the ring. He looked at the gloves. "They're clean. You can give them to Runyon's wife," Brown said.

In the dressing room, Sharkey said he had a concussion. At ringside, Runyon was writing that it was one of the hardest blows anybody ever had seen. Sharkey shuffled out of the dressing room, groped his way to the parking lot and when he found nobody there to watch him, he trotted to his car and drove through the night to Boston. Runyon got home at dawn to find Patrice jubilant. He slept most of the day. Patrice did not. She was seen walking with Carnera toward the Great Northern Hotel at noon. Carnera had a paper bag with $9,000 in singles in it. Madden had given it to him and told him it was his pay for winning the championship. "You're rich." He and Patrice bought thirteen pairs of shoes at the Florsheim store she had found for him. They went up the elevator to Carnera's sixth-floor suite so he could try on the shoes.

Runyon, the ultimate Broadway wise guy, knew nothing of this. But his personality was split between the two lives of illusion and writer. One day in the paper he had a column from nowhere about his father telling him about unrequited love. He said that people suffering from this often could be found at the bar, and if you played it right you could listen to them, then say you had to go, and immediately they would order a drink for you in order to keep you. This could go on all night, he said. In another column, he repeated Bugs Baer's famous line: "Love is the last word in a ten-word telegram." It was a puzzling column, but not so much so if your wife was going out with a giant prizefighter and you couldn't admit this to yourself in real life and allowed the subconscious to express itself through your typing fingers.

POSTAL TELEGRAPH COMMERCIAL CABLES
  TELEGRAMS TO ALL AMERICA TELEGRAMS TO ALL THE
WORLD
KN NEWYORK NY 14 712P
  MISS PATRICE GRIDIER
  ON BOARD TRAIN NO. 80 COMPARTMENT E CAR K 160 ARRIV-
ING JACKSONVILLE, FLA.
  DARLING I AM THINKING OF YOU ALL MY LOVE
  DAMON

WESTERN UNION
  MZA737 NL NEWYORK NY
  MISS PATRICE GRIDIER
  HOTEL DADE MIAMIBEACH FLO.
  DARLING GIRL I WAS DISAPPOINTED NO TELEGRAM THIS
MORNING I AM MAKING EVERY EFFORT TO GET AWAY NEXT WEEK
BECAUSE I MUST BE WHERE YOU ARE PLEASE GET ALL THE REST
YOU CAN AND WATCH YOUR HEALTH I LOVE YOU CARISSIMA MIA
ALWAYS
  DAMON

The movie *Lady for a Day* opened at the Radio City Music Hall on September 7, 1933. This was only a few days more than six months from the day Capra and Robert Riskin went to Palm Springs with the short story in their hands and hopes of being able to do a script. When one of his executives mentioned to Harry Cohn that it would make a great Christmas picture and should be held until then, Cohn exploded. "Go take another look at my movie. I say what day Christmas comes."

The first showing of the movie was at 11 A.M. on Thursday, September 7. On that morning, an hour and a half late because of her time of the day before, Apple Annie showed up under the fire escape of the Astor.

"I don't want to see the movie," she said. "I got a bad flu." The flu being a giant hangover. "Are you buyin' or bullshittin'?"

Runyon said he was going to the movie and that he would be back later on.

"No, you won't," she said.

"Go on."

"You go on. You won't spend another minute around me because you don't need me anymore."

He laughed and she did not.

His column that day was about the best nothing he could find, a conversation among fight trainers about the lightweight division. The lead story on the first page said that two additional warships arrived off Cuba, and Marine planes at the Quantico base were ordered on the ready to attack the island. President Roosevelt was pleased that he had received support from many Latin-American nations as he mobilized the American navy to bombard Cuba and protect the lives of Americans living there. Somewhere in the story the reason for possible war was given, that Communists were racing through Havana screaming "Down with Yankee imperialism," but the reason was not as important as the excruciating thrill of getting ready to go to war with a small country.

When Runyon called the office, the copyboy read off his phone messages, including a plea from a Mrs. Anna Cohen of Brooklyn, who owed her landlady back rent of $12.50 and because of this the landlady grabbed her eyeglasses and false teeth and would not give them back until she had the rent. There was another call from Frank Meier, who was Frank of the Ritz in Paris, chief bartender, who had just arrived on the SS *Manhattan*. Ben Reuben called to say that Bert Fish of Florida had just been named ambassador to Egypt. "Bert wants to know if that's the place where they got pyramids." It was no quip. Runyon wanted to buy an overcoat on sale for $45 at Rogers Peet at Fifth Avenue and 41st Street. Suits priced at $65 were listed at $40. Then Patrice arrived at the Parc Vendome with $125 worth of dresses and accessories to wear to the opening and he decided to forget the sale.

At six o'clock, the bellhop brought up the first editions of the *Daily News* and the *Mirror*, with the *News* giving the picture four stars and the *Mirror* claiming it was a Runyon triumph. At Radio City that night, he and Patrice sat in a loge with Columbia executives and May Robson, but Runyon, restless, went out for cigarettes several times. Afterward, he and Patrice walked up to Lindy's and waited for more reviews. Eddie Walker, the fight manager, now came running with the *Times*, which stated, " 'Lady for a Day' is a happy instance of welcome originality . . . It holds the spectator's attention with its surprises and gratifying freshness." The *Herald Tribune* said, "Hollywood got smart and didn't tamper with the unique Runyon touch."

"I win the heavyweight championship without having to feed the fighter," Runyon said.

When Patrice got up, Lou Goldberg, a Columbia press agent, said, "Pretty girl."

"She gave me the idea for the story," Runyon said.

"Does she write, or was it just a thing she said?" Goldberg asked.

"She's a Spanish countess," Runyon said.

"For real?"

"The lady not only has royal class, but she has a rock in a safe-deposit box that would knock your eyes out. The Amati diamond. It's over thirty carats. One of the nine or ten biggest rocks in the world. She's the real thing."

"Why didn't you tell us before? We could've used it," Goldberg said.

Patrice returned and started going through the papers, but stopped at a story from Los Angeles that said, "When Louis Soresi and William Duffy, bosses of champion Primo Carnera, arrived here for the filming of 'The Prizefighter and the Lady,' the first thing they said was that Carnera would not stand for being knocked out by Max Baer in the film. The ending had to be changed so that the fight ends in a draw in the American version and in the Italian version Baer gets stiffened."

"Très magnifique," she said.

"I thought you said she was Spanish," Lou Goldberg said.

"European royalty uses every language ever inscribed on stones," Runyon said.

At 3 A.M., when Lou Clayton walked around, he and Runyon dropped Patrice off at the Parc Vendome, and they headed for a crap game. She went up on the elevator. The maid was awakened by the sound of her abusing the operator because she wasn't being put through to her Los Angeles number quickly enough. When the maid mentioned this the next morning, she drew a glare from Patrice. Runyon seemed too interested in reading the paper to notice.

When Dick McCann wanted to marry Mary Runyon at the start of 1934, she called her father from Washington and he sent her money for the train to Miami. She came to the house on Hibiscus Island by cab, the driver waiting while she went inside for the fare. Mary remembered nothing of what she and her father spoke about while she was there because Runyon spent mornings in bed, afternoons at the racetrack and nights, starting right after dinner, typing. At dinner one night he was staring off, and when Mary tried to talk to him about plans for the wedding, Patrice touched her arm. "He has to think. This is when he actually writes." Patrice then put her back on a train to Washington for the wedding with a one-way ticket. Patrice's mascara was running. "You're just a little girl. You'll come back." Mary recalls being nervous and that she ate four bowls of oyster stew at the terminal. She was picked up at the Washington railroad station, she remembers, by Shirley Povich's wife. Mary always said, "He had been trying to tell us that he couldn't make it to the wedding. There was a big story in Miami. The date was January 16, 1934. A big story in Miami. Check it. He couldn't come to the wedding because of it."

Major news stories in the papers of January seventeenth, covering the activities of the sixteenth, included none from the whole state of Florida. There were stories about Congress' granting authority to seize gold in a revolt somewhere, about a housing act ruled illegal by the Supreme Court and, in New York, about Mayor La Guardia's denying he was using politics when he appointed a loyal campaign man to the board in charge of city bridges.

"I don't know why he wasn't here," Katherine Grau said. "All I know is that he didn't come. He wasn't much of a father."

The wedding was at the Sacred Heart Roman Catholic Church on 16th Street and Park Road in Washington. Mary wore a gray suit and appeared to be just another member of the large McCann family. There was no one on the bride's side of the church until the groom's relatives spread out. Katherine Grau remembers, "She had no one. We all gave her away." Afterward, she moved in with Dick in the family house and became another one of the children.

A baby came rapidly. Katherine Grau recalls, "She had a marvelous crib and she furnished the baby's room beautifully. Patrice sent Mary some money and she bought out Garfinckel's. But there wasn't much after that. Mr. Runyon came up when the baby was born. He stayed somewhere and we read in the paper that he was giving Dick and Mary a furnished house for a wedding and baby gift. Huh. He never bought them a cup of tea. Pardon my expression, but he was a bum as far as I was concerned. The rest of us took care of the baby. Poor Mary Elaine couldn't do it. She was a person who could pour tea but didn't know how to make it. I don't think she ever heard from her father. Once, around Christmas, he sent her a hundred dollars. She called me up and said, 'Let's go.' We went shopping downtown and she spent it all on underwear. It wasn't expensive stuff. She went to Lerner's. She just wanted a lot of it. She was a darling girl who didn't know how to be a mother. We all just stood around and waited to do something for her. She and Dick moved into an apartment on Connecticut Avenue and she called me up and said, 'Please help me. The colored socks just ruined the wash.' When I got there, I had to use Clorox to get the black color out of the sheets."

Her father's thoughts about her consisted of remembering the day he left her in the poolroom — "She's Runyon's marker." On those long nights in the Forrest and the Parc Vendome, Runyon had written a story about it that appeared in *Collier's Magazine*. He had his daughter as one character, and as another he used a guy who stood in doorways on 49th Street and took bets and hoped you'd lose because he had no way to make the payoff.

> The little doll is a very little doll indeed, the top of her noggin only coming up to Sorrowful's knee, although of course Sorrowful has very high knees, at that. Moreover, she is a very pretty little doll, with big blue eyes and fat pink cheeks, and a lot of yellow curls hanging down her back, and she has fat little legs and quite a large smile, although Sorrowful is lugging her along the street so fast that half the time her feet are dragging the sidewalk and she has a license to be bawling instead of smiling. . . .
>
> It seems that early in the afternoon a young guy who is playing the races with Sorrowful for several days pops into his place of business next door to the chop-suey joint, leading the little doll, and this guy wishes to know how much time he has before post in the first race at Empire. . . .
>
> "But," he says to Sorrowful, "to make sure I do not miss, you take my marker for a deuce, and I will leave the kid here with you as security until I get back."

The story runs in *Collier's*. In Hollywood here is this stage mother sitting with a six-year-old daughter who had curly hair and big eyes and who had taken singing and dancing lessons at Mrs. Meglin's School, Santa Monica, California. The mother had read this story about wise guys and a little girl who was left as a marker for a $20 loan. The mother loved it. A few days later she drove onto the Paramount movie lot with her little girl, Shirley Temple, seated next to her. The director of *Little Miss Marker* was named Hall. Shirley Temple remembers walking up to him and performing the act her mother had taught her so well, extending the right hand to shake with an adult. The director gave Shirley Temple a copy of the script and asked the mother to bring her back the next day. She did. And now Hall sat with Temple and he said, "Say, 'Aw nuts.' "

"Aw nuts!"

The director said, "Scram!"

"Scram!"

The director got up. "Okay."

"Okay," Shirley Temple repeated.

"No, kid, stop! We're finished. Let's go see your mother."

Shirley Temple has the lead role in *Little Miss Marker* and suddenly becomes the biggest movie star in the country, replacing Greta Garbo in box office receipts.

"Damon hated the song Shirley Temple sang," the songwriter Gerald Marks says. "It was 'Son of a Gun' and it was pretty famous."

All Runyon cards had the notation, "Winter months, c/o Reuben, 297 Hibiscus Island, Miami, Fla."

And then: "Winter months, Las Melaleuccas, 263 Hibiscus."

When Benito Mussolini watched the first screening of *Little Miss Marker* in all of Europe, the first thing he noticed was Shirley Temple's legs. "She has legs like one of the lions," he said. Four lion cubs slept outside on his terrace. Mussolini watched a movie every night and had become fanatical over Greta Garbo. Upon hearing that Shirley Temple had replaced Garbo as America's top box office draw, he told his cultural minister that he absolutely had to see this new little girl star. His villa, Via Nomentana, which was outside of Rome and behind high walls, had the first private screening room in Italy. Mussolini paid the owner, Prince Torlonia, rent of one lire a year, and the prince knew exactly how to receive the money. He kissed Mussolini's hand in gratitude.

Watching the movie, he was the man the pope had described as being halfway between heaven and earth. And that night it seemed he sure was. He was the revered head of Italy, and he was in love with Claretta Petacci, who was beautiful and twenty years old and supposedly engaged to an air force lieutenant, Riccardo Federici. She had seen Mussolini riding a motorcycle, and when introduced to him was trembling. Mussolini asked, "Are you cold?" She answered, "No, Duce. It is the emotion." At which moment the Duce fell grandly in love. But he was a man who needed everything, and as he watched this movie he became uneasy. He got up from his high-backed chair and tapped his friend, Roberto (the Slap Giver) Farinacci, whose political creed was, "Wind it up or we'll do what we haven't done yet." Mussolini and Farinacci went outside, and as the lion cubs snored softly, Mussolini again asked Farinacci about the troubling rumors of Primo Carnera and the Hearst writer's wife. Farinacci assured him that they were absolutely true and that there were diplomatic cables back at the office stating this. Mussolini exhaled loudly. "The man who wrote this Shirley Temple story."

"Runyon," Farinacci said.

Mussolini did not reveal his secret fear, that of losing the $1,600 a month paid to him for one major article that appeared in Sunday Hearst papers across America. Some would regard it as an honorarium, but to Mussolini, they would be people who lived in fiction. Had he known this early in his career, had he known that someone would pay such an unheard-of sum for writing a newspaper column, he would have looked differently on his long nights in the airless newsroom where he started his career. "I would have been too busy writing my dispatches for this money to take part in some political march," he once said.

That he was a dictator made him even hungrier. All politicians, from local council to absolute ruler, spend as much time gathering money as they do lying to people, or ordering them tortured. Mussolini had just replaced a little king, Vittorio Emanuele III, who wore faded and frayed uniforms on the most splendid of occasions, the reason for this being that he stole clothing allowances. By the time he was chased out, the king had a million and a half pounds in a London bank. Mussolini, having watched the Runyon film, understood that the overwhelming success the man was having would cause him to be more vindictive. "Because of this slob Carnera, he will punish me," he finally said to Farinacci. "He will complain to Hearst about me and I will lose the valuable voice in the United States. I must be published in America in order to move the entire nation into approval for our efforts." He would not mention anything as vile as money, particularly to Farinacci, who was so close to him that he might ask for some.

Once a week, Mussolini erupted into this insane energy and went to the pen, which in his career got him further than battalions of tanks. He wrote as he once did every night for his newspaper *Il Popolo* in Milan, wrote in big letters on clean paper. And if the paper ran out, rather than wait he continued writing on anything, an envelope, the back of a letter, walking around the room to any scrap, running the thought out. The chief of Hearst's Rome bureau came around to collect Mussolini's article and dispatch it to New York for use by Hearst papers throughout America. It appeared under white lettering on a black background: "Mussolini Speaks." Then, once a month, Hearst sent the check that more than ever Mussolini was terrified of losing.

Therefore, he had written:

"I Shall Regard Idle Rich in Italy as Outcasts," Is Mussolini's Warning
BY BENITO MUSSOLINI
(Special to Hearst newspapers via World Wide News Service)

ROME — One of the greatest enemies of the New Italy today, menacing the domestic life of the nation, is the idle rich. The Fascismo, in its new classification of the nation into syndicalist unions, will treat them as tramps.

The nation is grouped into categories. The password into the sacred premises of citizens is: "Do you contribute to the productiveness of the entire nation either by brain or the brawn — by your mental or muscle work?" Men and women who cannot pass this catechism will be ordered to take their places in line with tramps, vagabonds, paupers, thieves and idiots.

Those whose ancestors or parents amassed wealth, the greatest portion of which they left to their progeny whose spines grew soft in the midst of luxury, will today be given the opportunity to rehabilitate such spines with the elixir of the true God, and that is the sweat of a human body performing work without pause for anything except necessary human functions.

I shall stop the building of mansions, consuming cement and mortar, while the very builders of these luxuries are living in hovels. We shall soon see those who would live in such mansions standing on scaffolding and with their backs bent as they erect housing for the worthy workers of Italy.

If they do not perform such work, the doors of our prisons shall open to admit them and close with a most ominous noise behind them.

The next exclusive article for the Hearst papers said:

ROME — When I put a tax on bachelors and ordered the revenues thus derived to be set aside to aid mothers and their children, the whole world thought it was a joke. "This is another of Benito's fantasies," people said. In Italy, they no longer say this. The relentless force of my tax drives narcissistic young men away from their mirrors and to the sides of good Fascist women.

Under my edict, any man who attempts to live without a wife will face progressive taxes that at the end will take every lire of his wages and leave him roofless and starving. He will then face summary execution if found attempting to beg.

If I, Il Duce, Benito Mussolini, can live with a woman, then all of Italy's men can do the same.

If some man wants to practice the ultimate selfishness of living with himself, then he will starve to death in the streets because of his megalomania. As supreme leader, I prefer this to those who call for a more traditional remedy of castration, although I do not ban this word from my mind forever.

Long have I regarded loneliness as the dreaded enemy of a human being, and particularly a woman who grows up in a household with father and brothers. When the father dies and her brothers marry, she lives with the bare walls.

I understand the horror of this. I, Benito Mussolini, know that only Fascism can cure such a thing. Fascism is not a goal. It is a means to an end. Its first function was to cure Italy of her narcotics habit — to cure her of democracy and liberalism. A second function is to create more and more family life in Italy by having tax collectors chase these bachelors like rabbits and force them into life. As supreme ruler of all Italy, I order Italian men to marry Italian women!

This article was pasted on the walls of most beauty shops in New York. In the Cypress Hills neighborhood of Brooklyn, the pastor of the Church of the Blessed Sacrament ordered Mitzie's Beauty Shop on Fulton Street to remove the article from the window. The pastor said that the bachelor tax was an Italian problem and certainly one not to be found in his parish of decent Irishmen, who remained stuck together in saloons until they were too old to be of use to anybody.

The women who read and approved of Mussolini's ideas were not alone. Hearst applauded his work, particularly when he wrote, "A huge crowd is like a woman. It needs a strong man." Such people as Lincoln Steffens said he was truly great. Mussolini never quite mentioned the word "dictator," or that he wanted to kill all the Ethiopians and invade France.

Now, in his huge villa, he decided he must act immediately to save his paycheck. It was nine o'clock at night. "We leave now!" he said. He wanted to get to his office in Rome and try to call New York before everything there closed. He and Farinacci strode rapidly to the courtyard and got into a car that rushed them to the office at the Palazzo Venezia, the four-centuries-old, yellow stone palace at the foot of the Capitoline Hill. On the second floor, the Sala del Mappamondo, named for the ancient map of the world that covered the wall, he went to his desk at the far end of the room, which was seventy feet long and thirty feet wide.

The usher, Quinto Navarra, came in. Mussolini had him place a call to New York, to the offices of the Banco d'Italia on 116th Street, between First and Second avenues in the Italian neighborhood of East Harlem. The phone number was Lehigh 1200. The priority given to a chief of state allowed Mussolini's call to take up one of the twelve transatlantic lines. Peter Ferraro was president of the Banco d'Italia. In Mussolini's manner, he made all the people in the neighborhood call it "Banco Ferraro." Mussolini kept tourist and consulate funds in New York in the bank. When Ferraro came on, Farinacci at first did the speaking and relayed Ferraro's answers to Mussolini, who did not want to be on the phone with such an underling as a banker in an Italian neighborhood in New York. Farinacci told the banker that Carnera must be told to stay away from the writer Runyon's wife. Farinacci now relayed Ferraro's answer: "This he cannot do. He has no control over Carnera."

Mussolini grabbed the phone. "Ferraro. Do you not have Carnera's money in the bank?"

"Carnera is broke right now and doesn't have two lire in my bank."

Mussolini then said, "Tell Primo that the Duce implores him to stay away from that woman. It is his duty as a citizen not to touch that woman."

Ferraro now told Il Duce, "This is all over nothing. I know of what I speak. This writer Runyon is an old man. He is in his middle fifties. These things I hear. The girl is thirty years younger. What do you think. Of course she looks to be with a younger man. Why not Carnera? He is young and strong. He is not an old man like she has, this Runyon. Duce, you above all understand human nature and strength. Can you tell me how a man thirty years older can hope to satisfy a young woman?"

Mussolini, thirty years older than his girlfriend Claretta, was mute. Ferraro took this as a reason to continue. "Duce, it cannot be done. Is there one case anywhere on the face of the earth of a younger woman who does not become restless and seek out somebody her own age? Duce, even if she has to bring in the mailman. Duce, even if she has to go to the garbage man. Anything is better than an old man."

In Rome, all documentation shows, Mussolini leaped up in rage. He stuck out his jaw and chest and became so conscious of his five foot six height that he opened the French doors and stepped out one step and onto the balcony. "I order you to go to that big freak and from now on you take all his money from him and send it back to me. I will take care of Primo's money. Then you tell him that if he ever again touches her, I will travel to his town and burn his family at the stake."

Mussolini hung up. In New York, Ferraro immediately got into a taxi and went downtown to the Publicity building, where he found Madden about to leave for the day. He explained he was under personal orders of Benito Mussolini.

"I don't listen to Costello or Luciano," Owney said. "And they live right here. So why should I pay attention to that slob of yours don't even set foot in the town?"

Ferraro grimaced. "I promised him."

"Let's look at this sensible," Owney said. "You can't stop nature in an average guy. This here is a great huge animal don't know what to do with his prick. Let me show you something." He opened his desk and took out legal papers. "Nine paternity suits the bum got."

Ferraro was silent, then said, "I'll have to tell my country's leader."

"So what do you want?" Madden said.

"I'm one of the managers and I must get a piece of his purses," the banker said.

Ferraro the banker first sent a cable to Mussolini. "I have instructed your subject to do exactly as you demanded." Ferraro the banker then tucked a napkin under his chin and went after Carnera's money like it was fresh ravioli. When they matched Carnera with Max Baer, Ferraro asked only one question, "When people buy tickets in advance, who holds the money?" There was at this time no way to bull or bribe Baer. When the bell sounded, Duffy and Leon See put their hands over their eyes. Baer looked at this big giant, with a head that did not move and a jaw framed so beautifully, and for a moment he was indecisive. He didn't know whether to hit Carnera with a right hand or a left. He threw the hook. Carnera went down on his back. Baer burst into laughter as he went to a neutral corner. In the fifth row at ringside, sitting with Bill Reuben, Patrice Amati Runyon let out a shriek and implored Carnera to stay down. He never heard her or anything else. He stood up in shock, was hit again and went down right away. Eleven times that night Primo Carnera went down. At the end his face was blood, and from then on, he never thought of himself as anything but a victim.

The day after the fight, Carnera trudged into the Publicity Building and went to Madden's office. Owney told him that Ferraro the banker, on behalf of Mussolini, had his money. Carnera went to East Harlem, where Ferraro greeted him with a hug. He gave Carnera a paper bag filled with more one dollar bills. "Look at the size of your earnings. You are rich again!" Ferraro put a hand on Carnera's back and showed him to the door. A year later, when Mussolini withdrew all funds from the bank because Ferraro hadn't straightened out the thing with Runyon's wife, Ferraro emptied the bank vault, locked the front door and was gone. People in East Harlem called for his death. A large crowd gathered in front of the bank and began chanting: "Si tenete i soldi en la Banco Ferraro, si frigati!" Which meant, "If you have your money in the Banco Ferraro, you're freaked."

Runyon stood sideways in the shower with the water raining on his body. He kept his head out of the water and smoked an English Oval and stared out at Madison Square Garden. Wreathed in steam from the hot shower, holding a cigarette high in the air as the hand gestured, he looked out the window and announced to Jacobs Beach down below, "One evening along about seven o'clock I am sitting in Mindy's Restaurant putting on the gefilte fish, which is a dish I am very fond of, when in comes three parties from Brooklyn . . ."

He liked that. Ben Reuben's son Bill was in the living room. Runyon told him to get ready for the train ride to his father's house on Hibiscus Island.

At this time, there came to the streets of New York uncontrollable violence in the form of Ellsworth (Bumpy) Johnson. He had a head that had broken a thousand nightsticks. In each hand he carried a machete. And with each step he was signaling the start of change in the blacks in New York. It would take decades, but it had to start someplace, and so here came Bumpy, machetes at the ready.

This day had started when Dutch Schultz had kidnapped a numbers banker named Pompez from his home at 409 Edgecombe Avenue, on Harlem's Sugar Hill, and left his burned body in Central Park. Regret had made a point of remaining clear of this ugly violence, but now he had blundered and accompanied two Schultz hoodlums who were going to visit Madame Stephanie St. Clair, a tall woman from Jamaica who had the bearing of a monarch and the numbers business of a top hoodlum. Two hoodlums went to her door while Regret sat in the car. Madame St. Clair opened the door of her Stanford White renaissance townhouse on Strivers Row. The hoodlums threatened her. Slowly, the hand she held behind her opened the door. Mr. Johnson exploded onto the stoop and now was out on the cement and running. He was running too fast for Regret's taste.

Regret felt it was lousy thing to do, to push his foot down on the floor and make the car rush off and leave the two guys there on the street. Regret was afraid of one thing: running over somebody as he careened around the corner.

Bumpy Johnson walked into the 28th Precinct that day and said, "I want to report a robbery attempt. Two guys just jumped me."

The lieutenant sent two detectives with Bumpy. At 139th Street, down from Madame St. Clair's there was a crowd looking at two shredded bodies in the gutter.

"Two boys there tried to rob me," Bumpy said.

He was off a freighter from Charleston, South Carolina. He came in 1918 by sea because the law was looking for him by land. He was sixteen then and had a dozen whores working for him in Charleston, and when there was some trouble, he told the chief of police that he was going to kill him, then fuck his wife and his girlfriend. He was going to ruin a lot of lives in Harlem. He stole from people in Harlem and beat up people in Harlem, killed a few, too, and would wind up selling drugs in Harlem. But from the start he brought one thing with him that Harlem needed desperately. Bumpy Johnson was afraid of no white man ever born. Their heads open up just like anybody else's, he preached. There can be no way to obtain legitimate power until you first display strength on the street.

Now, on an early spring night, Bumpy Johnson stood with performers under their tree, the Tree of Hope, which had the first fresh green buds showing on the bare branches. The Tree of Hope was an elm tree whose roots were under the cement of Seventh Avenue at 132nd Street in Harlem, outside the entrance to the Lafayette Theater. "Rub the buds off," somebody said. "Tree won't give any luck unless you rub it bare." The first arrivals, the bass player, the chorus girl and the male dance team, grabbed a branch. The tree was supposed to get them a job, a gig. In the deepest winter, they came to the Tree of Hope at night, rubbed it and walked off in the cold. Once it became the least bit mild, only lashing rain kept the crowd from gathering every night. At any moment, a saloon owner could come by and grab a piano player. The booker for the Lafayette Theater's twelve daily acts steps out and calls for a dance team. Somewhere, a bass man failed to show and the band leader walks up to hire a replacement. Then, so often, nobody came to hire anybody. Still, the crowd started each evening under the elm, and the performers with jobs stopped by on their way to work. The great dancer Honi Coles remembered rubbing off buds for a job while looking enviously at Bub Miley, who played growl trumpet for the Duke Ellington band up at the Cotton Club, Freddy Guy, the guitar player, and Don Redman, a band leader, who were there for moral support before leaving for their jobs.

And so on this night one of them under the Tree of Hope said he had been invited to hear the Duke Ellington band play at the Cotton Club, an ugly little place on 142nd and Lenox Avenue that Ellington used as a bill payer while he developed recordings and radio shows. It was owned by Owney Madden, who did not allow a black into the place, except to go to work through the kitchen door. The white riffraff came uptown in limousines and had the thrill of being in Harlem and at the same time were protected from the black savages, who were kept outside, preferably on a rainy night so they would be driven off the streets, too. Not that anybody who lived in Harlem had the money to go in and spend fifty or sixty dollars, or who even wanted to sit with these white fop frauds from downtown.

At this time, however, anger had to be reserved for something more important than a cheap insult: the lynchings in the South were so furiously insane that even in Dallas the police and jail guards couldn't take it anymore and actually protected a black, firing at a mob of three hundred screaming for a prisoner's neck. Also in Harlem, there still was so much of the South in everybody's blood that nobody was disturbed by being barred from anyplace. The newspapers, the weekly *New York Age* and the *Amsterdam News*, took half-page ads from the white clubs and omitted editorials about the places being Mississippi with cornets. Luther (Red) Randolph, raised on the next corner from the Cotton Club, watched Harlem people pass on by as if keeping on their side of the square, right-hand side of the courthouse, Hayneville, Alabama. Lena Horne and Billie Holiday used the kitchen entrance and dressed behind a canvas curtain that separated them from the black male performers. The white riffraff from downtown sure did get a thrill from the Duke Ellington band, mostly because its leader was so elegant that with the least wave of the hand he turned a joint into a castle. They didn't understand the first bar of what they were hearing. Ellington, who comes up as the major composer in American history this far, was billed by the Cotton Club as playing "Jungle Music." Nobody in Harlem ever questioned any of this aloud until Bumpy Johnson came along and listened to the performers talking under the Tree of Hope.

The guy invited to hear Ellington said to Honi Coles, "I'll go in the front door."

"You will not."

"The Duke asked me to see the show. I come in like a customer."

"Ain't no colored man going through that front door."

"I am."

"That gray man at the top of the stairs throw you down without even looking."

The guy, doubtful now, said, "I'll sit at a table out front."

"You won't neither."

"Ellington said they have a table right there for people."

"That table," Honi Coles told the guy, "is way off on the side. The white people can't even see that table. That's where you get put. You come in the back door and you go out onto the side of the bandstand there. That table nobody can see is for other performers to watch these performers."

Now Bumpy Johnson said, "You want to go in the front door of the club?"

"I do," the guy who was going to see Ellington said.

"Some gray-haired man stop you?"

"He does," Honi Coles said.

"He does not," Bumpy said.

"Oh, you don't know them people."

"I know that when somebody is dead, they dead can't stop nobody."

"Come on now."

"You come on," Bumpy said. "What you're supposed to do is put on overalls and walk past there every night like a nigger and nod at the man at the door, go yessir and look down and walk on. One night you come by like usual and say yessir, and then you shoot that sonofabitch right in the head and you keep on walkin' same as before. You'd be surprised how fast that takes care of that."

"But then they close the place and the Duke loses a gig," Honi Coles said.

"Make the man lose a job," somebody else said.

"He got a whole band workin' in there. You can't blow the gig."

"You're all scared," Bumpy said.

"Not scared," Honi Coles said. "Just fellows who need a job ahead of everything else."

One night Runyon, Patrice and Regret were in the Cotton Club, and when Regret told him about Bumpy Johnson, Runyon insisted on seeing the guy. They went to Small's Paradise, where on this night Bumpy's favorite, Snake Hips Tucker, danced with a rhinestone belt whirling light across his middle as his hips wiggled. He came right up to a table and put that shaking front of his almost against some white lady's arm, and that was in the first pass around the room. The second time he moved, he threw that front of his right up against that white lady's arm, and he started wiggling those snake hips, and when the men took one look at that face of his, dead ready if you wanted to go with him right here, nobody minded what he was doing. He wiggled and rubbed, and the lady loved it and the men threw bills all over the floor for Snake Hips Tucker. Runyon kept Patrice away from the front of the room, although she was certainly interested, and with a growl almost at his lips, he left this obscene black. "Why don't we wait here for Bumpy?" Regret said.

"You know the fella, you wait for him," Runyon said.

"I don't know him," Regret said. "That's's why I wanted to meet him with you. He would like me then. Maybe take care of me up here."

Bumpy was not at Small's because a couple of his policy numbers runners were locked up by police at the 32nd Precinct on West 135th Street. Bumpy walked into the station house and announced to the desk lieutenant, "I paid you fellas my money and you double-cross me and lock up my men. I paid you fellas my fucking money."

The lieutenant tried to settle it with soft words, but among things for which Bumpy's temperament was not suited was calm. A couple of policemen came out of the squad room and walked Bumpy into the dayroom. Right away, Bumpy's hand went out and took the nightstick off the nearest cop. He gripped it tightly and said, "A couple of you boys don't get home alive."

The porter in the police station remembered that when an officer went for his gun, Bumpy's stick hit the guy right on the head and now he simply erupted. Nobody ever had seen a face like this before. All of them spilled out of the squad room, past the desk and out into the street and Bumpy Johnson was after them, swinging that nightstick.

One day after that, Lucky Luciano told people, "The toughest nigger ever to live is on 125th Street. His name is Bumpy Johnson. I like him."

Bumpy Johnson announced, "Lucky Luciano is the greatest Wop of them all."

He became the first black in New York who could sit down at a table

with the Mafia and be regarded as an equal. His first request was to
have Dutch Schultz killed. It was turned down, primarily because he
was the first black ever to ask for such a thing. "Someday," Bumpy
said.

As a big-city political system, particularly New York's, first had to be
cracked with physical intimidation by outsiders, every group of people
who left the soil of anywhere and came to the city first had to control
their own crime before even thinking of politics and education. The
Irish, afterward the Jews and then the Italians made it with knives and
guns in the streets before they reached the political clubhouse. Blacks,
the most peaceful of the immigrants to come to the city, brought the
most pleasant of customs to New York. They understood the soothing
gesture, and the notion that what you wear actually is a statement. On
Sunday mornings, the men would dress up, right to the derby hat, and
stand on the rooftops of the attached houses and wave to the crowds of
elegantly dressed people passing below on their way to church. Nobody allows you to thrive with that behavior.

As damaging as he was, Harlem needed Bumpy Johnson, who tried
to control crime where he lived. He couldn't do it all alone, and it took
decades before black gangsters finally stopped running numbers and
dope for whites and began doing it for themselves. But he set the ex-
ample, and once in control of their own crime, blacks, just like the
Irish who had lived in Harlem before them, could control their politics.

In his years in Harlem, Bumpy one day came out with that killer's
face and screamed, "They were supposed to shoot a man last night and
the lazy bastards didn't do it because they didn't get there on time!
Can't keep a fucking appointment." He went up to 125th Street and
shot a man at noon in front of a crowd and walked off. That night he
was on 135th Street and somebody said, "They're still up there operating on him."

"He's alive?" Bumpy said.

"Alive in the operating room, anyway."

Bumpy Johnson walked into the hospital and came raging through
the operating room doors in his street clothes and sent the doctors and
nurses flying out of the way. He pulled out a knife and stabbed the guy
to death on the table. A lieutenant named Boxer came to investigate,
but none of the doctors or nurses could remember more than their own
names.

Schultz, who lived in illusion himself, believed he could do whatever he wanted in Harlem because he paid Jimmy Hines, a Tammany leader. He did not care whether Bumpy Johnson lived or died; he thought Hines would handle it all. Hines represented a district in which both Runyon and Gene Fowler lived, and so they knew both Schultz and Hines. Hines attended the private dinners at Leone's with Runyon and Jimmy Walker. Out of which Runyon discovered that while at first it seemed irresistible to use politicians in his short stories, he was unable to fit them in, and for good reason.

At first, Hines seemed to have been born for Runyon. Hines, who began as a blacksmith, used a wood table in the back room of his clubhouse as an anvil. When angered, he pounded his thick arms on the table and everybody waiting in the outside room shuddered.

On one occasion, a man named Macrery, another one of the Protestants that Tammany used in those days, paid $10,000 to Hines for an appointment as a criminal court judge for five years. Hines took the money, then went to Jimmy Walker, the mayor, and whatever happened there is conjecture, although not so much really, for Walker appointed Macrery as judge for five years. Walker and Hines were so close that whenever they met, they clutched each other so fiercely that bystanders were afraid they would do themselves bodily harm. Yet appointing a judge transcended mere friendship. Humans are incapable of doing such a favor without getting paid.

Anyway, the money was no problem because the judges got it back from defendants. During his term, Macrery drank so much that his skull arteries turned into cement casing. This produced delusions, which propelled him into Hines's clubhouse one day to declare that he wouldn't pay Hines another $10,000 for his next five-year term. "I only pay once," Macrery said.

Hines lifted both thick arms over his head, locked his hands and brought the whole thing down like a pile driver. The wood table shook. Out in the waiting room, all those with hungry cousins decided that tomorrow seemed like a better day for imploring.

Sometime later, Macrery was found dead in a building at 934 Eighth Avenue, which was nowhere near his home. The medical examiner said nothing seemed amiss; the judge was out on a drunk. The examiner issued death certificate number 21089. The cause of death was listed as coronary sclerosis. Hines appeared at the wake with a hand over his heart. Immediately after the funeral, a Tammany lawyer made a stunning charge: that somebody from Tammany Hall, and by the very tone of his voice he meant Hines, had beaten Macrery to death over the

$10,000. The attorney demanded that the body be exhumed in order for justice to look it over.

Then the wife of another magistrate, George Ewald, appeared at the Hines clubhouse. Her husband still had some time before his reappointment came up, but she now believed that waiting was unhealthy. As she knew nothing about the clubhouse, and thus had no idea that nothing much was to be said outside the privacy of the back room, she announced to an old receptionist, and to the crowded waiting room: "I am here to pay the ten thousand dollars now. It is not time yet, but I would rather pay it now than have my husband killed later on."

Which produced two grand juries, followed by two indictments, both of which had to be thrown out. Finally, Hines came down to Lindy's one night and told Runyon, "All I know is that calling for an investigation was a great move. I never had to ask anybody for a dollar after that. So I wasn't an extortionist anymore. I didn't have to extort nobody. People gave me gifts."

Runyon never could make an amusing short story out of the incident because of a flaw in the central character: as politicians were not real people to begin with, he could not make a fictional character out of Hines. Certainly Hines was at the right level. He was not a mayor like Walker, or a presidential candidate like Al Smith, both too large and easily recognizable to use as characters. But the Runyon narrator in short stories always had a great love for crummy little criminals, of which politicians are, but the characters had to be real people first, as you cannot create a cartoon out of a cartoon. Politicians, Hines included, having the souls of ciphers, left Runyon unable to get a purchase on them. They were people who stole, but were secretive and not publicly proud of their scores. They never came up with a dollar out of them for anybody else.

In Hines's case, he took $10,000 off Ewald the judge's wife.

"Is it right to take from a lady?" Runyon asked in Lindy's.

"Are you referring to grabbing purses?" Regret said.

"No, at least that's taking the chance of being caught. This was done with protection," Runyon said.

"He can't get busted?" Regret said.

"Hardly."

"Puttin' the bull on a lady," Regret said.

"Indirectly."

"That's a mutt," Regret said. "Why didn't he wait for Ewald himself to come around?"

He never could even arrive at a nickname for Hines, which was necessary for ascent into a short story. The Runyon names, Butch and Regret and Sorrowful and Big Julie, all came out of an understanding and affection for his trade. Regret went out there with nothing in front of him except his belly, and so he was Abba Dabba, Regret or Avisack. But every time Runyon reached for a nickname for Jimmy Hines, his hand came out covered with poison ivy. He shook his head when he read stories about "colorful" politicians. While he liked Walker, and lived almost as secret a life, he knew it didn't sound right for a short story. The great gangster trait of being brazen was sadly lacking in Walker, who thrived on deceit.

We must at this point refer back one year, to the mayoral race of 1933, in order to underline its importance to the times in which it was held. In that election, Fiorello La Guardia ran for mayor on the platform of throwing out Tammany thieves such as Hines. The Tammany candidate was a man named Mahoney. The results in Jimmy Hines's own district, with all the neighbors voting, were:

La Guardia (Fusion) 18,701
Mahoney (Tammany) 11,709.

In the race for district attorney, Thomas E. Dewey, the Fusion candidate, ran on the promise that he would put Jimmy Hines in prison. The vote for district attorney in Hines's district:

Thomas E. Dewey (Fusion) 18,662
Harold W. Hastings (Tammany) 10,902.

"Maybe the guy never existed at all," Runyon said. He was nice enough about Hines when he covered the trial in which Dewey sent Hines to Sing Sing. But in all of Runyon's stories, Hines never was mentioned even in a line of dialogue. Then Runyon, without being exactly conscious of what he was doing, stepped in and used sports to perform a political act far larger than anything done by Hines, or by Jimmy Walker.

A few days before the Thanksgiving weekend of 1934, Jack Blackburn, an old trainer, called Runyon from Chicago as part of the publicity to help promote a match between Charley Massera of New York and a new heavyweight Blackburn was training, Joe Louis. Blackburn, who had been skating for a living, said to Runyon, "I always told you I was going to have a champion of the world. I have one now. You best get out here and take a look."

Then Ray Arcel, trainer, and Eddie Borden, manager, and their fighter, Charley Massera, were in Lindy's for an interview with Runyon. "I have to figure that my guy here is ready to fight anybody in the world, so we might as well take whatever they offer us," Borden said.

Runyon wanted to go to the fight, but he had a sore throat and thought he'd best stay home. "I can't wait for Florida this year," he rasped. "I have to shake these colds I keep getting." On Thanksgiving, he went to the estate in New Jersey of James Daugherty, called the Baron, with the playwright Howard Lindsay and his wife. Runyon and Lindsay were writing a Broadway play called *A Slight Case of Murder*. When he looked at Lindsay's wife, the actress Elaine Stritch, who at least looked many years younger than her husband, he was comforted. She seemed very much in love with Lindsay. At this time, Runyon had himself listed in *Who's Who* as a flat fifty, which was four years off his age. His wife was Countess Patrice del Grande of Calditas, Spain. Her age was twenty-eight. He felt secure and quite social. He and Lindsay slept in the same room, as they were scheduled to be up early to hunt birds in a Maryland game park. Runyon snored so loudly that Lindsay could not sleep. Muttering, he shook Runyon several times to try to get him to stop. At 6 A.M., Runyon woke up, glared at Lindsay and said, "You talked all night." Lindsay knew that while the second act of the play was thus far a brick wall, it was nothing compared to his coauthor.

They then went down to breakfast, served by a smiling black man, and when they left for the hunt, they had young black youths with fast legs and faster nods of assent to help them in picking up any shot birds. This thin, dour-faced man with the round wire-rim glasses appeared to treat them just as anybody else did, as if they were different.

In Chicago on November 30, Joe Louis walked out in the first round and jabbed. The jab was so fast and came with such frightful power, water drops spraying in the ring lights, eyes closing, nose immediately giving way, that Ray Arcel, crouched in the corner, was sorry the fight had ever started and thought right away of stopping it. At the end of the second, Massera, game as they come, refused to quit. He went out for the third and took a straight right hand. He did not know where he was, and Arcel was up at the ropes, arms waving, but the referee was moving in on his own.

A few days later, Ray Arcel assured Runyon that Louis would be a champion, and a good one for the business. "I think he can destroy any heavyweight I've ever seen," Arcel said.

That day, the promoter at Madison Square Garden, Jimmy Johnston, said he never would have anything to do with a black fighter. He said that he would inform Louis's managers that there were no matches available at the Garden.

On 49th Street, Runyon walked the ten yards from the Forrest Hotel, now just a hangout for him, to Mike Jacobs's ticket office. They had done business on the Hearst Milk Fund fights, and now Runyon proposed that they rent Yankee Stadium and promote a Joe Louis match. He and Jacobs would put the first black fighter in a main event in the history of New York. This would constitute a historic act, he told Jacobs.

"You do history in school," Jacobs said. "School is bum box office." He was a man with a complicated view of the world. He had left school when he saw that there were long lines at the aquarium. He and his brother got on line, bought tickets and then went and sold them at a higher price to people at the rear of the line. At the end of World War I, troopships returning to the West Side docks were met by a joyously waving Mike Jacobs, who stood on the bulkhead with a stack of cheap suitcases, which he sold to soldiers "so you could put your clothes in them and go back to Ohio." The suitcases cost Jacobs a quarter, and he sold them for a dollar and a quarter, and the thing was all right; the soldiers needed the suitcases and were happy with them, because carrying a suitcase made them feel like they were part of life again. Jacobs made a lot of money and this made him happy, too.

Runyon now talked to Jacobs about throngs of blacks paying to see Louis fight. Jacobs became social-minded. "It would give them a rootin' interest," he mused. When Runyon spoke of Louis winning and becoming heavyweight champion, with Jacobs and Runyon controlling his matches, and then Madison Square Garden, and finally all of boxing, Jacobs, out of deep human commitment, said, "We have to put him in with a big white guy and tell all the white people we got to save boxing from this savage. Who does he fight?"

Runyon blurted out, "Carnera." Usually Runyon thought for a long time about possible boxing matches, because he regarded himself as a genius at it. But this time he simply said "Carnera" and did not know why, but he felt very good saying it. Which is why the word "subconscious" is in the dictionary. Jacobs picked up a packet of tickets from one of his racks. He held them to his ear and shuffled them with his thumb. As the tickets ripped into his ear, he could tell by the sound if even one was missing. He always did this when he was considering a large financial move. Jacobs said he would put up the money to rent Yankee Stadium, and guarantee the purses.

Later, Madden, who sat in his second-floor office on Broadway, chewing gum and jingling loose change, ruled the idea preposterous. He said that while he did not mind Carnera's taking a few good belts, he did not want to see this big guy killed. But Runyon was strangely forceful. He told Madden that he had to have Carnera for Joe Louis. Madden shrugged. "Suit yourself," he said. He had decided that he wanted to get out of town for good and settle in Hot Springs, Arkansas, with a woman who was the daughter of the town postmaster. So freak Carnera. He shook hands on the match, which was scheduled for June.

EIGHTEEN

FEBRUARY 1935. At the Lindbergh kidnapping trial in Flemington, in the frozen fields of Hunterdon County in New Jersey, there is a pause while the judge's secretary comes in and hands the judge some papers. Damon Runyon, sitting in the front row, glances up from his writing pad and looks at Mrs. Bruno Richard Hauptmann, the wife of the defendant. She is being paid by Runyon's employer, Hearst. All she has to do is put on a beleaguered face and pose for pictures. This requires no acting, for Runyon figures that her husband has about as much shot of walking out of the room as he does of bringing back the baby. Now Runyon sees Walter Winchell standing up and posing in the courtroom. Everybody else remains seated. Of course there is a photographer over there on the side, standing on a chair under the windows, taking a picture of the courtroom. Runyon goes back to writing notes on his pad.

Winchell, the row behind Runyon, calls out, "Copy! Who can take my copy? I have to get this in early. Give them time to put it up front." Winchell holds up a sheet of paper as if it is the Magna Carta. A copyboy snatches the paper from Winchell.

Runyon, without looking up, says to the man next to him, Bob Musel of the United Press, "What do you think of this asshole? He actually thinks he's covering this thing."

Winchell's notes to his paper, the *New York Mirror*, described by William Randolph Hearst as "the worst newspaper in the country," read: "When Wilentz spoke tenderly of Col. Schwarzkopf and the 'boys' [the state troopers], Mrs. Schwarzkopf cried."

Runyon has been writing five thousand words a day on the trial for Hearst's *New York American* and papers around the country and it is probably the best American courtroom reporting ever done. As far as Runyon was concerned, Winchell belonged running around yapping away in his kennel. He had used Winchell as the character Waldo Winchester in two of his short stories, with the character being a fraud and a buffoon, and Runyon had made important money with both stories. Winchell, terrified of Runyon, told everybody that Runyon was a genius. Runyon dismissed this as humming from a mosquito. Winchell's ego smothered the tiniest doubt about himself. Runyon thought he was a preposterous sucker, for he had allowed a cheap saloon owner, Sherman Billingsley, to turn him into a shill. Billingsley gave him a special table and put a phone on it. At that time phone bills could run as high as $7.50 a month. Winchell put the name of the saloon in his column almost every day and thought the table and phone were more evidence that he was a major figure. "Your usual whore knows what she's doing," Runyon said.

In the courtroom, Runyon asked Bob Musel, "What do you think Hauptmann would rather do, sit where he is or spend the rest of his life listening to Winchell talk?"

"He'd jump into the electric chair," Musel said.

Runyon had saved Winchell's life a while before this. Trotting around the nightclubs, Winchell had been told by Texas Guinan, who had a motor mouth, that the guys were going to get rid of Vincent Coll, the scrawny Irish bedbug who slept on a couch at his mother's house and went around kidnapping gangsters. In one attempt, he shot five children, killing one, on the sidewalk in front of a place in East Harlem. Owney Madden had said that this was lousy, but he had no time for Coll, who then kidnapped Big Frenchy, and Owney had to pay $35,000 in ransom. He put everybody he had out on the streets after Coll. Guinan, hearing of this, told Winchell that "five planeloads came in from Chicago." Winchell put it in his Monday column in the *Mirror*. With timing that comes from energy, the early edition was on the street one hour before Arthur Bieler walked into a drugstore in the London Terrace buildings on West 23rd Street, saw Vincent Coll in the phone booth, waved goodbye to him and with a machine gun put an X in the phone booth door. When he got back to the Winona Club and saw the *Mirror*'s early edition, he decided that Winchell knew that he had done the shooting.

By this time, Winchell, shivering with excitement, had rushed to the newspaper to write a story for the late editions that would be all about himself and somewhat about Coll. He had finished and now was at the newspaper talking about himself to anybody who would listen. Bieler called. He warned Winchell not to write anything about the shooting. "It's on the presses," Winchell cried. "Then stop the presses or I fucking stop you," Bieler said. Winchell called Runyon, who was at the Winter Olympics at Lake Placid. Runyon was comatose from the cold fresh air. He had watched a speed skater, Irving Jaffe, win the deciding meet of the 10,000 meter skating race, and wrote, "The fast-closing Ballangrud, and the Canadian, Stack, almost tumbled over the sliding body of the American Hebrew." But on the phone, Winchell seemed in such terror that at four in the morning Runyon had to bargain over the phone with Madden and Bieler. Arthur was adamant. "That guy got my freedom in his hands. I can't have him walkin' around." Runyon negotiated a compromise. At 6 A.M. he called the newspaper. "Take a long vacation, Walter." Winchell announced he had a nervous breakdown and took off from the paper and went to California. After which, he left the gangsters to Runyon. But he still so wanted to be a newspaperman that here he was, rattling around a courtroom.

In the front of the room, the judge leaned to his right, and many of those on Runyon's side of the courtroom swiveled in their seats and went into a left oblique. As only five people in the courtroom wore eyeglasses, most had to twist around just to be able to make out the judge's shoulder. At this time, glasses still had a reputation for making wearers look ancient. "Men don't make passes at girls who wear glasses," Dorothy Parker said. Women all over were lurching off curbs and in front of moving buses. Men who wore glasses had on "cheaters" or were called "four-eyed." Long ago, Damon Runyon had figured the odds on glasses. Here in the courtroom, he had on his usual round glasses with wire frames. "Napoleon gets taken out in Russia," Runyon always said, "because he cannot see when they give him the weather report."

The judge now stands and walks to the door on his left, which leads to his office. The crowd shifts, left to right. The judge changes his mind, walks clear back to the other side of the bench, picks up something and returns to the office door. Some of the reporters spun so quickly that they wound up turning completely around and facing the back of the courtroom. Runyon thinks they would be better off covering the trial by radio.

For six weeks now, seeing through his glasses, he has been writing every day for the Hearst papers, and each night he is limp and the editors around the country send wires shrieking for more.

Runyon was here doing newspaper work because he was convinced in his sleep that if the short stories were fiction, then what if even the success did not exist? He had been a news reporter since age eleven, and he had seen too many newspaper families living with the lights shut off. Including his. He still kept at least one light on throughout the night. Now, at age fifty-five, he felt that without a regular job he would begin to go for scared money, and the writing would be that of a guy chasing scared money.

Right up front in the courtroom was Howard Lindsay, who was writing a play with Runyon that had nothing to do with Lindbergh and already was booked into a theater in the fall. Beautiful. What if it wasn't enough? He had race horses in Florida, but his filly Angelic, at Hialeah in Miami, had an injury that cost more money than a new car. He was the author of the famous line "All horse players die broke." No one knew it better. Whenever they finished the case against this Hauptmann, who sat up there as arrogant as the Kaiser, Runyon was going right to his white house on Hibiscus Island. By now, there was nobody over the footbridge on Palm Island. Capone had been carted off to Alcatraz. The bills don't quit and neither can you, Runyon always said. "The Payroll is a more important document than the Bible."

So here he is at the Lindbergh trial, a short wiry man who weighed 140 pounds and had wet hair slapped down. He practiced showing nothing with his face, but he had blue eyes that often gave chilly stares. Even here in this Jersey farm town, it took him an hour to get dressed in the morning. As he always regarded the selection of a suit as the first sentence of his day's story, he arrived in court in a Sunday blue that cost $50 at Nat Lewis's on Broadway and set him off by elegant understatement from all the slobs in the room. His shirt was pure silk and came from Charvet et Fils, 18 East 53rd Street. He had the initials *DR* stitched in red alongside the shirt label and also on the inside of his cuffs. He need not show off for inferiors; it was enough that he knew the initials were there. One of his men, sportswriter Hype Igoe of the *American*, was walking around Manhattan breaking in his latest pair of 5½B shoes.

In court, Damon Runyon is holding a large pad and a black newspaper copy pencil.

A New Jersey state trooper leaned into the row and said to Runyon, "The Western Union guy says that fella in there with him really is somebody named Regret."

"Sure is."

"Is he really the guy they had in the movie?" the state trooper asked.

"They had an actor play him. Lynne Overman."

"This is the first time I ever saw anybody who ever had a movie role named after him."

"Why don't you hang out with him today?" Runyon said.

"Isn't he a big gangster?"

"My friend, he couldn't be Shirley Temple's bodyguard. You might ask her one day. She said, 'Regret is softer than my pillow.' "

"What is Shirley Temple like?"

"She gets you all the money."

"Does Regret know her?"

"Sure."

"I'd love to have a beer with him when I get off."

"Come on, then."

He and the trooper went out into the hallway, at the head of a flight of stairs leading to the front door and the street. A room to the left was occupied by the jury. The one on the right was filled with Western Union wiremen tapping out Morse code on metal bugs that went to newspaper offices around the country. They could send 150 words a minute, and as no reporter knew the code, the wireman could be sitting right alongside the writer and tapping out, "This bastard is so slow we'll never get home."

Regret loitered in all this clatter. Runyon told him that the trooper would be honored to have a drink with him. Regret swallowed. "In fact, he would like to hang out with you from now on," Runyon said. "Him and all his buddies from the state police troop."

Runyon could find no seat for Regret in the courtroom. He already had two people in the room, Howard Lindsay and a guy who had been left in a seat requested by Mike Jacobs, Runyon's partner in promoting prizefights. Jacobs, who lived in Jersey, had come down himself to pick up an admission ticket from Runyon. He had told Runyon that he'd hired Yankee Stadium and the Polo Grounds for big outdoor fights that summer, starting with Louis and Carnera in June. They had the chance to become insanely rich by controlling the heavyweight championship of the world. It was a conflict for Runyon to be a newspaper reporter and a fight promoter, but what business was that of anybody's? Besides, rules like those are for the untalented, who must conform because they don't have the ability to do as they please.

Jacobs had peered into the crowded room and growled, "They let these people in free!" He put the blue admission ticket into his pocket and left to bring it to his friend.

And now, as Runyon went back to his seat, a man came up and introduced himself as the person who had received the ticket from Mike Jacobs. "Boy, this is sure worth the money," the guy said.

When the trial resumed, the judge charged the jury, and appeared to sink Hauptmann. The defense lawyer, Reilly, also was being paid by Runyon's employer, Hearst. Reilly, Runyon had concluded after observing the man's demeanor in the men's room, had a roaring case of venereal disease, which he was treating with whisky. Runyon wrote none of this.

When the jury began to deliberate, news reporters barged into the Western Union wire room and started a crap game. A *New York American* copyboy, Patrick Lynch, age seventeen, of 419 East 57th Street, couldn't wait to shoot dice with the big guys. He looked in and saw Walter Winchell throwing ten dollars down to get in the game. Winchell had his hat tilted back and a press card stuck in the hatband. He also would have worn a sandwich board — "I Am a Reporter!" — if it was allowed in court. Lynch went across the street to the Union Hotel and found Eddie Mahar, who was running the large Hearst staff of reporters and photographers, and asked for an advance on pay of ten dollars.

"You better go and see Runyon. He just squawked that you're not around," Mahar said.

"Where?" Lynch said.

"In the courtroom."

The room was empty and Runyon sat with a cigarette hanging from his mouth. He wrote in longhand on a yellow legal pad balanced on his knee.

"Coffee," Runyon said.

"There's a big crap game going downstairs," Lynch said.

"Coffee," Runyon said.

On the yellow pad, Runyon was writing the early scenes:

It is 11:16 this morning when the jurors retire into the jury room immediately at the conclusion of Justice Trenchard's charge. A short time later a light lunch of sandwiches, cake and coffee is taken in to them. Only twice after that is anything heard from them until they are ready to bring in the verdict.

The first time is early afternoon when they make a request for a magnifying glass. The lens is produced, carefully examined by State and defense counsel, and then sent in to the jurors.

Presumably they want to scrutinize the handwriting specimens, the

ladder, the "Jafsie" phone number scrawled on the board from Hauptmann's closet.

Lynch brought back a mug of black coffee from the Union Hotel. In
the hall outside the courtroom, he passed Winchell, who was leaning
against the wall. "I'm going a hundred at a clip in there and I'm getting
killed," he said. Inside, Runyon handed Lynch a couple of more handwritten pages. "You might as well get them started on this," he said.
"Be back in a few minutes."

Lynch stepped through the crap game and handed the copy to a
telegrapher named Visconti.

"I hear Winchell dropped a big number in here," Lynch said.

"Yeah, for ten fucking dollars," another telegrapher, Howie Smith,
said.

Visconti tapped out the copy, which went to the *American* office in
downtown Manhattan, a sand-colored building across the street from
Pier 40 on the East River. It was a replica of Hearst's national headquarters, which was uptown on Eighth Avenue. There, another telegrapher typed to the clicking of the Morse bug that sat on the desk. It
was the newest of news technology, replacing the carrier pigeon, and
good enough to pull Runyon's early edition copy out of the sky. A carbon went to the Hearst wire service, which sent the story to papers
around the nation.

"This guy is filing more words than they sent for the World War,"
Visconti said.

Some wag sits in the judge's chair and calls sharply for order, at which
everyone jumps. A checkers game is in progress at one end of the defense table. The lawyers are chatting and some of them sit in the jury
box.

The writer asks Reilly, "Did you ever lose a trial involving the death
sentence?"

He answers, "Lots of them."

"Any go to the chair?"

"Yes. If you take the kind of cases I do, you better be ready for the
worst."

"How does this one look to you?"

"Why, the jury can't wait to let him go," Reilly said, smiling.

Someone now starts the gentle pastime of making paper arrows and
sailing them around the room. Someone else produces a pair of green

dice, but is restrained from opening operations for fear it might bring even the jury out in a stampede.

Damon Runyon wrote in longhand for eleven hours and thirty-one minutes. Once, his hand remained still in the air as he thought of Lindbergh. He said to Lynch, "I covered the guy when he came home from Paris. Half a million people in Washington. He was so young. The youngest-looking hero we ever had. As slim as your finger. Look at me now. Writing about the guy who probably murdered his baby. If you want insides old before their time, this is the game."

He resumed writing and then put together a lead for the first editions of the paper.

> FLEMINGTON, Feb. 13 — Bruno Richard Hauptmann's fate rests with the jury tonight.
> As these lines are written at 9:23 P.M. the jurors have been out for ten hours, closeted in the barely furnished jury room for all that time, and there is still no indication they are near a verdict.

He stopped writing only when the jury came in with the verdict. In the back of the courtroom were two newsreel cameras, which everybody pretended were not there. All the court officers, and, most believed, the judge, too, were being paid by the newsreel companies.

When the guilty verdict was called out, Walter Winchell called out, "I said that in October. I predicted he'd be guilty. Oh, that's another big one for me! Come on fellas, put it in your stories. I was the first one to call it."

For the first time, Robert Musel of the United Press took the time to grumble anything. "How do they let a fucking child like this in the room?" Then he silently watched the depressing scene of Hauptmann's wife crying. Musel would go on to do his job for longer, and under more fire, than any reporter in World War II.

The moment the jury was dismissed and Hauptmann was sentenced and lugged off, Runyon went directly across the street to the four-story brick Union Hotel and typed with two fingers. Pat Lynch grabbed each page as Runyon pulled it from the typewriter.

> FLEMINGTON, Feb. 13 — Bruno Richard Hauptmann must die the week beginning March 18 for the murder of Charles A. Lindbergh, Jr.
> He is found guilty tonight of murder in the first degree, without

recommendation, and immediately sentenced by Justice Thomas W. Trenchard to be executed "in the manner provided by law."

In New Jersey this is electrocution.

The jury is out from 11:16 this morning until 10:45 tonight. . . .

Hauptmann, standing erect in front of the chair where he sat throughout the trial, handcuffed to Deputy Sheriff Low on one hand and Trooper O'Donnell on the other, receives his sentence. . . . Justice Trenchard remands him to the custody of the sheriff, and Low and O'Donnell start moving immediately, making such a quick start that Hauptmann stumbles as he moves. . . . He passes from the court with a strange half-step, as if the legs might crumble under him any moment. . . .

Some long moments earlier, during the wait for the jury to enter the room, Hauptmann's face is damp with perspiration. His wife comes in and takes a seat near him. They exchange no words. . . .

They sit and wait. Edward J. Reilly, chief of the defense counsel, and Attorney General Wilentz cannot sit down. A windowshade suddenly flying up makes everybody jump. An epidemic of coughing sets in as a result of the nervous strain while they are waiting on the judge.

At every stir in the crowd comes cries from the bailiff:

"Sit down!"

The troopers have their hands on their guns. Reilly stands smoothing the back of his hair. Wilentz paces up and down as they await the judge. Outside the flares, the mumbles of the crowd . . .

In the *American* office in Manhattan, they railroaded this late Runyon copy through to the composing room, where it was placed at the beginning of the many paragraphs that Runyon had done in longhand all day. The main edition went in at midnight. The next morning, the *American* and Hearst papers all over the nation had, in Runyon's trial story, one of the few newspaper stories ever to last past the first sundown.

The next night, he was with Patrice at the El Morocco on East 54th Street, which was the society place for a long moment in New York. Runyon couldn't wait for dark so he could be out with his young blonde. They were joined by Sam Becker, his lawyer. Becker was just up from Washington, where he had been a known name in the New Deal, because of which he soon had major clients in Manhattan because he was smart. He was short and bald and had these wonderfully alert little feet that could spin a big broad around a dance floor while he nestled his bald head between her chests. He also came out of his hotel suite each night with $1,500 on him because he never knew which big tall smack-up chorus girl he would meet while he was out with his new client,

Damon Runyon. He liked Runyon as a client ahead of the Ford Motor Company.

They began talking about the trial. "He shouldn't steal babies," Patrice decided. Becker drank bourbon, but Runyon ordered Coca-Cola for Patrice and coffee for himself. Becker noticed Patrice cock her head to the waiter, who brought her a Coke that obviously had something else in it. Runyon never noticed this. Becker said nothing. If Runyon were one of those dreadful corporate clients, he would tell the bum the truth at the drop of pencil, particularly if the truth could make the man wince. But here he was confronted with guys and dolls, and a third person always is safer keeping both feet on an earthquake than uttering one word. Becker let the woman sneak her gin in silence.

Runyon was ebullient. People all over the room looked at him, and some that he felt were truly important names, such as Jock Whitney, came over to ask about the trial. Runyon glowed when Whitney made a fuss over Patrice. Then he and Whitney talked about their horses and movies. Whitney said his latest project, a Civil War movie, would be "marvelous." Whitney, a partner with David O. Selznick, had received the galley proofs of a book nobody in Hollywood wanted, *Gone With the Wind*. He read the proofs on a plane going from La Guardia Field in New York to Hollywood. When it landed for fuel in St. Louis, Whitney went to the Western Union office and sent a wire to Selznick: "Send the Mitchell woman $50,000 as option on Gone With the Wind. Regards. Jock."

At the table, Whitney also mentioned that he was at Oxford when his father died. The butler called at 3 P.M. from Manhasset, Long Island, to England, and another student answered the phone and told the butler to hold on. The butler waited on the phone until midnight. Suddenly, the butler heard Whitney say hello. He had been out in London all night and, returning home at 6 A.M. London time, just happened to notice the phone off the hook. At that time there were only twelve transatlantic phone lines.

When Whitney left the table, Sam Becker wondered, "Did the butler ever think of hanging up?"

"What do you think he was, some cheap scullery man or a greenskeeper?" Runyon said. "He was the butler. That's a bigger job than being a general." He loved the customs of the rich almost as much as those of the gangsters.

On this night, Runyon had the glamour and excitement of the news business, great big headline heart-stopping murder trial, and yet he didn't have to live the grubby life of a reporter. He had a wife who had been dancing in Texas Guinan's chorus line between dethronings. And even though she was out of nightclubs, she wasn't a drinker. Runyon couldn't stand women who drank. His first wife had been an alcoholic. Next to him, Patrice drank more of her Coke drinks. When she left the table, Runyon's eyes followed her. Sam Becker was sure he was going to say something.

"Isn't she beautiful?" Runyon said to Sam Becker.

"Sure is," he said.

"She's here from Madrid," Runyon said. "Her uncle was a duke and they blew a decision with the king of Spain over something and she has to come over here. She is real Spanish royalty. How do you like that? A Runyon is married into royalty."

When she returned, Runyon stood, held her chair and patted her hand as he talked. Her other hand was busy tilting a glass with her seventh or eighth Coke. The countess, pure Castilian of course, spoke to the Mexican busboy in words that sounded to Becker as if they came from Tijuana.

"Why don't we dance?" Patrice said to Runyon. He smiled. He thought it was humorous that he couldn't dance.

"You don't dance because you're too old for it?" Patrice asked. Runyon thought that this was exceptionally funny. "Well, I'm not too old. I shouldn't be sitting here like this. I should be up dancing. This is for old people."

Runyon, age fifty-five, didn't seem to hear her. He listed himself with Patrice as being fifty-two, and would have loved to have chopped that down. At all other times, he was in open fear of the shame and disgrace of having his true age revealed. Yet as Patrice began to talk pointedly about age, Runyon didn't seem uncomfortable at all.

"Madame, would you care to dance?" Sam Becker finally said to Patrice.

She swallowed the rest of her drink, then got up and danced with Becker. He thought it was lucky that his feet were light enough to whirl her around as well as he could, for it saved his client a sure fight in public.

"You're Spanish," Becker said to her.

"Sí."

"The best I ever could do was Mexico."

"My mother's aunt comes from Tampico," she said.

"Where is your mother from?" Becker said.

She was good and stewed, but that question made its way through the alcohol. Alarm showed in her eyes. Her answer was a pout. She is a Mex, Sam Becker said to himself. Even Becker didn't realize that by now they were living "Madame La Gimp" and, to make it perfect, did not realize it. Runyon had castles whirling in his mind when he had her on his arm. By now, Runyon was sure he had left a wife and two children for royalty, never for some Mexican. Her Spanish countess story, that she had been dancing at Texas Guinan's nightclub as a result of a dethroning, was fine with Becker. "So he lies on his age, she lies about who she is. It's a Mexican standoff," Becker decided.

Runyon never seemed to realize that, alone and with empty paper in front of him, he had written the truth of his life. If somebody had come into the El Morocco right now and told Runyon that his wife was really Madame La Gimp, he would have looked for a gun.

Sam Becker could handle that all right, living in illusion, because he was doing that pretty good himself. But he was beside himself over the terms of the sale of "Madame La Gimp," which were made before he represented Runyon. The great shrewd Broadway wise guy had been paid by the gentle, loving Frank Capra the sum of exactly $1,500. "This thing is a big hit," Becker said. "Why, under the terms, they can make the picture again and give you nothing." Which is exactly what would happen. But it was more important to Runyon to be able to act as if he had made millions on the story, a story whose central character was on his arm, even if he no longer could recognize that it never happened.

He and Patrice went home to their apartment in the Parc Vendome on West 57th Street. The elegant building ran right up to the Hearst sandcastle, which stood on the corner of West 57th and Eighth Avenue. Runyon now worked there in a second-floor office and had to walk only yards to get home, which was a ninth-floor apartment with a two-story-high ceiling and a fireplace burning through the evenings. The round foyer led into a large living room with parquet floors covered partially with Persian rugs in blues and shades of rust. Comfortable club chairs flanked the fireplace, and the polished Queen Anne wood chests on either side caught the light and added to the ambiance of this high-ceilinged room crowned with beautiful molding. The room had a sofa covered in aging brocade, and several other period chairs and tables. Two beautiful wood tables were covered with polished silver-framed photographs of all sizes and a large round skirted table displayed a collection of Battersea enamel boxes. The one hunting shotgun that he demanded be in the room for effect was burnished so highly that it seemed rich furniture rather than an outdoor utensil. He had made it with gangsters on the street and bleeding prizefighters, and now she had him living like a Spanish count. Which was only right, for she was a countess.

The next afternoon, he, Patrice and Bill Reuben were in the dining car of the Florida East Coast Champion, going to Miami. Bill Reuben was twenty-one, and the son of one of Runyon's best friends. Patrice liked to have Bill around because Damon was always ducking off to write something, or leaving her while he sat up in a press row, and then she wanted someone young escorting her. Damon was the only older man she would tolerate, and she seemed to be at her most relaxed with him at time of jewelry. She drank Cokes and studied Trenton. Damon had coffee and cigarettes and read the newspapers. Winchell's column in the *Daily Mirror* was headlined "Number 13 on the Jury," and listed fifteen of his "scoops" during the Lindbergh case. The newspaper word of the time, "scoop," meaning an exclusive story, came from the ancient fishing trade, which described the use of nets to "scoop up everything before the others arrive." Newspaper reporters cried, begged and lied for an exclusive, then dashed madly about, locking doors so others wouldn't get out in time to report for their editions. There were few thrilling moments in any life that could match that of the reporter walking into the office in the morning with a scoop in the paper and all eyes following him as he moved through the desks. But here was Runyon reading a Winchell column in which he first reprinted his "scoop" about Mrs. Schwarzkopf crying in pride at the trial.

Reading this on the train, Runyon remembered the day in court when Winchell jabbered to everybody, "They are going to try to psycho the guy. I have the scoop in my column. Watch them try to psycho this guy. Just remember where you heard it first, boys!" He screamed in joy one day when the *World-Telegram* newspaper came out with the same story. Its reporter had been told to get a psychiatrist who would say anything for a headline — "Cain Hated Other Brother Too!" The reporter called nobody and made his story up. He quoted "a leading psychiatrist." He wrote, "Hauptmann is not legally insane but he is a distinct mental case." When Winchell read the *World-Telegram* newspaper, he couldn't keep his eyes still, and when he saw "not legally insane" he saw it as "not legally sane." Therefore, he claimed that his great scoop was confirmed by the *World-Telegram*.

Runyon now read the rest of Winchell's "scoops," one as childish and wrong as the next.

"What an asshole," Runyon said aloud.

"Who?" Bill Reuben said.

"The same at the half," Runyon said.

"Winchell," Patrice said.

Runyon reached for another paper. The train went around a curve and headed into 30th Street Station in Philadelphia, rocking enough to cause the silverware to sound softly, most pleasantly, with the elegance of chimes.

They were in Florida when one night Patrice came into Runyon's room while he was writing and demanded to know how anybody could let Primo Carnera get into the ring with this young, murderous Louis. When Runyon asked her how she knew about the match, which had not as yet been announced, she stammered and said that somebody in New York had told her. There was no further discussion. Back in New York in the spring, on June 25, 1935, Carnera stepped into the ring, eyes wide and trusting, then Joe Louis entered. When trainer Jack Blackburn took the robe off, his body looked like an electric chair. He was the first black ever to step into a New York ring as the main-event fighter, which made a weeded lane for the most powerful social act in America since the Civil War. Twelve years later, Branch Rickey of the Brooklyn Dodgers brought Jackie Robinson into baseball. The ring announcer, Harry Balogh, took out a speech written by Runyon and he tapped the microphone and called out to the crowded Yankee Stadium: "Ladies and gentlemen. We are all of New York. This is the center of intelligence. I would remind you at this time that we in this city have no room for prejudism."

There was laughter. Balogh read it again: "We have no room for prejudism."

He had to wait for even more laughter to stop. Balogh held up the paper and shouted, "This says 'prejudice.' That's exactly how I read it." He tapped the microphone. "But it comes out of here prejudism."

Patrice sat with Bill Reuben at the fight. At the first bell, as she first watched Louis, so young and lean, hands moving with terrifying speed, she got up and walked down the aisle with her back to the ring. The men in seats on both sides of her screamed at a slaughter she could not look at. She walked out of the stadium and up the street to the Concourse Plaza Hotel and was drinking gin and Coke until she saw Eddie Walker of Broadway coming in with a party after the fight. She got a cab and went to the Parc Vendome apartment. If, when Runyon came home at dawn and sat with a cigarette before going to bed, any natural impulses of envy or revenge still remained inside him, no one else ever knew of them. Providing that these feelings, which he kept so suppressed, as he did with those from much of the rest of his life, even were able to reveal themselves more clearly than as the vague uneasiness that he usually carried around with him.

Discord was to come into the open soon enough.

Dick McCann, 400 East 56th Street, New York City.

I absolutely forbid apprising his father of Damon [Junior]'s latest escapades. You are well aware that the reports last fall were equally alarming and after completely distracting the entire family securing more than the necessary funds to supply the so called urgent hospitalization the result was merely more concentrated indulgence on Damon's part. You and Mary and Damon's wife must assume any responsibility as you are all far closer to him than his father or I. His father has been with him so infrequently they are strangers usually yelling. He has little influence and Damon has shown repeatedly his utter disregard in following his father's wishes. Any suggestions by his father have only received the most violent criticism and contempt. I refuse to subject him to any further disrespect. This is absolute. I will gladly meet any reasonable financial obligations if Damon is placed under controlled supervision provided that I know the fixed amounts in advance. Surely Mary's fondness for her dad must make her support me in this decision. — Patrice.

First there was Trenton State Prison, when Damon Runyon had to watch Hauptmann's electrocution. By now he couldn't take it anymore. He was not sixteen and in Pueblo with a whore. He despised it and wrote that the death penalty was "the darkest era of human intelligence." But he studied the use of electricity in an execution. They used for the first shock 2,400 volts and 3 amperes. "Kindly reflect that 400 volts will move a trolley car," he wrote in the midst of his article about Hauptmann's death.

Then Regret went down with much noise. He claimed that he was being paid $10,000 a week from Dutch Schultz to fix the number. Schultz's numbers racket was based on a three-digit number derived from racetrack pari-mutuel betting. People betting the numbers were given 500-to-1 odds on a million-to-one shot. When the New York tracks closed for the winter, Schultz's number was based on betting at the Coney Island Race Track in Cincinnati.

Regret would stand at the track with his eyes riveted on the mutuel board. He claimed that numbers arrived in waves: "They travel in packs

like geese, and all you got to do is spot the lead bird, the wedge number, and that's the one to deal with." As people are dopes, they believed him. "I am putting everything into one little ray from my eyes
so I can only see the wave of numbers that is coming," he said.

Then his body shook. "He is letting the numbers talk to him," people in the grandstand marveled.

"Numbers don't talk. I see them!" Regret shouted.

He spun like a fat top; and rushed to bet a "wedge number," which
knocked out every policy number except the one that would make
everybody in Harlem lose. The idea that one specific bet at a track
could change anything, while hundreds of others were betting simultaneously, was insane. On Broadway, where one hallucinated or died,
everybody believed that Regret fixed the number for Schultz.

As Toney Betts, who lived with Regret for a time, recalled, "He told
people he won the battle of Waterloo. He caught Napoleon counting
his platoons wrong. We're living two in a hotel single and dining on
cheese sandwiches from the Greek downstairs. He could do multiplication about as well as your cat."

The owner of the Coney Island Race Track, Big Bill Dwyer, had a
mutuels clerk change the number with a pencil late each day and charged
the Dutch Schultz organization $2,500 a day for doing so. Regret's duties consisted of making one late afternoon phone call to New York,
where bet slips had been winnowed down and the potentially dangerous slips set aside. Whatever seventh-race number was needed to turn
the slips into gigantic winners could not be allowed to come up. Out at
the Cincinnati track, the mutuels manager used a pencil to change one
seventh-race number to one that ensured virtually no winners in Harlem. For his duty, Regret was paid a few hundred dollars a week and
bragging rights. He told everybody he was a wealthy genius. Driving
back to the hotel, the Schultz crew listened to a Cincinnati radio station that replayed old sports events. They bet among themselves on
the outcome. The station one day had on a famous Yankee game, and
Regret, who said he knew every Yankee for twenty years by heart, was
wrong with every guess. "He don't even know Babe Ruth," one hoodlum reported.

Regret was a bank vault for Runyon. He appeared six times in the
Broadway stories. He also was sure to be featured in a seventh story.
He believed his own lie, that he was a feared bodyguard and Schultz
needed him in order to stay alive. It didn't matter whether Regret, or
Abba Dabba, whichever name he was using, was effective or not. Schultz

was a gangster and they always get murdered no matter who they have
with them.

One day, in his offices in the Raleigh Clothes on Seventh Avenue,
gangster Louis (Lepke) Buchalter wondered why this cheap bedbug
Schultz was making money with numbers in Harlem. "Why is he still
around?" he asked an assistant, Jacob (Gurrah) Shapiro. Who went out
on Seventh Avenue and spoke to a purported bookmaker named Albert Anastasia. At this time, Albert was causing Gravesend Bay in
Brooklyn to become practically unnavigable because of all the dead
bodies. He was the head of the wholesale manslaughter company named
by a newspaperman, Harry Feeney of the *New York Sun*, as Murder, Inc.

Albert said, "Have you got an okay from everybody? We got rules
now. You got to see Luciano."

Lepke immediately went to see Luciano. "I got a nigger friend uptown don't like the bastard, either," Luciano said. "Go ahead and do
what you want. Just let me know so I can tell this nigger Bumpy that
he got a wish come true."

At a candy store on the corner of Saratoga and Livonia avenues in
the Brownsville neighborhood of Brooklyn, a woman named Midnight
Rose was at the sliding glass front window, selling Hershey bars and
Brooklyn Eagle newspapers. A short swarthy man with a perfectly dis-
gusting face, Abe Reles, swaggered into the store and went to the back
room. The woman, Midnight Rose, rearranged her candy bars. "Someone dies," she said. She didn't mind a little violence; in fact, she used
to cover her face with her hands and then spread her fingers so she
could see the guns go off. She was not in favor of this systematic killing
being conducted from the back of her store, but what was she to do,
not permit people into the place as customers and instead starve to
death right here in the candy store?

In the back room, playing cards and smoking cigarettes, were Charley (the Bug) Workman, Allie (Tick Tock) Tannenbaum, Blue Jaw Ma-
goon, Mende Weiss, Pittsburgh Phil Strauss, Happy Maione and Frank
(Dasher) Abbandando. A man named Piggy, who drove cars, was allowed to watch.

"We are going to make Dutch Schultz go away," Reles announced.
"He raped Lepke's wife."

"Why that sonofabitch."

"Lep should of killed him."

"That's why we're going to hit him," Reles said.

At that time, Dutch Schultz, who sensed he was a target for both cops and gangsters, was mobbed up in a busted-down apartment and spending his nights in a place called the Palace Chop House in Newark. Regret was in Cincinnati. The track owner, Big Bill Dwyer, chartered a plane to New York and invited Regret, who immediately called Runyon. "If you look up in the air tonight, you will see me flying over Broadway," he said.

"Remember as much of it as you can," Runyan said. "I could use the column."

"I can remember everything with my memory," Regret said.

Even as he spoke, Regret froze at the thought of flying. When it was time to leave for the airport, he was at Union Station. He bought a coach ticket to New York and rode east. He was not in the coach as a disguise or for any other reason except that he didn't have money for a berth. All through the night across Ohio, Regret made up stories to tell Runyon about how he flew home in a plane.

When the train from Cincinnati pulled into Newark station late in the afternoon of October 23, 1935, Regret stared out at the Jersey town. Of course he was going straight to Broadway. He would be the king of Lindy's, telling Runyon about the plane ride. Imagine passing that up just to sit with Schultz in some filthy saloon here in Newark all night. Filthy saloon with all guys and guns. Regret listened to the station noises. The conductor called, "New York Pennsylvania Station is the next stop." Maybe a couple of dirty whores. The train started. The Dutchman and whores! Regret was out of his seat and teetering in the open door. He had one instant to make a decision. The train had moved so far down the platform that now his car was only yards away from the end of the platform. There was a high yellow brick wall where the platform ended. Either his leap was fast and true, and way out from the train, or he would go smack against the wall and splatter his head. Whores! Mouth open, eyes closed, he sent his fat body flying out from the train door. He landed on the platform truly like a busted valise. Some minutes later, Regret emerged from a cab at the Palace Chop House at 12 East Park Street. He heard girls giggling. With a loud hurrah, Regret burst in. Dutch Schultz roared a welcome.

In the testimony of Allie (Tick Tock) Tannenbaum, in Superior Court, State of New Jersey, County of Essex, City of Newark, it was sometime later that night that Charley (the Bug) Workman complained, as the car seemed to be lost, "You're sure this is Newark and not Jersey City?"

"It's Newark," Piggy the driver said.

"I like to be sure of everything I do," Workman said.

Some minutes later Workman and the others sauntered into the chop house and started shooting Regret while he was in the middle of a story. Two others with Regret, Abe (Misfit) Landau and Bernard (Lulu) Rosenkrantz, also were filled with bullets. The other Murder, Inc. guys ran out of the place giggling. Charley Workman did not leave. He looked at the dead bodies. "No Schultz." He looked at the men's room door. He walked up to it, pulling out a second gun. He kicked in the door. Schultz was in front of him, screaming in terror. He shut up when Charley (the Bug) Workman began putting bullets into him.

When police went through Regret's pockets, they found he had $87.22 on him. It was said to be an honest count, for the officers were ashamed of stealing off the top of an amount that small.

Rather than a report on Regret's first plane trip, Runyon wrote, "Those of you who saw the movie, 'Little Miss Marker,' might remember a rotund jolly character who was named Regret." Runyon said Regret, or Abba Dabba, listed in the stories as a Schultz bodyguard, "could not be a bodyguard for a five-year-old."

The thing that killed more gangsters than a .38 was what was called their "eagles." "That Joe A., he got a real big eagle," they said of Joe Adonis on his streets, Third and Fourth avenues in Brooklyn. There, Joe A. walked with his head fixed straight ahead, chin high, never bothering to look one way or the other, for he knew that wherever he went, people looked at him.

His dream was to receive the same adulation over on the Big Street, Broadway. He had stepped out pretty good in the late nights at the Six-Day Bike Race, standing up and allowing an entire arena to see him, right up there, just like God, offering prizes. He could not wait, however, to get the same reaction from people during more normal hours in a more normal setting. He wanted to be a celebrity. In Adonis's case, this was like placing a baby in the vicinity of diphtheria.

He owned a neighborhood saloon at 260 Fourth Avenue in Brooklyn, which he used as a living room/headquarters for his business, which began with extortion and drugs and went through murder. The man was a gangster. What was he supposed to be doing, title searches? One night he looked at his neighborhood saloon and announced, "I'm too freaking big for this joint." He closed the place and opened a fine Italian restaurant on Pineapple Street in Brooklyn Heights, which is old and regal and at that time was Protestant in population and taste. In such a setting, Joe A. decided that he not only looked beautiful but, to go with it, he also knew absolutely everything.

And so he sat in his fine restaurant, dressed beautifully, his brain electric with great thoughts, and one evening in the spring of 1937, in walked William Randolph Hearst's old doctor, the city's former health commissioner and now U.S. senator, Royal Copeland. "Because you are such an important man, I am going to see to it that you live to be ninety-five," Copeland said.

Adonis sat bolt upright in ecstasy. He was one of the famous insiders who were going to be kept alive almost forever by Copeland.

Copeland's eyes now popped out and he began to rave. "I am going to rip the New Deal out by its roots," Copeland said, "Then I will go on to become President and change the nation with my first breath. I am going to begin by campaigning against the New Deal all over the city. You're not for giving people something for nothing, are you?"

"You bet I'm not," Adonis said.

"Fine. Then I want you with me. I am going to run for mayor."

"Against La Guardia?" Adonis said.

"I am going to run in both the Democratic and Republican primaries. I will win both primaries and be the mayor by acclamation. Then I will make plans to become President. You can ensure this by getting me Italian votes. Do you think you're more popular than La Guardia?"

Adonis's eyes glazed.

"Sure you are," Copeland said. "I can tell that by the way your own people look at you."

"I know Frank Costello hates La Guardia," Adonis said. "You can't blame Frank for hating him. He calls Frank a tinhorn gambler and tries to chase him out of town. But the man left me alone, I have to say that."

Copeland brushed this aside. "But you are more popular with Italians than La Guardia. You can cut down his Italian vote in this district and help me carry the day."

"Where does that leave me?" Adonis said.

"With the severe problem of friendship. For you are going to have to appoint at least two city commissioners by yourself, and that will mean making many people furious at you when you don't choose them."

When Copeland left, Adonis took a walk to Third Avenue. He looked over the Brooklyn dock workers and his finger beckoned to a man named Scarlato, who worked as a hiring boss at the Bush Terminal piers.

"Come here, commissioner, I want to see you."

Adonis thought it was a most effortless and delightful duty, picking his first commissioner, and he could not wait to pick his second commissioner.

Adonis then took his thrilling political news to Broadway, where he told Harry (Champ) Segal, "I am going to do the world a favor. I am going to get rid of the little bum La Guardia because he called Frank a cheap tinhorn."

"I think even Costello makes La Guardia a ten-to-one favorite over anybody," Segal said.

"You're crazy," Adonis said. "Copeland is going to be the next mayor."

"Who?" Segal said.

When Adonis explained to Segal who Copeland was, the Champ said, "I change the price. I make La Guardia an even twenty-two-thousand-to-one over this fucking quack of yours."

Adonis went into Lindy's and had a sandwich with Runyon, who had no interest in even the names of candidates since Jimmy Walker was chased out of town. He made a call to Dan McKetrick, who had worked for Tammany and understood the basics of the sport. McKetrick came down to counsel Adonis.

"You're asking Italians in South Brooklyn to vote for a man named Copeland over one of their native Italians?" McKetrick said softly.

"I don't ask, I tell them to," Adonis said.

"You won't get the lady next door," McKetrick said.

"You don't know how good a name I got with people," Adonis said.

McKetrick, unable to grapple with open insanity, fell silent. Runyon now tried. "Does Copeland want to help you get some dope you can sell?"

"No, the man don't even bring that up."

"Then he's of no use to you. Stay away from him. We're always safer with our own kind," Runyon said.

"Not me," Joe Adonis said. "I'm swank enough to have my own mayor."

"La Guardia didn't bother you the last couple of years," Runyon said.

"That's because of all the money I give him last time," Adonis said.

"Why don't you give him some more this time and let it go at that?" Runyon said.

"Because this time I am going the other way. I giveth and I taketh," Adonis said.

Adonis went home to Brooklyn, where he loudly announced that he was for Copeland against La Guardia. He put up large amounts of cash for Copeland's campaign. He began to read seven and eight papers a day to keep up with the political news, including the *New York Times* newspaper, which in those days cost two cents daily and a dime on Sunday. The political writers Adonis read were James Hagerty, who seemed very good, and Warren Moscow, who was another one of these people with a mind clerical in nature and who wrote long articles day after day and they all amounted to nothing.

One day Adonis told Runyon, "Hagerty is my favorite writer in this city."

Runyon stared at Joe A. with eyes that were colder than anything Joe had seen, even at a murder scene.

Joe A.'s adventure in politics made enemies in addition to Runyon.

At a little after 9 P.M. on primary night, September 14, a Tuesday, an election worker named Aunt Rosie Mondello emerged from a polling place in a barber shop on Fourth Avenue. The voting machines had just been opened and the tally taken. She was walking along with a slip that showed the vote totals. When she saw Joe Adonis and his man, the proposed commissioner, Scarlato, she called out, "Joey, you know what you ought to do?"

"What?"

"Put some money in your pocket and go over and tell one of La Guardia's people how much you like them."

That November, after he won the general election by a ton of votes, La Guardia told a jubilant election night crowd, "I am going to get this man Joe Adonis. He is a gangster, and the leader of the underworld."

As police, too, are aware of all major speeches, detectives soon rushed into the restaurant on Pineapple Street and arrested Adonis for hijacking. The complainant admitted he had never seen Adonis in his life. It didn't matter. Three automobile agencies owned by Adonis had their city licenses revoked. The restaurant was a goner. Next, he learned that he had to pay double to keep a crap game going.

That winter, the Brooklyn Democratic organization had its annual dinner at the Hotel St. George in downtown Brooklyn. On page 53 of the program there was a large silver page, usually bought only by big contributors. On the page was, in script, "Compliments of a Very Good Friend."

Everybody at the dinner who read the ad knew that it meant Joe A. was back in politics and that they should call him because he had a lot of money. And Joe A. sat by the phone and hoped that some big politicians would call him because he loved the game almost as much as he loved people getting shot. Sure enough, the politicians called him and he put up money and this time he got himself chased out of New York and into New Jersey, and then he wound up in federal crime hearings. Yet he loved politics all the way to the gangplank he walked up on the day they deported him to Italy.

In 1938, the Washington Senators moved their training camp from Biloxi, Mississippi, to Orlando, Florida. Dick McCann went to the camp to write stories for his paper. He brought Mary down with him, and Katherine Grau took care of Richard, their four-year-old son, for a month. When Mary came back, she made Kathy take a sheared beaver coat. "She had four fur coats," Katherine Grau recalled. "That's the only possessions she had. I didn't want it, except I was nice and thin and could wear it." Dick McCann got a job at the *Daily News* in New York, and he and Mary and the baby moved into the Alamac Hotel on West 71st Street and Broadway. The *News* building was on East 42nd Street. Mary, raised on "morning paper" hours, now simply went out into the night air and lived them herself while Dick sat in the *News* sports department, putting baseball scores into the second and third editions. Many nights, she was right around the corner with her old friend from the convent school, Rose Bernabei, in the Pen and Pencil or Danny's Hideaway, both on East 45th Street. "The only thing anybody ever asked me was, 'Rye or Scotch?' " Rose Bernabei remembered. "I told them I handle Scotch better."

In 1939, Shirley Povich came to New York with his wife for a few days around Christmastime. When they came to the Alamac they found Dick McCann out of his job at the *New York Daily News* and trying to write a book. Povich remembers coming into the hotel with his wife and Mary McCann was in a room, just a hotel room, with her son Richard. Povich looked around and didn't see a toy in the place. Mary called room service and Povich listened as she began to stammer and make excuses over the phone but still plainly was being rebuffed. "Then I knew what was going on."

While his daughter sat with his grandson in a hotel room without the bills being paid, Damon Runyon needed a valet to help dress him and keep track of his clothes. A chauffeur drove him, and he walked the street with bodyguards in order to keep the crowds away. "Runyon used to blame his life on his father," Shirley Povich said. "I think he was a louse on his own."

Two months later, the Poviches went to the Washington Senators'

training camp, and Mrs. Povich sent Mary McCann the fare for her
and her son to come down to the camp. "It was the first time the boy
ever saw grass," Shirley Povich remembered. Some years after that,
he recalled, he and his wife went to the old Toots Shor's on West 51st
Street, and the head waiter came over and said that Mr. Runyon wanted
to talk to him. "All these years I'd been around, Damon was the big
shot. Never a nod from him, not that I wanted one. On this particular
night I was going to the Yiddish Theater with my wife. I noticed that
for once he was not surrounded with these parasites. Anyway, I stopped
off and sat with him. He had no voice by now because of the cancer
and he wrote these notes to you. You wrote notes to him yourself instead of realizing that he could hear. So he wrote me a note saying,
'How is YOUR friend McCann?' "

The play Runyon wrote with Howard Lindsay, A *Slight Case of
Murder*, had made it onto Broadway and had come out as a big movie,
with Edward G. Robinson as the star. In New York, the *Times* called it
"the funniest show of the year." After which, Robinson could play with
complete confidence and all angry splendor any murderer he chose.

At the first chill wind along Broadway, he and another writer, Irving
Caesar, were at Hibiscus Island, writing lines for a script that began in
the Yale Bowl and wandered onto a racetrack and for a time featured the
Lindy's busboy as a singing busboy, but he was dropped. Runyon kept
the pages about the busboy. He and Caesar also decided that the script
weighed about a thousand pounds less than a play, after which they
turned it into a movie script. They titled it *Straight, Place and Show*, and
Runyon's agent, Paul Small, sent it to Darryl Zanuck at movie company Twentieth Century–Fox. Zanuck wired Runyon and asked him
to come out to the Coast to consult on changes and the filming itself.

"What's he say about me?" Irving Caesar said.

"He says hello," Runyon said.

"The hell with him."

"He also says we get $25,000."

"Tell him hello for me."

Runyon and Patrice moved into a cottage on the Twentieth Century
grounds. It was bare and had two bedrooms. It was all right in the
daytime, when movie casts walked by on the way to lunch, but you
could get insane in the emptiness at night. "The script is fantastic,"
Zanuck said. Harry Ritz said, "This is the best I ever read you!" He is
one of the three Ritz Brothers, who are to star in the movie. When
Straight, Place and Show comes out, there is not one line of Runyon's

or Caesar's in it. There is music, which is done by Ben Pollack, with Jule Styne coming in later. Runyon watches the film alone in a screening room and keeps grunting to himself, "Get the money. Just get the money." Back in New York, Irving Caesar is wildly angry. Runyon sends Caesar a wire from California telling him to count the money.

From *Variety:* " 'Straight, Place and Show,' the Ritz Brothers second starrer for 20th-Fox, emerges as a laugh hit that promotes the b.o. status of the three funnymakers."

Runyon moves into a house on the flats in Beverly Hills, along with a cat named Sheba and a dog named Nubbin. He keeps the shades drawn all day, rises late and sits facing a blank wall, where he talks to himself as he writes short stories about Broadway, one of which, about the Lindy's busboy, "Little Pinks," is taking him a lot of time. He says he writes them in a week, but this one has been around for a couple of years.

While contributing dialogue and consulting on scripts and the acting itself, Runyon has worked with many Hollywood people: Gregory Ratoff, Edward G. Robinson, Ethel Merman. Yet when he goes out, he pretends he is on Broadway and wears a shirt, tie and topcoat. At home, every time he opens the door, those who step in act as if they were just coming out of the subway.

"What is he doing?" Patrice said. A workman was rearranging the living room.

"He is putting up a screen," Runyon said.

"For what?"

"Ben Siegel says he wants me to watch an actor. He says I can use him in something."

Ben Siegel was a gangster with a brain that rocked like a boat, which is why he liked to ride around on them, as we will see. He was called Bugsy because people thought he was insane. Ben Siegel said he wasn't crazy at all, and that people should please refer to him only as "Ben" as he certainly was not insane. When somebody called him "Bugsy," his eyes popped out of his head and he tried to bite the man to death like a cannibal in broad daylight. He went to Hollywood as the gangster syndicate's big shot on the West Coast and became the founder of Las Vegas, until the guys in New York discovered that the founder was stealing, and that was the end of that game, but that is a long time ahead of this. Here, we are still in his Hollywood gangster period.

At eight o'clock, up the walk comes Siegel with a young woman whose very swing suggests that she desires that people should start a firefight.

Harry (Champ) Segal carries a can of film. Bodyguard Frankie Carbo's head was snapping around like a dog seeing rabbits. He never was in favor of ambushes by the other side.

Ben Siegel stood nervously as the projectionist got the film ready.

"You're going to discover a genuine star," Champ Segal said.

"If you two fellas are managing him, he winds up with five percent of his earnings," Runyon said.

When neither Siegel nor Segal reacted to the charge of their being crooked theatrical managers, Runyon was puzzled.

The woman and Frankie Carbo took seats in the corner. The woman seemed bored.

"I have to ask you to give me a word," Siegel said. "I don't want anybody in the world to know about this. I have to make up my own mind on what to do. I just thought that as a friend you could do me a turn and look this over."

The lights went out and the film zizzed in the background. Now on the screen came the striped clapboard title:

TEST: BEN SIEGEL
DIR: GEORGE RAFT

At least we don't use amateurs," the young woman noted.

"Shut up!" Siegel said.

On the screen, Siegel appeared. He wore a rich, subdued jacket, with breast kerchief and shirt and tie. The hair was black oil. He smoked a cigarette grandly. Even the smoke seemed to be cardboard.

"I told you I hate it when you smoke," the young woman said.

"What are you talking about?" the Champ said. "Who could breed smoke through the nose like that?"

"I said shut up! I can't see when you talk," Siegel said.

"I'm boostin' you!" the Champ said.

"Don't bother," the young woman said.

The side of Bugsy's neck pulsated.

On the screen, Siegel walked across a room and seemed to be thinking. He began to expound about problems of keeping up with the stockmarket. "Whenever I'm near a phone," he said, walking straight past a phone on a table, "I don't know whether to call up one of my girlfriends or one of my bankers. Let me tell you" — he almost said "yez" — "my banker is more understanding." He reached out for the phone, which was many paces behind him.

He attempted to smile. Then a voice called, "End test!"

"I hated it," the young woman said when Damon put on the lights.

"Why don't she shut up, Ben?" Champ Segal said. "I'll tell you how good you are in this here thing. Do you want to know how good you are?"

"Yes," Siegel said.

"Ben, you'll never have to steal again."

Runyon smoked in silence.

"Whaddya think?" Siegel asked him.

"Don't you shoot anybody?" Runyon said.

"I'm not there for mob guys. I'm for the broads! How do you think they'll like me?"

"I don't," the young woman said.

"I'm going to slap this broad," Siegel muttered. Runyon held up a hand to keep him seated.

"I should think you'd try to get the men first," Runyon said.

"Nah, that's if I want to play a wise guy. Forget about it."

"Oh, you don't want to play a tough guy?"

"No."

"Then what do you want to be?"

"A lead!"

"Then I can't do you any good at all."

"There's nowhere you could fit me in?"

"All they want me to write for them is about cold killers. Guys who kill the doll and don't even notice it on account of they got more important things to do."

"I can't be killin' nobody in a movie." Siegel said.

"Well," Runyon said.

"So there's no way you could fit me in."

"Fella, in the movies they pay me for, nearly all men must be carrying a John Henry or at least appear to be so."

"That's all you could do?"

"Ben, I never bite the hand that feeds me."

"I know. You're right. You'll do me one thing."

"Of course."

"Don't tell Georgie Raft I showed you this."

"Fear not," Runyon said. "I'll say one thing for your man, the Champ. He is loyal."

"Oh, I couldn't of got this far without him," Siegel said.

"I don't know about your princess. Maybe she thinks she is telling the truth."

"She gets a slap," Bugsy said.

The young woman was at the door. "Are we goin' or what?" she said.

As they left, Runyon thought for a moment about the size of the score that the Champ was taking from Siegel. He then concentrated on the young woman and the gangster. Great characters in a confrontation. She goes out with the busboy, he thought. A couple of days later, he met George Raft in the Brown Derby, and Raft told him about a home movie he had made with the Champ and Bugsy Siegel for Siegel's wife.

Soon, Bugsy Siegel was around again, this time because on one of Benny's boat rides, Harry (Champ) Segal was charged with mutiny on the high seas. Siegel took the Champ and a crew of twenty-six on a purported treasure-hunting trip through Central America on a chartered ship called the *Metha Nelson*.

Looking over the side, Champ Segal declared, "The water is festered with sharks."

He and Ben Siegel fired rifles at the sharks. Then they hung over the side and shot .45s. Ben Siegel, a homicidal maniac on normal days, completely lost control. He threw harpoons into wounded sharks, then announced, "I want to kill somebody who is alive."

This is why people called him Bugsy behind his back. And it also is why he somehow was carted off the ship at Guatemala. The Champ remained aboard. He was supposed to keep order on the trip home. Somewhere in the middle of the Pacific, he put a pistol in the ear of the ship's captain, a German named Hoffman. One crew member lost an eye and another was bound in chains and put in the hold. The radio man sent out an SOS.

The newspaper headline read: "WILD REVOLT ON 'HELL SHIP.'"

Listening to Ben Siegel, Runyon decided that the bookmaker character Case Ables in "Little Pinks" should resemble Siegel in words and actions, rather than Runyon's old friend Owney Madden, who was in the very front of Runyon's mind as he wrote the short story. What else was he supposed to do, sympathize and socialize with these ignorant gorillas and then not use them? What were they for? They were for exactly what he used them for, whenever he needed to use them.

Besides, shortly after this, Champ Segal was indicted for a murder. For some reason, this time Runyon had Bugsy drive him to the Western Union office in Beverly Hills, where he sent a telegram to Walter Winchell at the Majestic apartments, 115 Central Park West in New York City. He suggested that Winchell tell his dear friend J. Edgar Hoover that the Champ should not be in trouble, particularly if Hoo-

ver wanted to see the light comedy that Runyon planned to make out
of the ridiculous escapade.

In New York, Winchell was so overjoyed at receiving a wire from
Runyon that he was on Broadway assuring everybody, "The captain of
the ship called Champ a Jew. The captain is a Nazi. I'm going to have
Hoover rake this rat over the coals."

In Los Angeles, an FBI agent named Hansen, in questioning the
Champ, asked him more about horses and prizefighters than about
mutiny. Even when some rat prosecutor brought up the filthiest of
words, smuggling, the agent did not become angry with the Champ,
who was released.

There was a large welcome-home party at the Brown Derby hosted
by George Raft. Ben Siegel and the countess were there, as were
hoodlums. Patrice was irritable. She thought she would be in Hollywood glamour and instead this was just another table at Lindy's.

Next was a social evening with William O'Dwyer, the district attorney of Brooklyn, who came into town with his personal charm and smile
and the warmth of an old friendship, and even his slight business partnership in Mrs. Hearst's marvelous Free Milk Fund for Babies. Unfor-
tunately and despite this, he was in town on pure business. He had
with him, guarded and hidden somewhere, Allie (Tick Tock) Tannenbaum and Abe Reles from Saratoga Avenue in Brooklyn. They were to
testify on behalf of the state of California in a murder case against Bugsy
Siegel, and O'Dwyer insisted on calling him that, and also Frankie Carbo
and, "sad to say, your friend, the Champ."

"What can I say?" Runyon said.

"The next time you see the Champ, you can tell him to stop murdering people," O'Dwyer said.

"You can tell him that pretty good," Runyon said.

Finally, with enough gangsters all around him to give inspiration,
Runyon finished "Little Pinks" and was delighted by the reaction from
Collier's Magazine, and in particular the check for $5,000, because he
still needed money every minute. The story of 6,200 words was to go
far beyond one issue of a magazine and into an art form that at this time
he practically owned, the American gangster movie.

Advance copies of *Collier's Magazine* of January 27 reached the
mailroom of RKO Pictures, 780 North Gower Street, on January 18.
One copy went to William Koenig of the story department. He read it
a couple of times and then wrote a report for distribution around the
department:

Read by William Koenig
January 19, 1940

COLLIER'S — January 27 issue.

Short stories:
A MINK COAT EACH MORNING — Daniel Fuchs
LITTLE PINKS — Damon Runyon (Coverage)

One night in a New York nightclub, a big bookmaker named Case Ables gets mad at a red-headed chorus girl named Judy who is called Your Highness, slaps her and knocks her down a flight of stairs. Your Highness, who is on the make for a wealthy husband, is generally disliked because of her sharp tongue and high and mighty manner, but she has one champion in a little bus boy named Little Pinks, who gets beaten up himself for his gallantry. He also loses his job. It develops that Your Highness' spine is injured and she will never be able to walk again. Case Ables is too powerful to be blamed.

In the middle of a cold winter, Little Pinks is taking care of Your Highness in a basement where Little Pinks has secured a wheel chair for her. She is still high and mighty and has a cane with which she raps Little Pinks whenever he displeases her — which is often. Little Pinks is in love with her, but don't expect her to fall in love with a guy like him. He wants to take Your Highness to Florida, and he actually does start to push her there in a wheel chair. They get lifts however and reach Miami in about two weeks. . . .

A Runyon story. Always interesting, but a little too thin for the screen. This story is so touching, however, that development might be worth while. . . .

From March until October of 1941, three people wrote treatments, which are detailed stories that can be used as the basis for writing a script. None of the treatments was acceptable, but by now the idea of the story had become part of the studio hallways, and Leonard Spiegelgass, who had worked on Runyon movies before, was brought in. He did a treatment by the middle of October and was told to try a screenplay, and this was ready by November 13. In doing things this rapidly, Spiegelgass revealed for all to see that he was a man without a relative in a movie studio, and had to write for rent money.

The script ended with Runyon's Broadway philosophy:

TWO SHOT — Professor and Horsethief. Their eyes are quite wet.

HORSETHIEF
I would like to say as follows: this is pretty silly.

PROFESSOR B.
No. Pinks found what everybody else in the world is looking for.

HORSETHIEF
And lost it.

PROFESSOR B.
It is well known to one and all on Broadway that a citizen never loses
what he's got filed away in his ticker.

FADE OUT

RKO RADIO PICTURES, INC.
December 1, 1941

TO: All departments
Picture No. 367 (1865) has been assigned to the following:

"LITTLE PINKS" — Irving Reis, Director
              Damon Runyon, Producer

ACCOUNTING DEPARTMENT
BY G. B. HOWE

At this point in the progress of the movie, there was an interruption
in the usual life of the nation in that a war began. Sitting at home on
Sunday night, listening to news of Pearl Harbor on the radio, Runyon,
sixty-one, did not regard himself as being ready to compete. And on
Monday morning the cry came down the hallways of RKO Pictures:
"They'll need movies for the soldiers!"

For his newspaper columns he came within a paragraph of being the
only American to write of Japanese Americans as people being wronged:

> A slim young Japanese in the uniform of a private of the United
> States Army was helping his father and mother load a truck with
> household goods on San Pedro Street in Los Angeles' "Little Tokio"
> the other afternoon. The soldier was an American born youth, drawn
> into the army in the draft, the parents aliens under evacuation or-
> ders. . . .
>
> In the windows of all the Japanese stores were big signs reading
> "closing sales" and inside, crowds of Americans, Mexicans and Fili-
> pinos were taking advantage of the bargains. Little Japanese children
> played on the sidewalks of the sunny streets, one small boy on a tri-
> cycle towing another boy and two tiny girls around on a sort of bob-
> sled arrangement with iron wheels, 'mid much shrill laughter.

In several columns he pictured the Japanese as human beings. But
each time, right in the last paragraph, he went to the flag. "That there

are some rather pathetic aspects of the evacuation cannot be denied. In the liquidation of their businesses, the Japanese are lucky to get fifteen cents on the dollar. Yet in considering them the thought occurs that in Japan, evacuated Americans would probably not be permitted to liquidate."

Too bad that he didn't just complete the emotion and let millions scream, because you only get one shot at a thing like this, standing all alone and being absolutely right and everybody else wrong. The game usually runs out before you see another such chance. And here it was on the same page as his column in the New York paper, a two-column ad running down the page showing a bellhop bawling, "Call for Phillip Morris."

ALL SMOKERS INHALE — BUT
It needn't bother YOUR Throat!
CALL FOR PHILLIP MORRIS
America's FINEST Cigarette

By now, his throat was always raw and he swallowed all throat lozenges in a drugstore. He kept holding out his coffee cup when half empty so it always would be so hot as to be scalding. Each swallow was made in the hope that this mouthful of liquid heat finally was going to soothe the throat.

If he came up too old, at age sixty, in time of war, Patrice, thirty-three, did not. She heard marching songs and millions marching. "I want to shoot down Japanese planes," she announced. She got up one morning and went to the Los Angeles airport and looked up a flying school. She returned that night holding "Pilot Log Book Number IA." Date (Dec. 9, 1941) Aircraft Flown. (Make) Stinson. (Engine) Lycoming. Duration of flight. 30. She came home in a high degree of excitement, and when Runyon, preoccupied with his throat and his movie, didn't seem to be concentrating on what she was saying, she turned in the middle of a sentence and went into the bedroom, got out a bottle he didn't know she had, hid in the bathroom and had enough drinks to send her into a stupor.

The way to count money earned in 1940, many people with money insist, is to multiply it by ten. But these are people who live in dreariness, in banking and building, and know nothing of the real world, which is living in a dream, and the cost of that, of living in illusion, has increased more. "Little Pinks" was retitled *The Big Street,* and had a budget of $500,000. A movie made a half century after *The Big Street* uses the entire *Big Street* budget to pay for lodging, cars and drivers for the director and the stars. There are movie productions today of $25 and $30 million. Henry Fonda, who got $60,000 for starring in *The Big Street*, would have cost about twenty-five times higher today, cheap at $1.5 million for the role. The greatest change seems to be in the job of director. On *The Big Street*, Irving Reis was paid $9,320, less than the screenwriter, who received $11,419.80, and much less than Runyon received for the original story, $15,000. Directors today would tear up any paycheck that is under $1 million, and their names appear so prominently, almost as a religious symbol, as if they were stars. Whether this ton of money shaken into an incinerator every day, and all this direction by one person, puts out movies twenty-five times better might be a question.

An item Runyon saw in *The Big Street* budget, $25 for a dog to work with Lucille Ball, prompted him to take his own dog, Nubbin, to the veterinarian. While he was waiting, Runyon asked the veterinarian, Eugene Jones, if he had any cough drops; his throat was bothering him and his voice was hoarse. Everybody else had been noticing the voice, but this was the first time Runyon admitted something was wrong. The veterinarian had no cough drops, but suggested that as long as he was looking at the dog, he would take a look in Runyon's throat. Runyon loved the idea. "I bet all my money on animals, I might as well bet my life on a vet," he said. When Runyon opened his mouth, the veterinarian put a light down it. The veterinarian's eyes widened. He snapped off the light and told Runyon he better see a throat specialist. "I can't wait," Runyon muttered.

April 13 1942
FINAL SCRIPT   By Leonard Spiegelgass
   READ BY Lillian R. Bergquist for Feature Sales Dept.

THEME: A SELFISH, BEAUTIFUL BROADWAY ENTERTAINER IS PARALYZED FROM A BLOW RECEIVED FROM HER RACKETEER LOVER. A BUS BOY IS HOPELESSLY IN LOVE WITH HER, MAKES ENDLESS SACRIFICES FOR HER, AND PUSHES HER IN A WHEEL-CHAIR TO MIAMI WHERE SHE HOPES TO RECAPTURE A MIL-LIONAIRE ADMIRER. IN A DOUBLE-EDGED PLOT TO AVENGE HER ON THE RACKETEER, THE BUS BOY MAKES THE FORMER THROW A PARTY FOR HER. IT IS HERE THAT THE BOY'S LOVE FINALLY WINS THE GIRL, AND SHE WALKS A FEW STEPS ONLY TO DIE IN HIS ARMS. EVEN THOUGH HE FINALLY HAD TO LOSE IT, LITTLE PINKS DID FIND LOVE . . .

SCRIPT

FADE IN

EXT. BROADWAY — NIGHT

FULL SHOT

ANGLE TOWARD WINTER GARDEN AND LINDY'S. (MADE)

SHOT HOLDS for about fifteen feet then forms b.g. for a montage of Broadway in the 50's. (Made) When the montage reaches its peak, slowly the full inside feature page of a newspaper slips into view from bottom of screen. It progresses upward until it fills the screen completely, then CAMERA ZOOMS CLOSE on a column heading which reads:

DAMON RUNYON'S

THE BIG STREET

Simultaneously the montage clears and the music segues into picture's theme song.

CAMERA HOLDS for standard length of footage on column head, then WHIPS OVER to another column which has two typical newspaper photographs, and reads:

STARRING

HENRY FONDA

and

LUCILLE BALL

Runyon got $5,000 for the original story in *Collier's*, the $15,000 story fee from the production budget and a $40,000 fee as producer. He earned $60,000, millionaire's money today.

Runyon's pre-production work consisted of doing things he found delightful, such as easing the plight of William Orr, an actor who wanted to appear as tall as Henry Fonda. The studio had one pair of street shoes and one pair of dress shoes made that gave Orr three additional inches in height. "The man wants stilts," Runyon said. The shoes cost $30 each, and with tax of $1.80, the bill came to $31.80.

Eugene Pallette came down from Oregon to play his part and was without an overcoat. Runyon loved the maneuver, and refused to believe that Pallette was telling the truth when he said that he had lost the coat en route. His new coat cost $25.75. When somebody in the office said Pallette should pay for it, Runyon became angered. "He has found a way to get an overcoat without risking his limbs stealing one out of an Automat."

Harold Hendee of the New York office of RKO was sent to City Hall, where he was told that Grover Whalen, an assistant to the mayor, would help arrange for the movie crew to film at the Holland Tunnel entrance. Whalen always could arrange such things. Once, Whalen walked a lieutenant of police named Enright into the office of Commissioner Frederick Bugher. "Yes, lieutenant?" Bugher said.

Whalen thundered, "Wrong." He pointed to Enright. "He is the commissioner."

Bugher clicked his heels and left the office. The phone rang and Enright picked it up. "Lieutenant Enright speaking."

"You moron, you are the commissioner," Whalen shouted.

Now working with his third straight mayor, Fiorello La Guardia, Whalen rushed in and told his boss about the movie for the Holland Tunnel. All Whalen could see was a ton of great dinner parties with the stars of the movie. All La Guardia could see was the first filmed political commercial ever made, that of Jimmy Walker using Runyon's words while assuring movie audiences that La Guardia was a man who belonged in the cartoons that were to follow this commercial.

"I'll die before Damon Runyon gets anything in this city," La Guardia said.

"You're saying no?" Whalen asked.

"I'm saying never," La Guardia said.

When Whalen came out and informed Hendee of this, the old movie guy stood up and thanked him sincerely. "I heard a funny thing this morning," Hendee said. "Somebody from out on the Coast told me that Runyon went out and got his shoes shined and he found a dwarf with a lisp and he is going to put him in the movie as the mayor of New York."

WESTERN UNION
VERNON L. WALKER, RKO STUDIO

HAVE CONTACTED AUTHORITIES AND DO NOT THINK WE WILL HAVE ANY TROUBLE REGARDING PERMISSION TO SHOOT HOLLAND TUNNEL AS REQUESTED. ONLY STIPULATION THEY MADE WAS THAT WE MAKE ARRANGEMENTS WITH THEM FROM TWENTY FOUR TO FORTY EIGHT HOURS BEFORE TIME OF SHOOTING.
                                              HAROLD HENDEE

NINETEEN

April 15, 1942
WAR DEPARTMENT
ARMY AIR FORCES
Notification of Personnel Action. Mrs. Damon Runyon.
565th AAF Base Unit (3rd OTU)
Ferrying Division — ATC
Reno Army Air Base
Reno, Nevada.
Nature of action: Assignment.

She was consumed with storing her dresses and putting her jewelry in the bank strongbox, which of course she had rented on her first day in Hollywood because of the Amati diamond. She had one farewell party thrown by Darryl Zanuck. She had the bartender working the party in Zanuck's home lined up from the first Coke. He discreetly splashed enough gin in each drink to cause a tiger to stumble. She dimly heard the toasts in her honor, and Runyon said proudly that she had the quiet strength of a Rickenbacker. "She'll blow them all out of the sky if she gets the chance," he rasped. "Royalty always has it in the blood to fight wars with a little class."

They were great speeches, although the farthest he thought she was going was to Reno, which could be reached by motorcar. On the morning she left, he was up early, gave her a kiss and left for the studio. "I'll

see you in about a week," he said, and off she went to the world of the
young.

The first day's filming for *The Big Street* started at 11:15 A.M. on
April 22, 1942. Sometime during the day, there was a scene in which
Lucille Ball, clutching a dog, worked her way through a crowd in Lindy's. The day ended at 7:30 P.M.. The film was developed and the next
day after lunch it was shown in a small screening room. Right away, it
was clear that Spiegelgass, who came out of Brooklyn and had done a
couple of Runyon films before, knew exactly where to go to make sure
audiences laughed at the big-city characters.

GENTLEMAN
Personally, I find I now can make a very honest living by cheating
at cards.

It made everybody in the screening room laugh, even Runyon, who
had used the line a few hundred times in various forms. Now onto the
screen came Lucille Ball as Gloria — Your Highness — with the dog.

At first she was elegant:

Kindly clear the way.

Nobody seemed to hear. Her elegant bearing suddenly became hard:

Do you let me go through or do I start slugging?

She shows the right hand in the first five seconds, Runyon remembered. Remembered it always. In front of him on this screen was Lucille Ball, so young and beautiful, and with so much young talent that
you almost cried. Almost? Why, that was exactly what Runyon was doing,
crying. He dropped his head and had a fit of coughing so nobody in the
room would notice. Right away, he thought of Louisville. The place is
packed with people with cheeks wet as they watched Earl Sande ride
Gallant Fox through the stretch at Churchill Downs. That's just what
she is, he thought, a thoroughbred knocking them dead for all the
money.

When the lights went on, he was the first to speak. "I think that
when somebody looks her in the eye, she gives you the answer."

Everybody was elated. Good tough New York cynic. They went back
to the set with hopes that came true. When it was finished, Runyon
saw *The Big Street* about a hundred times in the projection room. He
sat alone and the projectionist could hear him cry. The life he thought

he saw and thought he lived on Broadway was there in front of him.
Damon Runyon's *The Big Street*.

Variety: " 'The Big Street,' typical top Damon Runyon story, shapes
up as the sturdiest b.o. from this studio in months."

It was booked into the RKO Palace on Broadway, as a single, with
no stage show accompanying it, and the reviews were all right, and the
box office all over the country was far better than kind words.

Runyon took a bow a minute in Lindy's and out on the sidewalk but
he would not walk into the Palace on 45th Street and sit in a crowded
movie and have people see and hear him cry as he watched the life he
imagined he had lived sparkle bright and hot on the screen.

"The movie goes the full Derby distance," he said. "Fifty years from
now, everybody is dead and the movie still runs somewhere." Years
later, when they buried Lucille Ball, somebody asked her daughter
about the life of the woman, and the daughter said, "Her favorite movie?
She didn't think anything was close to *The Big Street*."

That day in April 1944, the flower beds dividing Park Avenue into two
avenues were joyous with red and yellow tulips, causing him to realize
how much he loved the street. His name and fortune were partly based
on using it as a vile contrast to his Broadway, but now, waiting for the
traffic light to change, dressed in elegant dark blue suit and tie, with
his newest shoes glistening in the spring sun, he stood in the middle of
Park Avenue with all these tulips at his fingertips and he told himself a
slight truth: I am living in Pueblo, where they hang a man right in the
middle of the street, and I am sitting on the curb with a lady who can
not wait to love me. Then I am living on Park Avenue, where they put
flowers in the middle of street. You may not believe this when I say it
to you, but I am much happier on Park Avenue.

His newspaper's headline said that for the first time U.S. planes based
in Italy had bombed Austria. The Russians moved into Rumania. The
Dodgers and Yankees, with players who would be spectators at games
if there were no war, had a pre-season game scheduled for Atlantic
City. And in New York, Mayor La Guardia was accused of being mysterious about a plan for a transit tax. "Fella will deny he's having a
sandwich while he's chewing on it," Runyon said aloud. Later, he wrote
down the memory of the day, and recalled that his thoughts on the
mayor were based on a morning at Jamaica Race Track when La Guardia, as a private lawyer, showed up at the rail with Joe (the Boss) Mas-
seria and watched workouts. Joe the Boss' occupation was about what

the name indicated. "He is the boss in charge of everything," his people proclaimed. La Guardia became furious when his presence was reported. Runyon took this as an insult. If he could stand with Joe the Boss, then why did La Guardia feel he was so above something Runyon would do? When the track photographer came up and showed Runyon a picture of La Guardia and a line of gangsters watching the workout, he ran it in the paper. The light changed, and he was halfway across the uptown side of Park Avenue when the pain in his throat caused him to stop. His face was a wince. He looked down at the cigarette in his hand. He threw it away. The last, he said to himself.

Later, he would write that, crossing the street, he thought of the first cigarette he had ever smoked. He figured he was about nine or ten, certainly not much older, because he remembered cigarettes while he was writing his first poem, and that was at eleven. The first cigarette was in the alley behind the *Pueblo Chieftain*. One of the printers took out a pack of Camels, with that picture of the brown camel against the white pack, and as an afterthought shook the pack and popped up a cigarette for Damon, who jabbed it into his mouth. He remembered he got the end wet. The pressman lit the cigarette for him and he stood in the sun and watched the pressman inhale. Imitating, Damon took this deep breath and found that the smoke had gone down. Now he exhaled and it streamed out as if the smoke had nothing to do with him. Rather than become sick to his stomach, he found the cigarette, with its heavy taste in the cold morning, a delight, particularly because it made him feel like one of the guys when the presses began to rumble inside the *Chieftain* back shop.

While enjoying the first cigarette, he also was loosing the initial cigarette tar into his body. In this case, it fell in the form of smoke on the mucous membrane of the throat, a lining comprised of squamous cells. Unlike the skin of a human being, which by comparison has almost rocky covering, the throat tissue is vulnerable to attack from outside, which is one reason why human beings go around with their mouths shut. Throat tissue is virtually helpless against cigarette tar, which is comprised of polycyclic hydrocarbons. When condensed they are tar, such as found in snuff and chewing tobacco, and when dispersed are in smoke. Always, they are the deadly enemy of the squamous cell.

In his pain, the beauty of Park Avenue diminished and his eyes focused on grainy cement. High heels sounded on it when the rich women of the world walked out as white-gloved doormen held polished brass doors. The women greeted them with voices that sounded like water running over rocks. He walked to number 729 and went into the ground-floor offices of Dr. Hayes Martin, the doctor who had treated Babe Ruth. Runyon loved favorites and he knew Martin had the big name. And then the wise guy in him pointed out that the Babe had weighed ninety-five pounds when he went and Martin had attended the funeral. Runyon had a saying: Favorites only can win when they can win.

The nurse looked up as he came in, and said, "Oh, Mister Runyon." Martin now came out of the office, a man with a square face, which gave him a stern look, and small eyes. But, speaking gently, he said he remembered seeing Runyon on a couple of occasions. Martin didn't mention that one had to be the Babe's funeral. With great cheer, Martin brought him into an examining room and said casually that perhaps he ought to take off his coat. The nurse took it from him. He had Runyon sit in a chair and open his mouth. He looked into the throat with a laryngoscope, which caused Runyon to gag. He had to insert the tube a couple of times before Runyon, who pretended he was watching a heavyweight championship fight and was counting with the referee and not moving a muscle for he didn't want to miss an eyelash batting, sat in total stillness.

And in his concentration he caught the doctor with his breath slowing and even stopping. He had heard that breathing rhythm from a thousand prizefight managers when, in the first moments of the fight, their fighter traded jabs up in the ring and the other guy had so much reach and was so much faster that it was obvious that the thing was no good at all.

Looking into Runyon's throat, into the red tissue and mucous membrane, Martin saw what looked like a clump of limestone clinging to the roof of a cave. He removed the laryngoscope and said, "I'd like to investigate this a little bit more." Runyon sat quietly. The doctor called in the nurse. "Would you call over to Memorial and get a room for Mister Runyon? Schedule an x-ray. I'd like to do a procedure in the morning."

"Which morning?" Runyon said.

"Oh, tomorrow. That's why we're going to need you over there today."

"What did you just see?" Runyon said.

"Just that I do need to investigate a little bit more."

"I see. Have you got anything to stop the pain?"

Now he winced, and the doctor went to a cabinet and gave Runyon a pill. He asked the nurse to bring him a cup of water. Runyon swallowed the pill and the doctor said softly, "It'll work."

At four-thirty that afternoon, a man named Gillespie took developed x-rays and clipped them to a light board in the x-ray viewing section, a cramped space about the size of a crowded kitchen on the sixth-floor laboratories of Memorial.

Dr. Martin looked in. "Ready?"

"Yessir. He's been waiting for them, too."

Damon Runyon, in a hospital-blue robe, rose from a chair outside the doorway and came in. He took off his glasses and wiped them. Then he put them on and looked at the x-rays.

"The last one of these I saw, I got beat a dirty nose at Pimlico. First time they ever used them for a photo finish, too. I never trusted photos after that. Because when I looked at it, my horse had his nose in front. The judges said the other one was ahead. Said I was blind as a bat. Well, what do we have here?'"

"Why don't you wait in the room? I want to investigate this properly," the doctor said.

"I am making a rather large bet here. I could be playing with my life. More than somewhat." Filling anxiety and embarrassment with useless words.

Dr. Martin was looking at an inverted wishbone, the vocal cords, which when healthy appear on an x-ray with darkness beneath them, the darkness indicating clearness. On this film there was no darkness. An oval gray mass bulged out and was wrapped around the left vocal cord.

"What's it show?" Runyon asked.

"Oh, I'm not certain enough to give you a complete answer here. We're going to have to investigate a little more. These x-rays just don't tell you everything you want to know."

Dr. Martin knew one thing at a glance. The vocal cords, in inspiration, bend outward and allow breath through. But with the gray mass already partially blocking the passage, simple breathing soon would be a problem.

Runyon went back to his room. He called Lindy's on the phone and had them go outside and get Eddie Walker, the fight manager. He told Walker where he was, but that he was to tell nobody else. He sat and thought. He didn't know where to find his daughter or son on the phone. She was somewhere in the city. Drink. Damon Junior was in Cincin-

nati, working for the *Cincinnati Post*. Patrice was at Reno, and there
was no way to call her. Wartime long distance calls sometimes took a
week. Well, that took care of the family. He called the Hearst office on
Eighth Avenue and told them that he would be out for a few days with
minor surgery. "A wheel flew off the bike and they got to pin it back
on." "Right-o," the desk man, Bill White, said. White hung up. That
was it. Over, ball game, the end. Nothing else. Runyon had arrived in
New York in 1911 as a loner and now, in 1944, the loner suddenly felt
loneliness. He asked the nurse if she played cards. "I need somebody
with me here. I don't go to sleep till four, five in the morning." The
nurse smiled. At 9 P.M., she turned out his light. At 6:30 the next
morning, another nurse walked in and began talking to him. It was
time to get up. "O.R.," she said brightly.

Martin was in the operating room with a resident and two nurses
when they brought Runyon in. They had given Runyon phenobarbital
to calm him. Martin now went into his throat with both hands. One
held a dentist's mirror. In the other was a knife that had a scoop at the
end of it to catch the piece of tissue that he was cutting off.

As he was doing it, the foul smell coming up from the throat told
Martin as much as anything. The tumor was becoming necrotic, growing so fast Runyon's blood supply does not feed it and the tumor rots at
the edges. The first smell of death comes out of his body.

Runyon went back to his room and the piece of tumor was sent in a
jar to the laboratory, where it was labeled and placed in a freezer. When
it was frozen, it was taken out and a lab technician sliced it with a knife
and cut strips that were a couple of cells thick. He placed one of them
under the microscope. The cells that should be present in the throat,
squamous cells, are long and irregularly shaped. Here the cell he was
looking at had too many nuclei that were splitting too rapidly. The un-
controlled growth of cancer. These rapidly splitting cells had no function in a body, except to murder.

He remained in the hospital over a weekend. Eddie Walker came
with pastrami sandwiches and coffee. On Monday morning, he was
wheeled to the operating room. He was on a table outside, with a cap
on his slicked-back hair, and he began to think of Sheba the cat in Beverly Hills and the house vacant. He couldn't expect Patrice to close the
house. He would have to go out there himself. The cat was the thing
that stuck in his mind: the cat sleeping on a chair in the sun. He had to
get Sheba to Florida. He saw her crouching and moving across the grass
of the house in Beverly Hills.

On April 10, Martin cut through the side of the neck and began to dissect the neck, which has a sheath of muscles and cords that require hand and knife hours to get through. Then he reached the large tumor and took it out. A lymph node, which was supposed to be a little pink ball, was too large and too discolored. He took it out.

When Runyon awoke he tried to talk. A nurse had her finger to her lips. He tried to talk again. Nothing happened.

Hayes Martin came in and looked solicitously and said nothing about the voice. He said the wound was coming along fine. They were letting Runyon accept the loss of voice by making it de facto. Back in his room one day he wrote out a note and gave it to Martin.

"When do I get out of here? I have races to win."

Martin smiled. "We just want to look at one more aspect."

The look consisted of another major operation to cut out even more of the cancer, as had been discovered in the pathology taken of the cells and tissue around the first operation. At this time in the country, in the year 1944, there were no cancer departments in medical schools, and the cancer treatment specialty, oncology, was a word not yet heard. There were no drugs, except those used for attempted pain relief. When he was released in June, he was pale and thin, and the dark blue suit he wore on the day he entered the hospital hung from him. Hesitantly, he stepped out of the hospital and onto York Avenue, where Eddie Walker had a car waiting. He remembered few of the details, or his feelings. He tried disobeying the doctor. He went to Los Angeles in pain and maddening silence. When he was there, he barely could get out of the house. He shut the place down and came back to New York. He had given up the Parc Vendome, and the rich furniture was in Florida. He couldn't call anybody. He didn't want the memories of the Forrest. He took a suite at the Buckingham Hotel on Sixth Avenue and 57th Street. It once had been the Great Northern, and was the same place where his Patrice had dallied with Primo Carnera. It didn't matter to him. He tried eating huge amounts of food, but he had no taste. There are few highlights to dying.

Mrs. Damon Runyon
Riverside Hotel,
Reno, Nevada

My dear Mrs. Runyon:
    Mr. Runyon has asked me to write to you relative to our recent discussion of his future management. Last week, I discussed the sit-

uation fairly frankly with him for the first time since the last operation. I told him that I considered it unsafe for him to return to California since I wished to keep him under the closest observation. I told
him that I felt it was unfortunate that he went back to California last
summer against my advice, and that when I examined him on his return, my worst fears were realized, that is, that the disease was there
in a more advanced stage than would have been the case if I had been
able to follow him at short intervals.

I told him only enough of the facts of the situation to make my advice seem reasonable to him. I think he has decided to stay on in New
York and do whatever writing he can do here. I avoided giving him
any definite predictions as to the necessary length of his stay here and
tried to be as optimistic as possible.

When I operated upon him the last time, I found a return of the
growth in the lymph nodes, but not in the throat. The outlook for the
future is uncertain but not hopeless. There are many aspects of the
case that I cannot discuss in a letter and would be glad to go over
them in detail with you if you could come to New York.

Would you kindly write to your husband after receiving this letter
in as optimistic a frame of mind as possible and tell him that I have
written and explained the situation to you.

> With kindest regards, I am, sincerely yours,
> Hayes Martin

Her answer was a short note to Damon that wound up in the files of
his trust:

Dear Damon,

You know I enjoyed every split-second with you. How were we to
know there'd be a miserable war? We haven't seen each other in two
full years. I will not keep a secret and say there is nobody else. There
is. I might as well tell you I met someone here. Bill Coffin, from New
Bedford, Massachusetts. He took his primary training here. Naturally, he is younger. Before you ask your reporter's question, he is 26.
I have had a wonderful time. He's wonderful. And I hope to marry
him. Do take care of yourself.

> Fondly,
> Patrice

One afternoon, Eddie Walker brought the portable typewriter in the
red-and-white-striped case to Runyon, who set it on his lap and began
to type. It was excruciating because he could not move his neck, and
his head always rolled a little as he typed. Then there was the feeling

of something missing. The cigarette at the right hand. It was so much a part of his working rhythm: type noisily, hit the carriage with the left hand, reach for the cigarette, drag, put the cigarette down, start typing with smoke streaming from nose and throat. Working himself to death. Since 1908, for thirty-eight years, he had worked this way every day, seven days a week. The neck pain went from head to foot. Somehow, he would try to fight this. But typing without a cigarette robbed him of his confidence. He sat motionless in bed, afraid to write a sentence to his own wife.

Two days later, pressing one key at a time, he was able to write a short note to Patrice.

> I judge that your Mr. Coffin must be a very fine young man. I do not, however, envy your friendship. Let me explain. Patrice, what is romantic during time of war becomes commonplace thereafter. I am sure he does not know this at his age. You certainly do. Patrice, do not rob this young man of the years of his youth. I implore you to look at the difference in years. You cannot ask someone of 26 to live the life of a mature woman. You now must be, as I reckon, almost 40 years old. I understand about a war. I have some idea of it from the Philippines and France. The proximity of death destroys reason. Please, dear Patrice, do not take advantage of this period in life to take a full 14 or 15 years of a young man's life away from him. It is his youth. . . .

Even in his worst daydream, he had to admit to being sixty-four. He actually knew in his troubled heart that he was sixty-six. He had not seen Patrice in those last two years, except for one short afternoon when she drove down from Reno and met him in San Francisco. But as he grew sicker, he became more desperate for her. She had gone out with Primo Carnera and he thought of her as a most beautiful Madonna. He thought she could find a way to save his life by saving his heart.

The letter came back in an envelope from a lawyer in Miami. The lawyer was asking for an immediate divorce for his client, Patrice Amati Runyon.

"Everything," Runyon wrote on a notepad.

"What do you mean by that?" Sam Becker said.

Runyon tapped the pad.

"Well, what's everything? The house?" Violent nod, yes. "But you can't give the rights to your stories. Someday they could be worth a lot of money." Now he wrote on the pad, "I am."

He was sitting alone in Lindy's on the night that Harold Conrad re-

turned from war. Runyon grabbed Pincus the waiter, pointed to Conrad outside on the sidewalk and the waiter went out and brought him
in. Damon stood up to greet him. Conrad was a lanky, handsome man
who worked at the *Brooklyn Eagle,* where before the war he became
known for good descriptive writing and bad habits. A world war had
not changed his behavior: he was smoking a joint out on Broadway.
Conrad also was used to newspaper terseness, and Runyon wouldn't
have to wear his hand out writing him notes.

"I got a real war story to tell you," Conrad said. Runyon nodded.
"I'm only gone three and a half years," Conrad said. "I cheated on the
fucking country. I only did three and a half years in a war. So I get
home, and when I walk in, what is she doing? Getting dressed to go fly
to Europe with a USO show. She's standing there looking at herself in
the mirror. I say, 'Don't you ever kiss a poor serviceman hello?' She
says, 'I've got to be leaving at seven o'clock.' Home from a war and she
got to go away. These fucking broads."

Runyon started to write, "Fuckin' dis—"

And Conrad finished, "Just what it is, a fucking disease."

Runyon nodded vigorously in agreement.

"I'm working," Conrad said.

Runyon wrote; "All we have."

"The minute she leaves the house, I go back to work. Damon, I had
to. I don't have a fuckin' quarter. They pay you a million dollars to fight
Max Schmeling for a half hour in a ring. I go out for three and a half
years and fight the whole of Germany and they don't even give me
coffee when I get off the boat. She leaves the same night. So I'm out
covering a hockey game eight hours later. What am I supposed to do,
sit home and starve and moan at the same time?"

Runyon kept gesturing with his finger that he wanted Conrad to come
with him. They took a cab to Jimmy Ryan's, which was on the ground
floor of a brownstone on 54th Street between Park and Madison. It was
a small place, with candles on the tables and a bar loaded with people
who often drank until their heads hit the bar. Ryan, an old chorus boy
in Broadway shows, had the head that made the loudest noise. His
club was directly across the street from the Hotel Elysee, where actress Tallulah Bankhead often walked out in a fur coat with nothing
underneath and opened the coat to attract a taxi. Ryan's place had a
tiny piano against the wall. Runyon and Conrad took a small table for
two. Out of the kitchen came an immaculately dressed gray-haired man,
with a face busted up by all the nights. His name was Tommy Lyman,

and he was a singer out of speakeasies who ruined himself with enjoyment and never had a chance of making it. When he looked through the dimness and saw Runyon, he said something to the piano player and now, at 2 A.M., Tommy Lyman began to sing, "I saw you last night and got that old feeling . . ." Runyon sat in a trance.

"This guy is carrying the torch," Conrad said. Now he realized that Patrice was not with them and that he had never even asked Runyon about her.

Tommy Lyman sang the song twice, the second time while standing right over Runyon, who went into his pocket for some bills, which he pressed into Lyman's hand. Conrad almost fainted. "Damon is·paying!" Lyman then sang "That Old Feeling" a third time. After which, walking the room, but playing mostly to Runyon, he sang "Cocktails for Two."

When Lyman was finished, he went into the kitchen. Curly Harris, who was living in the Elysee across the street, came over with a woman named Princess Cindy Zee of Austria, whom he introduced as a hotel resident in from out of town. She is out on the turf now and then, Curly said. Princess Cindy Zee of Austria smiled. "As long as you don't smoke," Runyon wrote on the pad.

"Let's bring T to L's," Runyon wrote. Bring Tommy to Lindy's.

They went into the kitchen to get Lyman. He was there all right, sitting in an old easy chair in the corner, wedged between the end of the stove and the start of the sinks, smoking opium out of a long pipe while the Chinese dishwasher watched jealously.

"Want to come to Lindy's with us?" Conrad said.

"I can't. I'm right in the middle of walking across the Indian Ocean." He closed his eyes and smoked on.

Runyon and Conrad went back to Lindy's, and instead of going inside, Runyon waited on the sidewalk. "WW coming," he wrote. They waited a half hour and Walter Winchell, driving a Packard, pulled up. He wore a star reporter's snap-brim hat and had a cigarette hanging from his mouth. A police radio blared. Runyon and Conrad got in the back seat and Winchell, talking about himself, drove uptown. He pulled the car over for a moment and began to twist around in the front seat. "I'm just fixing my friend so it doesn't stab me in the side," Winchell said.

Conrad's eyes opened. "Has he got . . . ?"

Runyon held out a hand and pulled the index finger back to indicate a gun.

"You're kidding," Conrad said.

Runyon began to giggle. He wrote down on the pad, "Asshole."

Conrad shook his head.

"Asshole shoots —"

"Himself," Conrad said, finishing it. They rode uptown, into Harlem, and stopped at the 32nd Precinct on West 135th Street. Winchell swung into the municipal smell, his heels clicking on the cement floor. The famous radio voice called out, "Lieutenant." The desk lieutenant looked up, pleased and surprised. With great ceremony Winchell formally presented his press card. "What's doing?" he said. The lieutenant went over his blotter and showed that there were only domestic disputes, one much earlier ending in a homicide, plus two altercations outside a bar and three people reportedly being robbed. "Otherwise, we got nothing for you right now. It's a slow night. Looks like nothing," he said.

Runyon took out his pad. "Something will happen soon. I have faith in human nature."

From 3 A.M. until 5, they drove the streets of Harlem. There was one small amount of activity, that of people on a stoop fighting. Winchell pulled the car over and jumped out, his hand patting his gun under his jacket. Runyon, shaking his head, came out after him. Conrad was not that philosophical. He kept looking for police. If they came, he intended to point out that this little chatterbox was packing. Then they saw the women in their bare feet on the stoop while two men pushed each other. Winchell walked up to them.

"Used to happen in my house, too," Runyon wrote. Conrad noticed the "used to."

In New York in that year of the end of the war, 1945, there were 335 homicides, 2,115 assaults and 1,653 armed robberies. You had to ride many times down many streets before coming upon a crime scene. If they were around a couple of decades later, they could have covered double murders by looking out the front window.

The next night they are at the famous Stork Club and Winchell is talking. "The one shva is choking the other sonofabitch. Naturally, I have to get into it. I don't want to, but what am I going to do? I was born in Harlem. The return of the poor Jew. So the one guy is choking the other and I go to stop it and Damon runs up and holds out his pad: 'Stop! I never saw a man choked to death before.' "

Conrad saw that everybody laughed and that Runyon just smiled and didn't even refute it. That night, when the *Mirror* got on the streets, here was Winchell's column describing the fight that never happened and quoting Runyon's remark about choking. Winchell made it sound as if they rode in danger all night.

Winchell's girlfriend was Mary Lou Royce, a big blonde who danced at Billy Rose's Diamond Horseshoe. "I want a mink coat, you cheap sonofabitch," she told Winchell one night.

He laughed. "Listen to her."

"Cheap fuck," she pouted. "I'm going somewhere else with my life."

A week later, she walked into the Stork Club in this rich fur coat and she sat down and Winchell was up grabbing it. "How do you like this?" he said to Runyon.

Runyon wrote to Conrad, "Suckrs mst get f'd."

As the night went on, and Winchell talked nonstop, Mary Lou said, "Come on, let's go."

". . . so I walk in the back door, I always go in the back door of the White House, and here's this old shva to hold the door. How do you do, can I take your hat, and I say no, I keep my head covered in temple. I walk in and here's FDR and jeez, you want to die. He shakes like an old leaf. And I say to him, 'Mr. President, I wish you could have my life . . .' "

"Let's go," Mary Lou said.

". . . and FDR says, 'I got an item for you, Walt.' Hey!"

Mary Lou was walking out, dragging the coat across the floor as she went.

Winchell dashed after her and picked up the coat. "Chrissakes. I paid for that!"

"No you didn't, you little shlemiel. I did."

She turned around and walked out. Three weeks later, Winchell sat at the table and swore into the phone. Mary Lou Royce and her fur coat were elsewhere, wrapped in the arms of an announcer named Frank Gallop. "I got to get that guy thrown out of a job. Frank Gallop. Can you imagine that? A crummy fucking announcer steals my chick."

He made a hundred calls about Gallop's job, and one night he howled as he spoke on the phone, "He's out? You swear on your cock he's out? Arthur, I won't forget this. Never, never, never. You are a hero!" He slammed it down. "The guy won't be on the air tomorrow night. It's done. How do you like that? Play with my girl, you pay with your tookus."

The next night, when Conrad turned on a Perry Como radio show,

Frank Gallop was the announcer. When Conrad and Runyon got to the Stork, Winchell was oblivious.

"How do you stand with your chick?" he said to Runyon.

Damon's blue eyes grew cold.

At four o'clock the next day, Conrad walked to the Buckingham Hotel and went upstairs to find Runyon and his daughter Mary in the suite. She was there to live in the second bedroom and handle her father's phone calls. When Conrad looked at her, he saw whisky. He wondered about it as he and Runyon left the apartment.

Conrad walked in the winter wind on Sixth Avenue. This was in December of 1945, and he was living in an apartment at 307 Sixth Avenue, which was a riot scene each night. "The great thing about a war is if you get out of it alive, you can beat up your body all night and love every minute of it," Conrad enthused. The night before, the chorus girls had showed up at 5 A.M., and the way Conrad opened the door and greeted them with smile and deep warm voice made the girls mad that they hadn't ditched their dirty old Brazilian boyfriends earlier. Mary Lou Royce from the Diamond Horseshoe had given up listening to Walter Winchell, and she showed up at six and ran into the crowded apartment with her bottle of champagne, into smoke and noise and jokes that didn't get damp and people who were falling in love for a night. Including Harold Conrad, who by breakfast time thought he was married to Mary Lou.

At the end of one night, he happened to be alone and there was noise at the door. When he opened it, Mary Elaine Runyon burst in, wearing a fur coat and carrying a half bottle of gin. Conrad stayed out of reach and waited until she passed out. The next day he told Runyon, "I don't know how to put this, but I think she is drinking."

Runyon wrote, "How?"

"She was at my door with a bottle of gin. I had to let her in."

NC156 LG PD--EU   NEW YORK NY 2 1245P

1945 NOV 2 PM 2

16   DAMON RUNYON JR.

CINCINNATI POST CIN =

TAKE ANY AND ALL STEPS THAT MAY BE DEEMED NECESSARY MARYS CASE. THINK YOUR APPOINTMENT AS HER LEGAL GUARDIAN EXCELLENT IDEA NOT ONLY FOR PRESENT EMERGENCY BUT AGAINST EVENTUALITIES OF FUTURE SHOULD SHE REMAIN ILL. JAW INJURY MAY BE OF MONTHS STANDING AS SHE

HAD UNEXPLAINED CONTUSION WHEN SHE LEFT HERE FOR
MIAMI BUT ANYTHING MORE SERIOUS SEEMS TO HAVE ESCAPED
DOCTORS AND DENTISTS WHO TREATED HER HERE. HAVE YOU
BEEN ABLE ASCERTAIN WHERE SHE LEFT CLOTHES. LOVE TO
YOU BOTH = DAD.

DAMON RUNYON
BUCKINGHAM HOTEL, NEW YORKNEWYORK
MARY PLACED IN WOODSIDE MANOR NURSING HOME. ALL
WELL. DETAILS LATER.
AFFECTIONATELY, DAMON

On a clear, cold day, Harold Conrad walked in the sound of chimes
and tinkling bells of the first Santa Clauses of this Christmas. When he
got upstairs at the Buckingham, Runyon was at the dining room table.
He had on white pants and a pink shirt that was buttoned at the collar.
The gauze covering the hole in his throat showed above the collar. He
was self-conscious about it and fingered the collar. During his last hospital stint, they had done a tracheotomy and inserted the tube so he
could breathe. He smiled as he showed Conrad the white pants. His
lips formed a word. Conrad was unable to make it out. Runyon hummed
the word through the silver tube in his throat.

"Oh, Miami," Conrad said. "Well, you sure are dressed for Hialeah."

Runyon shook his head and scribbled. "Tropical! When learn Florida racing dates? Hialeah in January!"

Now he made another sound. When Conrad didn't understand,
Runyon gathered his breath and snarled through the tube, "Call her."

"What do you want me to say?" Conrad said.

Runyon went to the notepad. "Patrice. Home for Christmas."

"You're going to Miami for Christmas?"

He was angry as he wrote, "Her here for Christmas."

"Let me get another cup of coffee and we'll get at it," Conrad said.
"Here, we'll do your messages first." He reached for the pink hotel
phone slips on the table. Runyon's finger jabbed at the telephone. His
lips formed the word "call."

"Right now?" Conrad said.

The head nodded.

"Damon, let me ask you something," Conrad said. "Have you been
outside yet?"

Shake yes.

"Did you hear all the Santa Claus bells?"

Runyon scribbled. "One on corner. Stood with him all morning. No sleep last night."

"Damon, you're getting sentimental."

Runyon didn't even smile. He began jabbing at the phone again. Now Conrad saw the one thing he couldn't handle, the pleading in his eyes.

He dialed 211 and, the war over, was able to get the long distance operator quickly. He called Patrice at Hibiscus Island. She answered the phone too cheerily. There is only one reason that broad has a whistle in her voice, Conrad said to himself. "How are you?" he said.

"Wonderful."

"Damon wants to know when you're coming up for Christmas."

"Oh, I'm not coming up."

"He doesn't mean today. He means for Christmas."

"I said I'm not coming up."

"Patrice."

Runyon gave him a note: "Tell her to come now!"

"Patrice, he says he needs you."

"What can I tell you?" she said.

Conrad twisted in the chair so that his back would be to Runyon. There was an ugly sound. Runyon was gagging. He was so excited that the tube was clogged with phlegm. He stood up to go to the bathroom. Conrad wanted to wait until he heard Runyon running the water in the bathroom, but she said, "I guess I'll get off now."

"Patrice, for crying out loud, the guy is dying. All he wants is to see his wife for Christmas. Can't you come up once and see him? What do you want from him, he's dying."

"You keep him company. He'll be all right." She hung up.

Now Conrad realized that Runyon was in the bedroom doorway and had heard the death part. Runyon came to the table, grabbed a large sheet of paper and printed in big capital letters: "GODDAMMIT, WHEN IS SHE COMING?"

"Damon, stop yelling at me!"

Runyon began to laugh and gag at the same time.

Runyon stopped laughing and looked steadily at Conrad, looked hopefully, and right away the hope was replaced by terrible weakness, a frail, sick man panhandling with his eyes. For a moment, Conrad thought everything could be implied. He said nothing. Runyon kept his eyes riveted to him.

"Damon, she says she isn't going to come."
As he went into the bathroom, the frail shoulders shook.

As life during a mortal illness is a matter of constant acceptance of new
degrees of pain, humiliation and diminishing hope, he became an audience trying to understand as the doctor sat on the edge of an examining table and explained what he now was going to do. Martin hoped
that he was chasing "misbehaving cells" with cold steel and killing them.

When Hayes Martin could do exactly one thing: skillfully, sensi-
tively, he could cut Runyon's throat until nothing was left or the man
was dead.

The medical business thought that cancer was a localized disease,
and all you had to do was keep making excisions until the patient's life
was saved. This was ignoring any decent figures that showed, in 1940,
a study of 132 throat operations in New York and the follow-up done
on 106. This is because there were only 106 left to follow. Of these,
only 47 were alive at the end of the first year.

So, through all the long months, every time Runyon wheezed and
Hayes Martin looked at him and saw another tumor blocking the air
passages, Hayes Martin slit Runyon's throat.

Between operations, Runyon dressed each night, with a bib covering his slit neck and tube in the throat, and he went out and ate huge
amounts of food, at Moscowitz and Lupowitz and Polish places uptown. He could taste nothing, but he wanted to eat because he thought
something he would swallow would cure him. People never discussed
cancer around him and the doctor said little and everybody assumed
Runyon was living in another illusion. Then he wrote a column that
was to go into libraries:

Death came in and sat down beside me, a large and most distinguished-looking figure in beautifully tailored soft white flannels. His
expansive face wore a big smile.
"Oh, hello." I said. "Hello, hello, hello. I was not expecting you. I
have not looked at the red board lately and did not know my number
was up. If you will just hand me my kady and my coat. I will be with
you in a jiffy."

So many times compassion was either twisted at the outset or mis-
understood when advanced. Darryl Zanuck offered him money to simply write a paragraph that could become a movie. "Runyon doesn't write
paragraphs," he wrote angrily. One day his agent told him he abso-

lutely had to write a piece for *Collier's Magazine*. A new editor, Arthur Gordon, just out of the air force, took the story and saw its thinness, and perhaps the age of its ideas, and called the Buckingham to make an appointment with Runyon. He spoke and Runyon typed the answers. Gordon, doing his job, wanted a rewrite. "I want the old Runyon," he said.

Runyon had anger in his eyes. His lips were compressed bitterly. He typed, "The old Runyon doesn't live here anymore."

He was in Memorial in the spring of 1945 when Harold Conrad came in and told him, "You know Roosevelt died?" Runyon struggled out of bed and told Conrad to call the Hearst offices and say that he was going to cover the funeral. "Must do this alone!" he wrote to Conrad. Runyon traveled alone to Washington and wrote a story about an old man standing at the funeral and telling his young son that he had been wrong about Roosevelt: " 'I hated him politically,' the old man mused. 'Now I wonder why. He only did the best he could. No man could do more.' "

The old man was Hearst. It was Runyon's last favor for his boss.

Wherever he went, to shows or movies or restaurants, people looked at him and he began to write, "If one more person looks at me like I'm dying, I'll fade them. I'll kill myself at the table." In the end, Milton Berle handled it best. He was the head of the Friars Club, which at that time was housed in two rooms in the Edison Hall building on West 47th Street. It was over a haberdasher and the small elevator brought guests up to a place with two card tables and a pool table. Berle ran the place. Always, Walter Winchell and Benny Davis, a songwriter, argued. One night Runyon was playing gin at two cents a point with some guy and they got in an argument. Runyon wrote on his pad, "You prick, you cheated me. I'm not going to pay." The guy began to scream. Runyon wrote a direct threat on the pad. Berle announced, "Runyon and this shlemiel with him are expelled from the club." When Runyon found that he actually was suspended, he went around Broadway denouncing Berle on his notepad. Sam Becker, the lawyer, approached Berle one night. "Sam, don't talk to me," Berle said. "He doesn't get back in."

"Milton, I just wanted to tell you that you have him so crazy that he's staying alive."

Berle pursed his lips. "Isn't that sweet? Isn't it lovely that you're such a fuckin' genius that you figured it out by yourself?"

On December 6, 1946, writhing in pain, at the weight of one hundred pounds, he went into Memorial for the last time. The doctor was out in the hall when there was a commotion involving a younger man trying to get into the room. "I'm the son," the man said. Martin told Damon Junior, "He never told me he had a son."

Runyon by now was in a coma. He died on the tenth.

Sam Becker stood out in the hallway. "He said all horse players die broke," he said. "This one sure did. He comes into the world naked and he leaves naked."

When the *Herald Tribune* called, the son told them it was cancer. Until then, all the major names had died "after a long illness." The headlines over Runyon said, "Cancer." The next patient with a known name to have Hayes Martin for a doctor was a man named Lerner, who had several large department stores. He told everyone that he had cancer and wound up donating many millions to the cancer hospital.

Two days later, Eddie Rickenbacker flew a plane over New York, with Mike Todd, a producer, and Damon Runyon Jr. in it. When the plane was directly over Times Square, the son shook Runyon's ashes over the Big Street.

Sam Becker sat in his office and looked at a check for $25,000 from the film producer Alexander Korda. It was for a story Runyon had never written, and now it had to go back. Becker called Arnold Grant, who was Korda's lawyer. "Arnold, please let me grab $1,500 to file the will and open probate. If I don't, this Spanish countess of his will get everything that ever happens with the man's works. I've a family to protect." Grant said sure, and the filing fees were paid and the document that was to bring money to a family for decades was set up.

Milton Berle put on a telethon for the new Damon Runyon Memorial Cancer Fund a few months later, and as it was the first time anything like it was done on television, they all hoped to get a hundred thousand or so. Berle raised a million in one night. Included was a check for $5,000 from Frank Costello, Joe Adonis and Meyer Lansky, and a $250 pledge from Joseph (Joe Zocks) Lanza, boss of the Fulton Fish Market, who could give no more because at the moment he was in Sing Sing Prison, and it would have looked bad for a convict to be throwing thousands around.

TWENTY

ONE DAY IN 1948, the wife at the time of Ernie Martin, a producer, looked at an old green-bound book called *Guys and Dolls*. She told Ernie that it was a great title for a show. Ernie talked it over with his partner, Cy Feuer.

Feuer took the book and ran through the stories. He never had met Runyon, but he thought of himself as a "Brooklyn mug." He called Robbie Lantz, the theatrical agent who at the time represented the Runyon estate. "Is it taken?" Feuer asked. "No," Lantz said. Feuer and Martin put up $5,000 for an option. Feuer thought that Runyon's dialogue of the thirties sounded awkward, but he and Martin took offices on West 57th Street and began to read and discuss the book. The story Feuer liked the most was "The Idyll of Miss Sarah Brown," which was about the Salvation Army woman in Times Square. He took the dice game from another story, "Blood Pressure." Now, in the play, the wise guys rolled dice for their souls, and they lost and she saved their souls. In the Runyon tale in the book, Big Julie from Chicago grabs the derby hat from Jew Looey's head to roll dice in it. He rolls the dice and only he can look into the hat and see how they come out. "A ten!" He rolls again. "Ten." And then one of the players said, "A six and four?" And Big Julie growled, "Either way." Feuer loved it but didn't know how to make the dice visual for a play. He thought for a long time about the problem of showing the dice. They went first to the songwriter Frank Loesser and the Hollywood writer Jo Swerling. Loesser came around one day and played them the beginning of his score. He had a song about Nathan Detroit and a permanent floating crap game. Another song was called "A Bushel and a Peck." He played the show's theme, "Guys and Dolls": "When you see a guy reach for stars in the sky . . ."

The book by Swerling wasn't close to the music. They went to Abe Burrows, who had never done a show before. He was a short man, balding, who at first seemed to be a comic, and yet he had spent enormous time reading and studying the origins of words. He was delighted with his discoveries. "Cockamamy!" he yelled at them the first day. "Do you know where it comes from? In the old days on the East Side, they used to take decals and slap them on their foreheads and run around. It was a thing they did. They said it was 'decalomania.' Somebody couldn't speak right and he called it 'cockamania.' That's where it comes from." He slapped his forehead. He and Feuer worked each night from 9 P.M. until 3 A.M. in Feuer's house on East 64th Street in Manhattan.

Guys and Dolls opened at the 46th Street Theatre on November 25, 1950. Brooks Atkinson, in one of those restrained stories done in the face of tumult in the audience that must be fended off lest readers think you caved in to the cheers, said it was something that Broadway could be proud of. He said the genius of the play was that it preserved Runyon's friendly manner without patronizing. The score was dynamic. The city's best critic, John Chapman of the *Daily News*, said Abe Burrows's book for the play could hold up on its own, and with Loesser's perfect score, *Guys and Dolls* was a show that would last a long time.

It is still being shown somewhere in the world forty-plus years later.

On that opening night, Sam Becker had a big tall show broad, Charlotte Otis, from the Latin Quarter. When he saw what the play was doing to the opening night audience, Sam Becker reminded himself of how great he was in getting the will filed so Patrice wouldn't grab it all. At the end, Becker was so sure of the greatness of his act that he was disappointed he wasn't asked to take a bow in the crowded, happy theater.

At this time, Joseph (Joe Zocks) Lanza, boss of the Fulton Fish Market, had someone shovel a clearing for him in the waist-deep snow of the main yard of the Clinton Correctional Facility in Dannemora, New York, where he now resided. He had his bench pulled up in front of a fire blazing out of a fifty-five-gallon drum. The flames licked the sides of the drum and made Joe Zocks's boots sizzle.

Alongside him on the hill was the Cadillac car made of snow and ice that Sonny Gold of Manhattan had built. Every winter that he was here at Clinton Correctional Facility, and this was so many winters because

Sonny Gold had a behavior problem, he fashioned a complete Cadillac out of ice. It had a roof, taillights, headlights, grille, doors, and inside, seats, a dashboard, steering wheel and pedals. When convicts came out into the great yard, they walked up a slope to where Sonny's car sat, taillights against the wall. For a fee, which consisted of loose change or cigarettes, a guy could get a chance to sit in the car and dream. He would grip the wheel and pretend he was driving with some big broad right in the seat next to him, or had one waiting downtown. Joe Zocks got up and walked over to the car.

Richie LaRusso from East Harlem was at the wheel, and enthusiastic. "I'm drivin' down First Avenue to see my broad. Do you know what she is going to do to me?"

"Get out," Sonny said.

"I give you ten cigarettes for the ride. I'm not even at 86th Street yet."

"I said you should get out. Joe wants it."

Now Joe Zocks Lanza, boss of the Fulton Fish Market, gets into the ice car. "I drive to a big opening on Broadway."

"What opens?"

"Damon Runyon's show."

"He dies," somebody said.

"It's the show I'm going to see. He closes. The show opens," Joe said.

"You know the guy?" Richie LaRusso said.

"Many years. The guy beat the street. He married a Spanish countess. A beautiful-looking young broad."

"How young?"

"Way younger than he was, I'll tell you that. What do you want, him going out with some old broad?"

"Did he have a lot of money?"

"Man lived big. He had it from the movies. I know she got one of the biggest diamonds in the world. It's like one of the ten biggest diamonds in the whole world."

"How big?"

"I don't know. Thirty, forty carats. It's huge."

"That must look like something."

"You should see it. You wouldn't believe it," Joe Zocks said.

"You seen it, Joe?"

"Many times I was in their company and she had it on."

"Holy jeez, thirty carats!"

"Knock your eye out. You could axt anybody on Broadway about the ring."

"Anybody ever try to grab it?" Richie said.

"Who could steal off Damon Runyon?" Joe Zocks said.

Time passed. We are not dealing with the next hour or the next day here, because these were not nice people, and they were not in there for taking ice cream cones. Joe Zocks was still in charge of extortion at the Fulton Fish Market, which meant the halibut you ate cost much more per pound because Joe Zocks took money off the purchase price. You might as well know that young Richie LaRusso was in Dannemora because he had looked back at a loan company after holding it up and noticed the clerk staring hard at him, as in memorizing appearances. So he turned around and went back, and that was that for the clerk and his rat memory. And also for Richie, as they caught him.

While Richie was in jail, he received a letter from East Harlem saying that many people were moving out to the Bronx and along the Sound, to Connecticut and farther. His uncle had moved to one of the towns along the Sound and was a landscaper. He then sent Richie an announcement of the birth of a son. The proud father, Richie's uncle, put on the card that the baby boy would grow up to own his own landscaping business someday. "He is going to stay honest like you should of." The baby who was going to stay honest was Richie's cousin. Then, on a spring day in about the year of our Lord 1952, just after the melting Cadillac had been shoved down the hill for the traditional spring ride, crashing in the prison yard and melting away in a few days, LaRusso was near Joe Zocks's bench when Ruby the Reader ran up. In his hands was a folded copy of the *Law Journal*. One copy of the paper was distributed to the cellblock, and Ruby was in charge of reading it for all prisoners.

"You got reversed," he called to LaRusso.

"All these years? Never."

"It's right here. The state court of appeals. People versus Richard LaRusso. Reversed."

He showed it to LaRusso. The small print danced in LaRusso's eyes. "I'm out?"

"You're out. It got reversed."

"Does anybody else know?"

"I don't know," Ruby the Reader said. "Your lawyer should of sent you a telegram or come up to see you right away."

"The fuckin' lawyer."

"You didn't pay him, I'll bet," Ruby said.

"I don't give it all to him," LaRusso said.

"That's why he let you sweat a few extra days," Ruby said.

Two days later, a telegram arrived from the state court of appeals. Then, of a spring morning, LaRusso got up to go home. In the next cell, Joe, the old man, boiled water for the coffee on a hot plate. La-Russo sat on the bunk and pounded a baseball mitt. It was a good mitt. He had it oiled with neat's-foot oil and the pocket just nice. He wasn't going to take the glove home with him. You can't play third base on 116th Street. He decided he would give the glove to Jackie, who was four cells down. Jackie had five years to go. On the way out, he stopped and said goodbye to Joe Zocks, who had given him a job as gangster at the fish market.

"Don't be a hard-on," Joe Zocks said. "I don't want no hard-ons in my outfit."

Joe Zocks had established two separate trade associations for the fish market, which he hoped the parole board would soon allow him to run in person. They were the Fresh Water Merchants Association and the Salt Water Merchants Association. As the Fulton Fish Market sat on the East River, and yet the water came in from the ocean, Richie didn't know the difference and also didn't want anybody to think he was dumb.

Three years later, Joe Zocks was home, and he told Richie to inform the Fresh Water men that they now were selling their fish for forty cents a pound, as opposed to thirty cents. "The dime is for us," Joe Zocks said.

Richie went to codfish and halibut people, and then to whitefish and salmon and trout purveyors alike. When Joe Zocks's receipts were crazy, and he found out why, he hit Richie on the shoulder with a baseball bat. The blow was like to break Richie's bones. He was going to shoot Richie right there, but Richie, clutching his shoulder and whining, admitted that "I don't know the difference from salt water to fresh water."

Joe Zocks shook his head. This fucking moron was unbelievable. "Anybody knows what fresh water is. That's Jews. Anything they make gefilte fish out of, you dopey bastard. Salt-water fish is Italian. Anything you make calamari and scungilli out of. I'll tell you, I think you are the worst thing in the world. I think you are a hard-on."

That was that for Richie. He had just been called the one worst thing you could call him, a hard-on.

He stayed in the fish market, with the insult smoldering inside, for many years. Another time, Joe Zocks got mad at him, and again said, "Richie, did anybody ever call you the hard-on that you are?"

He walked off the job as gangster at the fish market and went out into the world to steal on his own. It was then that he heard about his baby cousin, now a full-grown young man, up there landscaping, which is a great word for lawn mowing, having this fight with the Runyon widow over a car. Richie's cousin barely knew who the President was, much less an old writer. But when Richie's cousin heard from Richie personal that the woman had a thirty-carat diamond, he was here on time, standing in the red light of the pizza stand at the turnoff for the road where Patrice Runyon lived. Some distance up the secluded road, Patrice was alone in the house, looking out at the dark sea. Her employer, Dougherty, was off to Lyford Cay, in Nassau, for the holidays. She had given him all her Christmas cards to mail from Nassau. Make her look good.

"You are sure she's alone?" he said to the cousin.

"Positive," the cousin said.

"Great," Richie said.

"One thing," the cousin said. "You don't get me in no trouble."

"Forget about it," Richie said.

She had just raced back home in her Jaguar after a a tour of the night joints, and they were waiting in the garage.

"What do you want?" Patrice screamed.

"Shut up," Richie said, hat down on his face. He grabbed her hands to tie them up. She bent down and bit him on the wrist so bad that he let out a yell. He whacked her on her blond head with his gun butt. His cousin was outside in the car. Richie dragged her into the house, blood sprinkling onto the carpet. Dazed, she slumped onto the floor with her hand on her strongbox. He went through the dresser and grabbed the big lighter and this citrine ring and a pound and half of jewelry, which she did not know came from Swifty Morgan. He walked over to the locked box that held the Amati diamond. "Give me the key," Richie said. She shook her head no. He took a cutter and snapped the chain and walked off with the box. Her scream followed him. "My family diamond!"

Richie knew he had what he was there for.

Later, his wrist bandaged because she had truly bit him right through to top of the bone, Richie was in the basement of a candy store on East 116th Street in East Harlem. Quiet Sal, a very good reverse locksmith in that he only wanted locks to open, broke open the box, and here inside it was a thin, beautifully formed layer of dust.

RUNYON WIDOW
Holdup Victim

Patrice Amati Runyon, widow of writer Damon Runyon, was held up at gunpoint and pistol-whipped in a palatial waterfront house last night. The gun man took the famous Amati diamond, at 30.10 carats now listed as the 10th largest diamond in the world.

Mrs. Runyon, who was taken to Greenwich General, told police that the diamond was so famous and easily recognizable that she feared the criminals would have it cut in order to sell it. There also were many heirlooms taken, she said, including a cigarette lighter given her husband by Pancho Villa.

Joe Zocks held court at four in the afternoon in Vesuvio, a restaurant on 48th Street just around the corner from where the little Lindy's had been. Oh, yes, so much time has passed that by now there was no more Lindy's. But there was Joe Zocks, and he looked at the first offering, the lighter from Pancho Villa, and he dropped it on the table. He didn't want it. He said to Richie, "What did you do with the ring?"

"It wasn't there."

Joe Zocks put down his fork. He picked up the napkin and wiped his mouth as if in thought. Calmly, he reached out, napkin covering the right fist, as a bullfighter uses cape on sword, and clouted Richie right between the eyes.

"You hard-on."

He left the restaurant with his face still stinging from the punch. He had about a week to produce the diamond or die. Joe Zocks wanted the diamond because he regarded Richie as being under his jurisdiction, and furthermore Richie had heard about the diamond from Joe Zocks first, all those years ago in the Dannemora prison yard, and Joe Zocks said this meant that the diamond was his, no matter who stole it.

Richie now reasoned that his cousin probably had copped the diamond from the strongbox, and because the cousin had known where the broad Patrice was living and had fingered the job, then the cousin deserved at least 20 percent of the diamond anyway, Richie reasoned.

It was not such good reasoning.

A couple of days later, Richie, following another sleepless night, heard knocking on the front and back windows of his ground-floor apartment at once. Cold with fright, he went under the mattress for his gun. He was looking for a place where he could play Alamo with Joe Zocks's men when out the front window he saw a patrol car. His breath came hissing out of him in relief. He threw the gun on the floor and opened the front door. He walked back to the bathroom, calling over his shoulder to the cops, "I just want to get dressed."

At his trial, Richie learned that some neighbor had seen him and his cousin, driving their own car, leaving the scene of the place where they dumped the stolen car used in the holdup.

"I have to wonder," Lopez the Lawyer, who was Richie's attorney, was saying, "how they can accept the fact that the big diamond was there when you tell me it wasn't."

"Believe me, it wasn't. Axt Quiet Sal."

"He would never lie," Lopez the Lawyer said wearily. "Well, I'll take his word and your word. I'll try to kill this broad on the witness stand."

Q. About this supposed diamond.
A. It was real.
Q. This supposed diamond, where was it purchased?
A. Oh, dear fellow, anything this historic never was really purchased. As I testified earlier, it has been in my family for generations. The Amati diamond originally was in Granada, and my great-great-aunt wore it to the palace in Madrid.

Lopez the Lawyer looked at the jury as she spoke. They believe every word she is saying, he thought.

Q. (To witness Swifty Morgan) Now, Mr. Morgan, have you gone over your testimony with anybody in authority before coming here?
A. (By witness Swifty Morgan) Yes.
Q. Who was that?
A. Frank Costello.
Q. Who?
A. Frank Costello. I hadda ask him about testifying here. He come up to me one day and says, "Everybody says go ahead. They are lousy rats that done that."
Q. What did this Mister Costello mean by that?
A. He meant it is better I should get up here than they have to do something.
Q. Do something?

A. Well.

Q. Over a diamond?

A. It was Runyon's wife's.

Q. Have you ever seen the diamond?

A. Can't you see? I'm half-blind on account of looking at it. The whole of Broadway has seed it.

When the jury went out, Lopez the Lawyer, Richie and his cousin, the landscaper's assistant, sat in the courtroom as the dust lazed in the air. Lopez the Lawyer poured water from a pitcher. He was in the midst of this when the court officer walked in and said, "A note." Lopez's hand shook. The judge came onto the bench, read the note and said, "We have reached a verdict." He told everybody to sit down and the jury filed in. The foreman, a plumber, got up and said, "Guilty."

The prosecutor leaned over and hissed at Lopez and LaRusso. "She wants the diamond back. You get the diamond back, you save years off your life."

"How many years?" Lopez asked.

"If we have the diamond, he gets two and a half for this right now. Not a day more. If we don't get the diamond, he's looking at seven and a half to fifteen."

"You mean a diamond don't exist costs me five years of my fucking life?" Richie said.

"Yessir."

"I give her back all she had. A ring and some fuckin' lighter. But there was no big diamond. I can't go to the can for something that wasn't there. This don't happen in real life."

And of course it did.

Some weeks later, a man and his wife had the heavy gold oval lighter on the counter on a red cloth.

"We thought we were just getting another piece of brass," the husband, Dick Peters, said.

"We got it as a throw-in," the wife, Laurie Peters, said.

A lashing fall rain sounded against the windows of their store, Roxy's Used Clothes, one flight over Thayer Street in Providence, Rhode Island.

"It was in the pile the woman didn't even want to show me," Laurie said. The woman was Patrice Amati Runyon, auctioning off her possessions. "It was in a dark room in the house, and she had these odd clothes on a blanket on the floor. That's what we were there for. It was a pre-auction sale. We already had bought all the gowns. I guess for about a thousand dollars. I said, 'Anything else?' She said, 'Well, I don't want to bother you with this.' As I'm telling you, the room was dark. I saw this ring on top of the clothes on the blanket and I said, 'This rhinestone we'll take.' Costume jewelry, worth about five dollars."

She held up the dull yellow stone ring, a citrine with eight diamonds on each side. "When I picked it up, I thought, nobody makes a piece like this for costume jewelry. They sure don't. It's a nineteen-and-a-half-carat citrine."

In the low light of the room, the stone was rich and lustrous.

"I decided to take the pile of clothes, too," she said. "The woman said, 'Here, take everything. Just leave me the blanket because I need that for the auction.' I said all right, and I was bunching the clothes together and I found the lighter. The room was so dark I thought it was just another piece of old brass. A five, ten dollar piece of brass. There are three different kinds of gold in it. Yellow, pink and green gold. The jeweler, we took it to Tilden Thurber, the best jeweler in Providence, felt it could've been made in England. It wasn't a stock piece by any means."

Dick Peters picked up the lighter. "We were driving home and Laurie was in the backseat looking at the ring and I said, 'What about the lighter?' She said, 'There's something written on the bottom.' I said, 'What does it say?' She said, 'I don't know. I can't read it. Here.' She put it in front of me, and I'm trying to drive and read the bottom of the lighter. I can't make it out, either. So I stopped the car and turned on the light and looked at it. Something, isn't it?"

> Damon Runyon
> Amigo Mío
> Salud
> Pancho Villa

And at the house on the point, Patrice walked around, her dress making a loud sound, and Bill Dougherty said, "What do you hear about the diamond?"

"Not a word," Patrice the Housekeeper said.

"What are you going to do?"

"Wait them out. He's not a very honorable guy who took my family diamond. It has been in the Amati family for centuries." She cried hard, real tears over the lost heirloom, even when the insurance company paid $200,000 for the loss.

And Richie LaRusso, B number 276435, is walking along cellblock

A, Clinton Correctional Facility, Dannemora, New York, and the first wind of winter is blowing down the walkway. Richie is holding on to his new clothes, and he also has magnetic hangers so he can slap them onto the metal ceiling of the cell. Richie has to hang up his shirts neat. A guy standing far up the walk, lounging in front of his cell, issues an angry call from which Richie thought that at least here he would be spared forever.

"Hey, hard-on!" Joe Zocks, the parole violator, snarled.

At this point in our story, August Belmont, the man who built the subways, is good and dead, and buried as deep they could get him. But the first aboveground railroad he owned, the Louisville and Nashville, had a train rumbling out of Des Moines, Iowa, that would end the old way of life in New York. The train, the Cotton Picker Special, did not go near New York City.

It left Des Moines in 1961 and went south with 108 flatcars, carrying a $4 million shipment of new and amazing green and yellow John Deere 99 cotton pickers. This was the biggest single shipment of farm machinery ever made by rail. Before this, two brothers named Hubbard had worked in the John Deere harvest analysis department to develop a line of machines that would mean less black hands pulling the cotton out of southern fields. The Hubbard had one early machine in the fifties that could do the work of forty field hands. Those pushed out of the cotton fields then headed north, to Brooklyn and the Bronx, and whites in turn moved to the suburbs. But still, in the 1955 movie *Guys and Dolls*, there are only two blacks and both of them were shining shoes as Marlon Brando and Frank Sinatra made gamblers' excuses to their women on white Broadway.

When the Cotton Picker Special reached Atlanta, it pulled into the Tilford Yards where, alongside the freight house, civic leaders, farmers and politicians crowded around it. The president of the Coca-Cola Company handed out free sodas. The president of the Atlanta board of aldermen, Lee Evans, announced, "Now it's the South's turn to conquer." One of the cotton pickers on the train could do the work of ninety field hands and would save $25 or more per bale at harvest time. In less than two and a half days, cotton-picking machines on the flatcars could pick enough cotton to encircle the earth. The shipment of 441 machines represented only half the number of cotton pickers that would be delivered to farmers in the South that year.

The Louisville and Nashville's Cotton Picker Special pulled out of Atlanta and rolled along 175 miles of track to Montgomery, its whistle blaring at the rows of shacks filled with black field hands. Soon they would be driven off the land by these machines glistening in the sun on the flatcars. At Montgomery, with the Confederate flag hanging in the listless air over the freight yard switching house, the shipment was broken up and cotton pickers rolled off for delivery throughout the South.

Broadway would no longer be the place of guys and dolls. Throngs of poor who were driven off the fields were at Trailways and Greyhound bus depots for the long ride to New York City, and the start of the new South was the finish of the old life in New York. The city and its political hacks and mediocre newspapers never knew what was happening. Hundreds of thousands of blacks from the fields moved into tenements that were vacated by hundreds of thousands of whites who ran for the suburbs. The blacks from the South did not like the desolate life in the tenements, and the whites who had fled still controlled the jobs of the city. It was an era that was to change the lives of most people in New York by asking them to live life as it actually is, as opposed to the twenties and thirties, when people felt the excitement was all about something that only existed when they laughed — the Broadway of Damon Runyon.